THE
WRITER'S
COMPASS

Instructor's Annotated Edition

THE WRITER'S COMPASS

A Sentence and Paragraph Text with Readings

SECOND EDITION

Kathleen T. McWhorter
Niagara County Community College

HOUGHTON MIFFLIN COMPANY   Boston   New York

Senior Sponsoring Editor: Mary Jo Southern
Senior Associate Editor: Ellen Darion
Project Editor: Christina Lillios
Senior Production/Design Coordinator: Jill Haber
Senior Manufacturing Coordinator: Priscilla Abreu
Senior Marketing Manager: Nancy Lyman
Editorial Assistants: Kate O'Sullivan, Lauren Gagliardi

Cover illustration: © 1998 by Celia Johnson

Cover design: Diana Coe

Photo Credits: Page 14, Associated Press/Wide World Photos; page 17,
Bill Bachmann/The Image Works; page 49, Courtesy of Allstate; page 72,
Spencer Grant/Stock Boston; page 131, Courtesy of Radio Shack; page
175, C. Okoniewski/The Image Works; page 262, John Yurka/Picture Cube;
page 268, courtesy of Ad Council/Education Excellence Partnership; page
274, courtesy of Bromleyaguilar and Associates; page 289, Bill Gallery/Stock
Boston; page 301, Courtesy of Napro; page 322, courtesy of Starbucks; page
323, Daniel MacDonald/Stock Boston; page 347, courtesy of State Farm
Insurance Companies; page 393, Gamma-Liaison.

Text credits begin on page 509.

Library of Congress Catalog Card Number: 98-72062

Student Edition ISBN: 0-395-87410-6

Instructor's Annotated Edition ISBN: 0-395-88544-2

123456789-BA-02 01 00 99 98

BRIEF CONTENTS

CONTENTS

CHAPTER **11**   **Drafting and Revising**   **267**

Part *VI*   *Paragraph Development*   **299**

CHAPTER **12**   **Developing, Arranging, and Connecting Details**   **300**

Part IX   Reviewing the Basics   447

Preface

The Writer's Compass, Second Edition, guides students toward effective writing with a unique and practical approach. It teaches fundamental sentence and paragraph writing skills by engaging student interest, keeping the focus on ideas rather than on rules, and stressing the interconnection of grammar and the writing process.

This book presents the study of grammar and the study of the "whole paper" as inseparable. Seven of *The Writer's Compass*'s sixteen chapters deal with grammar topics; in these chapters, students continue to examine student essays, read, respond to ideas, write, and revise paragraphs. In the book's nine rhetorical chapters, students are encouraged to apply what they have learned about sentence-level correctness to their own writing as they explore the logical development and organization of ideas. This lively, integrated approach leads to greater student interest and better, more fully assimilated, writing skills.

Each chapter of *The Writer's Compass* contains a brief, high-interest reading that sets up opportunities for writing and relates the chapter's lesson back to the student's own work. These readings encourage students to think, discuss, consider their own experiences, and respond to what they read in writing. They also strengthen students' confidence in the value and worth of their ideas. Additional readings in Part VIII provide options and extra opportunities to explore the reading/writing connection. Through the readings and the accompanying apparatus, the text stresses that effective writing must evolve from student interest and experience.

Special Features of This Text

The following features distinguish *The Writer's Compass.*

- *Balanced coverage*   The book presents both sentence- and paragraph-level material fully and in balance, with grammar presented as a vehicle for expressing ideas.
- *A strong reading-writing connection*   This book addresses reading and writing as essential, parallel skills and recognizes that students can improve their writing skills by strengthening their reading skills. The book contains a chapter that explores the reading-writing connection by presenting strategies for reading and writing about text.

The connection is reinforced throughout the book by the integration of readings within each chapter. These readings offer students models for writing, as well as a source of ideas, a basis for discussion, and an opportunity for collaborative learning or journal writing. Around the readings are structured prewriting activities, vocabulary development, and writing assignments.

- *A visual approach*   Advertisements, photos, charts, and revision maps enliven the text. With idea maps, students create visual representations of a paragraph or essay's content and organization to aid in the comprehension or revision process.

- *Clear, step-by-step chapter format*   Each chapter follows a consistent format. Each contains two primary divisions: *Writing* and *Writing about a Reading*. The *Writing* section presents writing strategies, instructional material, including writing samples and writing exercises. The *Writing about a Reading* section provides pre-reading questions, a brief reading, a *Getting Ready to Write* section that contains a vocabulary exercise, an idea map for students to complete, and questions that lead students to examine the reading and react to ideas presented in the reading. The section concludes with both paragraph and essay-level writing assignments.

- *Writing Success Tips*   Each chapter includes *Writing Success Tips* that offer practical advice on topics such as proofreading, word processing, keeping an error log, and taking competency tests.

- *Student writing*   Each chapter contains one or more pieces of student writing. These paragraphs and essays serve as examples of a particular writing strategy and as confidence-building models of effective, sustained student writing. Nine chapters include a *Student Essay* section that contains a complete, realistic student essay. Questions for analysis follow each reading.

- *Optional essay coverage*   In line with the book's "whole paper" approach, Chapter 1 presents basic essay-writing skills. Optional essay-writing assignments follow each of the readings.

Changes to the Second Edition

- *New Chapter*   A new chapter, *The Reading-Writing Connection* (Chapter 2), presents strategies for reading and writing about a reading assignment. It teaches students how to preview, how to connect the topic of the reading to their own experience, how to read paragraphs and essays, and how to handle difficult vocabulary. Students are also taught to annotate as they read, to use idea maps to analyze the relationships among ideas, and to develop ideas to write about in response to a reading.

- *Reorganization of Chapters*   The text has been reorganized to progress from sentence to paragraph level skills.
- *Idea Maps*   Idea maps present a visual representation of the content and organization of a reading. Idea maps now appear in every chapter reading. Portions of each map are left blank so students can supply the missing information. Early maps have many prompts; in later chapters the number of prompts diminishes, requiring students to participate in their production.
- *Skills Check*   Mastery exercises have been added to the end of each part. The revision exercises enable students to apply and integrate skills taught in the chapters.
- *Student Writing*   Nine student essays have been added on engaging topics such as test anxiety, cultural experiences, and athletics. The essays are intended as realistic, error-free samples of work students produce. Questions that follow each student essay guide the student in analyzing and evaluating the essay.
- *New Readings*   Nearly half (7 out of 16) of the end-of-chapter readings have been replaced. The readings are both accessible and relevant to students' lives; topics include job search strategies, parenting skills, and ethnic stereotyping.
- *Additional Practice Exercises*   Additional practice exercises have been added to most chapters.

Ancillary Materials

In addition to the student text and instructor's annotated edition, the following materials are available with adoption of *The Writer's Compass.*

- *Expressways student software*   *Expressways* is an interactive tutorial software program designed to teach the writing process and paragraph and essay writing. Each module provides condensed instruction on an important skill or rhetorical mode; numerous practice exercises; guided instructions as the students write their own papers on screen; a brief, on-screen reading; and supplementary assignments. *Expressways* is available in both Macintosh and PC versions.

- *PEER (grammar drill and practice) software*   This easy-to-use grammar drill and practice software is available in both Macintosh and PC versions.

- *The American Heritage College Dictionary,* **Third Edition**   The new hardcover edition of this acclaimed dictionary is available at a special low price when you order it with *The Writer's Compass.*

- *The Houghton Mifflin Developmental English Web Site*   This site features PowerPoint slides, an Expressways Demo, and links to selected Developmental English titles, including *The Writer's Compass,* Second Edition homepage, featuring downloadable tests and teaching tips.

Acknowledgments

I appreciate the advice, ideas, and suggestions of my colleagues who served as reviewers:

William Abernathy, Washtenaw Community College, MI

Alan Ainsworth, Houston Community College, TX

Paula Barber, Oklahoma State University, Oklahoma City, OK

Phyllis Boatman, Southern Arkansas University Tech, AR

Patricia Byrne, Camden County College, NJ

Aleta Chamberlim, Labette Community College, KS

Alice Cleveland, College of Marin, CA

Cathy Cole, Tulsa Junior College, OK

Mark Connelley, Milwaukee Area Technical College, WI

Pauline Corse, Chaffey College, CA

Nancy Cox, Arkansas Technical University, AR

Jane Focht-Hansen, San Antonio College, TX

Rita Gagelman, Barton County Community College, KS

Ted Gardner, Barton County Community College, KS

Jan Gerzema, Indiana University, NW, IN

Deborah Gilbert, Cleveland State University, OH

Paul Heilker, Virginia Tech, VA

Jennifer Hurd, Harding University, AR

Kathleen Jacquette, SUNY Farmingdale, NY

Anita C. Jones, Central State Community College, OH

Nancy Kelly, Fitchburg State College, MA

Nancy Laughbaum, Columbus State Community College, OH
Mike Likely, Nassau Community College, NY
Patricia Malinowski, Finger Lakes Community College, NY
Vivian Naylor, Meridian Community College, MS
Marcus H. Patton, Sacramento Community College, CA
Dee Pruitt, Florence Darlington Technical College, SC
Roberta Straight, University of New Mexico, Los Alamos, NM
Linda Tappmeyer, Southwest Baptist University, MO
Robert Walker, Daytona Beach Community College

The editorial staff with whom I have worked deserves praise and credit for their assistance throughout the writing of this text. In particular, I wish to thank Mary Jo Southern for her encouragement and continuing support and Ellen Darion and Harriett Prentiss for their guidance and creative insights. I also wish to thank Beverly Ponzi for her valuable assistance in keyboarding and manuscript management. Finally, I thank my students, who continue to challenge, motivate, and encourage me to write for them.

Kathleen T. McWhorter

GETTING
STARTED

1

An Introduction to Writing

On the first day of class, two students, Al and Maria, are talking as they wait for their writing class to begin.

Al   This class is going to be tough. My spelling is terrible, and I always make mistakes with grammar and punctuation. I might as well leave right now.

Maria   I know what you're saying. But my brother took this course last year. He said he improved a lot. He said you spend your time writing about interesting topics and readings. You write down your ideas and work on things like commas and fragments only as a way of making your ideas clearer. You don't spend your time memorizing rules for nothing.

Al   Hmm. That doesn't sound so bad. Maybe I'll stick around.

After the semester ends, Al meets Maria on campus.

Maria   So how did you do in writing?

Al   Things turned out better than I thought, and I got to like it, too. How about you?

Maria   Aren't you glad you decided to give it a try?

The story of Al and Maria illustrates that students can improve their writing and be successful in a writing class. So stick around, and let's get started on improving *your* writing.

In this book we will concentrate on writing as a means of expressing ideas. You will learn to plan, organize, and develop your ideas. You will learn to write sentences and paragraphs that express your ideas clearly and effectively. You will also learn how to avoid common problems in paragraph and sentence writing. Finally, you will discover that grammar, punctuation, and spelling do have a place in writing, but they are *not* its most important ingredients.

WRITING

What Writing Is and Is Not

The following list explains some correct and incorrect notions about writing:

Writing Is . . .	*Writing Is Not . . .*
• following a step-by-step process of planning, drafting, and revising.	• being able to pick up a pen (or sit at a computer) and write something wonderful on your first try.
• thinking through and organizing ideas.	• connecting words and sentences.
• explaining *your* ideas or experiences.	• developing new earth-shaking ideas no one has ever thought of before.
• being concerned with expressing your ideas clearly and correctly.	• being primarily concerned with grammatical correctness.
• using clear, descriptive, and accurate vocabulary.	• showing off a large vocabulary.
• constructing clear, understandable sentences.	• constructing long, complicated sentences.
• something that can be learned.	• something you are naturally either good or bad at.

EXERCISE 1-1 Suppose you are writing a letter to a toy manufacturer about a defective toy you purchased for your niece or nephew. You feel the toy is dangerous and unsafe for toddlers. Describe, step by step, how you would go about writing this letter. (What is the first thing you would do? What would you do after that? And so forth.) You are not actually writing the letter in this exercise or listing what you would say. You are describing your writing *process*.

The Writing Process: An Overview

Writing, like many other skills, is not a single-step process. Think of the game of football, for instance. Football players do not simply put on uniforms and rush onto the turf. Instead, they spend a great deal of time planning and developing offensive and defensive strategies, trying out new plays, improving existing plays, and practicing. Writing involves similar planning and preparation. It also involves testing ideas and working out the best way to express them. Writers often explore how their ideas might "play out" in several ways before settling upon one plan of action.

People have many individual techniques for writing, but all writing involves five basic steps:

1. generating ideas
2. organizing your ideas
3. writing a first draft
4. revising
5. proofreading

Each step in the process is described briefly below. You will learn more about each in later chapters.

Generating Ideas

Before you can write about a topic, you have to collect ideas to write about. Three helpful techniques to stimulate your thinking are (1) freewriting, (2) brainstorming, and (3) branching.

Organizing Your Ideas

Once you have collected ideas about your topic, the next step is to decide how to organize them. Ideas in a paragraph or essay should be logically organized. To achieve a logical organization, you will need to test various ways to group and arrange your ideas.

Writing a First Draft

A first draft expresses your ideas in sentence and paragraph form. Think of it as your first attempt to get your ideas down on paper without worrying about spelling, punctuation, capitalization, and grammar.

Revising

Revising is a process of *rethinking* your ideas. When you revise, you examine what you have written and make it better, clearer, more complete, and more interesting. Revising involves changing, adding, deleting, and rearranging your ideas and words. You might revise a paragraph or essay several times, going through several drafts, before you feel it has reached its final form.

Proofreading

Proofreading is checking for errors. Think of it as a final polishing of your work. Look for errors in grammar, spelling, punctuation, and capitalization. Errors such as these can distract your reader from your ideas.

NEED TO KNOW

The Writing Process
- Writing is a step-by-step process of explaining your ideas and experiences.
- Writing involves five basic steps: generating ideas, organizing your ideas, writing a first draft, revising, and proofreading.

EXERCISE 1-2 Write a paragraph on one of the following topics:

1. Describe a space alien's fear or surprise when stepping out of a spaceship onto Earth. Explain what the alien sees or hears and how he or she reacts to it.
2. Describe your reaction to your first day of college classes. Include specific examples to support your ideas.

Writing Essays

The sentence, the paragraph, and the essay are three basic building blocks in communicating your ideas. A **sentence** expresses one or more complete thoughts. A **paragraph,** which is usually made up of three or more sentences, expresses one idea and explains or supports that idea. An **essay,** which consists of two or more paragraphs, expresses and explains a series of related ideas, all of which support a larger, broader idea.

The emphasis in this text is on writing effective sentences and paragraphs. However, in some of your courses, your instructors may ask you to write essays or take essay exams. Some writing instructors prefer that their students write essays right away. Other instructors prefer that their students begin by writing single paragraphs and then progress to essay writing. Regardless of when you begin writing essays, the following introduction to essay techniques will be useful to you. It will show you why good paragraph-writing skills are absolutely necessary for good essays.

What Is an Essay?

An **essay** is a group of paragraphs about one subject. It contains one key idea about the subject, which is called the **thesis statement.** Each paragraph in the essay supports or explains some aspect of the thesis statement.

How Is an Essay Organized?

An essay follows a logical and direct plan: it introduces an idea (the thesis statement), explains it, and draws a conclusion. Usually, then, an essay has at least three paragraphs:

1. introductory paragraph
2. body (one or more paragraphs)
3. concluding paragraph

The Introductory Paragraph

Your **introductory paragraph** should accomplish three things:

1. It should establish the topic of the essay.
2. It should present the thesis statement of your essay in an appropriate way for its intended audience.
3. It should interest your reader in your essay.

The Body

The **body** of your essay should accomplish three things:

1. It should provide information that supports and explains your thesis statement.
2. It should present each main supporting point in a separate paragraph.
3. It should contain enough detailed information to make the main point of each paragraph understandable and believable.

The Concluding Paragraph

Your **concluding paragraph** should accomplish two things:

1. It should reemphasize but not restate your thesis statement.
2. It should draw your essay to a close.

In the following sample essay, the marginal notes indicate the function of each paragraph.

Sample Essay

College and the Marine Corps

this sentence builds interest ⟶   I have made two important decisions in my lifetime. They were to join the Marine Corps and to attend college. Each decision turned out to be the right one for me. Although the Marines and college are very different, each has had a similar effect on me.

thesis statement

introduction

supporting paragraph explaining Marine Corps' challenges and accomplishments

> There was only one reason for joining the Marine Corps. I had to make money to go to college. I needed it, and they offered it. The Marine Corps was more difficult and challenging than I had thought it would be. Boot camp was horrible. Each day was filled with obstacles, physical as well as mental. Each day, however, I felt a strong sense of accomplishment in making it through the day. At the end of boot camp I was proud to call myself a Marine.

body

supporting paragraph explaining challenges and accomplishments of college

> College has turned out to be the same as the Marine Corps in many ways. I chose to attend college for one reason: to have a career. I am enrolled in the Operating Room Assistant program, and it is much more difficult than I imagined it to be. Biology and Medical Terminology are hard courses. There are many obstacles, such as unannounced quizzes, labs, and exams. However, each time I earn a passing grade, I feel the same sense of accomplishment that I felt in the Marines. I know that when I graduate and walk into an operating room, I will be proud to be part of the medical team.

reemphasis of thesis statement

> Soon I plan to make a decision just as important as joining the Marine Corps or attending college. Next spring, I am planning to get married to a person I met in the Marines. I hope it, too, will work out.

conclusion

Practical Advice for Getting Started

Writing is a skill that can be learned. Like any other skill, such as keyboarding, playing football, accounting, or cooking, writing takes practice. Be sure to focus your attention on new techniques suggested by your instructor as well as the ones given in each chapter of this book. To improve, you often need to be open to doing things differently. Approach writing positively. Don't hesitate to experiment.

Consider the following points as ways to get off to a successful start:

1. Think first, then write.
2. Plan on making changes.
3. Give yourself enough time to write.
4. Develop a routine.
5. Allow sufficient time.
6. Take breaks.
7. Use full 8½-by-11-inch sheets of paper.
8. Keep a journal.

Think First, Then Write

Writing is a thinking process: it is an expression of your thoughts. Don't expect to be able to pick up a pen or sit down at a computer and immediately produce a well-written paragraph or essay. Plan to spend time generating ideas and deciding how to organize them before you write your first draft.

Plan on Making Changes

Most writers revise (rewrite, rethink, change, add, and delete) numerous times before they are pleased with their work. For example, I revised this chapter of *The Writer's Compass* five times before I was satisfied with it.

Give Yourself Enough Time to Write

For most of us, writing does not come easily. It takes time to think, select a topic, generate ideas, organize them, draft a piece of writing, revise it, and proofread it. Reserve a block of time each day for writing. Use the time to read this book and to work on its writing exercises and assignments. Begin by reserving an hour per day. This may seem like a lot of time. However, most instructors expect you to spend at least two hours outside of class for every hour you spend in class. If your writing class meets for a total of three hours per week, then you should spend at least six hours per week working on writing.

Develop a Routine

Try to work at the same time each day. You will develop a routine that will be easy to follow. Be sure to work at peak periods of concentration. Don't write when you are tired, hungry, or likely to be interrupted.

Allow Sufficient Time

Begin assignments well before they are due. You will need time to plan, organize, draft, revise, and proofread. Plan to let your drafts "sit" awhile—preferably a day—before you begin to revise. Necessary changes will become much more obvious after some time away from your work.

Take Breaks

If you get stuck and cannot think or write, take a break. Clear your mind by going for a walk, talking to a friend, or having a snack. Set a time limit for your break, though, so you return to work in a reasonable time. When you begin again, start by rereading what you have already written. If you still cannot make progress, use freewriting, brainstorming, and branching techniques (see page 252) to generate more ideas about your topic.

Use Full 8½-by-11-Inch Sheets of Paper

By using standard-sized 8½-by-11-inch paper, you will be able to see better how your ideas connect. Write on only one side of the paper so that you can spread out the sheets and track the development of ideas.

Keep a Journal

A writing journal is an excellent way to improve your writing and keep track of your thoughts and ideas.

How It Works

1. Buy an 8½-by-11-inch spiral-bound notebook. Use it exclusively for journal writing.
2. Reserve ten to fifteen minutes a day to write in your journal. Write every day, not just on days when a good idea strikes.

3. Write about whatever comes to mind. You might write about events that happened and your reactions to them or describe feelings, impressions, or worries.

If you have trouble getting started, ask yourself some questions:

- What happened at school, work, or home?
- What world, national, or local events occurred?
- What are you worried about?
- What positive experience did you have lately? Maybe it was eating a good meal, making a new friend, or finding time to wash your car.
- What did you see today? Practice writing descriptions of beautiful, funny, interesting, or disturbing things you've noticed.
- What is the best or worst thing that happened today?
- Whom did you talk with? What did you talk about? Record conversations as fully as you can.

Sample Journal Entries

The following student journal entries will give you a better picture of journal writing. They have been edited for easy reading. However, as you write, do not be concerned with neatness or correctness.

Jeffrey The best thing that happened today happened as soon as I got home from work. The phone rang. At first, I wasn't going to answer it because I was tired and in one of those moods when I wanted to be by myself. It rang so many times I decided to answer it. Am I glad I did! It was MaryAnn, a long-lost girlfriend that I'd always regretted losing touch with. She said she had just moved back into the neighborhood, and . . . I took it from there.

Malcolm This morning while walking across campus to my math class, I stopped for a few minutes under a chestnut tree. Perfect timing! I've always loved collecting chestnuts, and they were just beginning to fall. When I was a kid, I used to pick up lunch bags full of them. I never knew what to do with them once I had them. I just liked picking them up, I guess. I remember liking their cold, sleek, shiny smoothness and how good they felt in my hand. So I picked up a few, rubbed them together in my hand, and went off to class, happy that some things never change.

Allison This morning my new seven-week-old puppy tore up the house. I went upstairs to get dressed, and I forgot to take her with me. She got into my houseplants. When I came down, there were dirt, moss, and leaves spread all through the living room and kitchen. I was furious until I looked at her. She sat in the middle of the mess, wagged her tail, and looked at me with *those* eyes. All of a sudden, all was forgiven.

Benefits of Journal Writing

When you write in your journal, you are practicing writing and becoming better at expressing your thoughts in writing. You can feel free to practice without pressure or fear of criticism. Besides practice, journal writing has other benefits:

1. Your journals will become a good source of ideas. When you have a paper assigned and must select your own topic, review your journal for ideas.
2. You may find that journal writing becomes a way to think through problems, release pent-up feelings, or keep an enjoyable record of life experiences. Journal writing is writing *for yourself*.

Peer Review

Not everything you write in a college writing class needs to be graded by your instructor. Instead, you can get valuable "peer review," or feedback, from other members of your class. Peers (classmates) can tell you what they like and what they think you need to improve in your writing. You can also learn a lot from reading and commenting on the work of other students.

If your instructor wants you to choose your own reviewer, look for someone who is reliable, serious, and conscientious. It is not necessarily a good idea to work with close friends, since they may feel reluctant to give you honest criticism. With friends, it is easy for conversation to drift away from the task at hand, too. If you are on the giving end of peer review, take your job seriously. The following tips tell you how to use the peer review process.

Tips for the Writer

1. Prepare your draft in a readable form. Double-space your work; be sure to use full 8½-by-11-inch sheets of paper. Use only one side of the paper.
2. Keep a copy of your paper for yourself, if possible.

3. When you receive your reviewer's comments, weigh them carefully, but do not feel you have to accept every suggestion that is made.
4. If you have questions or are uncertain about the advice your reviewer gave you, talk with your instructor.

Tips for the Reviewer

1. Read the draft through at least once before making any judgments.
2. Read the draft two or more times before you make specific comments.
3. As you read, keep in mind the writer's intended audience (see Chapters 10 and 14). The draft should be appropriate for the audience for whom it was written.
4. Offer positive comments first. Say what the writer did well.
5. Use the Revision Checklists that appear at the end of Chapters 11 through 15 as a guide.
6. Avoid general comments. Don't just say that a sentence is unclear. Instead, explain what it lacks or how it could be improved, but do not make actual corrections for the writer.

NEED TO KNOW

Peer Review

- You can get valuable help with your writing from class members by using peer review.
- You should weigh a reviewer's comments seriously, but not feel obliged to accept every suggestion.
- As a reviewer, you should read the work several times and offer positive comments as well as specific suggestions for improvement.

WRITING ABOUT A READING

Thinking before Reading

The following reading by Bill Cosby humorously describes a parent-child conflict from his childhood. Before you read, connect the reading to your own experience by answering the following questions:

1. Why do children often have different attitudes, opinions, and tastes from their parents'?
2. What parent-child conflicts do you recall experiencing?

READING

The Way It Was
Bill Cosby

When I was thirteen, my father used to sit in our living room and listen on our Philco radio to strange music by people named Duke Ellington, Count Basie, and Jimmie Lunceford. Sometimes when I walked by, I saw him leaning back in his armchair and smiling blissfully. My mission was to sneak *past* that living room before he caught me and made me come inside for a music appreciation lesson on the old-timey music that I couldn't stand. 1

"Come here and sit down," he'd say. "Now this is Jimmie Lunceford." He pointed to the Philco and smiled, while I tried to adjust my ears to the low volume. And when the piece was over, he'd say, "Now *that's* music. I don't know what you call the crap you hear upstairs, but *that's* music." 2

During each of these command performances, I would smile respect-fully and move my head back and forth in rhythm as if I really enjoyed this junk; and after my own performance was over, I would pat my father on the knee, say, "Thank you, Dad," and tell him I had some-thing important to do. The something important, of course, was to get away from that music. And then I would go upstairs and wonder how I could negotiate these walks past the living room and out of the house without having my father use his Philco to damage my brain. For a while, I considered putting a ladder against my window, but it also would have let a burglar in. 3

Had a burglar made it into my room, he would have had a wonder-ful time hearing Sonny Rollins, John Coltrane, Dizzy Gillespie, Miles Davis, Thelonious Monk, Bud Powell, and Philly Joe Jones. He would have been able to hear them right through any ski mask because I always played them at top volume. The greatest advantage of top vol-ume was that I couldn't hear the grownups when they came in to tell me to turn that crap down. 4

From time to time my father would come by, kick the door open, and then stand there under the assault of the music. He had the look of a sailor standing on deck in a typhoon. And then his lips would start to move. I couldn't hear him, but I didn't have to, for he was sending an ancient message: 5

Turn that crap down. 6

I then would turn the sound down about halfway, moving him to say, "Turn it down, I said." I'd then turn the dial to the three-quarters point and he'd say, "More." Giving him more, I would say, "Dad, it's off." 7

"And that," he would [8] say, "is what I want."

Music has changed so [9] drastically since the days when I first heard the wonders of John Coltrane and Bud Powell. Today a guitar is a major appliance whose volume guarantees that the teenager playing it will never be aware of the start of World War III. This teenager will merely see the explosions and will probably think that they are part of a publicity campaign for a new English group called the Armageddons.

I know I don't sound [10] hip talking like this, but no matter *how* he talks, a father cannot sound hip to his children. (I wonder if even the Duke sounded hip to Mercer Ellington, or if Mercer just humored the old man.) He can give high fives until his palms

bleed; he can say "Chilly down" so much that he sounds like a short order cook; but the father will still be a man who lost all of his hipness at the age of twenty-three.

The day he started paying rent. [11]

Remember Cosby's First Law of Intergenerational Perversity? Well, [12] it also applies to being hip. Anything that *you* like cannot possibly be something your kids like too, so it cannot possibly be hip. You know what would end Madonna's career? If enough parents suddenly started to like her.

From Bill Cosby, *Fatherhood.*

Getting Ready to Write

Strengthening Your Vocabulary

Write a brief definition for each of the following words from the preceding reading. If you cannot figure out the meaning of a word from the way it is used in the reading, look the word up in a dictionary.

1. blissfully (paragraph 1)   very happily
2. negotiate (paragraph 3)   arrange, manage
3. intergenerational (paragraph 12)   occurring between generations
4. perversity (paragraph 12)   stubbornness

Examining the Reading

1. What did Bill Cosby think of his father's musical tastes? What did Cosby's father think of Cosby's musical tastes?
2. What does Cosby think of currently popular music?
3. Explain Cosby's Law of Intergenerational Perversity.
4. Describe Cosby's attitude toward his father.

Reacting to and Discussing Ideas

Get ready to write about the reading by discussing the following questions:

1. Is Cosby correct that parents and children often disagree about music?
2. Do you agree or disagree with Cosby's Law of Intergenerational Perversity?
3. In what areas other than music do parents and children often disagree?
4. Why do parents and children frequently have different tastes and preferences? Do children need to be different from their parents?

Writing about the Reading

The Paragraph Option

Write a paragraph describing a parent-child conflict you have observed or experienced. Explain the central issue. Describe the opinions of the parent and of the child. How was the conflict resolved?

The Essay Option

Write an essay contrasting your musical preferences to those of your parents or friends.

WRITING SUCCESS TIP 1

Today many students use a computer when they write. With a computer, you can type your papers onto a disk and print them out using a printer connected to the computer. Computer word processing programs let you add or delete words, sentences, or even entire paragraphs without retyping the whole paper. Drafting, revising, and correcting errors are all easier and less time consuming.

1. **Investigate computer availability on your campus.** You don't have to own a computer to do word processing. Many colleges have computer labs or writing labs with computers available for your use and with assistants present to help you.

2. **Learn a word processing system.** You may need to spend some time learning how to work a word processing system. You will also need basic typing skills. You do not need to type fast, but you do need to be familiar with the keyboard. Many colleges offer keyboarding workshops or credit courses that teach the basics. Any time you spend learning to use a word processing system will be saved many times over as you begin to use a computer to write your papers. Experience with word processing will also be an asset when you apply for jobs.

3. **Save your work frequently.** You can instruct the computer to make a permanent copy of what you are writing at any time by using a "save" command. Save your work often—every ten or fifteen minutes. This practice will prevent your work from being accidentally erased by a power failure or a mistaken command.

4. **Work with printed copy.** At various stages in the writing process, you may find it easier to work with printed copy than with what appears on the screen. Most screens display only about twenty lines of print at a time. Therefore, when you are evaluating the overall organization of a lengthy paragraph or essay, it may be easier for you to see the flow of your ideas on a printed copy of your work.

5. **Use a spell-check program.** Some word processing programs come with a built-in spell-check program. Spell-checkers have a vocabulary of common words and can identify any misspellings of these words; some can give you the correct spelling as well. Spell-checkers are not 100 percent accurate, however, so you should still always look for misspellings. Also, spell-checkers only confirm that a word exists; they do not indicate whether you have used it correctly.

2 The Reading-Writing Connection

Scott is taking a writing course in which the instructor assigns readings as sources of ideas for writing. Each time a reading is assigned, Scott complains: "I like to write, and the readings are interesting, but it takes me so long to read them. I have trouble remembering what I read, so I have to read them three or four times. By the time I've finished, I don't feel like writing anymore."

Do you, like Scott, wish you could get more out of reading assignments? Do you want to avoid spending unnecessary time rereading and reviewing? This chapter explains skills and techniques that can make an immediate, noticeable change in how well you understand and remember what you read. As you work through this chapter, you will see that there is a strong connection between reading and writing. Improving one skill often improves the other. You will also discover that there is more to reading an assignment than opening your book to the correct page, reading, and closing the book. You will learn a number of strategies and techniques for reading essays more effectively, for remembering what you read, and for finding ideas to write about.

EXPLORING THE READING-WRITING CONNECTION

At first, reading and writing may seem like very different, even opposite, processes. A writer starts with a blank page and creates and develops ideas, while a reader starts with a full page and reads someone else's ideas. Although reading and writing may seem very different, they are actually parts of the same communication process.

Writers begin with a message they wish to communicate; readers attempt to understand that message. Drawing from their knowledge and experience, writers create a message; readers grasp its meaning by connecting it to their own experience. The written word is the means through which the message is transmitted from one person's mind to another—in sentence, paragraph, and essay form.

Because reading and writing work together, improving one often improves the other. By learning to read more effectively, you'll become a better writer as well as a better reader. For example, as you learn more about writing paragraphs, you will be able to read them more easily. Similarly, as you learn more about how an essay is organized, you will find it easier to organize your own ideas into essay form.

You can see, then, that reading and writing are part of the same process, in much the same way as speaking and listening are part of the same process. In each situation a message is transmitted from one person to another. The purpose of this chapter is to strengthen your reading-writing connection—to provide a starting point for reading and writing and to build skills in both areas.

> **NEED TO KNOW**
>
> **The Relationship of Reading and Writing**
> - Reading and writing are parts of the same communication process.
> - Writers begin with a message they want to communicate.
> - Readers try to understand the message by connecting it to their experience.

This text uses readings to help you become a better writer. Every chapter concludes with a reading that illustrates the skills taught in the chapter and provides ideas to write about. This chapter offers strategies and skills for approaching reading assignments. It will "walk you through" a reading assignment, offering tips at each stage and suggesting what to do before, while, and after reading to strengthen your comprehension, help you remember more of what you read, and show you how to find ideas to write about.

Previewing before Reading

To make an assignment easier to read and remember, as well as to make it more interesting, take a few minutes to find out what the reading is about and to discover what you already know about the topic before you begin reading. Do this by previewing the reading and then connecting what you discover to your own experience.

Previewing is like looking at a map before you begin to drive in an unfamiliar city. It familiarizes you with the organization and content of a reading. Then, when you read the selection, you are able to understand it more easily. Previewing is not time consuming. You can preview a brief selection in several minutes by following these basic steps:

1. **Read and think about the title.** What does it tell you about the subject? Does it offer any clues as to how the author feels about the subject or how the author will approach it? What do you already know about the subject?

2. **Check the author.** Is the author's name familiar? If so, what do you know about the author?

3. **Read the first paragraph.** Here the author often introduces the subject. Look for a statement of the main point of the entire reading. If the first paragraph is lengthy, read only the first few sentences.

4. Read all dark-print headings. Headings divide the reading into sections and announce the topic of each section.

5. Read the first sentence under each heading. This sentence often states the main point of the section.

6. If the reading lacks headings, read the first sentence of a few paragraphs on each page. You will discover many of the main ideas of the article.

7. Read the last paragraph. Often this paragraph summarizes or concludes the reading. If the last paragraph is lengthy, read only the last few sentences.

The more you practice previewing and get in the habit of previewing, the more effectively it will work. Use the preview strategy for all your college textbooks, as well as for assigned chapters and readings in this book. In this book, you will notice a section titled "Thinking Before Reading," which comes before each reading and reminds you to preview.

Demonstration of Previewing

Now, preview the following reading, "Ways to Improve Your Memory." The portions you should preview have been highlighted. Preview this reading now, reading only the shaded portions.

Ways to Improve Your Memory

Before taking office, President Clinton invited five hundred business leaders to an economic summit in Little Rock. When it was over, many of the guests marveled at Clinton's ability to address them all by name. I have always been impressed by stories like this one—by stories of stage actors who memorize hundreds of lines in only one week of rehearsal, of people who fluently speak five languages, and of waiters who take dinner orders without a note pad. How can these accomplishments be explained? 1

Over the years, psychologists have stumbled upon a few rare individuals who seemed equipped with extraordinary "hardware" for memory. But often the actors, waiters, multilinguists, and others we encounter use memory tricks called mnemonics—in other words, they vary their memory's "software." Can you boost your recall capacity through the use of mnemonics? Can you improve your study skills as a result? At this point, let's step back and consider several ways you can improve your memory. 2

Practice time: To learn names, dates, vocabulary words, formulas, or the concepts in a textbook, you'll find that practice makes perfect. In general, the more time spent studying, the better. In fact, it pays to over-learn—that is, to review the material even after you think you have it mastered. It's also better to spread out your studying over time than to cram all at once. You will retain more information from four two-hour sessions than from one eight-hour marathon.

Active thinking: The sheer amount of practice time is important, but only if it's "quality time." Mindless drills may be helpful in the short run, but long-term retention requires that you think actively and deeply about material—about what it means and how it is linked to what you already know. Ask yourself critical questions about the material. Think about it in ways that relate to your own experiences. Talk about the material to a friend, thus forcing yourself to organize it in terms that can be understood.

Organization of information: Once you have information to be learned, organize it as in an outline. Start with a few broad categories, then divide these into more specific subcategories and sub-subcategories. This is how many experts chunk new information, and it works. Thus, when Andrea Halpern (1986) presented subjects with 54 popular song titles, she found that recall was greater when the titles were organized hierarchically than when they were scrambled. The implication for studying is clear: organize the material in your notes, preferably in the form of an outline—and make sure to review these notes later.

Verbal mnemonics: Sometimes the easiest way to remember a list of items is to use verbal mnemonics, or "memory tricks." Chances are, you have already used popular methods such as *rhymes* ("*i* before *e*, except after *c*" is my favorite; "thirty days hath September, April, June, and

3

4

5

6

Slogans and Products

Read the slogans and product names listed below. How many of the slogans can you match to the correct advertised products?

_____ 1. Like a good neighbor	(a) General Electric
_____ 2. Be all that you can be	(b) State Farm
_____ 3. You deserve a break today	(c) Busch Beer
_____ 4. Head for the mountains	(d) Allstate
_____ 5. We bring good things to life	(e) McDonald's
_____ 6. You've got the right one, baby	(f) Diet Pepsi
_____ 7. You're in good hands	(g) U.S. Army

Answers: 1(b), 2(g), 3(e), 4(c), 5(a), 6(f), 7(d)

November" is another) and *acronyms* that reduce the amount of information to be stored (for example, *ROY G BIV* can be used to recall the colors of the light spectrum: *r*ed, *o*range, *y*ellow, *g*reen, *b*lue, *i*ndigo, and *v*iolet). Relying on verbal mnemonics, advertisers create slogans to make their products memorable (see table on page 22).

Interference: Because one learning experience can disrupt memory for another, it is wise to guard against the effects of interference. This problem is particularly common among college students, as material learned in one course can make it harder to retain that learned in another. To minimize the problem, follow two simple suggestions. First, study right before sleeping and review all the material right before the exam. Second, allocate an uninterrupted chunk of time to one course, and then do the same for your others as well. If you study psychology for a while, then move to biology, and then on to math and back to psychology, each course will disrupt your memory of the others—especially if the material is similar. 7

Study environment: Information is easier to recall when people are in the setting in which it was learned. That's why actors like to rehearse on the stage where they will later perform. So the next time you have an important exam to take, it may help to study in the room where the test will be administered. 8

These are just a few ways to improve your memory. Experiment with each to discover those that work for you. 9

From Kassin, *Psychology*

Although you may not realize it, you learned a great deal about improving your memory in the minute or two you spent previewing.

EXERCISE **2-1** | Without referring to the above reading, "Ways to Improve Your Memory," make a list of ideas or suggestions you recall.

Connecting the Reading to Your Own Experience

Once you have previewed a reading, try to connect the topic to your own experience. Take a moment to recall what you already know or have read about the topic. This activity will make the reading more interesting and easier to write about. Here are a few suggestions to help you make connections:

1. Ask questions and answer them. Suppose you have just previewed a reading titled "Advertising: Institutionalized Lying." Ask questions such as: Do ads always tell the truth? If not, why not? What do I already know about deceptive advertising?

2. Brainstorm. Jot down everything that comes to mind about the topic on a sheet of scrap paper or a computer file. For example, if the topic of a reading is "The Generation Gap," write down ideas as they occur to you. You might list reasons for such a gap, try to define it, or mention names of families in which you have observed it. For more about brainstorming, see Chapter 10, page 252.

3. Think of examples. Try to think of situations, people, or events that relate to the topic. For instance, suppose you have previewed a reading titled "Fashions, Fads, and Crazes." You might think of recent examples of each: athletic clothing as casual attire, Barbie dolls, in-line skating, or the macarena.

Each of these techniques will help you identify ideas or experiences that you may share with the writer and that will help you focus your attention on the reading. In this book, the section titled "Thinking Before Reading," which comes before each reading, lists several questions that will help you draw connections to your own experience.

EXERCISE ▷ 2-2 | Based on your preview of "Ways to Improve Your Memory," use one or more of the above techniques to connect the reading to your own experience. You might think of memory tricks you already use or things you find difficult (or easy) to remember.

Reading for Meaning

Reading is much more than moving your eyes across a line of print. To get the most out of a reading, you should search for, grasp, and react to the author's ideas. To do so, you'll need to know how essays and paragraphs are organized, how to develop strategies for dealing with difficult or confusing sentences or passages, and how to handle unfamiliar vocabulary.

What to Look for in Essays

If you know what to look for as you read, you'll find reading is easier, goes faster, and requires less rereading. When you read the essays in this book, be sure to pay attention to each of the following parts:

1. The title. In some essays, the title announces the topic of the essay and may reveal the author's viewpoint. In others, the meaning of the title becomes clear only after you have read the essay.

2. The introduction. The opening paragraph of an essay should interest you, announce the subject of the essay, and give necessary background information.

3. The author's main point. The main point is often called the *thesis statement*. It is the one big idea that the entire essay explains. Often it appears in the first paragraph, but it can be placed anywhere in the essay.

4. Support and explanation. The body of the essay should explain, give reasons for, or offer support for the author's main point.

5. The conclusion. The last paragraph brings the essay to a close. Often, it will restate the author's main point. It may also suggest directions for further thought.

Now, reread "Ways to Improve Your Memory," which has been marked here to identify each of the above parts.

Ways to Improve Your Memory

Before taking office, President Clinton invited five hundred business leaders to an economic summit in Little Rock. When it was over, many of the guests marveled at Clinton's ability to address them all by name. I have always been impressed by stories like this one—by stories of stage actors who memorize hundreds of lines in only one week of rehearsal, of people who fluently speak five languages, and of waiters who take dinner orders without a note pad. How can these accomplishments be explained? — 1 } introduction

Over the years, psychologists have stumbled upon a few rare individuals who seemed equipped with extraordinary "hardware" for memory. But often the actors, waiters, multilinguists, and others we encounter use memory tricks called mnemonics—in other words, they vary their memory's "software." Can you boost your recall capacity through the use of mnemonics? Can you improve your study skills as a result? At this point, let's step back and consider several ways you can improve your memory. — 2 } thesis statement

Practice time: To learn names, dates, vocabulary words, formulas, or the concepts in a textbook, you'll find that practice makes perfect. In general, the more time spent studying, the better. In fact, it pays to overlearn—that is, to review the material even after you think you have it mastered. It's also better to spread out your studying over time than to cram all at once. You will retain more information from four two-hour sessions than from one eight-hour marathon. — 3 } support and explanation

Active thinking: The sheer amount of practice time is important, but only if it's "quality time." Mindless drills may be helpful in the short run, but long-term retention requires that you think actively and — 4

deeply about material—about what it means and how it is linked to what you already know. Ask yourself critical questions about the material. Think about it in ways that relate to your own experiences. Talk about the material to a friend, thus forcing yourself to organize it in terms that can be understood.

Organization of information: Once you have information to be learned, organize it as in an outline. Start with a few broad categories, then divide these into more specific subcategories and sub-subcategories. This is how many experts chunk new information, and it works. Thus, when Andrea Halpern (1986) presented subjects with 54 popular song titles, she found that recall was greater when the titles were organized hierarchically than when they were scrambled. The implication for studying is clear: organize the material in your notes, preferably in the form of an outline—and make sure to review these notes later.

Verbal mnemonics: Sometimes the easiest way to remember a list of items is to use verbal mnemonics, or "memory tricks." Chances are, you have already used popular methods such as *rhymes* ("*i* before *e*, except after *c*" is my favorite; "thirty days hath September, April, June, and November" is another) and *acronyms* that reduce the amount of information to be stored (for example, *ROY G BIV* can be used to recall the colors of the light spectrum: *red, orange, yellow, green, blue, indigo,* and *violet*). Relying on verbal mnemonics, advertisers create slogans to make their products memorable (see table below).

support and explanation

Slogans and Products

Read the slogans and product names listed below. How many of the slogans can you match to the correct advertised products?

_____ 1. Like a good neighbor
_____ 2. Be all that you can be
_____ 3. You deserve a break today
_____ 4. Head for the mountains
_____ 5. We bring good things to life
_____ 6. You've got the right one, baby
_____ 7. You're in good hands

(a) General Electric
(b) State Farm
(c) Busch Beer
(d) Allstate
(e) McDonald's
(f) Diet Pepsi
(g) U.S. Army

Answers: 1(b), 2(g), 3(e), 4(c), 5(a), 6(f), 7(d)

Interference: Because one learning experience can disrupt memory for another, it is wise to guard against the effects of interference. This problem is particularly common among college students, as material learned in one course can make it harder to retain that learned in another. To minimize the problem, follow two simple suggestions. First, study right

before sleeping and review all the material right before the exam.
Second, allocate an uninterrupted chunk of time to one course, and then
do the same for your others as well. If you study psychology for a while,
then move to biology, and then on to math and back to psychology,
each course will disrupt your memory of the others—especially if the
material is similar.

} support and explanation

Study environment: Information is easier to recall when people are
in the setting in which it was learned. That's why actors like to rehearse
on the stage where they will later perform. So the next time you have
an important exam to take, it may help to study in the room where the
test will be administered.

8

These are just a few ways to improve your memory. Experiment
with each to discover those that work for you.

9
conclusion

What to Look for in Paragraphs

A paragraph is organized around a topic sentence. This sentence states
what the entire paragraph will be about and is the main point of the paragraph. Every other sentence in the paragraph is a detail that explains or
supports it. Details may be facts, statistics, examples, or descriptions. You
can visualize a paragraph as follows:

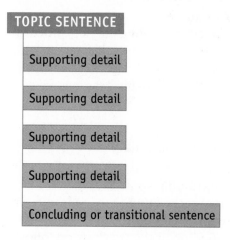

In this diagram the topic sentence appears first. The first sentence is the
most likely place to find the topic sentence, but it can appear anywhere in
the paragraph. (You will learn much more about the topic sentences and
supporting details in Chapters 11 and 12.)

Now, let's look at a sample paragraph and notice how the writer states
and then explains ideas. Again, refer to the marginal notes as you read.

Verbal mnemonics

topic sentence { *Sometimes the easiest way to remember a list of items is to use verbal mnemonics, or "memory tricks."* Chances are, you have already used popu-

supporting detail { lar methods such as *rhymes* ("*i* before *e*, except after *c*" is my favorite; "thirty days hath September, April, June, and November" is another) and *acronyms* that reduce the amount of information to be stored (for example, *ROY G BIV* can be used to recall the colors of the light spectrum: *r*ed,

concluding sentence { orange, *y*ellow, *g*reen, *b*lue, *i*ndigo, and *v*iolet). Relying on verbal mnemonics, advertisers create slogans to make their products memorable.

As you read, search for the topic sentence of each paragraph and notice how the other sentences in the paragraph explain it. This search process will help you keep your mind on the reading and will direct your attention to the reading's key points. Try underlining or highlighting each topic sentence as you find it.

In this book you will find an exercise titled "Examine the Reading" following each reading. It is designed to help you check your understanding of the reading—both main ideas and details.

EXERCISE 2-3 ▷ | Underline the topic sentence of each paragraph of the reading "Ways to Improve Your Memory," on page 21.

How to Handle Difficult Readings

All of us at one time or another come across a piece of material that is difficult or confusing. An entire reading may be difficult, or just a paragraph or two within an otherwise comfortable reading may be troublesome. Don't give in to the temptation to skip over difficult parts or just give up. Instead, try to approach challenging readings using the methods in the box on page 29.

How to Handle Difficult Vocabulary

As you are reading, you will probably come across some unfamiliar words or phrases. Before interrupting your reading to look them up in a dictionary, try to get a general sense of what they mean from how they are used in the sentence. Often, you can find a clue to a word's meaning in the sentence in which it is used or in the previous or following sentence. These clues are called *context clues*. (The words that surround an unknown word are known as its *context* and offer clues to its meaning.)

Using Context Clues

There are four types of context clues: definition, example, contrast, and inference.

TIPS FOR READING DIFFICULT MATERIAL

1. **Analyze the time and place in which you are reading.** If you have been reading or studying for several hours, mental fatigue may be the source of the problem. If you are reading in a place with numerous distractions, lack of concentration may contribute to poor comprehension.

2. **Look up unfamiliar words.** Often, a few unfamiliar words can block understanding. Keep a dictionary handy and refer to it as needed. For additional suggestions, see the next section, "How to Handle Difficult Vocabulary."

3. **Do not hesitate to reread difficult or complicated sections.** In fact, sometimes several rereadings are appropriate and necessary.

4. **Rephrase each paragraph in your own words.** You might approach extremely complicated material sentence by sentence, expressing each idea in your own words.

5. **Read aloud sentences or sections that are particularly difficult.** Hearing ideas aloud often aids comprehension.

6. **Make a brief outline of the major points of the reading.** An outline will help you see the overall organization and progression of ideas.

7. **Slow down your reading rate if you feel you are beginning to lose comprehension.** On occasion, simply reading more slowly will boost your comprehension.

8. **Summarize.** Test your recall by summarizing each section after you read it.

9. **Work with a classmate.** Working through and discussing the reading with a classmate often will increase your understanding of it.

Definition Clues.

When a writer thinks you may not understand a word, he or she provides a brief definition or synonym in the sentence. Sometimes you may find a direct definition: a sentence written specifically to define the word. Other times a synonym or brief definition may be inserted in the sentence. Synonyms may be separated from the sentence by commas, parentheses, or dashes.

Status refers to one's position in society.

Deviance, an act that violates what society expects, is too complex to assess.

There are two **variables,** or factors, to consider.

Hieroglyphics (pictures that represent words) were used in ancient languages.

Limericks—five-line rhyming poems—are often humorous or witty.

Once you figure out a word using context clues, jot its meaning in the margin. Writing will help you remember it, and it will be there for easy reference and study.

Example Clues.

Often a writer includes an example that helps explain or clarify a word. Suppose you did not know the meaning of **condiments** in the following sentence:

> The fast-food restaurant offers a limited choice of **condiments:** catsup, mustard, and relish.

From the three examples of condiments—*catsup, mustard,* and *relish*—you can figure out that *condiments* are seasonings added to food. Here are a few more examples:

> **Involuntary reflexes,** such as breathing and beating of the heart, should be carefully monitored.
> **Homonyms**—words such as *their* and *there,* and *deer* and *dear*—are easily confused.

Contrast Clues.

Sometimes you can figure out the meaning of an unknown word from a word or phrase that has the opposite meaning. In the following sentence, notice how an opposite word (underlined) suggests the meaning of the word in boldface print.

> The college president **denounced** certain changes in financial-aid regulations, while praising others.

Although you do not know the meaning of *denounced,* you know that it means the opposite of *praised.* (The word *while* suggests the two words are opposites.) *Denounce,* then, means to openly condemn or attack. Try to identify the contrast clues in the following examples:

> In Western society, men marry only one woman at a time; in other cultures, **polygamy** is common.
> During the ceremony the children were quiet, but at the reception they were **boisterous.**

Inference Clues.

There are times when you can figure out an unknown word by reasoning from the information contained in the sentence, as in the following example:

> After he tasted five types of pizza, James found his appetite was completely **satiated.**

NEED TO KNOW

Context Clues

- Sometimes you can figure out the meaning of an unknown word through context clues.

- "Context" refers to the words that surround an unknown word: words in the same sentence or in the previous or following sentence.

- There are four kinds of context clues: definition, example, contrast, and inference.

You can reason that after tasting five different pizzas, a person would not feel like eating more. Thus, you could infer that *satiated* means "full" or "satisfied." Here are a few more examples; does the underlined information provide a clue to meaning?

> The **ludicrous** sight of the basketball team dressed as <u>Santa's elves</u> forced us to <u>burst out laughing</u>.
>
> Maria is quite **versatile**: she is a strong <u>public speaker</u>, an excellent <u>dancer</u>, a caring <u>parent</u>, and a <u>community leader</u>.

As you become skilled in their use, you will find context clues are a handy, efficient way to figure out unknown words. In this book you will find a section following each reading titled "Strengthening Your Vocabulary." This exercise, which lists several words from the reading and directs you to write brief definitions for them, provides an opportunity for you to practice using context clues and to review the meanings of these words. If you are unable to figure out the meaning of a word from its context, be sure to look up the word in the dictionary.

EXERCISE 2-4 Use context clues to figure out the meaning of the following boldface words. Write a brief definition in the space provided.

1. In most societies, people have **patrilocal residences**—homes in which the married couple lives with the husband's family.
   <u>homes in which the married couple lives with the husband's family</u>

2. A student review panel **exonerated** the team of any possible misconduct.
   <u>freed from blame</u>

3. Large corporations are self-interested and exist to make profits, despite their **altruistic** claims.
   <u>unselfish concern for the welfare of others</u>

4. **Homophobia**, fear of homosexuals, was a topic of several recent campus-newspaper editorials.

fear of or aversion to homosexuals

5. Recent menu **innovations** included tofu, fajitas, and stir-fried vegetable dishes.

newly introduced changes

6. The climate was in a continual **flux**; one week it was warm, the next week frigid.

change

7. A gang may recruit through **deception**; potential members may be promised safety and protection but soon discover themselves involved in violence.

lying or trickery

8. Speakers use **nonverbal communication**, such as smiles or gestures, to clarify their meaning.

communication without words; body language

9. To **simulate** the restrictions of space ships, astronauts are trained in confined spaces.

to create a similar situation or condition; to duplicate

10. Under stress, people tend to act **impulsively** rather than make reasoned decisions.

swayed by emotions or impulses

EXERCISE ▶ 2-5 ◀   Write a brief definition of each of the following words from the reading "Ways to Improve Your Memory," on page 21.

1. mnemonics (paragraph 2)   _memory tricks_

2. marathon (paragraph 3)   _test of stamina or endurance_

3. categories (paragraph 5)   _class or group_

4. implications (paragraph 5)   _ideas that are suggested or implied_

5. acronyms (paragraph 6)   _words formed from the first letters of_

groups of words

6. allocate (paragraph 7)   _reserve, set aside for a particular purpose_

7. administered (paragraph 8)   _given_

Checking Dictionary Meanings

When a word's context does not provide any clues to its meaning, you will need to look up its meaning in a dictionary. Keep a dictionary handy as you read. Refer to Writing Success Tip 5, "Buying and Using a Dictionary," page 123.

When using a dictionary, be sure to find the meaning that fits the way the word is used in the reading. For example, the word *exercise* has ten meanings, but only one makes sense in the following sentence:

The accused "dead beat dad" *exercised* his right to a hearing.

In this sentence, *exercised* means "to make use of." Other meanings, such as "a lesson" or "a ceremony," do not fit the way the word is used in the sentence.

To find the correct meaning of an unknown word, follow these steps:

1. Finish reading the sentence in which the word appears so you understand its full context.
2. Try to figure out the part of speech of the unknown word. In a dictionary, a word's meanings are usually grouped by part of speech. In the above example, *exercised* is a verb, so you would only need to look at the meanings labeled "v.," for verb.
3. Substitute in place of the unknown word each meaning listed until you find one that makes sense.
4. Jot the meaning in the margin so you can refer to or review it later.

EXERCISE ▶ 2-6 ▶ Working in pairs or in teams, use a dictionary to find the meaning of each of the following boldfaced words. Write the definition in the space provided.

1. The next witness is expected to **corroborate** the testimony of the first witness.

   support or confirm, attest to the truth

2. Peter was **despondent** because he learned he would lose his job next month.

   depressed, in low spirits

3. The physician applied an **emollient.**

   substance that softens and smooths

4. The visiting diplomat, ignoring **protocol,** talked informally with the spectators.

   etiquette or rules followed by heads of state

5. Brenda felt **compelled** to file a report about the incident.

   forced, driven, duty bound

After each reading in this book, you will find an exercise on using context clues and/or a dictionary to define several words from the reading. These exercises are designed to give you additional practice using the words and will help you build your vocabulary.

Keeping a Vocabulary Log

Many students find it helpful to keep a log of vocabulary words they want to learn and use in their writing. This log can be part of your writing journal (see "Keep a Journal," page 9). Alternatively, you can use index cards, writing the words on the front and their meanings on the back. Study and review these words frequently; after you have used a word at least once in your writing, place a checkmark next to it.

How to Record Your Thinking: Annotation

Annotation is a way of jotting down your ideas, reactions, opinions, and comments as you read. Think of annotation as recording your ideas about what you are reading. It is a personal way to brainstorm and "talk back" to the author—to question, challenge, agree, disagree, or comment. Annotations are particularly useful when you will be writing about what you have read.

You can also use annotation to clarify meaning by marking key parts of the essay. To clarify meaning, you might:

- underline or highlight key ideas.
- place an asterisk (*) by key terms or definitions.
- number key items of supporting information.
- define unfamiliar words.
- paraphrase a complicated idea.
- bracket ([ ]) a useful example.
- mark with an asterisk (*) useful summary statements.
- connect ideas with arrows.
- highlight statements that reveal the author's feelings or attitudes.

Here are some ways you might "talk back" to the author:

Ask questions.	Why would...?
Challenge the author's ideas.	If this is true, wouldn't...?
Look for inconsistencies.	But the author has already said that...
Add examples.	For instance...
Note exceptions.	This isn't true in the case of ...

Disagree with the author.   How could...?
Make associations with   This is similar to...
other sources.
Make judgments.   Good point...

Overall, you will find annotation useful for meaning and interacting with the author's words and ideas. When you have to write an essay about a reading, you will understand it much better and thus be able to go right to the part you need to make your point. Here is the annotation one student did as she read "Ways to Improve Your Memory." Study it to see how she recorded her responses to and impressions of the reading.

EXERCISE 2-7 Reread the following excerpt from "Ways to Improve Your Memory" and annotate it to reflect your thoughts about and responses to it.

but it takes time!

Practice time: To learn names, dates, vocabulary words, formulas, or the concepts in a textbook, you'll find that practice makes perfect. In general, the more time spent studying, the better. In fact, it pays to over-learn—that is, to review the material even after you think you have it mastered. It's also better to spread out your studying over time than to cram all at once. You will retain more information from four two-hour sessions than from one eight-hour marathon.

Active thinking: The sheer amount of practice time is important, but only if it's "quality time." Mindless drills may be helpful in the short run, but long-term retention requires that you think actively and deeply about *examples?*—material—about what it means and how it is linked to what you already know. Ask yourself (critical questions) about the material. Think about it in ways that relate to your own experiences. Talk about the material to a friend, thus forcing yourself to organize it in terms that can be understood.

use outline form?

Organization of information: Once you have information to be learned, organize it as in an outline. Start with a few broad categories, then divide these into more specific subcategories and sub-subcategories. This is how many experts chunk new information, and it works. *how did she organize the titles?*—Thus, when Andrea Halpern (1986) presented subjects with 54 popular song titles, she found that recall was greater when the titles were organized than when they were scrambled. The implication for studying is clear: organize the material in your notes, preferably in the form of an outline—and make sure to review these notes later.

there must be a limit to how many of these a person can remember

Verbal mnemonics: Sometimes the easiest way to remember a list of names is to use verbal mnemonics, or "memory tricks." Chances are, you have already used popular methods such as *rhymes* ("*i* before *e,* except after *c*" is my favorite; "thirty days hath September, April, June, and November: is another) and *acronyms* that reduce the amount of information to be stored (for example, *ROY G BIV* can be used to recall the colors of the light spectrum: *r*ed, *o*range, *y*ellow, *g*reen, *b*lue, *i*ndigo, and *v*iolet). Relying on verbal mnemonics, advertisers create slogans to make their products memorable.

Using Idea Maps

Many students have difficulty remembering what they have read and find they have to reread frequently in order to write about a reading. One solution to this problem is to draw an idea map: a diagram that helps you both understand and remember how the writer's ideas relate to one another and how the essay is organized. Idea maps work because they force you to think about and analyze the relationship of ideas. They also are effective because they require you to express ideas from the reading in your own words; this activity increases your recall of those ideas.

Here is a sample idea map for the reading "Ways to Improve Your Memory." Notice that it includes all of the key ideas.

THERE ARE SEVERAL WAYS TO IMPROVE YOUR MEMORY.

- Practice time
- Active thinking
- Organization of information
- Verbal mnemonics
- Interference
- Study environment
- Experiment to discover which ones work.

In each of the remaining chapters in this book, you will find a partially completed idea map. These chapters will gradually teach you how to draw an idea map. As you go along, more and more will be left for you to fill in. By the time you reach the final chapter, you will have learned how to draw your own idea maps and will be asked to draw the entire map.

Once you are comfortable using idea maps, do not hesitate to begin drawing your own for reading assignments in other courses. You will find that idea maps make a big difference in how much you can remember of what you read.

How to Write about a Reading

Once you have finished reading an essay, be sure you have understood what you have read. Define any unfamiliar words, and make sure you have found the author's thesis statement and key supporting ideas. In this book, you will find a set of questions following each reading. Called "Examining the Reading," these questions will help you check your understanding of the key points of the reading. To answer them, do not hesitate to refer back to the reading frequently, especially to the parts you've highlighted and annotated. For certain questions, you may need to reread to clarify ideas or check details. Once you are confident that you have grasped the full meaning of the reading, you are ready to react to the reading's ideas through discussion and journal writing.

Class Discussion: An Opportunity to Explore Ideas

Class discussions are valuable sources of ideas to write about. By talking to classmates about a reading and listening to their ideas, you often discover ways to apply the reading, uncover new ways of looking at ideas, or see relationships or connections you had not previously thought of. Be sure to get involved in the discussion. Don't just listen; you will learn more if you participate. By expressing your ideas orally, you will also be better prepared to express them in writing.

During a discussion, try to take only brief notes. Jot down key words and phrases to help you recall striking, new, or unusual ideas that develop in your discussions. Detailed notes are usually not a good idea because you spend all your time writing and don't participate in the discussion. When class is over, however, try to fill in your notes, recording ideas more completely and adding ideas as you recall them. Your instructor may begin class discussions with the questions listed in the section titled "Reacting to and Discussing Ideas," which follows every reading. Be sure to read these questions before class and think about possible responses.

EXERCISE 2-8 If your instructor conducts a class discussion of the reading "Ways to Improve Your Memory," take brief notes during the discussion and fill them in when the class is over. Possible discussion questions are:

1. Are some types of material more difficult to memorize than others? Give some examples.
2. What positive (or negative) experiences have you had with memorizing information? When has your memory failed you or served you well?
3. Do you know anyone with extraordinary memory skills? Describe his or her skills.

Journal Writing: An Opportunity to Test Your Ideas

Responding to a reading by writing in your journal gives you a chance to explore ideas and experiment with ways of expressing them. Use the questions in the section titled "Reacting to and Discussing Ideas" as starting points to help you discover your own ideas about the reading, as well as to clarify those of the author. Don't limit yourself to these specific questions; here are some general questions that may help you develop a response to the reading.

QUESTIONS TO DIRECT YOUR THINKING

- Why did the author write the essay? What was his or her purpose?
- For whom (for what audience) was the essay written?
- What issue, problem, concern, or question does the essay address?
- What is the author's main point or position on that issue?
- How well did the author explain and support the position?
- Do you agree or disagree with the author's position? Why?
- Do ideas in the essay apply or connect to your life? If so, how?
- What in your experience is similar to or different from what the author describes in this essay?

EXERCISE 2-9 Select two or more techniques suggested in "Ways to Improve Your Reading." Write a journal entry in response to the following question: How can you apply these techniques to your studies?

Writing Assignments: Expressing Your Ideas

In this book, the section "Writing About the Reading" offers both paragraph and essay assignments on topics related to the reading. When your instructor gives you an assignment, use the following suggestions to help you produce a solid, well-written paper.

1. Read the assignment several times before you begin. Express in your own words what the assignment requires. If you have a choice of assignments, take a fair amount of time to choose. It is worthwhile spending a few minutes thinking about and weighing possible topics. You don't want to work your way through a first draft and then realize that you don't have enough to say or you cannot work well with the topic.

2. Try discussing the assignment with a classmate. By talking about it, you can make sure you are on the right track, and you may discover new or additional ideas to write about. Also consider asking the classmate to react to your paper once you have a draft.

3. Review your journal entries and notes of class discussions for possible topics or approaches to the assignment. (Chapter 10, "Planning and Organizing," offers several strategies for discovering and selecting ideas to write about.)

4. Don't be satisfied with the first draft that you write. As you will discover in Chapter 11, "Drafting and Revising," you need to rethink and revise both what you have said and how you have said it.

WRITING ABOUT A READING

Thinking before Reading

In the following reading, John Rosemond, a noted child psychologist and writer, discusses three styles of parenting and tells us which one he believes works best. While reading this essay, notice how the author makes all the parts of the essay work together. Refer to page 24 of this chapter and page 5 of Chapter 1 for the parts of an essay.

1. Preview the reading, using the steps listed on page 20.
2. After you have done your preview, connect the reading to your own experience by answering the following questions:
   a. How were you raised as a child? What did your parents usually do to get you to do what they wanted?
   b. What different styles or ways of parenting have you seen?

READING

The Job Isn't for Wimps—or Dictators
John Rosemond

This may cause great dismay among parents everywhere, but it's a fact: No matter what your child's age, no matter how hard you try, no matter what disciplinary techniques you use, you cannot control your child. If you try to control your child, you'll only become frustrated and stressed-out, and you'll create more problems than you solve, if you manage to solve any at all. The only thing you can effectively control is your relationship with your child. It this regard, there are three kinds of parents.

1. Parents who try to control their children. These parents—termed authoritarian—are dictatorial and rigidly restrictive. Because they are attempting to do the impossible, and because they do not accept children for what they are, authoritarian parents are frequently angry and frustrated, and they almost always overdiscipline, using a hammer when they could have used a fly swatter.

2. Parents who fail to control their relationships with their children. These parents are often termed "permissive." I prefer wimp. They try to be friends with their children, let their children make decisions they're incapable of making, try to keep their children happy, compromise and capitulate in the face of conflict, and are generally at their children's beck and call.

3. Parents who make no attempt to control their children but are in complete control of their relationships with their children. These parents are authoritative. They make rules and enforce them dispassionately. They supervise well but are not highly involved with their kids. They describe their own boundaries to their children, thus helping their children learn to stand on their own two feet. They care deeply for their kids, but they don't care what their kids think of them at any given moment. They understand that one cannot both lead and fraternize, that it's either one or the other.

Most unfortunately, the majority of today's parents fall into one of the first two categories. In both cases, we're talking about parents who are ruled by emotion. The authoritarian parent is ruled by frustration and anger, the permissive parent by anxiety and guilt. The authoritative parent, by contrast, rules. He is not in the sway of emotion, but neither is he unemotional. Quite the contrary, because he understands and accepts children for what they are (as opposed to having either unrealistic expectations or a sentimental perspective), he is capable of showing his children more love and compassion than either of his hyper emotional counterparts—and it is the showing that counts.

"Can you give us some concrete examples of trying to control one's relationship with a child vs. simply controlling?" Sure. The authoritative parent, for example, realizes that (a) while he cannot make a 4-year-old share toys with playmates (sharing, by definition, is not compelled), he can confiscate those toys the youngster refuses to share; (b) while he can't prevent a 10-year-old from misbehaving in school, he can revoke privileges at home, and (c) while he can't make a teen-ager get good grades, he can refuse to let the youngster get a driver's license until grades improve.   6

In each case, the parent controls circumstances in the child's life, thereby controlling the parent-child relationship. In no case does the parent get bent out of shape. He also knows that regardless of what he does, the child in question may not change his or her behavior. He is simply resolved to teach the child that choices result in consequences. Whether the child "gets the message" is not a simple matter of how well he teaches. It is also a matter of how willing the child is to learn, which is what is meant by children have minds of their own.   7

From *Buffalo News*.

Getting Ready to Write

Strengthening Your Vocabulary

Write a brief definition for each of the following words from the reading. If you cannot figure out the meaning of a word from the way it is used in the reading, look the word up in a dictionary.

1. authoritarian (paragraph 2)

   dictatorial, favoring strict obedience to authorities

2. permissive (paragraph 3)

   allowing freedom of behavior, tolerant

3. compromise (paragraph 3)

   to settle by making concessions or adjustment

4. capitulate (paragraph 3)

   to give in, surrender

5. dispassionately (paragraph 4)

   calmly, impartially

6. fraternize (paragraph 4)

to associate with and treat as an equal

7. compelled (paragraph 6)

forced

8. confiscate (paragraph 6)

to seize or take away

9. revoke (paragraph 6)

withdraw, cancel

Reviewing the Reading Using an Idea Map

Review the reading by completing the missing pieces of the idea map shown below.

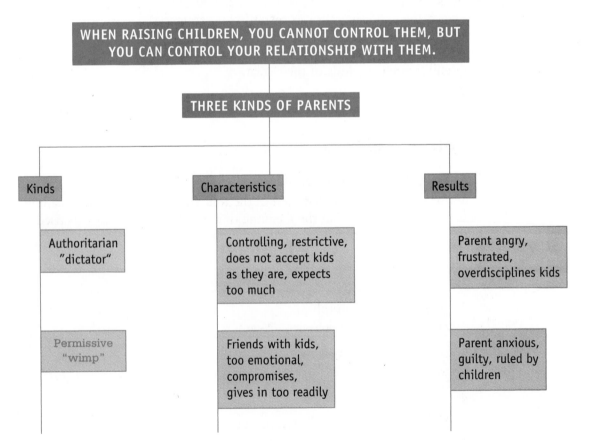

| Authoritative | Sets and enforces fair rules, guides, teaches consequences, shows love, controls own emotions | Parent controls relationship; kids learn responsibility, independence |

| Authoritative gets best results (implied). |

Examining the Reading

1. What are the three styles of parenting discussed in this reading? Explain each.

2. Which style of parenting does the author support? Why?

3. Why does Rosemond call one type of parents "wimps"?

4. What does the author mean when he says that some parents use "a hammer when they could have used a fly swatter"?

5. Why are many parents often angry and frustrated?

Reacting to and Discussing Ideas

1. Do you think that trying to be friends with your children is a mistake? Explain your answer.

2. Do you agree with John Rosemond's approach to parenting? Why or why not?

3. Which type of parent do you think you are or will be? Why do you think so?

Writing about the Reading

The Paragraph Option

1. Write a paragraph explaining what you would do or did do differently from your parents in raising a child.

2. Have you ever seen, in a supermarket or other public place, a situation in which a parent wanted a child to do something that the child didn't want to do? Write a paragraph describing the parenting style you saw and explaining what made you think so.

The Essay Option

The author says that when it comes to loving children, "it is the showing that counts." Write an essay describing an experience in your life that supports this idea.

Organizing a
Place and Time
to Read and
Write

Organizing a
Place to Read
and Write

WRITING SUCCESS TIP 2

You may find that you read and write more easily if you do so in the same place and at the same time each day. Use the following tips to organize a place and time to read and write.

1. If you live at home or in an apartment, try to find a quiet area that you can reserve for reading and writing. If possible, avoid areas used for other purposes, such as the dining room or kitchen table, because you'll have to move or clean up your materials frequently. If you live in a dorm, your desk is an ideal place to write, unless the dorm is too noisy. If it is, find a quiet place elsewhere on campus.

2. You'll need a table or desk; don't try to write on the arm of a comfortable chair. Choose a space where you can spread out your papers.

3. Eliminate distractions from your writing area. Photos or stacks of bills to pay will take your mind off your writing.

4. Be sure that lighting is adequate and your chair is straight and comfortable.

5. Collect and organize supplies: plenty of paper, pens, pencils, erasers, stapler, white-out, and so forth. If you write on a computer, keep spare disks on hand.

6. Organize completed and returned papers, quizzes, class handouts, and so on in separate folders.

7. Keep a dictionary nearby, as well as any other reference materials recommended by your instructor—a thesaurus, for instance. (See Writing Success Tip 5 for advice on what type of dictionary to buy.)

8. Use this place for reading, studying, and writing for your other courses, as well.

Organizing
Time to Read
and Write

1. Reserve a block of time each day for reading this book and working on writing exercises and assignments. Also reserve time for writing in your journal.

2. For now, reserve an hour a day for writing. This may seem like a lot of time, but most instructors expect you to spend a minimum of two hours outside of class for every hour you spend in class.

3. Try to work at the same time each day. You'll establish a routine that will be easy to follow.

4. Choose a time during the day when you are at the peak of your concentration. Don't try to write when you are tired or likely to be interrupted.

5. Begin assignments well ahead of their due dates so that you have time to plan, organize, write, revise, and proofread. It's best to leave a day or more between finishing your first draft and beginning to revise.

SENTENCE BASICS

Complete Sentences Versus Fragments

When you read the caption next to the picture in the following advertisement—"Killer cocktail"—does it make sense? Does it tell you what message Allstate is trying to communicate? No doubt your answer is yes. From the caption and the picture, you know that Allstate is urging safe and sober driving and warning that the use of alcohol before driving is dangerous.

Now suppose you saw the caption alone, without the accompanying photograph. Would it make sense? Would you understand the message of the advertisement? Probably not. It would seem to be a title or name of an alcoholic beverage. The caption is a sentence fragment. It has a subject—cocktail—but it lacks a verb. We do not know what the cocktail does or what action is performed.

How can you make the caption into a complete sentence? You must add a verb. Here are a few ways to make the caption a complete sentence:

FRAGMENT: Killer cocktail

                             subject   verb

COMPLETE SENTENCE: A cocktail is dangerous.

                             subject   verb

COMPLETE SENTENCE: A cocktail can kill.

The new version now makes sense even without the photograph. This version has a subject and a verb and expresses a complete thought.

Following are a few more statements taken from magazine ads. Each is a sentence fragment because each lacks a subject and a verb and does not express a complete thought. As you read the fragments, notice how difficult they are to understand. Try to guess what product each sentence fragment describes. Correct answers appear at the bottom of page 50.

Fragment	Product
1. "Comfort, warmth, quiet"	1. _____
2. "Because you and your family deserve the very best"	2. _____
3. "Bye-bye, Crocodile"	3. _____
4. "Introducing color so rich you can feel it"	4. _____

WRITING

Because advertisers use pictures to complete their messages, they do not have to worry about the confusing nature of sentence fragments. Also, no one requires writers of ads to use complete sentences. Your instructors, however, expect you to write sentences that are complete and correct. You will, therefore, need to know how to spot and correct sentence fragments. To do so, you need to understand three sentence elements:

1. subjects
2. verbs
3. dependent clauses (also called subordinate clauses)

NEED TO KNOW

Subjects, Verbs, and Sentence Fragments

- A **subject** of a sentence tells you who or what the sentence is about—who or what receives the action of the verb.

- A **verb** expresses action or state of being. Sometimes a verb consists of only one word. (The doorbell *rang.*) Often, however, the main verb has a helping verb. (The guest *had arrived.*)

Subject	*Verb*
Heat	rises.
Joyce	laughed.
Weeds	grow.
Opportunities	exist.

- A **sentence fragment** is an incomplete sentence because it lacks either a subject or a verb, or both. It needs to be connected to a nearby sentence, or to be expanded into a new sentence.

Subjects

The **subject** of a sentence is usually a **noun.** (For a review of nouns, see Part VIII, "Reviewing the Basics," page 450.)

The Babylonians wrote the first advertisements.

The advertisements were inscribed on bricks.

The kings conducted advertising campaigns for themselves.

Answers to sentence fragments on page 49: (1) BMW car; (2) Alpha SH (sinus-headache medication); (3) Lubriderm (dry-skin lotion); (4) Cover Girl lipstick.

The subject of a sentence can also be a **pronoun,** a word that refers to or substitutes for a noun (for example, *I, you, he, she, it, they, we*). (For a review of pronouns, see Part IX, page 252.)

Early <u>advertisements</u> were straightforward. <u>They</u> carried the names of temples.

The <u>wall</u> was built. <u>It</u> was seen by thousands of people.

The subject of a sentence can also be a group of words:

<u>Inscribing the bricks</u> was a difficult task.

<u>Uncovering the bricks</u> was a surprise.

<u>To build the brick wall</u> was a time-consuming task.

Compound Subjects

Some sentences contain two or more subjects joined together with a coordinating conjunction (*and, but, or, nor, for, so,* or *yet*). The subjects that are linked together form a **compound subject.**

compound subject

<u>Carter's Little Liver Pills</u> and <u>Ivory Soap</u> are examples of early brand-name advertising.

Note that when there are two subjects, there is no comma before the *and.* When there is a series of subjects, however, commas appear after each subject except the last.

compound subject

<u>Calendars</u>, <u>toys</u>, <u>posters</u>, and <u>clocks</u> carried advertisements for early brand-name products.

Distinguishing Subjects from Prepositional Phrases

Do not mistake a noun in a prepositional phrase for the subject of a sentence. The subject of a sentence is *never* in a prepositional phrase. A **prepositional phrase** is a group of words that begins with a preposition (such as *after, in, of*). A prepositional phrase usually ends with a noun or pronoun that tells what or whom (the object of the preposition).

preposition   noun telling what

<u>on</u> the <u>house</u>

preposition   noun telling whom

<u>from</u> my <u>instructor</u>

Here are a few more prepositional phrases using common prepositions. For a review of prepositions and more examples, see Part IX, page 467.

<u>across</u> the lawn   <u>until</u> last night
<u>throughout</u> history   <u>to</u> Maria
<u>before</u> the judge   <u>between</u> friends

Remember, the noun within a prepositional phrase is *never* the subject of a sentence.

prepositional phrase   subject

Beneath the chair, the c<u>at</u> dozed.

subject   prepositional phrase

The <u>students</u> in the art class painted a mural.

prepositional phrase   subject

Inside the house, the <u>temperature</u> was seventy-five degrees.

It is especially easy to mistake the noun in the prepositional phrase for the subject of the sentence when the prepositional phrase comes between the subject and verb.

subject   prepositional phrase

The <u>idea</u> of killing animals disturbs Brian.

EXERCISE 3-1

Circle each prepositional phrase. Then underline the subject in each of the following sentences.

EXAMPLE: The superintendent (of our school) was quoted (in the newspaper.)

1. A <u>crowd</u> (of teenagers) had purchased tickets for the concert.
2. <u>Rows</u> (of birds) perched (on the telephone wires) (in the cornfields.)
3. The <u>strap</u> (on my backpack) was tattered.
4. <u>Trash</u> (from the festival) covered the grounds (inside the park.)
5. <u>Patches</u> (of blue sky) are visible (above the horizon.)

EXERCISE 3-2

Write a sentence using each of the following words as subjects. Then circle any prepositional phrases in your sentence.

EXAMPLE: sister   My sister has the best sense (of humor)

1. history   <u>The history (of the Civil War) fascinates us (to this day.)</u>

2. movie actresses   Movie actresses appear (on talk shows.)

3. dancing   Dancing is a human activity performed (in all cultures.)

4. telephone calls   Telephone calls (at midnight) are annoying.

5. studying   Studying on the bus is a good use (of my time.)

Fragments Without a Subject

A common sentence-writing error is to write a sentence without a subject. The result is a sentence fragment. Writers often make this mistake when they think the subject of a previous sentence or a noun in a previous sentence applies to the next sentence as well.

complete sentence	fragment
Marge lost her keys on Tuesday.	And found them on Wednesday.

[The missing subject is *Marge.*]

complete sentence	fragment
The instructor canceled class.	But did not postpone the quiz.

[The missing subject is *instructor.*]

complete sentence

Relieved that it had stopped raining, Teresa rushed into the mall. Then remembered her car window was open.

fragment

[The missing subject is *Teresa.*]

You can revise a fragment that lacks a subject in two ways:

1. **Add a subject, often a pronoun referring to the subject of the previous sentence.**

   FRAGMENT: And found them on Wednesday.

   subject
   ↓
   REVISED: She found them on Wednesday.

   FRAGMENT: Then remembered her car window was open.

   subject
   ↓
   REVISED: Then she remembered her car window was open.

2. Connect the fragment to the previous sentence.

FRAGMENT: And found them on Wednesday.

                    subject verb   verb
                        ↓   ↓   ↓
REVISED: Marge lost her keys on Tuesday and found them on
                    Wednesday.

FRAGMENT: But did not postpone the quiz.

                    subject   verb   verb
                        ↓   ↓   ↓
REVISED: The instructor canceled class but did not postpone the quiz.

Each of these sentences now has a subject and a compound verb. (See Part
IX, page 474.)

EXERCISE 3-3   Each of the following items consists of a complete sentence followed by a
sentence fragment that lacks a subject. Make each fragment into a com-
plete sentence by adding a subject. You may need to take out or add new
words, or to capitalize words or make them lower case as you revise.

                                                         He
EXAMPLE: Bert threw the basketball. ~~And~~ cheered when it went in the
                    hoop.

                                                                    he
1. The president waved as he left the building. Then got in the car and
   drove away.

                                        It w
2. The novel was complex. Was also long and drawn out.

                                                 They w
3. The scissors were not very sharp. Were old and rusty, you see.

                                                                    They m
4. Hundreds of students waited to get into the bookstore. Milled
   around until the manager unlocked the door.

                                                            She g
5. My roommate Tonya is an excellent skater. Gets teased sometimes
   about her name.

                                                                    it
6. The computer printed out the list of names. Then beeped loudly.

                                            They
7. Fans crowded the stadium. ~~And~~ cheered for each touchdown.

8. Many guests arrived early for the wedding. Unfortunately, ₍guests₎ were not seated until ten o'clock.

9. The delivery man put the large package down. Then ₍he₎ rang the doorbell.

10. The big black dog sat obediently. ₍It₎ ~~But~~ growled nonetheless.

EXERCISE ▶ 3-4 Write a paragraph describing an advertisement you have seen or heard recently. Explain to whom the advertisement appeals and why. After you have finished revising and proofreading your paragraph, underline the subject of each sentence. Exchange papers with a peer reviewer, and see if you agree on the choices of subjects. Discuss any differences of opinion with another peer reviewer or with your instructor.

Save your paper. You will need it for another exercise in this chapter.

Verbs

A **verb** is a word or word group that indicates what the subject does or what happened to the subject. Most verbs express action or state of being (for example, *run, invent, build, know, be*). (For a review of verbs, refer to Part IX, page 455.)

Advertising <u>is</u> bland without a slogan.

Slogans <u>promote</u> a specific product.

Sometimes a verb consists of only one word.

The announcer <u>speaks</u>.

Often, however, the main verb is accompanied by one or more **helping (auxiliary) verbs** (such as *will, can,* and forms of *be, have,* or *do*). (See Part IX, page 456, for a review of helping verbs.)

helping main
verb   verb
  ↓   ↓
The announcer <u>will</u> speak.

helping   main
verb   verb
  ↓   ↓
The announcer <u>will be</u> speaking.

helping   main
verb   verb
↓   ↓

The first trademark <u>was</u> <u>registered</u> in 1870.

helping   main
verb   verb
↓   ↓

<u>Do</u> any companies <u>use</u> animals as trademarks?

helping main
verb   verb
↓   ↓

The lion <u>has</u> <u>been</u> MGM's trademark for a long time.

Compound Verbs

Some sentences have two or more verbs joined together with a coordinat-ing conjunction (such as *and, or,* or *but*).

subject   compound verb
↓   ↙   ↘

The "Uncle Sam Wants You" poster <u>stirred</u> patriotism and <u>increased</u> enlistments.
↑
coordinating conjunction

compound verb
↙   ↘

The posters <u>appeared</u> on billboards and <u>hung</u> on buildings.
↑
coordinating conjunction

EXERCISE ▶ 3-5   Underline the verb(s), including any helping verb(s), in each of the fol-lowing sentences.

> EXAMPLE: The lectures in psychology <u>have been focusing</u> on instinctive behavior lately.

1. Preschools <u>teach</u> children social and academic skills.
2. Exercise clubs <u>offer</u> instruction and provide companionship.
3. Millions of people <u>have watched</u> soap operas.
4. Essay exams <u>are given</u> in many college classes.
5. The audience <u>will be suprised</u> by the play's ending.

Fragments Without Complete Verbs

Fragments often occur when word groups begin with words ending in *-ing* or with phrases beginning with the word *to.* These words and phrases are verb forms and may look like verbs, but they cannot function as verbs in sentences.

"-ing" Fragments

Note the *-ing* word in the fragment below:

FRAGMENT: <u>Walking</u> across campus after lunch.

In this word group, *walking* has no subject. Who is walking? Now let's add a subject and see what happens:

Alice <u>walking</u> across campus after lunch.

The word group still is not a complete sentence; the verb form *walking* cannot be used alone as a sentence verb. You can make it complete by adding a helping verb (for example, *is, was, has been*) or by using a different verb form (*walked* or *walks*).

helping verb added

REVISED: Alice <u>was</u> walking across campus after lunch.

verb form changed to present tense

REVISED: Alice <u>walks</u> across campus after lunch.

Now the word group is a complete sentence.

You can correct fragments beginning with *-ing* words in four ways:

1. Add a subject and change the verb form to a sentence verb.

fragment

FRAGMENT: Morris was patient. Waiting in line at the bank.

subject   verb changed to past tense

REVISED: Morris was patient. <u>He</u> <u>waited</u> in line at the bank.

2. Add a subject and a form of *be* (such as *am, are, will be, has been, is, was, were*) as a helping verb.

fragment

FRAGMENT: Juan was bored. Listening to his sister complain about her boyfriend.

subject   form of *be*   main verb

REVISED: Juan was bored. <u>He</u> <u>was</u> <u>listening</u> to his sister complain about her boyfriend.

3. Connect the fragment to the sentence that comes before or after it.

fragment

FRAGMENT: Mark finished lunch. Picking up his tray. Then he left the
cafeteria.

modifies *he*
↓

REVISED: Mark finished lunch. Picking up his tray, he left the cafeteria.

**4. If the *-ing* word is *being,* change its form to another form of *be (am,*
*are, is, was, were).***

fragment

FRAGMENT: Sally failed the math quiz. Her mistakes being careless errors.

verb form changed
↓

REVISED: Sally failed the math quiz. Her mistakes were careless errors.

Fragments with *To* Phrases

A phrase that begins with *to* cannot be the verb of the sentence. When it
stands alone, it is a sentence fragment.

FRAGMENT: To review for the psychology test.

This word group lacks a subject and a sentence verb. To make a complete
sentence, you need to add a subject and a sentence verb.

subject verb
↓   ↓

REVISED: Jeff plans to review for the psychology test.

You can revise fragments that begin with *to* in two ways:

1. Add a subject and a sentence verb.

FRAGMENT: To reach my goal.

subject verb
↓   ↙

REVISED: I hope to reach my goal.

2. Connect the *to* phrase to a nearby sentence.

FRAGMENT: To earn the highest grade. Libby studied eight hours.
REVISED: To earn the highest grade, Libby studied eight hours.

EXERCISE 3-6   Each of the following word groups is a fragment. Revise each to form a
complete sentence.

Andrea was w
EXAMPLE: Walking along the waterfront.

Sal was p   all day.
1. Photographing the wedding. _____

_____

Sarah and Joe hope t   after they graduate.
2. To have a family. _____

_____

Anthony hung
3. ~~Hanging~~ up the suit in the closet._____

_____

Lucas d   ed
4. Deciding what to have for dinner._____

_____

We wanted t
5. To attend the awards ceremony. _____

_____

Pat was w   in the library.
6. Writing the speech. _____

_____

The student attempted t
7. To sketch a diagram. _____

_____

Sally unexpectedly decided t
8. To quit her job. _____

_____

Anne will be m   in her next draft.
9. Making the paper less repetitious. _____

_____

The car is
10. ~~Being~~ old and in disrepair. _____

EXERCISE ▶ 3-7 | Go back to the paragraph you wrote in Exercise 3-4, and circle the verb or verbs in each sentence. Exchange papers with a peer reviewer, and check each other's work.

Clauses: An Overview

A sentence must not only contain a subject and a verb; *it must also express a complete thought.* That is, a sentence should not leave a question in your mind or leave an idea unfinished. To spot and avoid sentence fragments in your writing, you must be able to recognize the difference between independent and dependent (or subordinate) clauses. An **independent clause** expresses a complete thought and can stand alone as a complete sentence. A **dependent** (or **subordinate**) **clause** does not express a complete thought. When a dependent clause stands alone, it is a fragment.

A **clause** is a group of related words that contains a subject and its verb. There are two kinds of clauses:

1. independent
2. dependent (or subordinate)

Independent Clauses

An **independent clause** has a subject and a verb and can stand alone as a complete and correct sentence. It expresses a complete thought.

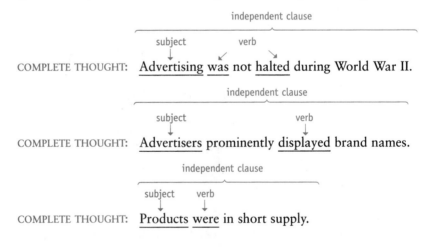

COMPLETE THOUGHT: Advertising was not halted during World War II.

COMPLETE THOUGHT: Advertisers prominently displayed brand names.

COMPLETE THOUGHT: Products were in short supply.

Dependent (or Subordinate) Clauses

A **dependent clause** has a subject and a verb but cannot stand alone as a complete and correct sentence. It does not express a complete thought. A dependent clause makes sense only when it is joined to an independent clause. When a dependent clause stands alone, it is a **dependent clause fragment.** A dependent clause fragment leaves an unanswered question in your mind.

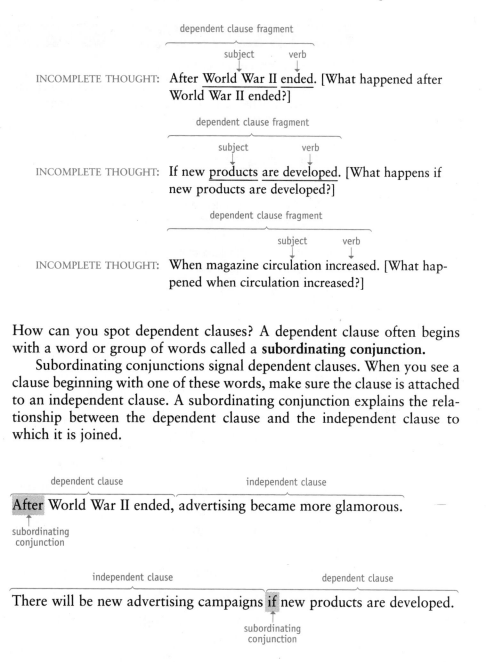

INCOMPLETE THOUGHT: After World War II ended. [What happened after World War II ended?]

INCOMPLETE THOUGHT: If new products are developed. [What happens if new products are developed?]

INCOMPLETE THOUGHT: When magazine circulation increased. [What happened when circulation increased?]

How can you spot dependent clauses? A dependent clause often begins with a word or group of words called a **subordinating conjunction.**

Subordinating conjunctions signal dependent clauses. When you see a clause beginning with one of these words, make sure the clause is attached to an independent clause. A subordinating conjunction explains the relationship between the dependent clause and the independent clause to which it is joined.

After World War II ended, advertising became more glamorous.

There will be new advertising campaigns if new products are developed.

When magazine circulation increased, magazines became a popular new advertising medium.

NEED TO KNOW

Subordinating Conjunctions

A clause beginning with a subordinate conjunction is a dependent clause. It cannot stand alone. It must be connected to an independent clause. Here is a list of common subordinating conjunctions.

after	if	though
although	inasmuch as	unless
as	in case	until
as far as	in order that	when
as if	in order to	whenever
as long as	now that	where
as soon as	once	whereas
as though	provided that	wherever
because	rather than	whether
before	since	while
during	so that	
even if	than	
even though	that	

EXERCISE ▶ 3-8 Decide whether the following clauses are independent or dependent. Place "I" for independent or "D" for dependent before each clause.

_____D_____ 1. While Arturo was driving to school.

_____I_____ 2. *Sesame Street* is a children's educational television program.

_____I_____ 3. Samantha keeps a diary of her family's holiday celebrations.

_____D_____ 4. Because Aretha had a craving for chocolate.

_____I_____ 5. Exercise can help to relieve stress.

_____D_____ 6. When Peter realized he would be able to meet the deadline.

_____I_____ 7. A snowstorm crippled the eastern seaboard states on New Year's Eve.

_____D_____ 8. Unless my uncle decides to visit us during spring break.

_____ I _____ 9. Long-distance telephone rates are less expensive during the evening than during the day.

_____ D _____ 10. As long as Jacqueline is living at home.

Correcting Dependent Clause Fragments

You can correct a dependent clause fragment in two ways:

1. Join the dependent clause to an independent clause to make the dependent clause fragment part of a complete sentence.

FRAGMENT: Although competition increased.
COMPLETE SENTENCE: Although competition increased, the sales staff were still getting new customers.

FRAGMENT: Because market research expanded.
COMPLETE SENTENCE: The company added new accounts because market research expanded.

FRAGMENT: Although statistics and market research have become part of advertising.
COMPLETE SENTENCE: Although statistics and market research have become part of advertising, consumers' tastes remain somewhat unpredictable.

2. Take away the subordinating conjunction, and the dependent clause fragment becomes an independent clause that can stand alone as a complete sentence.

                               C
COMPLETE SENTENCE: ~~Although~~ competition increased.
                               M
COMPLETE SENTENCE: ~~Because~~ market research expanded.
                               S
COMPLETE SENTENCE: ~~Although~~ statistics and market research have become part of advertising.

Note: When you join a dependent clause to an independent clause, you need to think about punctuation:

1. If the *dependent* clause comes first, follow it with a comma. The comma separates the dependent clause from the independent clause and helps you know where the independent clause begins.

dependent clause   independent clause

COMMA NEEDED: After World War II ended, humor and sex were used in commercials.

2. If the *independent* clause comes first, do *not* use a comma between the two clauses.

independent clause

NO COMMA NEEDED: Humor and sex were used in commercials after World War II ended.

dependent clause

EXERCISE 3-9   Make each of these dependent clause fragments into a sentence by adding an independent clause before or after the fragment. Add punctuation if necessary.

EXAMPLE: After we got to the beach, we put sunscreen on.

1. Since the surgery was expensive. , Arthur applied for a loan. _____

   _____

2. As long as my boss allows me. to do so, I will leave at three o'clock. ____

   _____

3. Because I want to be a journalist. , I am majoring in English. _____

   _____

You can expect leaks u

4. Until the roof is repaired. _____

   _____

My backpack was nearly empty o

5. Once I returned the library books. _____

   _____

I arrive on campus early s

6. So that I do not miss class. _____

   _____

7. Provided that Marietta gets the loan. , she will buy a used car. _____

   _____

We will go bowling u

8. Unless you would rather go to the movies. _____

   _____

9. If the thunderstorm comes during the barbecue. ‿ , we will
   eat indoors.

10. Although we visited Pittsburgh last summer. ‿ , we are planning to
    return this summer.

Dependent Clauses Beginning with Relative Pronouns

Dependent clauses also may begin with **relative pronouns.** For more
information on relative pronouns, see Part IX, on page 454.)

Relative Pronouns

Relative pronouns that refer to people
who   whom   whose
whoever   whomever

Relative pronouns that refer to things
that   what   whichever
which   whatever

The relative pronoun that begins a dependent clause connects the
dependent clause to a noun or pronoun in the independent clause.
However, the verb in the dependent clause is *never* the main verb of the
sentence. The independent clause has its own verb and expresses a complete thought.

The following sentence fragments each consist of a noun followed by
a dependent clause beginning with a relative pronoun. They are not complete sentences because the noun does not have a verb and the fragment
does not express a complete thought.

FRAGMENT: The slogan that we saw on the billboard.

FRAGMENT: An athlete who endorses a product.

FRAGMENT: The newspaper that carried advertisements on its front page.

You can correct this type of fragment by adding a verb to make the noun the subject of an independent clause. Often the independent clause will be split, and the dependent clause will appear between its parts.

Part of independent clause	dependent clause	remainder of independent clause.

subject of independent
clause   dependent clause   verb of independent clause

The slogan that we saw on the billboard has been removed.

relative pronoun

Part of independent clause	dependent clause	remainder of independent clause.

subject of independent
clause   dependent clause   verb of independent clause

An athlete who endorses a product earns a lot of money for doing so.

relative pronoun

Part of independent clause	dependent clause	remainder of independent clause.

subject of independent
clause   dependent clause   verb of
independent clause

The newspaper that carried advertisements on its front page filed for bankruptcy.

relative pronoun

EXERCISE 3-10 ▶ Make each of these fragments into a complete sentence. Add words, phrases, or clauses and punctuation as needed.

EXAMPLE: The usher who was available. ⟋ led us to our seats.

1. The radio that Trevor had purchased last night. ⟋ was defective.

_____

We could not find t
2. The official who had signed the peace treaty. _____

_____

3. The athlete who won the tennis tournament. ⟋ received an award.

_____

4. Mark, whose nose had been broken in a fight. ✐, needs surgery. ___

_____

He disregarded t
5. The advice that his lawyer gave him. _____

_____

6. The student who needed the scholarship the most. ✐ came in second.

_____

We cannot rely on t
7. The answering machine that is in the kitchen. _____

_____

8. Sarah, whom I knew in high school. ✐, married my brother. _____

_____

No one finished t
9. The problems that the professor assigned. _____

_____

10. The men who signed the Declaration of Independence. ✐ have _____
become famous. _____

NEED TO KNOW

How to Spot Fragments

Use the following questions to check for fragments:

1. **Does the word group have a subject?** The subject is a noun or pronoun that performs or receives the action of the sentence. To find the subject, ask *who* or *what* performs or receives the action of the verb.

2. **Does the word group have a verb?** Be sure that the verb is a complete and correct sentence verb. Watch out for sentences that begin with an *-ing* word or a *to* phrase.

3. **Does the word group begin with a subordinating conjunction** (*since, after, because, as, while, although,* and so forth) **introducing a dependent clause?** Unless the dependent clause is attached to an independent clause, it is a fragment.

4. **Does the word group begin with a relative pronoun** (*who, whom, whose, whoever, whomever, that, which, what, whatever*) **introducing a dependent clause?** Unless the dependent clause forms a question, is part of an independent clause, or is attached to an independent clause, it is a fragment.

How to Spot and Revise Fragments: A Brief Review

Now that you have learned to identify subjects, verbs, and dependent clauses, you will be able to spot and correct fragments. Following is a brief review.

NEED TO KNOW

How to Revise Fragments

Once you spot a fragment in your writing, correct it in one of the following ways:

1. **Add a subject if one is missing.**

   FRAGMENT: Appeared on television ten times during the game.
   REVISED: The advertisement for Pepsi appeared on television ten times during the game.

2. **Add a verb if one is missing.** Add a helping verb if one is needed, or change the verb form.

   FRAGMENT: An action-packed commercial with rap music.
   REVISED: An action-packed commercial with rap music advertised a new soft drink.

3. **Combine the fragment with an independent clause to make a complete sentence.**

   FRAGMENT: Because advertising is expensive.
   REVISED: Because advertising is expensive, companies are making shorter commercials.

4. **Remove the subordinating conjunction or relative pronoun so the group of words can stand alone as a sentence.**

   FRAGMENT: Since viewers can "zap" out commercials on video-recorders.
   REVISED: Viewers can "zap" out commercials on videorecorders.

EXERCISE 3-11 ▶ Make each of the following sentence fragments a complete sentence by combining it with an independent clause, removing the subordinating conjunction or relative pronoun, or adding the missing subject or verb.

EXAMPLE: Many environmentalists are concerned about the spotted owl. Which is almost extinct.

COMPLETE SENTENCE: Many environmentalists are concerned about the spotted owl, which is almost extinct.

1. *Margaret* Renting*ed* a tape of the movie *Citizen Kane*. _____

   _____

2. Spices that had been imported from India. *were on sale at Tops*
   .Market. _____

3. The police officer walked to Jerome's van. *t*To give him a ticket.

   _____

4. My English professor, with the cup of tea he brought to each class.
   , perched on his desk. _____

   _____

5. After the table was refinished. *, it looked like a priceless antique.*

   _____

6. Roberto memorized his lines. *f*For the performance tomorrow night.

   _____

7. *Inez bought a* A tricycle with big wheels, painted red. _____

   _____

8. On the shelf, *sat* an antique crock used for storing lard. _____

   _____

9. Because I always wanted to learn to speak Spanish. *, I registered*
   for Beginning Spanish. _____

10. Looking for the lost keys, I was late for class. _____

    _____

EXERCISE 3-12 Read the following paragraph. Underline all the fragments you find (you should find five.) Revise them as complete sentences.

Advertising in movies is big business. The next time you go

to a movie, look at all the products being shown. Maybe the

                                          o
detective is sitting in her car/ Øn a stakeout. She's sipping a can

of Coke. Maybe the movie is a comedy about a whacky family. In

one scene, they're having breakfast. What do you think is on the
                  They are having
table?ΛTropicana orange juice and Cheerios. Or suppose there's
                        w
a street scene/ With the main characters just walking along.

They pass signs advertising everything from Nike shoes to Tums

and Meow Mix cat food. You probably don't even realize all the
                                            b
advertising that's done in a movie/ Because it's so subtle.

Advertisers pay a lot to get their products in films, and they
                        i
know it pays off/ In increased sales.

EXERCISE 3-13 ▶ | Review the paragraph you wrote for Exercise 3-4, checking for sentence fragments. If you find a fragment, revise it.

WRITING ABOUT A READING

Thinking before Reading

The following reading tells of the pain and embarassment felt by someone who didn't learn to read until he was middle-aged. It describes his life and how he made his breakthrough. As you read, notice that the writer uses complete, well-developed sentences.

1. Preview the reading, using the steps listed on page 70.

2. After you have done your preview, connect the reading to your own experience by answering the following questions:

   a. Have you ever known someone who couldn't read? How did he or she try to hide this from others?
   b. Do you know or have you heard of a person who couldn't read but who still became successful?
   c. How could someone graduate from college and become a teacher without being able to read?

READING

John Corcoran—The Man Who Couldn't Read
Gary Smith

For as long as John Corcoran could remember, words had mocked him. The letters in sentences traded places, vowel sounds lost themselves in the tunnels of his ears. In school he'd sit at his desk, stupid and silent as a stone, knowing he would be different from everyone else forever. If only someone had sat next to that little boy, put an arm around his shoulder and said, "I'll help you. Don't be scared."   1

But no one had heard of dyslexia then. And John couldn't tell them that the left side of his brain, the lobe humans use to arrange symbols logically in a sequence, had always misfired.   2

Instead, in second grade they put him in the "dumb" row. In third grade a nun handed a yardstick to the other children when John refused to read and write and let each student have a crack at his legs. In fourth grade his teacher called on him to read and let one minute of quiet pile upon another until the child thought he would suffocate. Then he was passed on to the next grade and the next. John Corcoran never failed a year in his life.   3

In his senior year, John was voted homecoming king, went steady with the valedictorian and starred on the basketball team. His mom kissed him when he graduated—and kept talking about college. College? It would be insane to consider. But he finally decided on the University of Texas at El Paso, where he could try out for the basketball team. He took a deep breath, closed his eyes . . . and recrossed enemy lines.   4

On campus John asked each new friend: Which teachers gave essay tests? Which gave multiple choice? The minute he stepped out of a class, he tore the pages of scribble from his notebook, in case anyone asked to see his notes. He stared at thick textbooks in the evening so his roommate wouldn't doubt. And he lay in bed, exhausted but unable to sleep, unable to make his whirring mind let go. John promised he'd go to Mass 30 days straight at the crack of dawn, if only God would let him get his degree.   5

He got the diploma. He gave God his 30 days of Mass. Now what? Maybe he was addicted to the edge. Maybe the thing he felt most insecure about—his mind—was what he needed most to have admired. Maybe that's why, in 1961, John became a teacher.   6

John taught in California. Each day he had a student read the textbook to the class. He gave standardized tests that he could grade by placing a form with holes over each correct answer and he lay in bed for hours on weekend mornings, depressed.   7

Then he met Kathy, an A student and a nurse. Not a leaf, like John.   8
A rock. "There's something I have to tell you, Kathy," he said one night
in 1965 before their marriage, "I . . . I can't read."

"He's a teacher," she thought. He must mean he can't read well.   9
Kathy didn't understand until years later when she saw John unable to
read a children's book to their 18-month-old daughter. Kathy filled out
his forms, read and wrote his letters. Why didn't he simply ask her to
teach him to read and write? He couldn't believe that anyone could
teach him.

At age 28 John borrowed $2,500, bought a second house, fixed   10
it up and rented it. He bought and rented another. And another. His
business got bigger and bigger until he needed a secretary, a lawyer
and a partner.

Then one day his accountant told him he was a millionaire. Perfect.   11
Who'd notice that a millionaire always pulled on the doors that said
PUSH or paused before entering public bathrooms, waiting to see which
one the men walked out of?

In 1982 the bottom began to fall out. His properties started to sit   12
empty and investors pulled out. Threats of foreclosures and lawsuits
tumbled out of envelopes. Every waking moment, it seemed, he was
pleading with bankers to extend his loans, coaxing builders to stay on
the job, trying to make sense of the pyramid of paper. Soon he knew
they'd have him on the witness stand and the man in black robes would
say: "The truth, John Corcoran. Can't you even read?"

Finally in the fall of 1986, at age 48, John did two things he swore   13
he never would. He put up his house as collateral to obtain one last

construction loan. And he walked into the Carlsbad City Library and told the woman in charge of the tutoring program, "I can't read."

Then he cried.   14

He was placed with a 65-year-old grandmother named Eleanor   15
Condit. Painstakingly—letter by letter, phonetically—she began teaching him. Within 14 months, his land-development company began to revive. And John Corcoran was learning to read.

The next step was confession: a speech before 200 stunned business- 16
men in San Diego. To heal, he had to come clean. He was placed on the board of directors of the San Diego Council on Literacy and began traveling across the country to give speeches.

"Illiteracy is a form of slavery!" he would cry. "We can't waste   17
time blaming anyone. We need to become obsessed with teaching people to read!"

He read every book or magazine he could get his hands on, every   18
road sign he passed, out loud, as long as Kathy could bear it. It was glorious, like singing. And now he could sleep.

Then one day it occurred to him—one more thing he could finally   19
do. Yes, that dusty box in his office, that sheaf of papers bound by ribbon . . . a quarter-century later, John Corcoran could read his wife's love letters.

From Canfield and Hanson, *Chicken Soup for the Soul*

Getting Ready to Write

Strengthening Your Vocabulary

Write a brief definition of each of the following words, used in the preceding reading. If you cannot figure out the meaning of a word from the way it is used in the reading, look the word up in a dictionary.

1. dyslexia (paragraph 2)   the inability to learn to read

2. lobe (paragraph 2)   section or part

3. suffocate (paragraph 3)   choke, not be able to breathe

4. insecure (paragraph 6)   lacking self-confidence, unsure

5. foreclosures (paragraph 12) legal actions to seize property

6. coaxing (paragraph 12)   persuading with soothing words or flattery

7. collateral (paragraph 13)   security for a loan

8. revive (paragraph 15)   come back to life, recover

9. sheaf (paragraph 19)   bundle, packet, stack

Reviewing the Reading Using an Idea Map

Review the reading by completing the missing pieces of the idea map shown below.

JOHN CORCORAN DIDN'T LEARN TO READ UNTIL AGE 48.

Early life

John had dyslexia

No help in grade school; just passed on

High school and college

High-school basketball star and homecoming king

Bluffed his way through college

After graduation

Found ways around dyslexia as a teacher

Married: unable to read to daughter

Second career

Started business and became millionaire

Business began to fail

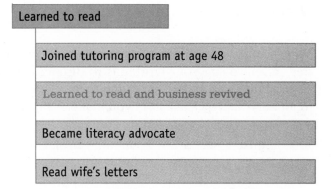

Learned to read

Joined tutoring program at age 48

Learned to read and business revived

Became literacy advocate

Read wife's letters

Examining the Reading

1. How was John Corcoran treated in elementary school?

2. How was he able to function as a teacher with his reading disability?

3. How did he become successful without knowing how to read?

4. What finally caused him to enroll in a tutoring program?

Reacting to and Discussing Ideas

1. How would you go about teaching an illiterate person how to read?

2. How might you feel if you couldn't read?

3. If you could not read, what things would you be unable to do that you can do now? Try to be specific.

Writing about the Reading

The Paragraph Option

1. Write a paragraph describing how you learned to read.

2. Write a paragraph explaining what characteristics a person would need to possess in order to finally learn to read as an adult.

The Essay Option

1. Write an essay describing what impact the ability to read has had on your life. Mention specific personal accomplishments and how reading has played a part in them.

2. Write an essay that explains John Corcoran's statement "Illiteracy is a form of slavery!" Include reasons why you agree and examples of how it is true.

WRITING SUCCESS TIP 3

Most writers make certain types of errors and not others. The first step in improving your writing is to discover what errors you make. Then you can work on correcting them. An error log is an easy way to identify the types of errors you make. To make an error log, follow these simple steps:

1. Organize a section of your journal or a sheet of paper into two columns using the following headings:

Types of Errors	Assignment					
	1	2	3	4	5	6

2. Whenever your instructor returns a corrected paper, spend time reviewing your errors.

3. If you do not understand why something is marked as an error, ask your instructor to explain it.

4. Fill in your error log by listing each error you made. Be as specific as possible. Group your errors into four categories: sentences, grammar, punctuation, and misspelled words (see the sample error log shown on the next page). Add a paragraph-development or essay-development category if you are writing essays. For more information on types of errors, consult Part VIII, "Reviewing the Basics."

5. After you have filled in the errors for several assignments, look for a pattern in your errors. The student who produced the following log needs to concentrate on run-on sentences, subject-verb agreement, verb tenses, and commas.

6. Not all instructors mark all errors on every paper. Some mark more serious errors when they first start correcting your papers. Once you've corrected those errors, you instructor may mark different types of errors.

Sample Error Log

Types of Errors	Assignment			
	1	2	3	4
Sentences				
run-on	one	two	one	
fragments	one	0	0	
Grammar	subject- verb agreement	—	subject- verb agreement	
	verb tense	- verb tense	verb tense	
	pronoun ref.		pronoun ref.	
Punctuation	comma	comma quotation	comma semicolon	
Misspelled Words	favorite relies knowledge	chemicals majority especially leisure	necessary hoping definitely	

4

Run-on Sentences and Comma Splices

CHAPTER OBJECTIVES

In this chapter you will learn to

1. recognize and correct run-on sentences.

2. recognize and correct comma splices.

Have you ever heard a tape played on fast forward? What happens to the message? Does it seem garbled and incomprehensible? The information seems to run together without any spacing between words, phrases, and sentences. The same confusion can occur in writing if you run your ideas together without pauses or separations. In this chapter you will learn how to separate your ideas to make them as clear and understandable as possible. Specifically, you will learn to avoid writing run-on sentences and comma splices.

WRITING

The Function of Punctuation

All punctuation serves one primary purpose—to separate. Periods, question marks, and exclamation points separate complete sentences from one another. Think of these punctuation marks as *between*-sentence separators. All other punctuation marks—commas, colons, semicolons, hyphens, dashes, quotation marks, and parentheses—separate parts *within* a sentence. To correct and avoid run-on sentences and comma splices, you need a good grasp of both between-sentence and within-sentence punctuation.

Between-Sentence Punctuation

The period, question mark, and exclamation point all mark the end of a sentence. Each has a different function.

Between-Sentence Punctuation

Punctuation	Function	Example
Period (.)	Marks the end of a statement or command	The lecture is about to begin. Please be seated.
Question mark (?)	Marks the end of a direct question	Are you ready?
Exclamation point (!)	Marks the end of statements of excitement or strong emotion	We are late! I won an award!

Within-Sentence Punctuation

Commas, colons, semicolons, hyphens, dashes, quotation marks, and parentheses all separate parts of a sentence from one another. For a complete review of how and when to use each, refer to Part IX, "Reviewing the Basics," pages 490–496.

The **comma** is the most commonly used within-sentence punctuation mark and also the most commonly misused. The comma separates parts of a sentence from one another. In this chapter, we'll be concerned with just one type of separation: the separation of two complete thoughts. (*Note:* Some instructors refer to a complete thought as an independent clause. An independent clause has a subject and a verb and can stand alone as a sentence. For a review of independent clauses, see Chapter 3, pages 60–62.)

The comma can be used to separate two complete thoughts within a sentence *if and only if* it is used along with one of the coordinating conjunctions *(and, or, so, for, but, yet, nor)*. Coordinating conjunctions are words that link and relate equally important parts of a sentence. The comma is not a strong enough separator to be used between complete thoughts without one of the coordinating conjunctions.

complete thought   coordinating conjunction   complete thought

I work now for a big company, but I am hoping someday to take over my father's business.

complete thought   coordinating conjunction   complete thought

I am undecided about a career, so I am majoring in liberal arts.

When you do not insert punctuation and a coordinating conjunction between two complete thoughts, you create an error called a **run-on sentence**. (This is sometimes called a **fused sentence** because two sentences are incorrectly fused, or joined together.) When you use *only* a comma to separate two complete thoughts, you make an error called a **comma splice**.

Run-on Sentences

When you do not separate two complete thoughts (two independent clauses) with the necessary punctuation, the two clauses run together and form a run-on sentence.

How to Recognize Run-on Sentences

1. Read each sentence aloud. Listen for a break or change in your voice midway through the sentence. Your voice automatically pauses or slows down at the end of a complete thought. If you hear a break but have no punctuation at that break, you may have a run-on sentence. Try reading the following run-on sentences aloud. Place a slash mark (/) where you hear a pause.

RUN-ON: The library has a copy machine it is very conveniently located.

RUN-ON: The Career Planning Center on campus is helpful one of the counselors suggested I take a career-planning course.

RUN-ON: My major is nursing I do enjoy working with people.

Did you mark the sentences as follows?

The library has a copy machine **/** it is very conveniently located.

The Career Planning Center on campus is helpful **/** one of the counselors suggested I take a career-planning course.

My major is nursing **/** I do enjoy working with people.

The pause indicates the need for punctuation.

2. Look for a sentence that contains two complete thoughts (independent clauses) without punctuation to separate them.

complete thought (independent clause)

RUN-ON: Houseplants are pleasant additions to a home or office they add color and variety.

complete thought (independent clause)

complete thought
(independent clause)   complete thought
(independent clause)

RUN-ON: My sister decided to wear black I chose red.

complete thought
(independent clause)

RUN-ON: Having a garage sale is a good way to make money
          it unclutters the house, too.

complete thought
(independent clause)

complete thought
(independent clause)   complete thought
(independent clause)

RUN-ON: We bought a portable phone then we had to connect the base
          unit into our phone line.

3. Look for long sentences. Not every long sentence is a run-on, but run-ons do tend to occur more frequently in longer sentences than in shorter ones.

RUN-ON: Choosing a mate is one of the most important decisions you will
          ever make unless you make the right choice, you may be
          unhappy.

RUN-ON: I plan to work in a day-care center some days taking care of my
          own kids is enough to make me question my career choice.

EXERCISE 4-1 Read each sentence aloud. Place a check mark in the blank before each sentence that is a run-on. Use a slash mark to show where punctuation needs to go. Not all of these sentences are run-ons.

_____✓_____ 1. Parking spaces on campus are limited/ often I must park far away and walk.

_____ 2. Before exercising, you should always stretch and warm up to prevent injury.

_____✓_____ 3. Theodore's car wouldn't start/ fortunately Phil was able to use jumper cables to help him get it started.

_____✓_____ 4. The skydiver jumped from the plane/ when she had fallen far enough she released her parachute.

_____ 5. Radio stations usually have a morning disc jockey whose job is to wake people up and cheer them up on their way to work.

_____✓_____ 6. It continued to rain until the river overflowed/ many people had to be evacuated from their homes.

_____✓_____   7. Calla bought a bathrobe for her brother as a birthday
              gift/ it was gray with burgundy stripes.
_____✓_____   8. The rooms in the maternity section of the hospital have
              colorful flowered wallpaper/ they are cheerful and
              pleasant.
_____   9. Because my cousin went to nursing school and then to
              law school, she is going to practice medical malpractice
              law.
_____✓_____   10. We rented Rocky to watch on the videorecorder/ later we
              practiced boxing moves.

NEED TO KNOW

How to Correct Run-on Sentences

You can correct run-on sentences in four ways:

Method 1   Separate the two complete thoughts into two sentences.

Method 2   Separate the two complete thoughts with a semicolon.

Method 3   Join the two complete thoughts with a comma and a coordinating
            conjunction *(and, or, but, for, nor, so, yet)*.

Method 4   Make one thought dependent upon the other by using a subordinat-
            ing conjunction (see the list on page 62).

How to Correct Run-on Sentences

1. Create two separate sentences. Split the two complete thoughts into
two separate sentences. End the first thought with a *period* (or a *question
mark* or an *exclamation point* if one is needed). Begin the second thought
with a capital letter.

              Complete thought.   Complete thought.

RUN-ON: Many students do not have a specific career goal they do have
           some general career directions in mind.

CORRECT: Many students do not have a specific career goal. They do have
           some general career directions in mind.

RUN-ON: Some students choose courses without studying degree require-
           ments these students may make unwise choices.

CORRECT: Some students choose courses without studying degree require-
           ments. These students may make unwise choices.

RUN-ON: Some people love their jobs they are delighted that someone is willing to pay them to do what they enjoy.

CORRECT: Some people love their jobs. They are delighted that someone is willing to pay them to do what they enjoy.

RUN-ON: Some people hate their jobs going back to school may be a good idea in these cases.

CORRECT: Some people hate their jobs. Going back to school may be a good idea in these cases.

The separation method is a good choice if the two thoughts are not closely related or if joining the two thoughts correctly (by one of the methods described next) creates an extremely long sentence.

EXERCISE 4-2 ▶ Revise the run-on sentences you identified in Exercise 4-1 by creating two separate sentences in each case.

2. Use a semicolon. Use a **semicolon** (;) to connect two complete thoughts that will remain parts of the same sentence.

> Complete thought.   ;   Complete thought.

RUN-ON: Our psychology instructor is demanding he expects the best from all his students.

CORRECT: Our psychology instructor is demanding; he expects the best from all his students.

RUN-ON: Sunshine is enjoyable it puts people in a good mood.

CORRECT: Sunshine is enjoyable; it puts people in a good mood.

RUN-ON: A course in nutrition may be useful it may help you make wise food choices.

CORRECT: A course in nutrition may be useful; it may help you make wise food choices.

Use this method when your two complete thoughts are closely related and the relationship between them is clear and obvious.

EXERCISE 4-3 ▶ Place a check mark in the blank before each sentence that is a run-on. Correct each run-on by using a semicolon. Not all of these sentences are run-ons.

_____✓_____   1. The economic summit meeting was held in Britain many diplomats attended.

_____ ✓ _____ 2. I especially enjoy poetry by Emily Dickinson; her poems are intense, concise, and revealing.

_____ 3. The Use and Abuse of Drugs is a popular course because the material is geared for nonscience majors.

_____ ✓ _____ 4. The food festival offered a wide selection of food; everything from hot dogs to elegant desserts was available.

_____ 5. Since the flight was turbulent, the flight attendant suggested that we remain in our seats.

_____ ✓ _____ 6. The bowling alley was not crowded; most of the lanes were open.

_____ ✓ _____ 7. Swimming is an excellent form of exercise; it gives you a good aerobic workout.

_____ 8. When the space shuttle landed, the astronauts cheered.

_____ ✓ _____ 9. The two-lane highway is being expanded to four lanes; even that improvement is not expected to solve the traffic-congestion problems.

_____ ✓ _____ 10. Before visiting Israel, Carolyn read several guidebooks; they helped her plan her trip.

3. Use a comma and a coordinating conjunction. Use a **comma** and a **coordinating conjunction** to separate two complete thoughts placed within one sentence. (*Note:* When you separate two complete thoughts by using a coordinating conjunction, you must also use a comma.) The seven coordinating conjunctions are listed below:

Complete thought.	, and	complete thought.
	, but	
	, for	
	, nor	
	, or	
	, so	
	, yet	

When you use a coordinating conjunction to separate two complete thoughts, be sure to use the right one. Since each coordinating conjunction has a particular meaning, you should choose the one that shows the right relationship between the two thoughts. For example, the conjunction *and* indicates the ideas are equally important. The words *but* and *yet* indicate that one idea is contrary to or in opposition to the other. *For* and *so* emphasize cause-effect connections. *Or* and *nor* indicate choice.

NEED TO KNOW

How to Use Coordinating Conjunctions

There are seven coordinating conjunctions. Choose the one that shows the right relationship between the two complete thoughts in a sentence.

Coordinating Conjunction	Meaning	Example
and	added to, in addition, along with	Budgeting is important, *and* it is time well spent.
but	just the opposite, on the other hand	I had planned to visit Chicago, *but* I changed my mind.
for	since, because	Sarah is taking math, *for* she is a chemistry major.
nor	and not, or not, not either	Sam cannot choose a career, *nor* can he decide upon a major.
or	either	I will major in liberal arts, *or* I will declare myself "undecided."
so	as a result, consequently	Yolanda enjoys mathematics, *so* she is considering it as a career.
yet	despite, nevertheless	I plan to become a computer programmer, *yet* a change is still possible.

The following examples show how to use a comma and a coordinating conjunction to correct a run-on sentence:

RUN-ON: Interests change and develop throughout life you may have a different set of interests twenty years from now.

comma and conjunction *so* used to show cause-effect relationship

CORRECT: Interests change and develop throughout life, so you may have a different set of interests twenty years from now.

RUN-ON: Take courses in a variety of disciplines you may discover new interests.

comma and conjunction *for* used to show cause-effect relationship

CORRECT: Take courses in a variety of disciplines, for you may discover new interests.

RUN-ON: Alexis thought she was not interested in biology by taking a biology course, she discovered it was her favorite subject.

comma and conjunction *but* used to show contrast

CORRECT: Alexis thought she was not interested in biology, but by taking a biology course, she discovered it was her favorite subject.

RUN-ON: The weather forecast threatened severe thunderstorms just as the day ended, the sky began to cloud over.

comma and conjunction *and* used to show addition

CORRECT: The weather forecast threatened severe thunderstorms, and just as the day ended, the sky began to cloud over.

This method of correcting run-ons allows you to indicate to your reader how your two ideas are connected. Use this method for correcting run-on sentences when you want to explain the relationship between the two thoughts.

EXERCISE 4-4 ▶ Correct each of the following run-on sentences by using a comma and a coordinating conjunction. Think about the relationship between two thoughts, and then choose the best coordinating conjunction. (These are the coordinating conjunctions: *and, or, but, for, nor, yet, so.*)

EXAMPLE: I thought I had left for class in plenty of time, [but] I was two minutes late.

1. Jameel got up half an hour late [, so] he missed the bus.

2. My creative-writing teacher wrote a book [, but] our library did not have a copy.

3. Ford is an interesting first name [, but] we did not choose it for our son.

4. Smoking cigarettes is not healthy [, for] it can cause lung cancer.

5. My paycheck was ready to be picked up [, yet] I forgot to get it.

6. The window faces north [, so] the room gets little sun.

7. I may order Chinese food for dinner͵ I may bake a chicken.
   `, or`

8. Miranda had planned to write her term paper about World War͵ I she switched her topic to the Roaring Twenties.
   `, but`

9. The journalist arrived at the fire͵ she began to take notes.
   `, and`

10. The table is wobbly͵ we keep a matchbook under one leg to stabilize it.
    `, so`

4. Make one thought dependent. Make one thought dependent by making it a dependent clause. A **dependent clause** depends on an independent clause for its meaning. It cannot stand alone because it does not express a complete thought. In a sentence, a dependent clause must always be linked to an independent clause, which expresses a complete thought. By itself, a dependent clause always leaves a question in your mind; the question is answered by the independent clause to which it is joined.

dependent clause raises a question

Because I missed the bus   [What happened?]

independent clause answers the question

Because I missed the bus, I was late for class.

dependent clause raises a question

When I got my exam back   [What did you do?]

independent clause answers the question

When I got my exam back, I celebrated.

Did you notice that each dependent clause began with a word that makes it dependent? In the above sentences, the words that make the clauses dependent are *Because* and *When.* These words are called **subordinating conjunctions.** Subordinating conjunctions let you know that the sense of the clause that follows them depends on another idea, an idea you will find in the independent clause of the sentence. Some common subordinating conjunctions are *after, although, before, if, since,* and *unless.* For a more complete list, see page 62.

You can correct a run-on sentence by changing one of the complete thoughts into a dependent clause and joining the ideas in the two clauses with a subordinating conjunction. This method places more emphasis on the idea expressed in the complete thought (independent clause) and less emphasis on the idea in the dependent clause.

RUN-ON: Aptitudes are built-in strengths they are important in career planning.

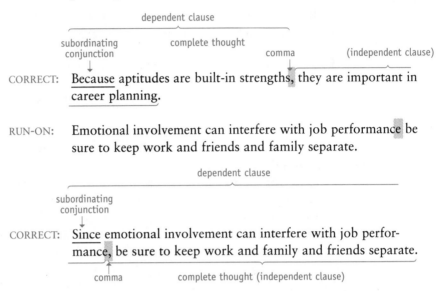

CORRECT: Because aptitudes are built-in strengths, they are important in career planning.

RUN-ON: Emotional involvement can interfere with job performance be sure to keep work and friends and family separate.

CORRECT: Since emotional involvement can interfere with job performance, be sure to keep work and family and friends separate.

Note: A dependent clause can appear before or after an independent clause. If the dependent clause appears first, it must be followed by a comma, as in the examples above. No comma is needed when the complete thought comes first.

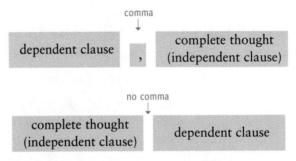

RUN-ON: Personal relationships are enjoyable they should be minimized in the workplace.

CORRECT: Even though personal relationships are enjoyable, they should be minimized in the workplace.

complete thought
(independent clause)   no comma

CORRECT: Personal relationships should be minimized in the workplace
even though they are enjoyable.

↑
subordinating conjunction

dependent clause

EXERCISE 4-5 ▶ In each of the following run-on sentences, make one thought dependent on the other by using the subordinating conjunction in boldface. Don't forget to use a comma if the dependent clause comes first.

Until w

EXAMPLE: We called the plumber we were without water.   **until**

1. David wants a leather jacket it is very expensive.   **even though**

2. Margery runs ten miles every day she can try out for the cross-country squad in the spring.   **so that**

3. The television program ended, Gail read a book to her son.   **when**

4. The pool was crowded it was 95 degrees that day.   **because**

5. Industry is curbing pollution, our water supply still is not safe.   **although**

6. I always obey the speed limit speeding carries a severe penalty in my state.   **because**

7. The crowd fell silent the trapeze artist attempted a quadruple flip.   **while**

8. The Cold War with the USSR is over, there are greater opportunities for cultural exchange.   **since**

9. The storm approached, I stocked up on batteries.   **as**

10. The moon is full, our dog is restless.   **Whenever**

EXERCISE 4-6 ▶ Write five sentences, each of which has two complete thoughts. Then revise each sentence so that it has one dependent clause and one complete thought (independent clause). Use a comma, if needed, to separate the two clauses. You may wish to refer to the list of subordinating conjunctions on page 62.

Comma Splices

Like run-ons, comma splices are serious sentence errors that can confuse and annoy your readers. Also, like run-ons, they are easy to correct once you know what to look for. In fact, they are corrected in the same way that run-ons are. A comma splice occurs when you use *only* a comma to separate two complete thoughts. A comma alone is not sufficient to divide the two thoughts. A stronger, clearer separation is necessary. You can visualize a comma splice this way:

COMMA SPLICE: Complete thought. , complete thought.

COMMA SPLICE: Spatial aptitude is the ability to understand and visualize objects in physical space, it is an important skill for engineers and designers.

COMMA SPLICE: Some people have strong mechanical ability, they often prefer hands-on tasks.

COMMA SPLICE: Verbal reasoning is important to many careers, it is the ability to think through problems.

How to Recognize Comma Splices

To avoid comma splices, you have to make sure that you do not place *only a comma* between two complete thoughts. To test a sentence to see if you have written a comma splice, take the sentence apart at the comma. If the part before the comma is a complete thought and the part after the comma is a complete thought, then you need to check whether the second clause starts with a coordinating conjunction *(and, or, so, for, but, yet, nor)*. If you do not have a coordinating conjunction to separate the two complete thoughts, then you have a comma splice.

NEED TO KNOW

How to Correct Comma Splices

Correct comma splices the same way you correct run-on sentences:

Method 1   Separate the two complete thoughts into two sentences.

Method 2   Separate the two complete thoughts with a semicolon.

Method 3   Join the two complete thoughts with a comma and a coordinating conjunction *(and, but, for, nor, or, so, yet)*.

Method 4   Make one thought dependent upon the other by using a subordinating conjunction (see the list on page 62).

How to Correct Comma Splices

To correct comma splices, use any one of the four methods you used to correct run-ons:

1. Separate the thoughts into two complete sentences, deleting the comma.

> Complete thought.   Complete thought.

2. Separate the two thoughts with a semicolon, deleting the comma.

> Complete thought. ; complete thought.

3. Separate the two thoughts by adding a coordinating conjunction after the comma.

> Complete thought , and complete thought.

> , but
> , for
> , nor
> , or
> , so
> , yet

4. Make one thought dependent on the other by using a subordinating conjunction to separate the two thoughts. (See page 110 for a complete list of subordinating conjunctions.)

> Subordinating conjunction dependent clause , independent clause .

> Independent clause subordinating conjunction dependent clause .

EXERCISE 4-7 Some of the following sentences have comma splices. Correct each comma splice by using one of the four methods described in this chapter. Write "OK" in the blank before each sentence that is correct.

_____ 1. The stained glass window is beautiful,⟋ it has been in the church since 1880.

_____ 2. Replacing the spark plugs was simple,⟋ replacing the radiator was not.

                                                                because
_____   3. School buses lined up in front of the school,/ three
            o'clock was dismissal time.

                                                                    ;
_____   4. The gymnast practiced her balance-beam routine,/ she did
            not make a single mistake.

                                                          . I
_____   5. A huge branch fell on the driveway,/ it just missed
            my car.

                                                      and
_____   6. The receptionist answered the phone, ⌄she put the caller
            on hold.

___OK___   7. The couple dressed up as Raggedy Ann and Andy for
            Halloween, but their red-yarn wigs kept falling off.

                                                    . H
_____   8. Bill left his notebook in the cafeteria,/ he was confused
            later when he was unable to find the notebook.
                                                          but
_____   9. The strawberries were red and sweet, ⌄the blueberries
            were not ripe yet.

___OK___   10. There had been a severe drought, so the waterfall
            dried up.

EXERCISE 4-8 ▶ In the blanks, identify each sentence as a run-on sentence (RO), a comma
splice (CS), or a correct sentence(C). Then correct the faulty sentences
using one of the four methods.

EXAMPLE: ___CS___ When the children chased the ball into the street,
          cars screeched to a halt.

                    When
___RO___   1. ⌄Inez packed for the camping trip,⌄she remembered every-

            thing except insect repellant.

                                                              and
___CS___   2. A limousine drove through our neighborhood, ⌄everybody

            wondered who was in it.

                                                    , but
___RO___   3. The defendant pleaded not guilty ⌄the judge ordered him

            to pay the parking fine.

_____RO_____ 4. Before a big game, Louis, who is a quarterback, eats a lot of pasta and bread. he says it gives him energy.

_____CS_____ 5. Four of my best friends from high school have decided to go to law school, but I have decided to become a legal secretary.

_____RO_____ 6. Felicia did not know what to buy her parents for their anniversary, so she went to a lot of stores and she finally decided to buy them a camera.

_____RO_____ 7. After living in a dorm room for three years, Jason found an apartment. The rent was very high, so he had to get a job to pay for it.

_____CS_____ 8. The cherry tree had to be cut down because it stood right where the new addition was going to be built.

_____C_____ 9. Amanda worked every night for a month on the needlepoint pillow that she was making for her grandmother.

_____CS_____ 10. Driving around in the dark, we finally realized we were lost. Dwight went into a convenience store to ask for directions.

EXERCISE 4-9 Find and correct the run-on sentences and comma splices in the following paragraph. You should find two run-ons and three comma splices

Everyone has heard of "IQ," but have you ever heard of "EQ"? "EQ" stands for "emotional intelligence." A psychologist named Daniel Goleman believes that IQ is not nearly as impor-

tant as EQ for successful living. People with a high EQ know how to manage their own emotions, for example, high EQ people
^F — *(marked above "for")*

how to manage their own emotions, for example, high EQ people

don't procrastinate. They don't put off paying their bills or go to

the movies instead of studying for an exam. High EQ people also

set goals and persevere they keep trying if something is impor-

tant to them. High EQ people care about others they are aware

of people's feelings and respect differences of opinion. They

have good relationships with others, they are also better par-

ents. Goleman thinks that emotional intelligence should be

taught as a separate course in grade school and high school. He

believes we would have less violence in our society if people

were more emotionally healthy, what do you think?

WRITING ABOUT A READING

Thinking before Reading

Have you ever imagined what it would be like to become a millionaire and what you would have to do to become one? Would it take a run of good luck, an innovative idea, or a stroke of genius? The following reading provides an answer that you may not have expected: Hard work is the key to financial success. As you read, you'll see that the reading is easy to understand. The author has made sure that each idea is clear and separated from other ideas correctly. Notice how the author sometimes uses commas to separate elements within sentences.

Before you read:

1. Preview the reading, using the steps listed on page 20.

2. After you have done your preview, connect the reading to your own experience by answering the following questions:

   a. What types of careers do you think lead to financial success?
   b. Do you enjoy work, or do you know someone who does? What is there about work that is enjoyable for you or that person?
   c. Do you think becoming a millionaire is a worthwhile goal?
   d. Is becoming a millionaire a realistic goal? Why or why not?

READING

How to Become a Millionaire
William M. Pride, Robert J. Hughes, and Jack R. Kapoor

$1,000,000 is a large and magical number. Besides winning a lot-   1
tery, being a superstar athlete, or being born into an extremely
wealthy family, how does one become a millionaire? When you
examine the lives and lifestyles of millionaires, you might be surprised to
find out how they do it.

Contrary to popular belief, most current millionaires didn't inherit   2
their wealth. About 80 percent of American millionaires come from
middle- or working-class families. Doctors, lawyers, and business executives have highly prestigious jobs, but they don't necessarily make the
most money. Owners of small, often mundane businesses have a much
greater chance of becoming millionaires. Close to 85 percent of
America's millionaires own their own companies or own sizable
portions of private firms. Athletes, entertainers, and artists do not
represent a large proportion of American millionaires—in fact, less
than 1 percent!

Thomas J. Stanley, a marketing professor at Georgia State University   3
and an expert on the American rich, has come up with a list of businesses that he thinks might bring the industrious, hard-working, ambi-
tious individual his or her first million. The list includes: operation of a
dry-cleaning chain; computer program design; commercial printing; jewelry retailing; specialized tool-and-die manufacturing; real estate-related
businesses; plumbing, heating, and air-conditioning contracting; money
managing; and independent insurance brokerage services.

Millionaires are typically workaholics: Sixty-eight percent claim that   4
they don't ever plan on retiring. Rich people work even though they
don't have to. Not only do millionaires work hard; but they save, too.

They do not spend their money carelessly or extravagantly. Fewer than half of the millionaires in this country send their children to private elementary or high schools. Most millionaires don't own expensive watches or yachts. Intense saving, not spending, might be the key to making your first million.

So if you have ideas about reaching that million-dollar plateau, it   5
might be a wise idea to forget about the fancy cars and cancel that plane reservation to Las Vegas. If you do go to Vegas, spend less time inside the casinos and more time checking out the acts.

From William M. Pride, Robert J. Hughes, and Jack R. Kapoor, *Business* (3rd ed.).

Getting Ready to Write

Strengthening Your Vocabulary

Write a brief definition for each of the following words, used in the preceding reading. If you can't figure out the meaning of a word from the way it is used in the reading, look the word up in a dictionary.

1. prestigious (paragraph 2)   important, commanding respect

2. mundane (paragraph 2)   ordinary

3. industrious (paragraph 3)   making an earnest effort

4. intense (paragraph 4)   extreme

5. plateau (paragraph 5)   stable level

Reviewing the Reading Using an Idea Map

Review the reading by completing the missing pieces of the idea map shown below.

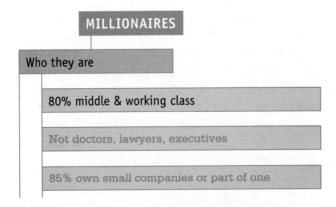

MILLIONAIRES

Who they are

80% middle & working class

Not doctors, lawyers, executives

85% own small companies or part of one

1% athletes, entertainers, artists

Businesses to become one

Dry-cleaning chain
Computer program design
Commercial printing
Jewelry retailing
Specialized tool-and-die manufacturing
Real estate
Plumbing, heating, air conditioning contracting
Money managing
Insurance brokerage

How they do it

Workaholics
68% say they won't ever retire
Work even though they don't have to
Don't spend carelessly; save

Examining the Reading

1. According to Professor Stanley, which careers are likely to lead to financial success?

2. Describe the lifestyle of a typical millionaire.

3. How did *most* millionaires in this country acquire their wealth?

Reacting to and Discussing Ideas

Get ready to write about the reading by discussing the following questions:

1. Is $1,000,000 a magical number? Why or why not?

2. Do you think all millionaires are happy? Discuss whether or not money is important to happiness.

3. Why do many millionaires keep on working once they have made their first million? Discuss the value and importance of work.

4. Do you think you could become a millionaire?

Writing about the Reading

The Paragraph Option

1. Write a paragraph describing your job or career goals. Include information about what you would like to do and why. Assume your reader is a career-planning counselor with whom you have an appointment.

2. Millionaires have an obligation to help people less fortunate than they. Write a paragraph supporting or disagreeing with this statement.

The Essay Option

Write a brief article for your local or campus newspaper in which you advise other students about a career or job area that you think may lead to financial success. What area do you see becoming profitable as our world changes?

**Proofreading
Tips**

WRITING SUCCESS TIP 4

Proofreading is checking for errors. Think of proofreading as giving your work an important final polish. Carefully study what you have written, and be concerned with correctness. Use Part IX, "Reviewing the Basics," as a reference for checking points of grammar, punctuation, and mechanics. Check each paragraph for just one kind of error at a time so you can focus on that error.

1. Check for errors you commonly make by consulting your error log (see Writing Success Tip 3, "Keeping an Error Log," on pages 76 and 77). Read your paragraph through once for each type of error.

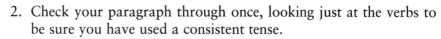

2. Check your paragraph through once, looking just at the verbs to be sure you have used a consistent tense.

3. Read your paragraph through once to check if you have used pronouns correctly.

4. Read your paragraph again, checking for subject-verb agreement. Each time you spot a singular subject, be sure you have used a singular verb. Each time you spot a plural subject, check to be certain you have used a plural verb.

5. Read your paragraph another time for mechanics. Check capitalization and punctuation.

6. To spot spelling errors, read your paragraph backwards, from the last word to the first word. This process removes you from the flow of ideas so you can focus on spotting errors. Check your dictionary for the spelling of any questionable words.

7. Read each sentence aloud, slowly and deliberately. Reading aloud will help you catch missing words, endings you have left off verbs, or missing plural endings.

8. Check for errors again as you rewrite or type your paragraph in final form. Prepare your final draft when you are fresh; if you are tired, you might introduce new mistakes.

5

Combining and Expanding Your Ideas

Try an experiment. Ask a friend or classmate what he or she plans to do this weekend. Then, when the person answers, notice the length of his or her sentences. Are they long or short? You probably discovered that many sentences were very short. Some may not even have been complete sentences. (Incomplete sentences are common in casual speech but should not be used in formal writing.) We usually speak in short sentences for a number of reasons. First, we tend to express ideas as they come to us, often in their simplest form. Second, without any written or taped record, listeners have to carry in their minds what the speaker has said and is saying. Short spoken sentences are easier to grasp and remember than longer ones.

Sample Spoken Answer

One student recorded the following answer to a question about weekend plans:

> I'm hoping to relax. Catch up on homework, too. We might see a movie Friday night. Just depends. Ramón may have to work late. I'm not sure. On Saturday I'm going to the mall, at least I hope so. I've got to get a dress for my sister's wedding. It's next month. Sunday is for homework. There's a test coming up in psych. It's a big one. I've just got to start reviewing.

If you heard this answer out loud, the sentences would probably seem quite normal, but how did it feel to *read* the answer? Did it seem too simple? Did it seem choppy? Did ideas seem to start and stop, start and stop? Was it dull? Did it seem to take a long time to convey a relatively small amount of information?

Now read a revised version of this answer.

Revised Written Answer

I'm hoping to relax and catch up on homework this weekend. If Ramón does not work late, we'll see a movie on Friday evening. On Saturday I'm going to the mall to get a dress for my sister's wedding next month. On Sunday I am planning to study for an important psychology test.

Here the same information in the choppy spoken answer appears in organized written form. The sentences are longer. Several sentences were combined, and connections between the ideas were made clearer. In writing, you need to make your expression tighter, more condensed, and more interesting than you do in speech.

In this chapter you will learn to combine your ideas to make your sentences more effective as well as more interesting. You will also learn how to use sentence arrangement to show relationships between and among ideas. To do so, you'll need to understand and be able to write independent and dependent clauses.

WRITING

Understanding Independent and Dependent Clauses

If you are financially independent, you alone accept full responsibility for your finances. If you are financially dependent, you depend on someone else to pay your living expenses. Clauses, too, are either independent or dependent. (A clause is a group of words that contains a subject and a verb.) Clauses either stand alone and accept responsibility for their own meaning, or they depend on another clause to complete their meaning. Independent clauses can stand alone as sentences. Dependent clauses can never stand alone because they are not complete sentences. The key to combining and expanding your ideas is to know this difference between independent and dependent clauses.

The various combinations of independent and dependent clauses shown in the box below allow you to link your ideas to one another. In this chapter you will learn how to combine your ideas so that the logical connection between them is clear.

NEED TO KNOW

Independent and Dependent Clauses

Sentences are made up of various combinations of independent and dependent clauses. Here are the possible combinations.

1. **Simple sentence.** A simple sentence has one independent clause and no dependent clauses.

   independent clause

   Richard hurried to his car.

2. **Compound sentence.** A compound sentence has two or more independent clauses and no dependent clauses.

   independent clause   independent clause

   Richard hurried to his car, but he was already late for work.

3. **Complex sentence.** A complex sentence has one independent clause and one or more dependent clauses.

   independent clause   dependent clause

   Richard hurried to his car because he was late for work.

4. **Compound-complex sentence.** A compound-complex sentence has two or more independent clauses and one or more dependent clauses.

   dependent clause   independent clause

   As Richard hurried to his car, he knew he would be late for work, but
   he hoped that he would not be docked an hour's pay.

   independent clause   dependent clause

Combining Ideas of Equal Importance

Many times ideas are of equal importance. For example, in the following sentence, it is just as important to know that the writer never has enough time as it is to know that she always rushes.

I never have enough time, so I always rush from task to task.

Complete thoughts (independent clauses) of equal importance are combined by using a technique called **coordination**. *Co-* means "together." *Coordinate* means to work together. When you want two complete thoughts to work together equally, you can combine them into a single sentence by using coordination.

NEED TO KNOW

How to Join Independent Clauses

There are two basic ways to join two ideas that are equally important:

Method 1. Separate them by using a **comma** and a **coordinating conjunction** (*and, or, but, for, yet, so, nor*).

Complete thought , coordinating conjunction complete thought .

Method 2. Separate them by using a **semicolon.**

Complete thought ; complete thought .

Method 1: Use a Comma and a Coordinating Conjunction

The most common way to join ideas is by using a comma and a coordinating conjunction. Use a semicolon only when the two ideas are *very* closely related and the connection between the ideas is clear and obvious. In this section, we will concentrate on using a comma and a coordinating conjunction.

The following two sentences contain equally important ideas:

Samatha works twenty hours per week.

Samatha manages to find time to study.

You can combine these ideas into one sentence by using a comma and a coordinating conjunction.

idea 1   comma   conjunction   idea 2

Samatha works twenty hours per week, but she manages to find time to study.

Following are a few more examples:

SIMPLE SENTENCE:	Time is valuable. I try to use it wisely.
COMBINED SENTENCE:	Time is valuable, so I try to use it wisely.
SIMPLE SENTENCE:	Many students try to set priorities for work and study. Many students see immediate results.
COMBINED SENTENCE:	Many students try to set priorities for work and study, and they see immediate results.
SIMPLE SENTENCE:	I tried keeping lists of things to do. My friend showed me a better system.
COMBINED SENTENCE:	I tried keeping lists of things to do, but my friend showed me a better system.

As we saw in the section on correcting run-ons (see Chapter 4, pages 82–89), a **coordinating conjunction** joins clauses and adds meaning to a sentence. A coordinating conjunction indicates how the ideas are related. Following is a brief review of the meaning of each coordinating conjunction and the relationship it expresses:

Coordinating Conjunction	*Meaning*	*Relationship*
and	in addition	The two ideas are added together.
but	in contrast	The two ideas are opposite.
for	because	One idea is the cause of the other.
nor, or	not either, either	The ideas are choices or alternatives.
so	as a result	The second idea is the result of the first.
yet	in contrast	The two ideas are opposite.

Note: Do *not* use the words *also, plus,* and *then* to join complete thoughts. They are *not* coordinating conjunctions.

EXERCISE 5-1 | For each of the following sentences, add the coordinating conjunction that best expresses the relationship between the two complete thoughts.

EXAMPLE: I never learned to manage my time, _____so_____ I am planning to attend a time-management workshop.

1. I might study math, _____or_____ I might review for my history exam.
2. The average person spends fifty-six hours a week sleeping, _____and_____ the average person spends seven hours a week eating dinner.
3. Watching television is tempting, _____but_____ I usually shut the set off before I start studying.
4. I do not feel like typing, _____nor_____ do I feel like reviewing math.
5. I am never sure of what to work on first, _____so_____ I waste a lot of time deciding.
6. A schedule for studying is easy to follow, _____for_____ it eliminates the need to decide what to study.
7. My cousin has a study routine, _____and_____ she never breaks it.
8. Frank studies his hardest subject first, _____and_____ then he takes a break.
9. I know I should not procrastinate, _____yet_____ I sometimes postpone an unpleasant task until the next day.

10. I had planned to study after work, _____but_____ my exam was postponed.

EXERCISE 5-2 Complete each of the following sentences by adding a second complete thought. Use the coordinating conjunction shown in bold. Be sure to insert a comma before the coordinating conjunction.

> EXAMPLE: I feel torn between studying and spending time with friends, **but** I usually choose to study.

1. My psychology class was canceled , **so** _I studied in the library._

2. I waste time doing unimportant tasks , **and** _then I feel guilty._

3. The phone used to be a constant source of interruption , **but** getting an answering machine solved the problem.

4. I had extra time to study this weekend , **for** _my three sons visited their_ grandmother.

5. I had hoped to finish reading my biology chapter , **but** _I still have_ ten pages to go.

6. Every Saturday I study psychology , **or** _I review for an upcoming exam._

7. I had planned to finish work early , **yet** _my boss asked me to stay until_ five o'clock.

8. I can choose a topic to write about , **or** _I can use one my instructor_ suggested.

9. I had hoped to do many errands this weekend , **but** _a winter storm_ has changed my plans.

10. I tried to study and watch television at the same time , **but** _I could_ not concentrate on my reading.

EXERCISE 5-3 Combine each of the following pairs of sentences by using a comma and a coordinating conjunction (*and, but, yet, for, so, nor, or*). Change punctuation, capitalization, and words as necessary.

EXAMPLE: a. I have a free hour between my first and second classes./ ', so

b. (I use that ~~free~~ hour to review my biology notes.

1. a. Some tasks are more enjoyable than others./ , so

          w   the   ones

    b. We tend to put off unpleasant ~~tasks.~~

2. a. Many people think it is impossible to do two things at once./ , but

        b

    b. Busy students soon learn to combine routine activities.

3. a. Marita prioritizes her courses./ , and

        she

    b. ~~Marita~~ allots specific blocks of study time for each.

4. a. Marcus may try to schedule his study sessions so they are several hours apart./ , or

        he

    b. ~~Marcus~~ may adjust the length of his study sessions.

5. a. Sherry studies late at night./ , so

        she

    b. ~~Sherry~~ does not accomplish as much as she expects to.

6. a. Marguerite studies without breaks./ , and

        she

    b. ~~Marguerite~~ admits she frequently loses her concentration.

7. a. Alfonso studies two hours for every hour he spends in class./ , so

        he

    b. ~~Alfonso~~ earns high grades.

8. a. Deadlines are frustrating./ , for

        they

    b. ~~Deadlines~~ force you to make hasty decisions.

9. a. Juan thought he was organized./ , but

        he

    b. ~~Juan~~ discovered he was not.

10. a. Monica sets goals for each course./ , and

        she

    b. ~~Monica~~ usually attains her goals.

Method 2: Use a Semicolon

A semicolon can be used alone or with a transitional word or phrase to join independent clauses. These transitional words and phrases are called

conjunctive adverbs. Conjunctive adverbs are adverbs that *join*.

Independent clause. ; therefore, independent clause.
; however,
; consequently,

independent clause   independent clause

semicolon   conjunctive adverb

I had hoped to earn a good grade; however, I never expected an A.

independent clause   independent clause

semicolon   conjunctive adverb

I lost my wallet; consequently, I had to cancel two credit cards.

As you can see in these examples, a comma follows the conjunctive adverb.

Use this method when the relationship between the two ideas is clear and requires no explanation. Be careful to choose the correct conjunctive adverb. Here is a list of conjunctive adverbs and their meanings.

Conjunctive Adverb	Meaning	Example
therefore, consequently, thus, hence	cause and effect	I am planning to become a nurse; consequently, I'm taking a lot of science courses.
however, nevertheless, nonetheless, conversely	differences or contrast	We had planned to go bowling; however, we went to hear music instead.
furthermore, moreover, also	addition; a continuation of the same idea	To save money I am packing my lunch; also, I am walking to school instead of taking the bus.
similarly, likewise	similarity	I left class as soon as I finished the exam; likewise, other students left.
then, subsequently, next	sequence in time	I walked home; then I massaged my aching feet.

Note: If you join two independent clauses with only a comma and fail to use a coordinating conjunction or semicolon, you will produce a comma splice. If you join two independent clauses without using a punctuation mark and a coordinating conjunction, you will produce a run-on sentence. (See page 80.)

NEED TO KNOW

How to Use Conjunctive Adverbs

Use a conjunctive adverb to join two equal ideas. Remember to put a semicolon before the conjunctive adverb, and a comma after it. Here is a list of common conjunctive adverbs.

also	in addition	otherwise
as a result	instead	similarly
besides	likewise	still
consequently	meanwhile	then
finally	nevertheless	therefore
further	next	thus
furthermore	now	undoubtedly
however	on the other hand	

EXERCISE 5-4

Complete each of the following sentences by adding a coordinating conjunction or a conjunctive adverb and the appropriate punctuation.

EXAMPLE: Teresa vacationed in Denver last year __; similarly,__ Jan will go to Denver this year.

1. Our professor did not complete the lecture __, nor__ did he give an assignment for the next class.
2. A first-aid kit was in her backpack __; consequently,__ the hiker was able to treat her cut knee.
3. An opening act performed at the concert __; next,__ the headline band took the stage.
4. I always put a light on when I leave the house __, and__ I often turn on a radio to deter burglars.
5. Sue politely asked to borrow my car __; futhermore,__ she thanked me when she returned it.
6. My roommate went to the library __; therefore,__ I had the apartment to myself.
7. Steve and Todd will go to a baseball game __, or__ they will go to a movie.
8. Cheryl looks like her father __; however,__ her hair is darker and curlier than his.

9. Maureen took a job at a bookstore <u>; subsequently,</u> she was offered a job at a museum.
10. Our neighbors bought a barbecue grill <u>; likewise,</u> we decided to by one.

 EXERCISE 5-5 Write five compound sentences about how you study for tests or how you spend your weekends. Each sentence should contain two complete thoughts. Join the thoughts by using a comma and a coordinating conjunction. Use a different coordinating conjunction in each sentence.

 EXERCISE 5-6 Write a paragraph evaluating how well you manage your time. Use at least two compound sentences.

Combining Ideas of Unequal Importance

Consider the following two simple sentences:

Pete studies during peak periods of attention.

Pete accomplishes a great deal.

Reading these sentences, you may suspect that Pete accomplishes a great deal *because* he studies during peak periods of attention. With the sentences separated, however, that cause-effect relationship is only a guess. Combining the two sentences makes the relationship between the ideas clear.

Because Pete studies during peak periods of attention, he accomplishes a great deal.

The combined sentence makes it clear that one event is the cause of another.

Let's look at another pair of sentences:

Yolanda analyzed her time commitments for the week.

Yolanda developed a study plan for the week.

You may suspect that Yolanda developed the study plan *after* analyzing her time commitments. Combining the sentences makes the connection in time clear.

After Yolanda analyzed her time commitments for the week, she developed a study plan.

In each of these examples, the two complete thoughts were combined so that one idea depended on the other. This process of combining ideas so that one idea is dependent on another is called **subordination.** *Sub* means "below." Think of subordination as a way of combining an idea of lesser or lower importance with an idea of greater importance.

Ideas of unequal importance can be combined by making the less important idea depend on the more important one. Notice how, in the following sentence, the part before the comma doesn't make sense without the part after the comma.

While Malcolm was waiting for the bus, he studied psychology.

If you read only the first half of the sentence, you'll find yourself waiting for the idea to be completed, wondering what happened while Malcolm was waiting. The word *while* (a subordinating conjunction) makes the meaning of the first half of the sentence incomplete by itself. Thus the first half of the sentence is a **dependent clause.** It depends on the rest of the sentence to complete its thought. A dependent clause never can be a complete sentence. It must always be joined to an *independent* clause to make a complete thought. The dependent clause can go at the beginning, in the middle, or at the end of a sentence.

See the following list for other words that are commonly used to begin dependent clauses. Such words are called **subordinating conjunctions.** Use these words to indicate how a less important idea (a dependent clause) relates to another, more important idea (an independent clause).

Subordinating Conjunction	*Meaning*	*Example*
before, after, while, during, until, when, once	time	*When* you set time limits, you are working toward a goal.
because, since, so that	cause or effect	*Because* I felt rushed, I made careless errors.
whether, if, unless, even if	condition	*If* I finish studying before nine o'clock, I will read more of my mystery novel.
as, as far as, as soon as, as long as, as if, as though, although, even though, even if, in order to	circumstance	*Even if* I try to concentrate, I still am easily distracted.

Note: Relative pronouns (*who, whom, whose, that, which, what, whoever, whomever, whichever, whatever*) can also be used to show relationships and to join a dependent clause with an independent clause. The topic of relative pronouns is covered in detail in Chapter 7 (pages 168–170).

When you combine a dependent clause with an independent clause, use a comma to separate the clauses if the dependent clause comes *first* in the sentence.

| Dependent clause | , | independent clause. |

dependent clause   independent clause

When I follow a study schedule, I accomplish more.

comma

When the dependent clause comes in the *middle* of the sentence, set it off with a *pair* of commas.

| First part of independent clause | , | dependent clause | , | remainder of independent clause |

subject of independent clause   dependent clause   remainder of independent clause

comma   comma

Malcolm, while he was waiting for a ride, studied psychology.

If the dependent clause comes at the end of the sentence, do not use a comma to separate it from the rest of the sentence.

| Independent clause | dependent clause |

independent clause   no comma   dependent clause

I accomplish more when I follow a study schedule.

EXERCISE 5-7 For each of the following sentences, add a subordinating conjunction that makes the relationship between the two ideas clear. Try to use as many different subordinating conjunctions as possible.

EXAMPLE: _____When_____ I finish studying, I am mentally exhausted.

1. _____Because_____ math requires peak concentration, I always study it first.

2. _____When_____ Terry starts to lose concentration, he takes a short break.

3. Julia never stops in the middle of an assignment _____unless_____ she is too tired to finish.

4. _____Since_____ she likes to wake up slowly, Shannon sets her alarm for ten minutes before she needs to get up.

5. _____After_____ Maria took a five-minute study break, she felt more energetic.

6. Alan worked on his math homework _____while_____ he did the laundry.

7. _____Even if_____ Jason increases his study time, he may not earn the grades he hoped to receive.

8. _____Once_____ Marsha completes an assignment, she crosses it off her "To do" list.

9. _____Since_____ Robert did not know where he wasted time, he kept a log of his activities for three days.

10. _____So that_____ noises and conversation do not interfere with my concentration, I wear a headset with soft music playing.

EXERCISE 5-8 Make each of the following sentences complete by adding a complete thought. Be sure the meaning fits the subordinating conjunction used in the sentence.

EXAMPLE: _____I edited my essay_____ while the ideas were fresh in my mind.

1. _____I fed my fish_____ after I finished studying.

2. Because my job is part-time, _____I can work on my journal only in the evening._____

3. Once I finish college, _____I am going to shorten my hair._____

4. _____The accident occurred_____ while I was studying.

5. If you schedule blocks of study time, _____you will accomplish more._____

6. _____I forget my own birthday_____ unless I carry a pocket calendar.

7. Although English is my favorite subject, <u>I do think 7 a.m. is too</u>

early for the class to meet.

8. <u>There is no mystery Poirot cannot solve</u> as far as I can tell.

9. Even if I finish by eight o'clock, <u>there is no way I can get to the</u>

bowling alley on time.

10. As soon as I decide what to do, <u>I will tell you.</u>

EXERCISE 5-9 Combine each of the following pairs of sentences by using a subordinating conjunction and a comma. Change punctuation, capitalization, and words as necessary. You may wish to refer to the list of subordinating conjunctions on page 62.

EXAMPLE: Because
a. Ann is taking voice lessons. ,
she
b. ~~Ann~~ always sings scales in the shower.

1. Since
a. Christine has a six-month-old child. ,
b. She must study while the baby sleeps.

2. Because
a. George jots stray thoughts on a notepad to clear them from his mind. ,
he
b. ~~George~~ can concentrate through a fire drill.

3. When
a. Gary finished a difficult biology assignment. ,
he
b. He rewarded himself by ordering a pizza.

4. Because i
a. It takes Anthony forty-five minutes to drive to school. ,
he
b. ~~Anthony~~ tape records lectures and listens while he drives.

Since she
5. a. ~~Molly~~ felt disorganized, ,

 b. Molly made a priority list of assignments and due dates.

As
6. a. Juanita walked from her history class to her math class.

 b. ~~s~~he observed the brilliant fall foliage.

Rather than   eat
7. a. ~~Kevin~~ skipped meals and ~~ate~~ junk food, ,

 b. Kevin signed up for a cooking class.

When
8. a. Barbara joined the soccer team, ,

   she
 b. ~~Barbara~~ became the first woman to do so.

During
9. a. ~~John ate~~ dinner on Saturday night, ,

 b. John reviewed his plans for the week with his less-than-fasci-
    nated date.

While
10. a. Frank waited for his history class to begin, ,

   he
 b. ~~H~~e wondered if he was in the right room.

EXERCISE **5-10**   Write ten complex sentences on a subject that interests you. Each must
contain one dependent clause and one independent clause. Use a comma
to separate the clauses when the dependent clause comes first. Use two
commas to set off a dependent clause in the middle of the sentence. You
do not need a comma when the dependent clause comes last.

EXERCISE 5-11   Write a paragraph on one of the following topics. Include at least two
complex sentences.

1. renting videos
2. catalog shopping
3. visiting the dentist or doctor
4. advantages or disadvantages of credit cards
5. a favorite possession or a favorite piece of clothing

Writing Compound-Complex Sentences

A compound-complex sentence is made up of two or more independent clauses and one or more dependent clauses. This type of sentence is often used to express complicated relationships. Examples of three compound-complex sentences follow:

dependent clause   independent clause

Even though Marsha needed to be better organized, she avoided weekly study plans, and she ended up wasting valuable time.

independent clause

[Here a dependent clause is followed by two independent clauses.]

first part of   dependent   remainder of
independent clause   clause   independent clause

The students who had just registered wanted a tour of the town, but Lamar told them that he had no time.

independent   dependent
clause   clause

[Here an independent clause containing a dependent clause is followed by a second independent clause containing a dependent clause.]

independent clause
dependent clause   dependent clause

Although Amanda changed her work schedule, she found that she still needed more time to study, and she ended up quitting her job.

independent clause

[Here the sentence is made up of a dependent clause, an independent clause containing a dependent clause, and another independent clause.]

The key to writing effective and correct compound-complex sentences is to link each clause to the one that follows it in the correct way. The rules you have already learned in this chapter apply. For example, if you have two independent clauses followed by a dependent clause, link the two independent clauses as you would in a compound sentence by using a comma and a coordinating conjunction. Then link the second independent clause to the dependent clause by using a subordinating conjunction.

independent clause   independent clause   dependent clause

I got up early, and I left the house before rush hour because I wanted to be on time for my interview.

EXERCISE 5-12 ▶ Each of the following sentences is made up of at least three clauses. Read each sentence, and then make it correct by adding the necessary subordinating and/or coordinating conjunctions in the blanks.

EXAMPLE: ____Because____ they both got home from work late, Ted grilled hamburgers ____while____ Alexa made a salad.

1. ____Because____ Sarah's sociology class required class discussion of the readings, she scheduled time to review sociology before each class meeting ____so that____ she would have the material fresh in her mind.

2. ____Although____ making a "To Do" list takes time, Jill found that the list actually saved her time, ____so____ she accomplished more when she sat down to study.

3. ____When____ Terry's history lecture was over, he reviewed his notes, ____and____ if he discovered any gaps, he was usually able to recall the information.

4. Many students have discovered that distributing their studying over several evenings is more effective than studying in one large block of time ____because____ it gives them several exposures to the material, ____and____ they feel less pressured.

5. We have tickets for the concert, ____but____ we may not go ____because____ Jeff has a bad cold.

EXERCISE 5-13 ▶ | Write a compound-complex sentence. Then label its dependent and independent clauses.

The following student essay is a good example of how to combine ideas to create interesting and effective sentences. As you read, notice how Tumiel shows relationships and connects events by combining independent clauses with each other or with dependent clauses.

STUDENT ESSAY

Miracles Made, Prayers Answered
Jennifer Tumiel

When my Aunt Susan had a double lung transplant, it affected   1
her life as well as mine. This procedure proved to be an eye-
opening brush with death for her, but it changed my life as well.

Susan Tumiel Smith was born with a disease called cystic fibrosis, a
hereditary disease that affects the respiratory system. At the time of her
birth, doctors predicted that for her to live past the age of sixteen would
be a triumph in itself. She fought this disease through her teen years by
practicing healthy ways of living and by educating herself to the fullest
extent possible about how to control her symptoms. Finally she reached
her sixteenth birthday; she had passed this phase of "the test."

By the time Susan reached thirty-two years old, she became oxygen-
tank dependent. When this happened, she immediately became a candidate for a double lung transplant. Once the transplant was approved by
a panel of doctors, Susan's name was placed on a waiting list, a list of
desperate people, all of whom needed a lung transplant in order to sur-
vive. She waited more than two years for her phone to ring with that
"miracle call" that she hoped and wished for daily. Susan patiently
waited for her "gift of life"; however, it brought terrible anxiety to her
and her husband.

Finally, in April of 1994 her phone rang. The voice on the other
end of the line summoned her immediately to Pittsburgh University
Presbyterian Hospital, where her new lungs awaited her. She arrived
with tremendous fear, only to be sent back home. The lungs that she
was to receive contained blood clots and were useless.

At home in Buffalo, it was back to endless waiting for Susan. This
was a disappointment not only to her, but to our whole family, who was
by her side through the long journey. Once again, Susan and our family
sat on the edges of our chairs, awaiting a simple phone call. Our prayers
were answered in July of 1994. My family immediately went to
Pittsburgh hoping for the best. The surgery was successfully completed
on the fourth of July, and everything went well for a few weeks.

Just when we thought Susan had passed her final "test," things took
a turn for the worse. We were informed that Susan's kidneys were failing and that she was fading fast. My family returned to Pittsburgh for
what we thought would be our final good-byes. As I entered the room
where my aunt lay helpless, reality hit me hard. From the looks of her, I
knew she would not be returning to Buffalo with us. The machines with
all the tubes and monitors scared me in such a way that I wanted to run
home and forget the whole situation. But instead, I walked closed to her
and grabbed her hand as slept peacefully. Everyone told me, "Don't be
upset if she doesn't respond, she's not awake, and she's very weak. To
my surprise, however, she opened her eyes, mustered a smile, and
squeezed my hand.

During our stay in Pittsburgh, events took another turn. Susan's kidneys began to work on their own, and the doctor said there was a good
possibility that she would come through. I visited her every two hours.

After about a month Susan returned home, and the surgery was considered a success.

This event made me look at life in a whole new way. I look at it more as a "gift" now. It's something that I have to take care of. I don't take much for granted anymore. Not only did Susan's transplant affect my relationship with her because it brought us closer, it also affected my relationship with myself. To see someone you love come that close to death makes you realize that life is a precious thing. Life is too short to react over the small things because there is always the possibility that they could be worse. 8

Susan is now thirty-six years old, and she travels to high schools and colleges, educating others about organ and tissue donation, and sharing her story. She is truly a gift to our family and an important asset to our society as a role model and as a teacher. 9

Evaluating the Essay

1. Underline the sentence in paragraph 2 in which two complete thoughts are combined. Which method is used to combine them?

2. Underline a sentence in paragraph 3 that contains one independent and one dependent clause.

3. In paragraph 6 underline two complex sentences.

4. In paragraph 7 underline a sentence that combines two independent clauses.

5. Locate a sentence in the essay that combines two complete thoughts using a semicolon and conjunctive adverb.

WRITING ABOUT A READING

Thinking before Reading

In the following reading, bigoted comments made during an online chat between her mother and a stranger prompt Angela Bouwsma to discuss racial attitudes and affirmative action. As you read, notice that Bouwsma uses numerous compound and complex sentences to show the relationships among her ideas.

1. Preview the reading using the steps provided on page 20.

2. After you have done your preview, connect the reading to your own experience by answering the following questions:

a. Have you ever initiated a friendship with someone and later discovered that he or she held racist or sexist beliefs?

b. Have you ever experienced or observed someone else experiencing racism or sexism in a subtle way?

READING

Showing His True Colors
Angela Bouwsma

I was ecstatic when my mother finally turned off the information dirt road and brought a PC a couple of years ago. Last summer she went all out and signed up for America Online. She subscribed because she wanted access to the Internet, not because she wanted to make friends. But as a result of the distinctive name she choose for herself, she often logs on and receives messages from strangers who are intrigued by her AOL handle.

Not long ago, my mother told me about a conversation she'd had online with a stranger, a computer engineer from the Midwest. They discussed a variety of topics, and toward the end the subject of beauty came up, followed by race. The man, feeling comfortable after almost an hour of chitchat and not knowing that my mother was black, went on to give her his honest impressions of her kind.

She couldn't recall precisely what he said, but the key words were "ignorant," "lie," "cheat," and "smell." My mother, stunned but in the comfort of anonymity, gathered herself and tried to reason with her new friend. He found her efforts to defend black people noble but incredibly naive. "One of these days you'll find out how black people really are," he wrote.

With that, my mother gave up reasoning and resorted to the easiest tactic to convince him that his beliefs were based on ignorance; she revealed that she herself was black. The man professed shock and endlessly apologized. Giving her what I suppose was intended as a compliment, he expressed his happy surprise at finally meeting an intelligent black person.

I won't recite my mother's academic and professional accomplishments here. Although her achievements and those of many other black Americans would make her friend look like a sheltered fool as well as a bigot, they're beside the point. The man, relying only on words as clues, assumed my mother was white, someone who would be sympathetic and to whom he could speak freely.

What my mother did not ask her computer acquaintance was   6
whether he regarded himself as a racist. He was extremely contrite, even
embarrassed, when she revealed her ethnicity. I'll speculate that because
he was apologetic and didn't type "You're a lying cheat," he congratulated himself that he'd judged fairly. He might say that his ideas were
based on experience. Once he saw how normal she was, the many interests they shared, he was willing to acknowledge her as someone deserving respect.

Stories like this have always infuriated me, but my mother's made   7
me sad. She told me that all she could think of as she responded to this
intelligent, college-educated man was me. Her talented, educated daughter, to whom she believed she'd given every advantage, for whom she
had so many hopes, might be seen on the street by this man and reflexively judged as a stupid, lying cheat.

For a large group of black Americans, particularly those of us trying   8
to make it in corporate America, racism is not experienced the way it's
depicted in movies; rednecks brandishing six-packs, bad haircuts and
baseball bats. It's better explained by the absence of minorities in certain
areas of life—boardrooms, film directors' chairs or editors' desks. In
these instances, black Americans are generally denied the opportunity to
participate—with a few heralded exceptions—where they are not explicitly required. That kind of racism is subtle and insidious, not something
that can be photographed, like a corpse swinging from a tree or a burning cross. It's a racism that smiles at you, shakes your hand, wishes you
luck. But its effects are clear and measurable.

To say that affirmative action should be scrapped because racial   9
preferences are ideologically intolerable is alarming and insulting. It
spits in the face of the reality we all share, one where implicit racial—
and gender—preferences not only exist but, at the highest echelons, are
the rule of thumb. As a result, more often than not, being black or being
a woman pulls a little farther from your reach the top levels of success.

Last November my home state of California abolished affirmative   10
action in state-run agencies and schools. Despite the temporary restrain-
ing order issued against it by a federal judge, Proposition 209 scares me
a great deal. I'm convinced that, as the mood of the nation dictates, the
Supreme Court will uphold it.

If that happens we'll begin a slide backward after 130 years of slow,   11
painful progress. Such a decision will further polarize us into two separate Americas, one in which racism effectively disappeared the day the
Civil Rights Act was signed, and another where it is as much a part of
life as breathing. And though I'll urge her to pursue whatever success
she desires, as I do, I'll be wondering whether strangers are dismissing
my daughter the way my mother wonders today.

From *Newsweek*

Getting Ready to Write

Strengthening Your Vocabulary

Write a brief definition for each of the following words, used in the preceding reading. If you can't figure out the meaning of a word from the way it is used in the reading, look the word up in the dictionary.

1. anonymity (paragraph 3)   condition of being unknown

2. naive (paragraph 3)   inexperienced, uninformed

3. reflexively (paragraph 7)   automatically, without thinking

4. heralded (paragraph 8)   widely known, notable

5. explicitly (paragraph 8)   clearly, definitely, unmistakably

6. insidious (paragraph 8)   sly and cunning, hard to discover

7. ideologically (paragraph 9)   based on ideas or opinions

8. implicit (paragraph 10)   not directly stated, understood

9. polarize (paragraph 11)   divide, draw apart

Reviewing the Reading Using an Idea Map

Review the reading by completing the missing pieces of the idea map shown below.

> **BIGOTRY STILL EXISTS**
>
> Bouwsma's mother has online conversation with stranger
>
> Stranger makes bigoted remarks about blacks
>
> Mother tries to reason with him, fails
>
> Mother reveals she is black
>
> Man apologizes; says she's an exception
>
> What Bouwsma thinks about the conversation

Man assumed mother would agree with his remarks

He probably thought remarks fair

He saw mother deserved respect

All other blacks: stupid, lying cheats

Racism and sexism hidden everywhere

Affirmative action still needed

Affirmative action abolished in California

If Supreme Court upholds: further division of nation

Examining the Reading

1. How did Bouwsma's mother respond when her online acquaintance made demeaning remarks about black people?

2. How did this man react when he realized Bouwsma's mother was black?

3. What did the author think of the man's action?

4. What is the author's opinion of California's Proposition 209?

5. What does the author believe will happen if affirmative action is not supported?

6. Why did the author write this piece?

Reacting to and Discussing Ideas

Get ready to write about the reading by discussing the following questions:

1. Do you think affirmative action is positive or negative? Why?

2. How do you think you would have reacted to the man if you were Bouwsma's mother?

3. Bouwsma writes about the man: "Once he saw how normal she was, the many interests they shared, he was willing to acknowledge her as someone deserving respect." What does this statement reveal about the man and his beliefs?

Writing about the Reading

The Paragraph Option

1. Write a paragraph describing an experience you've had with racism or sexism.

2. Write a paragraph explaining what information you would want to have about a person before establishing an online friendship with him or her.

The Essay Option

Write an essay explaining the pros and cons of affirmative action and whether you agree or disagree with the current affirmative action laws. Be sure to include your reasons for agreeing or disagreeing.

WRITING SUCCESS TIP 5

Buying and Using a Dictionary

Every writer needs a dictionary, not only to check spellings, but also to check meanings and appropriate usages of a word. You should have a desk or collegiate dictionary plus a pocket dictionary. If you have difficulty with spelling, a misspeller's dictionary is another valuable reference. It can help you locate correct spellings easily. Two commonly used ones are *Webster's New World Misspeller's Dictionary* and *How to Spell It: A Handbook of Commonly Misspelled Words*.

Here is a brief review of the information a dictionary entry contains:

1. **Pronunciation.** The pronunciation of the word is given in parentheses. Symbols are used to indicate certain sounds. Refer to the pronunciation key printed on each page or on alternate pages of your dictionary.

2. **Grammatical information.** The part of speech is indicated, as well as information about different forms the word may take. Most dictionaries include
   - principal forms of verbs (both regular and irregular).
   - plural forms of irregular nouns.
   - comparative and superlative forms of adjectives and adverbs.

3. **Meanings.** Meanings are numbered and are usually grouped by the part of speech.

4. **Restrictive meanings.** Meanings that are limited to special situations are labeled. Some examples are:

- *Slang*—casual language used only in conversation.
- *Informal*—language used only in casual writing.
- *Nonstandard*—words not used in standard speech and writing.
- *Biol.*—words used in specialized fields, biology in this case.
- *Regional*—words used in only certain parts of the United States.
- *Obs.*—words that are obsolete (that is, no longer used).

5. **Synonyms.** Word with similar meanings may be listed.

6. **Word history.** The origin of the word (its etymology) is described. (Not all dictionaries include this feature.)

Beyond definitions, a dictionary contains a wealth of other information as well. For example, in the *American Heritage Dictionary,* Third Edition, you can find the history of the word *vampire,* the population of Vancouver, and an explanation of the New England expression "Vum!"

Pronunciation

Grammatical information

—parts of speech

—verb forms

Meanings

Restrictive meanings

Word history

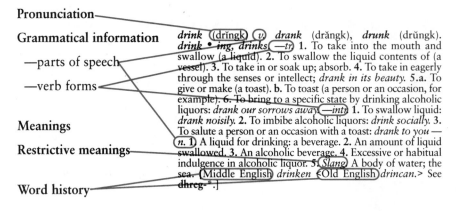

SKILLS CHECK

Paragraph 1

The following student paragraph has been revised to correct all errors except sentence fragments. Finish the revision by correcting all sentence fragments.

Anyone who has been to a professional hockey game in the last five years has a right to be disgusted. Since the players are permitted to bash each other on the ice and get away with it, And in some cases, players are even encouraged to do this. People are now starting to object to paying good money in order to watch what can only be considered a street fight. Because it is a contact sport, It is understandable that arguments will break out among players. This will cause tempers to flare. However, it is unfair to subject fans to a dramatic show of violence when they have paid to watch a sport, Especially since these players are making so much money. If the National Hockey League would suspend players each time they got into a fight, they would soon be playing hockey with appropriate sportsmanlike conduct instead of fighting.

SKILLS CHECK   CONTINUED

Paragraph 2

The following student paragraph has been revised to correct all errors except run-on sentences and comma splices. Finish the revision by correcting these two kinds of errors. Use the four methods you have just been reading about.

It seems that the Internet is having problems with certain messages being posted. There are people who argue that anyone has the right to say anything on the Internet, because people do have the right to freedom of speech. However, but the line should be drawn when it comes to hate messages. It is immoral—and should be illegal—to make remarks that are racist, sexist, and anti-Semitic. After all, these verbal actions are no longer tolerated in the classroom or in the workplace. Why should the Internet be different? The problem with the Internet is that there seems to be no established sense of etiquette among users. Maybe there should be some guidelines about what people should and should not say on the Internet. Why should people be subjected to hate-filled speech in order to preserve the right of free speech?

SKILLS CHECK   CONTINUED

Paragraph 3

The following student paragraph has had all errors corrected, but it consists mainly of simple sentences and lacks details. Revise it by expanding or combining the sentences. See the Selected Answer Key on page 515 for answers.

Many people are homeless. Our country has a problem. Now is the time for the government to take action on the problem of homelessness. The media have focused a great deal of attention on the homeless. This has been happening for the past several years. Many college campuses have been holding "sleepouts." These call attention to the problems of the homeless. Religious groups have been trying to help. They have been opening shelters for them. Still, this is not enough. The problem is only getting worse. The government needs to be pushed to do something about this problem now. Students should write their government officials. Religious groups should put pressure on members of Congress. They should urge them to act upon the problems of the homeless. Concerned citizens should become involved now. This problem is a disgrace to our country.

SENTENCE DEVELOPMENT

6 Using Adjectives and Adverbs to Describe

CHAPTER OBJECTIVES

In this chapter you will learn to

1. use adjectives to add descriptive detail.

2. use adverbs to describe actions more vividly.

A djectives and adverbs are essential parts of our language. They enable us to describe—to give our listeners and readers vivid details that help them visualize our topic. Even advertising writers, who have the benefit of art and photographs, rely on adjectives and adverbs to produce an effective ad. Read the ad for Radio Shack's wireless phones on the following page.

If we remove the adjectives and adverbs from the ad's opening line, we are left with the following:

Phones are being offered in places with contracts and plans.

With the adjectives and adverbs removed, the ad's opening sentence loses its meaning, and the connection between the photographs and captions are lost. Adjectives and adverbs, then, are essential to clear and effective communication. In this chapter you will learn how to make your sentences lively and descriptive by using adjectives and adverbs effectively.

WRITING

Using Adjectives to Describe

Adjectives describe nouns and pronouns. Notice that the following sample student paragraph uses very few adjectives.

Sample Paragraph

The congregation had just finished singing a hymn as the minister stepped up to the pulpit. Just as the man

asked the congregation to pray, a boy screamed. The grandmother tried to calm the child as she placed a hand over the lips of the child. The child obviously didn't enjoy this because he bit the hand. The minister continued with the prayer and tried to ignore the cries of the boy. Somehow the boy slipped away from the grip of the grandmother and ran down the aisle to the front of the church. The minister walked down from the pulpit and picked up the child. "Lord," he said as he continued the prayer, "help all the children of this world and bless all of the grandmothers, ministers, and members of the congregation who have to put up with them! Amen." With that he ended the service.

This paragraph gives the bare bones of an interesting story, but how well does it enable you to visualize the people involved? Adjectives give you details about the nouns and pronouns they modify.

They can add four kinds of information to your writing:

WHICH: the <u>young</u> man, the <u>largest</u> stove

WHOSE: <u>Sam's</u> application, <u>my</u> mug

WHAT KIND: the <u>job</u> interviewer, the <u>traffic</u> helicopter

HOW MANY: <u>thirty</u> résumés, <u>no</u> cookies

Thus, we say that adjectives *describe* and *identify* (which? whose?), *qualify* (what kind?), or *limit* (how many?) nouns and pronouns. (For more on adjectives, see Part IX, "Reviewing the Basics," page 461.) The following revised version of the above paragraph uses adjectives (underlined) to add interesting and important information.

Revised Paragraph

The congregation had just finished singing a <u>sacred</u> hymn as the <u>tall</u>, <u>young</u> minister stepped up to the <u>well-lit</u> pulpit. Just as the man asked the <u>reverent</u> congregation to pray, a <u>red-headed four-year-old</u> boy screamed. The <u>embarrassed</u> grandmother tried to calm the <u>angry</u> child as she placed a <u>firm</u> hand over <u>his quivering</u> lips. The <u>squirming</u> child obviously didn't enjoy this because he bit his <u>grandmother's</u> hand. The <u>calm</u> minister continued with the prayer and tried to ignore the <u>little boy's loud</u>, <u>shrill</u> cries. Somehow, the <u>determined</u>, <u>tearful</u> boy slipped away from his <u>grandmother's firm</u> grip and ran down the <u>long center</u> aisle to the front of the church. The <u>patient</u> minister walked down from the pulpit and picked up the <u>screaming</u> child. "Lord," he said as he continued the prayer, "help all the children of this world and bless all of the <u>loving</u> grandmothers, <u>patient</u> ministers, and <u>long-suffering</u> members of the congregation who have to put up with them! Amen." With that he ended the service.

EXERCISE ▶ 6-1 *The Adjective Contest:* The time limit for this exercise is three minutes. List as many positive adjectives that describe one of your instructors as you can. This is your chance to flatter an instructor! Exchange lists with a partner, verify that each word listed is an adjective, and count the words on the list. The winner is the student who has listed the most adjectives.

"*The face of the pear-shaped man reminded me of the mashed turnips that Aunt Mildred used to serve alongside the Thanksgiving turkey. As he got out of the strawberry-hued car, his immense fists looked like two slabs of slightly gnawed ham. He waddled over to the counter and snarled at me under his lasagna-laden breath, 'Something, my little bonbon, is fishy in Denmark.' Slowly, I lowered my grilled cheese sandwich . . .*"

Using Adjectives Correctly

To use adjectives effectively, you must also use them correctly. Keep the following points in mind:

1. Adjectives are usually placed in front of the word they describe.

the *wet* raincoat

the *purple* dragon

2. An adjective can follow a linking verb, such as *is, are, seems, feels.* A linking verb expresses a state of being.

Serafina seems <u>sleepy</u>. [*Sleepy* describes Serafina.]

The room was <u>warm</u>. [*Warm* describes the room.]

3. Several adjectives can describe the same noun or pronoun.

George's <u>three</u> <u>biology</u> assignments

The <u>worn</u>, <u>ragged</u> <u>denim</u> jacket

4. When two or more adjectives describe the same noun or pronoun, there are specific rules concerning when to use a comma between the adjectives. First, however, *never* place a comma between an adjective and the noun or pronoun it describes.

no comma

a soft-spoken, understanding counselor

no comma

an interesting, appealing job

Do place a comma between two adjectives when each describes the same noun (or pronoun) separately.

comma

a soft-spoken, understanding counselor

Do not place a comma between two adjectives when the adjective closest to the noun (or pronoun) describes the noun and the other adjective describes the combination of those two words.

no comma

a | worn | English dictionary |

no comma

a | broken | glass bottle |

no comma

an | accurate | job description |

Use the following test to decide whether you need to place a comma between two adjectives: if the word *and* makes sense when placed between the two adjectives, a comma is needed.

MAKES SENSE: a soft-spoken <u>and</u> understanding counselor

USE A COMMAN: a soft-spoken, understanding counselor

DOES NOT MAKE SENSE: a new <u>and</u> Mexican restaurant

DO NOT USE A COMMA: a new Mexican restaurant

EXERCISE 6-2 ▶   Add commas to each of the following phrases if needed.

EXAMPLE: the lazy, sleepy pot-bellied pig

1. a California senator
2. the gentle, quiet waves

3. a folded used newspaper
4. the educated cancer specialist
5. the sharp cat's claw
6. valuable family photographs
7. a weathered twisted pine tree
8. excited happy children
9. brown leather wallet
10. worthless costume jewelry

Using Adjectives to Expand Sentences

Adjectives are powerful words. They can create vivid pictures and impressions in the mind of your reader. Consider the following sentence:

EXAMPLE: The applicant greeted the interviewer.

This sentence has two nouns: *applicant* and *interviewer*. Without adjectives, however, what do we know about them or the situation? With adjectives, the same sentence becomes more informative.

REVISED: The eager, excited applicant greeted the friendly, welcoming job interviewer.

REVISED: The nervous, insecure applicant greeted the cool, polished job interviewer.

Now can you imagine the people and the situation each sentence describes?

Let's take another sentence and expand it several ways by using adjectives.

EXAMPLE: The building houses the lab.

REVISED: The ivy-covered brick building houses the well-equipped, up-to-date biology lab.

REVISED: The dilapidated, unpainted building houses the time-worn, outdated biology lab.

As you can see from the above examples, you can drastically alter and expand your meaning by using adjectives. Think of adjectives as words that allow you to choose details that create the impression you want.

EXERCISE ▶ 6-3 ◀ Expand and revise each of the following sentences in two different ways by adding adjectives. Each of your two revisions should create a different impression. Underline your adjectives.

EXAMPLE: The interviewer asked Julie a question.

REVISED: The <u>skillful</u> interviewer asked Julie an <u>indirect</u> question.

REVISED: The <u>young</u>, <u>inexperienced</u> interviewer asked Julie a <u>personal</u> question.

1. Mr. Lindgren's parrot was able to speak several words.

   a. Mr. Lindgren's <u>annoying</u>, <u>nasty</u> parrot was able to speak several <u>shrill</u> words.

   b. Mr. Lindgren's <u>witty</u>, <u>lively</u> parrot was able to speak several <u>humorous</u> words.

2. The store made sales.

   a. The <u>large</u> <u>department</u> store made <u>few</u> sales.

   b. The <u>small</u> <u>department</u> store made <u>many</u> sales.

3. The Wildlife Rehabilitation Center sponsored an exhibit.

   a. The <u>remote</u> Wildlife Rehabilitation Center sponsored a <u>reptile</u> exhibit.

   b. The <u>popular</u> Wildlife Rehabilitation Center sponsored a <u>children's</u> <u>awareness</u> exhibit.

4. A professor published an article on campus reform.

   a. A <u>well-known</u> professor published a <u>controversial</u> article on campus <u>curriculum</u> reform.

   b. An <u>unpopular</u> professor published a <u>little-read</u> article on campus <u>curriculum</u> reform.

5. The chef prepared a dish.

   a. The <u>tired</u>, <u>overworked</u> chef prepared an <u>uninteresting</u>, <u>tasteless</u> dish.

   b. The <u>innovative</u> <u>young</u> chef prepared an <u>exciting</u> <u>Chinese</u> dish.

6. The diner serves food throughout the night.

   a. The <u>popular</u> <u>forties-style</u> diner serves <u>tasty</u> food throughout the night.

   b. The <u>dingy</u> <u>old</u> diner serves <u>bland and starchy</u> food throughout the night.

7. The disc jockey plays music.

   a. The <u>lively</u> disc jockey plays <u>contemporary</u> music.

   b. The <u>soft-spoken</u> disc jockey plays <u>classical</u> music.

8. The book was read by each member of the club.

   a. The fly-fishing book was read by each member of the fishing club.

   b. The costume-jewelry book was read by each member of the crafts club.

9. The newspaper lay on the table.

   a. The unread newspaper lay on the coffee table.

   b. The well-read newspaper lay on the lunchroom table.

10. The teacher calmed the child by showing her books.

    a. The concerned teacher calmed the frightened child by showing her comic books.

    b. The busy teacher calmed the frightened child by showing her picture books.

EXERCISE 6-4

Rewrite the following paragraph by adding adjectives. You can also add new phrases and sentences anywhere in the paragraph—beginning, middle, or end—as long as they have adjectives in them. Underline the adjectives.

I had been looking forward to my *tropical* vacation for *three long winter* months. I was going to lie on the *sandy* beach all day and dance all night. I didn't get off to a good start. On the *long* flight to Miami, I had the middle seat between a big *heavy-breathing* man and a*n anxious* mother with a *cranky* baby. Then we sat on the ground for two *endless* hours because of *thick* fog. It was hot and noisy. When we did get off the ground, the *long* flight was very bumpy. Finally we got to Miami. I waited and waited for my *oversized* suitcase.

Needless to say, it didn't arrive. I could just picture all my new *light-weight summer* clothes sitting in some other city. Actually, though, all I needed for my week in Miami was *my trusty* a raincoat, because it rained every day. I didn't need my *newly purchased* party clothes either because the first morning, I slipped getting out of the shower and sprained my

right
my_∧ankle. I need a vacation from my vacation.

EXERCISE 6-5 | Write a paragraph on one of the following topics. After you have written your first draft, revise your paragraph by adding adjectives. Underline your adjectives.

1. a full- or part-time job you held
2. a trip you took
3. a valued possession
4. searching for _____
5. interviewing for _____

NEED TO KNOW

Adjectives

- Adjectives describe nouns and pronouns.
- An adjective is usually placed before the word it describes.
- An adjective can follow a linking verb.
- Use adjectives to add interest and detail to your sentences.

Using Adverbs to Describe

Adverbs describe, qualify, or limit verbs, adjectives, or other adverbs. The following paragraph uses no adverbs.

Sample Paragraph

> The old door opened on its rusty hinges. A young woman entered the attic. She searched for the box of costumes. She saw a carton on the shelf across the room. She lifted the box and undid its dusty strings. She opened it. She began laughing. A huge chicken costume was in the box!

Did this paragraph give you enough details to visualize the scene? Imagine you are directing this scene in a movie: How would the rusty door hinges sound? How would the young woman walk when she entered the attic? Where would she look for the costumes? Adverbs give you details about the verbs, adjectives, and other adverbs they modify.

Adverbs can add five kinds of information to your writing:

HOW?	He announced cautiously.
WHEN?	We will leave tomorrow.
WHERE?	We searched everywhere.
HOW OFTEN?	I exercise daily.
TO WHAT EXTENT?	The caller was very polite.

The following revised version of the above paragraph uses adverbs to add details that let you visualize the scene more fully.

Revised Paragraph

The old door opened creakily on its rusty hinges. A young woman quickly entered the attic. She searched everywhere for the box of costumes. Finally, she saw a carton on the shelf across the room. Gingerly, she lifted the box down and undid its dusty strings. Very carefully she opened it. She began laughing gleefully. A huge chicken costume was in the box!

From this revision, you can see that adverbs help bring actions alive.

EXERCISE 6-6

The Adverb Contest: The time limit for this exercise is ten minutes. Expand the "attic" paragraph above, and see how many more adverbs you can add. You can add new phrases and sentences anywhere in the present paragraph—beginning, middle, or end—as long as they have adverbs in them. Underline your adverbs, and exchange your expanded stories with a partner to verify how many adverbs you have added. The winner is the student who has added the most adverbs.

Using Adverbs Correctly

To use adverbs effectively, you must also use them correctly. Keep the following points in mind:

1. Many adverbs end in -ly. Some do not, however, such as *often, now, always,* and *not.* To determine if a word is an adverb, look at how it functions in your sentence.

2. Adverbs can modify verbs, adjectives, or other adverbs.

Adverb describing a verb (a verb expresses action or state of being):

verb

Clara patiently waited for the appointment.

verb

The building crumbled quickly.

verb

The winning team proudly watched the videotape of the playoff game.

Adverb describing an adjective (an adjective modifies a noun or pronoun):

adjective

An extremely long interview is tiring.

adjective

The reporters asked briskly efficient questions.

adjective

Microscopically small plankton live in the ocean.

Adverb describing another adverb:

adverb

Read a want ad very carefully.

adverb

Microscopes allow one to view an object more closely.

adverb

The automated door opened quite easily.

3. Adverbs can be placed almost anywhere in a sentence. Three common placements are

AT THE BEGINNING OF THE SENTENCE: Briefly, Mark explained.

IN FRONT OF THE VERB: Mark briefly explained.

AFTER THE VERB: Mark explained briefly.

4. Adverbs should be followed by a comma only when they begin a sentence.

comma

Slowly, Jim walked into the reception area.

comma

Cautiously, he asked to see Mr. Stoneface.

When adverbs are used elsewhere in a sentence, they are *not* set off by commas.

no comma   no comma

Jim walked slowly into the reception area.

He asked cautiously to see Mr. Stoneface.

no comma   no comma

Using Adverbs to Expand Sentences

Like adjectives, adverbs are powerful words. Adverbs can create a more complete impression of the action within a sentence. Consider the following sentence and its two revisions:

EXAMPLE: The car runs.

REVISED: The car runs <u>smoothly</u>.

REVISED: The car runs <u>haltingly</u>.

In one revised sentence, the car runs well; in the other revision, the car barely runs at all. Notice how adverbs, like adjectives, let you change your meaning.

In the following examples, adverbs give you extra details about the action:

EXAMPLE: The president prepared his State of the Union address.

adverb   adverb   adverb

REVISED: The president <u>very</u> <u>carefully</u> and <u>thoroughly</u> prepared his State of the Union address.

EXAMPLE: The swim team accepted the gold medal.

adverb   adverb

REVISED: <u>Proudly</u> and <u>excitedly</u>, the swim team accepted the gold medal.

Like adjectives, adverbs allow you to choose details that expand your sentences and refine your meaning.

EXERCISE ▶ 6-7   Expand and revise each of the following sentences in two different ways by adding adverbs. Each revision should create a different impression. Underline your adverbs.

EXAMPLE: The employment agency lists hundreds of management positions.

REVISED: The employment agency <u>usually</u> lists hundreds of management positions.

REVISED: The employment agency <u>seldom</u> lists hundreds of management positions.

1. The gymnast performed his routine.

   a. <u>The gymnast performed his routine easily.</u>

   b. <u>The gymnast carefully performed his routine.</u>

2. The chemistry experiment was completed.

   a. <u>Finally, the chemistry experiment was completed.</u>

   b. <u>The chemistry experiment was gradually completed.</u>

3. Botanists study newly discovered plant life.

   a. <u>Botanists study newly discovered plant life thoroughly.</u>

   b. <u>Botanists eagerly study newly discovered plant life.</u>

4. The furniture in our office breaks.

   a. <u>The furniture in our office breaks frequently.</u>

   b. <u>The furniture in our office rarely breaks.</u>

5. The business people in my office use cellular phones.

   a. <u>The business people in my office often use cellular phones.</u>

   b. <u>The business people in my office rarely use cellular phones.</u>

6. The professor will post the exam grades.

   a. <u>The professor will post the exam grades promptly.</u>

   b. <u>The professor will eventually post the exam grades.</u>

7. Mirrors should be handled carefully.

   a. <u>Mirrors should be handled very carefully.</u>

   b. <u>Mirrors should be handled quite carefully.</u>

8. People in the Depression lived.

   a. <u>People in the Depression lived frugally.</u>

   b. <u>People in the Depression lived cautiously.</u>

9. Seatbelts have saved thousands of lives.

   a. <u>Fortunately, seatbelts have saved thousands of lives.</u>

   b. <u>Not surprisingly, seatbelts have saved thousands of lives.</u>

10. The boat left the dock.

   a. <u>The boat left the dock hastily.</u>

   b. <u>The boat slowly left the dock.</u>

N E E D   T O   K N O W

Adverbs

- Adverbs qualify or limit verbs, adjectives, or other adverbs.
- Many adverbs end in -*ly,* but some do not.
- Use a comma after an adverb only when the adverb begins the sentence.
- Use adverbs to qualify and expand your ideas.

EXERCISE 6-8

Write a paragraph on one of the following topics. After you have written your first draft, revise your paragraph by adding adverbs. Underline your adverbs.

1. a long-lasting or vivid memory
2. the lack of privacy in apartments
3. how to make a(n) _____
4. learning to _____
5. how to avoid _____

EXERCISE 6-9

Rewrite the following paragraph by adding adjectives and adverbs. You can also add phrases and sentences anywhere in the paragraph-beginning, middle, or end-as long as they have adjectives and adverbs in them. Underline the adjectives and circle the adverbs.

Every family has someone who's eccentric—someone who's

lovable but ⟨rather⟩ strange. In my family, that's Aunt Irma. Aunt Irma

lives in an tiny one-bedroom apartment filled with unique souvenirs from her many trips.

She has souvenirs of all kinds—big and small—from everywhere

in the world. If you want to sit down at Aunt Irma's, you have to

move a souvenir, and, probably, what you're sitting on is a sou-

venir, too. Aunt Irma also has unusual eating habits. She eats
(extremely)

hot   cold
only soup and sandwiches. She always makes her own soups
        Can you imagine beet, leek,   One of her strangest is a sour dill
        (really) and corn soup with garlic   pickle and peanut butter sandwich
and they are unusual. The sandwiches are strange, too. You'll
        that croutons?   smothered with taco sauce.
never see one on a menu. Aunt Irma is also an exercise nut. She

has several sets of weights in different rooms. She runs in place

whenever she watches TV. Finally, Aunt Irma has a distinctive
                                                  n (incredibly)

way of dressing. I have seen her wear some really strange out-
        Last week she wore a (vividly) purple plaid jumper, a black polka-dot
fits. But she is lovable and, when all's said and done, what
blouse, and yellow-striped sneakers.
would we do without Aunt Irma stories?

Using Adjectives and Adverbs to Compare

Adjectives and adverbs modify, describe, explain, qualify, or restrict the words they modify. **Adjectives** modify nouns and pronouns. **Adverbs** modify verbs, adjectives, and other adverbs; adverbs can also modify phrases, clauses, or whole sentences.

> ADJECTIVES: <u>red</u> car; the <u>quiet</u> one
>
> ADVERBS: <u>quickly</u> finish; <u>only</u> four reasons; <u>very</u> angrily

Comparison of Adjectives and Adverbs

Positive adjectives and adverbs modify but do not involve any comparison: *green, bright, lively.*

Comparative adjectives and adverbs compare two persons, things, actions, or ideas.

> COMPARATIVE ADJECTIVE: Michael is <u>taller</u> than Bob.
>
> COMPARATIVE ADVERB: Antonio reacted <u>more calmly</u> than Robert.

Here is how to form comparative adjectives and adverbs. (Consult your dictionary if you are unsure of the form of a particular word.)

1. If the adjective or adverb has one syllable, add *-er*. For some two-syllable words, also add *-er*.

> cold → colder   slow → slower   narrow → narrower

2. For most words of two or more syllables, place the word _more_ in front of the word.

reasonable → more reasonable   interestingly → more interestingly

3. For two-syllable adjectives ending in _-y_, change the _-y_ to _-i_ and add _-er_.

drowsy → drowsier   lazy → lazier

EXERCISE 6-10 ▶ | Fill in the blank with the comparative form of the adjective or adverb given.

1. seriously   Mary was injured __more seriously__ than Tom.

2. lively   I feel a lot ____livelier____ than I did yesterday.

3. pretty   This bouquet of flowers is ____prettier____ than that one.

4. interesting   My biology teacher is __more interesting__ than my history teacher.

5. softly   Speak ____more softly____ or you'll wake the baby.

Superlative adjectives and adverbs compare more than two persons, things, actions, or ideas.

SUPERLATIVE ADJECTIVE: Michael is the tallest member of the team.

SUPERLATIVE ADVERB: She studied most diligently for the test.

Here is how to form superlative adjectives and adverbs.

1. Add _-est_ to one-syllable adjectives and adverbs and to some two-syllable words.

cold → coldest   fast → fastest   narrow → narrowest

2. For most words of two or more syllables, place the word _most_ in front of the word.

reasonable → most reasonable   interestingly → most interestingly

3. For two-syllable adjectives ending in _-y_, change the _-y_ to _-i_ and add _-est_.

drowsy → drowsiest   lazy → laziest

EXERCISE 6-11 ▶ | Fill in the blank with the superlative form of the adjective or adverb given.

1. beautiful   It was the __most beautiful__ wedding I'd ever seen.

2. slow   I always get in the ____slowest____ checkout line at the grocery store.

3. early   This is the _____earliest_____ Jana has ever arrived.

4. difficult   That is the ___most difficult___ trick the magician
                 performs.

5. loud   It was by far the _____loudest_____ band that played
                 last Saturday.

Irregular Adjectives and Adverbs

Some adjectives and adverbs form their comparative and superlative
forms in irregular ways.

Positive	*Comparative*	*Superlative*
Adjectives		
good	better	best
bad	worse	worst
little	littler, less	littlest, least
Adverbs		
well	better	best
badly	worse	worst
Adjectives and Adverbs		
many	more	most
some	more	most
much	more	most

EXERCISE 6-12 Fill in the blanks with the correct positive, comparative, or superlative
form of the adjective or adverb given.

1. good   Bob's barbecue sauce is _____better_____ than
                 Shawna's, but I think Leo's recipe is

                 _____best_____ of all.

2. little   Please give me just a _____little_____ piece of pie.

                 You can give me even _____less_____ ice cream.

3. well   I don't feel _____well_____ today, but I'm still

                 _____better_____ than I was yesterday.

4. much   I have _____more_____ homework this semester
                 than last semester. Of all my classes, I get the

                 _____most_____ homework in math.

5. bad   It rained _____worst_____ on Thursday than on

                           Friday, but it rained the _____worst_____ on
                           Saturday.

Common Mistakes to Avoid

1. Do not use adjectives to modify verbs, other adjectives, or adverbs.

INCORRECT: Peter and Mary take each other serious.
CORRECT: Peter and Mary take each other seriously. [Modifies the verb *take.*]

2. Do not use the adjectives *good* and *bad* when you should use the adverbs *well* and *badly.*

INCORRECT: Juan did good on the exam.
CORRECT: Juan did well on the exam. [Modifies the verb *did.*]

3. Do not use the adjectives *real* and *sure* when you should use the adverbs *really* and *surely.*

INCORRECT: Jan scored real well on the exam.
CORRECT: Jan scored really well on the exam. [Modifies the verb *well.*]

INCORRECT: I sure was surprised to win the lottery.
CORRECT: I surely was surprised to win the lottery. [Modifies the verb *was surprised.*]

4. Do not use *more* or *most* with the *-er* or *-est* form of an adjective or adverb. Use one form or the other, according to the rules above.

INCORRECT: That was the most tastiest dinner I've ever eaten.
CORRECT: That was the tastiest dinner I've ever eaten.

5. Avoid double negatives—that is, two negatives in the same clause.

INCORRECT: He did not want nothing in the refrigerator.
CORRECT: He did not want anything in the refrigerator.

6. When using the comparative and superlative forms of adverbs, do not create an incomplete comparison.

INCORRECT: The heater works more efficiently. [More efficiently than what?]
CORRECT: The heater works more efficiently than it did before we had it repaired.

7. Do not use the comparative form for adjectives and adverbs that have no degree. It is incorrect to write, for example, *more square, most perfect, more equally,* or *most straight.* Do not use a comparative or superlative form for any of the following adjectives and adverbs.

Adjectives

complete	equal	infinite	pregnant	unique
dead	eternal	invisible	square	universal
empty	favorite	matchless	supreme	vertical
endless	impossible	parallel	unanimous	whole

Adverbs

endlessly	infinitely	uniquely
equally	invisibly	universally
eternally	perpendicularly	
impossibly	straight	

EXERCISE 6-13 ▷ Revise each of the following sentences so that all adjectives and adverbs are used correctly.

EXAMPLE: I answered the question polite~~ly~~.

1. Michael's apartment was more expensive, than Ellen's.

2. When I heard the man and woman sing the duet, I decided that the woman sang ~~best.~~ better.

3. Our local movie reviewer said that the film's theme song sounded ~~badly.~~ bad.

4. The roller coaster was exciting~~er~~ more than the merry-go-round.

5. *The Scarlet Letter* is ~~more good~~ better than *War and Peace*.

6. Susan sure, ly gave a rousing speech.

7. Last week's storm seemed ~~worst~~ worse than a tornado.

8. Some women thought that the Equal Rights Amendment would guarantee that women are treated ~~more~~ equally.

9. Taking the interstate is the ~~most~~ fast, est route to the outlet mall.

10. Professor Reed had the ~~better~~ best lecture style of all my instructors.

STUDENT ESSAY

The following student essay is a good example of how to use adjectives and adverbs to add interest and detail. As you read, notice how Molly Falk helps you visualize or imagine the coffee drinks, both their taste and their preparation, through the use of adjectives and adverbs.

Nancy's Coffee Cafe
Molly Falk

I work in a coffee cafe. I know a lot about coffee, types of coffee   1
drinks, and their preparation. Surprisingly, there is a lot to learn
about coffee—more than I ever imagined.

Coffee is one of the most popular drinks, and it has been around a   2
long time. By the 16th century, coffee was known throughout the world,
but grown only in Yemen and Java. Coffee was considered a medicine
and used as a mild stimulant. Gradually, people started using it daily.
Soon coffeehouses became popular around the world. Europeans were
the people who spread the popularity of coffee. They planted coffee tree
seedlings in countries that they colonized. By the late 1800's, coffee trees
grew in most tropical regions. From this beginning, coffee became
America's favorite hot beverage following the Boston Tea Party, and
today the Americans happily consume nearly one-third of all the coffee
grown in the world.

There are many different kinds of coffee drinks. The names of some   3
specialty coffee drinks are cappuccino, café mocha, café latte, café au
lait, red eye, hot cloud, and café Americano. These drinks are all made
with espresso, except the café au lait and hot cloud. Steamed milk is the
key ingredient used in making these drinks. To steam milk, you pour
some milk into a cold metal pitcher. Then you put the wand or nozzle
from the cappuccino machine into the cup of milk. As you turn the
knob slowly to the right, the wand gets hot. You slowly keep moving
the cup up and down, keeping the tip of the wand in the milk. This
process will foam the milk. The temperature of the milk should always
be 140 degrees. The only hot drink that is made with steamed chocolate
milk is café mocha. This drink is very popular among chocolate lovers!

The strongest hot drink is an espresso. Espresso has a very strong   4
flavor with an aftertaste to it. It has a lot of flavor even though a cup is
only a couple of ounces. People's reactions are funny when I give them
their espresso, because they don't expect it to be so small! The most
important part of an espresso is the "crema." The "crema" is the top
layer of the espresso. It helps hold in the flavors and aromas of the coffee. If the "crema" forms incorrectly or does not cover properly, then
the espresso tastes differently. Espresso comes in single shots and double
shots. A single shot is 7 grams of coffee and water. Fourteen grams of
coffee and water equals a double shot of espresso.

There are many tasty dessert drinks and iced drinks made from cof-   5
fee. The most popular dessert drink is the caramel turtle. This drink
consists of a squirt of caramel flavoring syrup, half hazelnut coffee, and
half hot chocolate. The drink is garnished with whipped cream, caramel,

and chocolate drizzle. Another good drink is café au chocolate. This drink is half brewed coffee and half hot chocolate. This drink is garnished with whipped cream and chocolate drizzle. Iced drinks are also very popular. There is iced mocha, iced cappuccino, cappuccino cooler, iced coffee, Italian soda, and French soda. All of the iced drinks consist of cold espresso, ice, and milk. These drinks come either over ice or blended like a slushy. The cappuccino cooler is a favorite. It's just like a milkshake. This drink is made with a powdered mix, ice, and water. Then it is carefully blended until thick and garnished with puffy whipped cream. The Italian soda is made with a flavored syrup shot, ice, and soda water. This drink can be made over ice cubes or crushed ice and garnished with whipped cream. The French soda is made with a flavored syrup shot, ice, dairy creamer, and soda water. It is served over ice and garnished with whipped cream.

Even though the specialty drinks are great, many people just enjoy   6
brewed coffee. There are all kinds of coffee flavors. They range from the weakest blend to the strongest blend. Mocha Java, Tip of the Andes, New Orleans, Kenya, Hazelnut, French Vanilla, Caramel Toffee, and Raspberry are just a few popular coffees. When brewing coffee, never let it sit more than ten minutes. The fresher it is, the better it will taste!

With its great taste and aroma, coffee is a beverage that will never   7
go out of style. As my boss always tells us employees, "There's nothing like great gourmet coffee in your cup!"

Evaluating the Essay

1. Evaluate the structure and content of the essay.

   a. Does the essay follow a logical plan? Describe its organization.
   b. What is the author's thesis statement?
   c. In what ways does the writer support her thesis?
   d. Evaluate the effectiveness of the title, introduction, and conclusion.

2. How well does the author use adjectives and adverbs to describe her subject?

   a. Underline at least ten adjectives that you feel are particularly effective and descriptive.
   b. Underline at least three adverbs.
   c. In what sentences or paragraphs could more adjectives or adverbs have been used?
   d. Add an adjective to the title of the essay: "Nancy's _____ Coffee Cafe."

WRITING ABOUT A READING

Thinking before Reading

The following reading, "The Struggle to Be an All-American Girl," uses adjectives and adverbs effectively to bring vividness and realism to the events of the author's childhood story.

Before you read:

1. Preview the reading, using the steps provided on page 20.

2. After you have done your preview, connect the reading to your own experience by answering the following questions:
   a. Think about your family heritage or ethnic background. What is your attitude toward it?
   b. Consider your childhood education. Do you have mostly positive or mostly negative memories?

READING

The Struggle to Be an All-American Girl
Elizabeth Wong

It's still there, the Chinese school on Yale Street where my brother and I used to go. Despite the new coat of paint and the high wire fence, the school I knew ten years ago remains remarkably, stoically the same.   1

Every day at 5 P.M., instead of playing with our fourth- and fifth-grade friends or sneaking out to the empty lot to hunt ghosts and animal bones, my brother and I had to go to Chinese school. No amount of kicking, screaming, or pleading could dissuade my mother, who was solidly determined to have us learn the language of our heritage.   2

Forcibly, she walked us the seven long, hilly blocks from our home to school, depositing our defiant tearful faces before the stern principal. My only memory of him is that he swayed on his heels like a palm tree, and he always clasped his impatient twitching hands behind his back. I recognized him as a repressed maniacal child killer, and knew that if we ever saw his hands we'd be in big trouble.   3

We all sat in little chairs in an empty auditorium. The room smelled like Chinese medicine, an imported faraway mustiness, like ancient mothballs or dirty closets. I hated that smell. I favored crisp new scents,   4 like the soft French perfume that my American teacher wore in public school.

There was a stage far to the right, flanked by an American flag and the flag of the Nationalist Republic of China, which was also red, white and blue but not as pretty.

Although the emphasis at the school was mainly language—speaking, reading, writing—the lessons always began with an exercise in politeness. With the entrance of the teacher, the best student would tap a bell and everyone would get up, kowtow,[1] and chant, "Sing san ho," the phonetic for "How are you, teacher?"

Being 10 years old, I had better things to learn than ideographs[2] copied painstakingly in lines that ran right to left from the tip of a *moc but*, a real ink pen that had to be held in an awkward way if blotches were to be avoided. After all, I could do the multiplication tables, name the satellites of Mars, and write reports on *Little Women* and *Black Beauty*. Nancy Drew, my favorite book heroine, never spoke Chinese.

The language was a source of embarrassment. More times than not, I had tried to disassociate myself from the nagging loud voice that followed me wherever I wandered in the nearby American supermarket outside Chinatown. The voice belonged to my grandmother, a fragile woman in her seventies who could outshout the best of the street vendors. Her humor was raunchy; her Chinese rhythmless, patternless. It was quick; it was loud; it was unbeautiful. It was not like the quiet, lilting romance of French or the gentle refinement of the American South. Chinese sounded pedestrian. It sounded public.

In Chinatown, the comings and going of hundreds of Chinese on their daily tasks sounded chaotic and frenzied. I did not want to be though of as mad, as talking gibberish. When I spoke English, people nodded at me, smiled sweetly, said encouraging words. Even the people in my culture would cluck and say that I'd do well in life. "My, doesn't she move her lips fast," they would say, meaning that I'd be able to keep up with the world outside Chinatown.

My brother was even more fanatical than I about speaking English. He was especially hard on my mother, criticizing her, often cruelly, for her pidgin speech—smatterings of Chinese scattered like chop suey in her conversation. "It's not 'What it is,' Mom," he'd say in exasperation. "It's 'What *is* it, what *is* it!'" Sometimes Mom might leave out an occasional "the" or "a," or perhaps a verb of being. He would stop her in mid-sentence: "Say it again, Mom. Say it right." When he tripped over

1. Kneel, touching forehead to ground
2. Symbol representing idea or object

his own tongue, he'd blame it on her: "See, Mom, it's all your fault. You set a bad example."

What infuriated my mother most was when my brother cornered her 11 on her consonants, especially "r." My father had played a cruel joke on Mom by assigning her an American name that her tougue wouldn't allow her to say. No matter how hard she tried, "Ruth" always ended up "Luth" or "Roof."

After two years of writing with a *moc but* and reciting words with 12 multiples of meanings, I finally was granted a cultural divorce. I was permitted to stop Chinese school.

I though of myself as multicultural. I preferred tacos to egg rolls; I 13 enjoyed Cinco de Mayo[3] more than Chinese New Year.

At last, I was one of you; I wasn't one of them. 14

Sadly, I still am. 15

3. Mexican holiday celebrating the defeat of Napoleon III in the Battle of Puebla

From Elizabeth Wong, "The Struggle to Be an All-American Girl."

Getting Ready to Write

Strengthening Your Vocabulary

Write a brief definition for each of the following words from the preceding reading. If you cannot figure out the meaning of a word from the way it is used in the reading, look the word up in a dictionary.

1. stoically (paragraph 1)   <u>without feeling, unchanging</u>

2. dissuade (paragraph 2)   <u>persuade not to do something</u>

3. repressed (paragraph 3)   <u>held back, unconscious</u>

4. maniacal (paragraph 3)   <u>insane</u>

5. disassociate (paragraph 8)   <u>to break contact with</u>

6. chaotic (paragraph 9)   <u>confusing</u>

7. frenzied (paragraph 9)   <u>wildly excited</u>

Reviewing the Reading Using an Idea Map

Review the reading by completing the missing pieces of the idea map shown below.

ELIZABETH WONG RECALLS HER EXPERIENCES
ATTENDING CHINESE LANGUAGE SCHOOL.

At age 10 Elizabeth and her brother forced to attend Chinese school

Learned speaking, reading, writing Chinese

Didn't want to attend

Her language embarrassed her

Thought Chinese was ugly: loud, quick, rhythmless

Not refined like French or English spoken in South

She wanted to speak English well

People encouraged her

Chinese said she would be successful outside Chinatown

Brother more fanatical about English

Criticized mother for pidgin English

Blamed her for his errors

Allowed to stop Chinese school after two years

Now, in her twenties, she is sad about her rejection of Chinese culture

Examining the Reading

1. Underline several particularly descriptive adjectives and adverbs in the reading.

2. At the end of the essay, Wong says, "At last, I was one of you; I wasn't one of them." To whom do the *you* and the *them* refer?

3. Summarize Wong's attitude toward her Chinese heritage.

4. Why do you think Wong's mother insisted she attend Chinese school?

Reacting to and Discussing Ideas

Get ready to write about the reading by discussing the following questions:

1. Why do you think Wong's brother criticized his mother's inability to speak English?

2. Why does Wong say she prefers tacos to eggrolls?

3. Explain the meaning of the title of the essay.

4. Explain the meaning of the last line of the essay: "Sadly, I still am."

Writing about the Reading

The Paragraph Option

1. Wong was embarrassed by her Chinese heritage. Write a paragraph describing a situation in which you were proud of or embarrassed by your heritage or by the cultural behavior of a member of your family.

2. Write a paragraph in which you describe a family tradition. Use adjectives and adverbs in your description.

The Essay Option

1. Wong states that Nancy Drew, the main character in an American mystery novel series, was her heroine. Write an essay describing a person, real or fictional, that you admire. Be sure to describe the specific characteristics that make this person your hero or heroine.

2. Clearly, Wong and her brother viewed their heritage from a different perspective than that of their parents and grandparents. Write an essay in which you evaluate generational differences within your own family. Choose one topic or issue, and consider how different generations view the matter.

WRITING SUCCESS TIP 6

How can you improve your spelling? The following practical tips will help.

1. **Don't worry about spelling as you write your first draft.** Checking a word in a dictionary at this point will interrupt your flow of ideas. If you don't know how a word is spelled, spell it the way it sounds. Circle or underline the word so you remember to check it later.

2. **Develop a spelling awareness.** Your spelling will improve just by being aware that spelling is important. When you encounter a new word, notice how it is spelled and practice writing it.

3. **Pronounce words you are having difficulty spelling.** Pronounce each syllable distinctly.

4. **Keep a list of words you commonly misspell.** You can make this list part of your error log (see Writing Success Tip 3, "Keeping an Error Log," on pages 76–77) or part of your writing journal. Every time you catch an error or find a misspelled word on a returned paper, add it to your list.

5. **Study your list.** Ask a friend to quiz you on the list. Eliminate words from the list after you have passed several such quizzes.

6. **Review basic spelling rules.** Your college library or learning lab may have manuals, workbooks, or computer programs that review basic rules and provide guided practice. Also see Part IX, page 506, for more information on spelling rules.

7. **Have a dictionary readily available when you write.** See Writing Success Tip 5, "Buying and Using a Dictionary" (pages 123–124), for more information on using a dictionary in your writing.

8. **Use the spell-checker on your computer.** If you are writing on a computer that has a spell-checker program, get into the habit of using this feature as a final step before printing your writing.

9. **Read your final draft through once just for spelling errors.** Before you hand in an assignment, check any spellings you are not sure of.

Using Modifiers to Add Detail

Modifiers are words and phrases that change or limit the meaning of another word or word group. They help convey your exact meaning. They also add information and make your writing flow more smoothly. Note how the following paragraph uses very few modifiers and therefore lacks specific details.

CHAPTER OBJECTIVES

In this chapter you will learn to add detail by using

1. prepositional phrases.
2. *-ing* phrases.
3. *who, which,* and *that* relative clauses.

Sample Paragraph

> Eyes produce tears. Tears wash the eye. Tears clean away dust and germs. People cry sometimes when happy, sad, or in pain. No one knows why. The eye also waters if something touches it or if the person has a cold or other infection. Used tear fluid drains away. It goes to a chamber in the nose. Crying produces a runny nose.

Did this paragraph seem choppy and underdeveloped to you? Now read the revised paragraph below. To add information and improve flow, the writer has used modifiers, such as prepositional phrases, *-ing* phrases, and relative clauses.

Revised Paragraph

> Eyes produce tears <u>in the lachrymal glands behind the upper eyelids</u>. <u>Cleaning away dust and germs with every blink</u>, tears wash the eye. <u>For reasons not well understood</u>, people <u>who are happy, sad, or in pain</u> sometimes produce extra tears, <u>which flood down their cheeks</u>. The eye also waters if something touches it or if the person has a cold or other infection. Used tear fluid drains away <u>through two tiny holes</u> <u>in the eyelids</u> <u>near the nose</u>, <u>entering small tubes that are called the tear</u>

157

ducts. These ducts empty into a chamber in the nose. This fact explains why someone <u>who is having a good cry</u> will often get a runny nose as well.

In this chapter you will learn to write more interesting, effective sentences by using three types of modifiers: prepositional phrases; *-ing* phrases; and *who, which,* and *that* relative clauses.

WRITING

Using Prepositional Phrases to Add Detail

A **preposition** links its object (a noun or pronoun) to the rest of the sentence. Prepositions often show relationships of *time, place, direction,* or *manner.*

TIME:	Let's study after class.
PLACE:	Meet me behind Hayes Hall.
DIRECTION:	Who's that coming toward us?
MANNER:	I acted according to my principles.

Prepositions show other relationships as well, usually variations on *time, place, direction,* or *manner.*

DURATION:	We walked until dark.
REASON:	They were late because of the snow.
RELATION:	She looks like her sister.
QUALIFICATION:	Everyone attended except Suzanna.
ORIGIN:	In the beginning, I thought I couldn't write.
DESTINATION:	We're going to the Grand Canyon in May.
LOCATION:	The book is in my car.

Become familiar with the following common prepositions. They will help you link your ideas and make your sentences more varied and interesting.

Common Prepositions

about	beneath	in spite of	round
above	beside	instead of	since
according to	between	into	through
across	beyond	like	throughout
after	by	near	till
against	concerning	next to	to
along	despite	of	toward
along with	down	off	under
among	during	on	underneath
around	except	onto	unlike
as	except for	out	until
aside from	excepting	out of	up
at	for	outside	upon
because of	from	over	with
before	in	past	within
behind	in addition to	regarding	without
below	inside		

A **prepositional phrase** consists of a preposition and the object of the preposition (a noun or pronoun). It may also include words that modify the object.

preposition   object of preposition

Sam sat beside me.

preposition   modifier   object of preposition

Turn left at the red barn.

You can add a prepositional phrase to a sentence to describe a noun, pronoun, verb, or adjective.

Prepositional Phrase
Describing a

noun

noun   The man with the suitcase boarded the train.

pronoun

pronoun   Both of the skaters wore red.

verb

verb   I swam in the ocean.

adjective

adjective   I was pleased with my exam grade.

Using Prepositional Phrases to Expand Sentences

Now let's look at how you can use prepositional phrases to add detail to and expand your sentences:

BASIC SENTENCE:	I met an old friend.
ADDITIONAL DETAIL:	My old friend was from California. [location]
	We met at a quiet restaurant. [place]
	We met on Saturday night. [time]
EXPANDED SENTENCE:	On Saturday night, I met an old friend from California at a quiet restaurant.
BASIC SENTENCE:	Molly got a job.
ADDITIONAL DETAIL:	Her job is at the bakery. [place]
	The bakery is on Seventh Street. [place]
	She got the job during the week. [time]
EXPANDED SENTENCE:	During the week, Molly got a job at the bakery on Seventh Street.

Punctuating Prepositional Phrases

To use prepositional phrases effectively, you must also punctuate them correctly. Keep the following points in mind:

1. A preposition is never separated from its object by a comma.

comma

INCORRECT: According to, the newspaper

no comma

CORRECT: According to the newspaper

2. A prepositional phrase is never a complete sentence. It lacks both a subject and a verb. Be sure you do not punctuate a prepositional phrase as a sentence. To do so is to create a fragment.

INCORRECT:	We went for a walk. Along the road.
CORRECT:	We went for a walk along the road.

3. A prepositional phrase that introduces a sentence is set apart from the rest of the sentence by a comma, unless the prepositional phrase is very short (two or three words).

comma

COMMA: According to my sister and my cousin, the party lasted until midnight.

no comma

NO COMMA: On Tuesday I missed class.

4. When a prepositional phrase interrupts a sentence and is not essential to the meaning of the sentence, it is set apart from the sentence with commas.

comma   comma

The president, unlike those before him, intends to establish new policies.

EXERCISE 7-1   Underline each prepositional phrase. Add punctuation if it is needed.

> EXAMPLE: The mayor according to the television news report has vetoed the school budget.
>
> The mayor, according to the television news report, has vetoed the school budget.

1. The family walked toward the museum.

2. Throughout the film, the man next to me kept sneezing.

3. A tree branch crashed to the ground and blew down the hill.

4. Over the past few years, the sculptor has created many works.

5. Barbara bought a VCR instead of a CD player with her bonus check.

6. After dinner Dominic gave me a gift.

7. Over the phone the salesman tried to convince me to buy his product.

8. The dog and the squirrel ran around the tree.

9. We were busy talking, and drove past the restaurant.

10. Firemen broke into the building and rescued seven people.

EXERCISE 7-2   Expand each of the following basic sentences by using prepositional phrases to add additional detail. Your new sentence should have only one subject and one verb. Add punctuation if it is needed. Underline the prepositional phrases.

EXAMPLE

BASIC SENTENCE: I ordered a pizza.

ADDITIONAL DETAIL: I ordered it from Mazia's.
                    I ordered it with mushrooms and anchovies.
                    I ordered it before noon.

EXPANDED SENTENCE: <u>Before noon</u> I ordered a pizza <u>with mushrooms
                    and anchovies</u> <u>from Mazia's.</u>

1. Basic Sentence: Maria plays the drums.
   Additional Detail: She plays in a band.
                        The band plays at the Rathskeller.
                        She plays on weekends.

   Expanded Sentence: <u>On weekends</u> Maria plays the drums <u>in a band</u>

                        <u>at the Rathskeller.</u>

   _____

2. Basic Sentence: The construction crew is building a sky-
                        scraper.

   Additional Detail: They are building it next to a church.
                        They are building it on Ivy Street.

   Expanded Sentence: The construction crew is building a skyscraper

                        <u>on Ivy Street</u> <u>next to a church.</u>

   _____

3. Basic Sentence: The folders should be organized and filed.
   Additional Detail: They should be organized by subject.
                        The folders are beside the phone.
                        They should be filed under "Marketing
                        Ideas."

   Expanded Sentence: The folders <u>beside the phone</u> should be orga-

                        nized <u>by subject</u> and filed <u>under "Marketing</u>

                        <u>Ideas."</u>

4. Basic Sentence: Jason will buy a house.
   Additional Detail: The house is in Williamsville.
                        He will buy it as an investment.
                        The house has a two-car garage.

Expanded Sentence: As an investment, Jason will buy a house in Williamsville with a two-car garage.

5. Basic Sentence:
    Additional Detail:

The library is a popular place.
It is popular for socializing.
The library is in the Humanities Building.
Many students study there during the exam period.

Expanded Sentence: Located in the Humanities Building, the library is a popular place for socializing and studying during exam time.

6. Basic Sentence:
    Additional Detail:

The vice-president was honored.
He was honored for his volunteer work.
He was honored after the staff meeting.
He volunteered throughout his career.

Expanded Sentence: After the staff meeting, the vice-president was honored for his volunteer work throughout his career.

7. Basic Sentence:
    Additional Detail:

Tamara joined a sorority.
She joined along with her friend Marion.
This was unlike her sister Shara.
She joined despite her busy schedule.

Expanded Sentence: Despite her busy schedule, Tamara, unlike her sister Shara, joined a sorority along with her friend Marion.

8. Basic Sentence:
    Additional Detail:

The movie is playing at the theater.
The theater is behind the mall.
The movie is about dinosaurs.
It is playing during the afternoon only.

Expanded Sentence: The movie about dinosaurs is playing at the theater behind the mall but only during the afternoon.

9. Basic Sentence: Women are waiting to get married.
   Additional Detail: They are waiting until they are older and have careers.
   This is happening throughout the country.
   This is true according to a recent survey.

   Expanded Sentence: According to a recent survey, women throughout the country are waiting to get married until
   they are older and have careers.

10. Basic Sentence: The museum is famous.
    Additional Detail: The museum is outside the city.
    It is famous for its Monet paintings.
    It is famous despite its out-of-the-way location.

    Expanded Sentence: Despite its out-of-the-way location outside
    the city, the museum is famous for its Monet
    paintings.

EXERCISE 7-3

Expand each of the following sentences by adding at least two preposi-tional phrases anywhere in the sentence. Underline your prepositional phrases.

EXAMPLE

BASIC SENTENCE: Jack rented an apartment.

EXPANDED SENTENCE: Jack rented an apartment with a beautiful view of the waterfront.

1. The bank was recently taken over. The bank in the shopping plaza was recently taken over by First Federal.

2. The grocery store closed permanently. The grocery store on the corner closed permanently in June.

3. The publisher uses only recycled paper. Except for business stationery, the publisher uses only recycled paper in the business office.

4. The children heard a story. During class, the children heard a story about wolves.

5. Lightning struck the old oak tree. <u>During the storm lightning struck the old oak tree beside the farmhouse.</u>

6. The tanker spilled oil. <u>Throughout the night, the tanker spilled oil into the Gulf of Mexico.</u>

7. Alaskan brown bears catch salmon. <u>Despite swift currents, Alaskan brown bears catch salmon in local rivers.</u>

8. The road was being paved. <u>Despite the bad weather, the road was being paved by the county work crew.</u>

9. The Bach sonata was being played. <u>The Bach sonata was being played at the outdoor concert in New Orleans.</u>

10. The show dog won a ribbon. <u>The show dog with the red collar won a ribbon at the field trials.</u>

EXERCISE 7-4

Write a paragraph on one of the following topics. After you have written your first draft, make sure your paragraph includes at least five prepositional phrases. Underline these phrases.

1. when the unexpected happened
2. something simple that became difficult
3. a lost and never-found item
4. signs of laziness
5. a phobia (fear) of _____

Using *-ing* Phrases to Add Detail

Another way to add detail to your writing is to use *-ing* phrases to expand your sentences. An *-ing* phrase begins with the *-ing* verb form (*running, calling*) and functions as an adjective—that is, it modifies a noun or pronoun.

<u>Walking slowly</u>, the couple held hands.

<u>Sitting on the sofa</u>, Sally watched a video.

The phrase *walking slowly* describes the couple. The phrase *sitting on the sofa* describes Sally.

You can also use *-ing* phrases to combine ideas from two sentences into a single sentence.

TWO SENTENCES: Matt grilled a steak.
He was standing on the patio.

COMBINED: Standing on the patio, Matt grilled a steak.

TWO SENTENCES: The couple discovered an injured pelican.
The couple searched for sea shells.

COMBINED: Searching for sea shells, the couple discovered an injured pelican.

TWO SENTENCES: The photographer slipped off his stepstool.
He fell two feet.

COMBINED: The photographer slipped off his stepstool, falling two feet.

Punctuating -ing Phrases

Remember the following rules for punctuating -ing phrases:

1. A comma must follow an -ing phrase that appears at the beginning of the sentence. Its purpose is to separate the -ing phrase from the independent thought that follows.

comma

Driving home, I saw a shooting star.

2. If the -ing phrase appears at the end of the sentence, a comma separates the -ing phrase from the independent thought that comes before the phrase.

comma

I explored the flooded basement, wishing I had worn my boots.

3. When the -ing phrase interrupts a sentence and is not essential to the meaning of the sentence, it is set apart from the sentence with commas.

comma   comma

The cows, munching grass, all stood with their backs to the wind.

EXERCISE 7-5 Combine each pair of sentences into a single sentence that begins with an -ing phrase. Underline these phrases.

EXAMPLE

TWO SENTENCES: a. Art wished it would stop raining.
b. Art was walking home without a raincoat.

COMBINED: <u>Walking home without a raincoat,</u>   Art
                    wished it would stop raining.

1. a. Kedra did not listen to the lecture.
    b. Kedra was thinking about her essay.

    Combined: <u>Thinking about her essay, Kedra did not listen to the lecture.</u>

    _____

2. a. Kenyon was driving to the bookstore.
    b. Kenyon was singing to himself.

    Combined: <u>Driving to the bookstore, Kenyon was singing to himself.</u>

    _____

3. a. The plumber entered the house.
    b. The plumber carried a toolbox.

    Combined: <u>Carrying a toolbox, the plumber entered the house.</u>

    _____

4. a. The baby was crying for her mother.
    b. The baby was standing in her crib.

    Combined: <u>Standing in her crib, the baby was crying for her mother.</u>

    _____

5. a. The press secretary held a press conference.
    b. The press secretary was wearing a navy pin-striped suit.

    Combined: <u>Wearing a navy pin-striped suit, the press secretary held a</u>

    <u>press conference.</u>

EXERCISE 7-6 ▶ Expand each of the following sentences by adding an *-ing* phrase. You may add your *-ing* phrase at the beginning, the middle, or the end of the sentence. Underline these phrases.

EXAMPLE: The man stood on a ladder.

EXPANDED SENTENCE: <u>Painting his garage,</u> the man stood on a ladder.

1. The programmer sat at her desk. <u>Working at a computer,</u> the program-

   mer sat at her desk.

2. The doctor walked through the hospital. The doctor walked through

   the hospital, <u>checking on each of her patients.</u>

3. Rafael climbed the tree. <u>Rafael, trying to reach the stranded cat, climbed</u>

<u>the tree.</u>

4. The teenagers walked through the mall. <u>Wearing headsets, the</u>

<u>teenagers walked through the mall.</u>

5. The instructor returned the exams. <u>Explaining her grading system, the</u>

<u>instructor returned the exams.</u>

6. Ellen waited for a bus. <u>Humming softly, Ellen waited for a bus.</u>

7. The clerk bagged the groceries. <u>Talking constantly, the clerk bagged</u>

<u>the groceries.</u>

8. The movie star accepted the award. <u>Smiling graciously, the movie star</u>

<u>accepted the award.</u>

9. They spent a quiet evening. <u>They spent a quiet evening, ordering a</u>

<u>pizza and watching a video.</u>

10. The kitten was curled up on the sofa. <u>Purring softly, the kitten was</u>

<u>curled up on the sofa.</u>

EXERCISE ▶ **7-7** | Review the paragraph you wrote for Exercise 7-4. Double-underline any *-ing* phrases. If you have not used any *-ing* phrases, revise your paragraph to include at least one.

Using *Who, Which,* and *That* Relative Clauses to Add Detail

A **clause** is a group of words that has a subject and a verb. Clauses that begin with the pronoun *who, which,* or *that* are called **relative** (or **adjective**) **clauses** because they relate one idea to another. The pronoun

who refers to people.

which refers to things.

that refers to people or things.

Relative clauses add variety to your writing, as well as interesting detail. Following are a few examples of relative clauses used to expand sentences by adding detail:

BASIC SENTENCE:	My sister is a football fan.
ADDITIONAL DETAIL:	She is ten years old.
EXPANDED SENTENCE:	My sister, <u>who is ten years old</u>, is a football fan.

BASIC SENTENCE:	My favorite movie is *Star Trek: Lost in Space*.
ADDITIONAL DETAIL:	I saw *Star Trek: Lost in Space* ten times.
EXPANDED SENTENCE:	My favorite movie is *Star Trek: Lost in Space*, <u>which I've seen ten times</u>.

BASIC SENTENCE:	I own a large van.
ADDITIONAL DETAIL:	The van can haul camping equipment.
EXPANDED SENTENCE:	I own a large van <u>that can haul camping equipment</u>.

Placement of Relative Clauses

Who, which, and *that* clauses usually come directly after the words they relate to or modify.

My math instructor, <u>who lives in Baltimore</u>, has a British accent.

Mickey's, <u>which serves thirty-two varieties of coffee</u>, is part of a national chain.

Punctuating Relative Clauses

Note the following guidelines for punctuating relative clauses:

1. A relative clause is never a sentence by itself. Alone, a relative clause is a fragment. It must be combined with a complete sentence.

FRAGMENT:	That has two fireplaces.
REVISED:	The house <u>that has two fireplaces</u> is for sale.

FRAGMENT:	Who lives next door.
REVISED:	The woman <u>who lives next door</u> is a plumber.

SENTENCE + FRAGMENT:	I needed my notebook. Which I left at home.
REVISED:	I needed my notebook, <u>which I left at home</u>.

2. If the relative clause is necessary to the meaning of the sentence, no punctuation is needed.

Pens <u>that have refillable cartridges</u> are expensive.

The above sentence states that not all pens are expensive. Only those pens that have refillable cartridges are expensive. Here the relative clause is essential to the meaning of the sentence, so no commas are needed.

3. If the relative clause is *not* essential to the meaning of the sentence, then it should be separated from the remainder of the sentence by commas. To discover if the clause is essential, try reading the sentence without the clause. If the basic meaning does not change, the clause is not essential.

My car, <u>which is a Nissan</u>, has over 100,000 miles on it.

In this sentence, the additional information that the car is a Nissan does not change the basic meaning of the sentence.

My computer, <u>which has a single disk drive</u>, is outdated.

Dogs <u>that bark constantly</u> are annoying.

In this sentence, the clause is essential: only dogs that bark constantly are annoying.

EXERCISE ▶ **7-8**   Underline each relative clause. Add punctuation if it is needed. Circle the word to which each clause relates.

     EXAMPLE: My bicycle which I rode all summer needs repair.

     REVISED: My bicycle, <u>which I rode all summer</u>, needs repair.

1. An (apartment) <u>that has three bedrooms</u> is expensive.

2. The (tape) <u>that I handed you</u> has a concert on it.

3. (Becky,) <u>who has been there before,</u> said the food is terrific.

4. (Trees) <u>that lose their leaves</u> are called deciduous.

5. (Animals) <u>that live both on land and in water</u> are called amphibians.

6. The (fence) <u>that was put up to keep rabbits out of the garden</u> is becoming rusted.

7. My (car,) <u>which I bought at an auction,</u> is seven years old.

8. The professor asked a question of (Michael,) <u>who had not done the reading</u>.

9. Bettina reconditions outboard (motors,) <u>which she buys at marinas</u>.

10. (Brady,) <u>who visited France last year,</u> speaks six languages fluently.

EXERCISE ▶ **7-9**   Combine each pair of sentences into a single sentence that has a relative clause. Underline the relative clause, and circle the word to which each clause relates.

EXAMPLE:

     TWO SENTENCES: a. Sam Arrowsmith lives in New Orleans.

b. Sam Arrowsmith travels around the country demonstrating computer software.

COMBINED: (Sam Arrowsmith,) who lives in New Orleans, travels around the country demonstrating computer software.

1. a. The trunk was old.
   b. The trunk contained antique clothing.

   Combined: The (trunk) which was old, contained antique clothing.

   _____

2. a. The coins were valuable.
   b. The coins had sunk on a boat hundreds of years ago.

   Combined: The (coins) that had sunk on a boat hundreds of years ago were valuable.

3. a. The students attended the Garth Brooks concert.
   b. The students enjoy country and western music.

   Combined: The (students) who enjoy country and western music attended the Garth Brooks concert.

4. a. Einstein stated the theory of relativity.
   b. Einstein was a very humorous man.

   Combined: (Einstein,) who was a very humorous man, stated the theory of relativity.

5. a. The truck got a flat tire.
   b. The truck was going to the repair shop.

   Combined: The (truck) that was going to the repair shop got a flat tire.

   _____

6. a. The wreath was hung on the door.
   b. The wreath was made of dried flowers and leaves.

   Combined: The (wreath,) which was made of dried flowers and leaves, was hung on the door.

7. a. An appointment book was found on the desk.
   b. The appointment book was filled with writing.

   Combined: An (appointment book,) which was filled with writing, was found on the desk.

8. a. Roberto was hired as an accountant.
   b. Roberto has a degree from this college.

Combined: (Roberto,) who has a degree from this college, was hired as an

accountant.

9. a. The pool sold for fifty dollars.
   b. The pool had a tear in its lining.

Combined: The (pool,) which had a tear in its lining, sold for fifty dollars.

10. a. Test questions should be approached systematically.
    b. Some test questions are multiple choice.

Combined: (Test questions) that are multiple choice should be approached

systematically.

EXERCISE 7-10 Review the paragraph you wrote for Exercise 7-4. Bracket any relative clauses. If you have not included any relative clauses, revise your paragraph to include at least one.

EXERCISE 7-11 Expand each of the following sentences by adding a relative clause. Underline all relative clauses, and set off unessential ones with commas.

EXAMPLE: Mr. Schmidt had a heart attack.

EXPANDED SENTENCE: Mr. Schmidt, who had always been healthy, had a
                     heart attack.

1. "The Three Little Pigs" is a popular children's story. "The Three
Little Pigs," which I read to my daughter frequently, is a popular children's
story.

2. Our dog is afraid to climb the spiral staircase. Our dog is afraid to
climb the spiral staircase, which leads to the attic.

3. A paper plate lay in the garbage. A paper plate, which was strewn
with wilted salad, lay in the garbage.

4. The stereo was too loud. The stereo that was perched above the show
case was too loud.

5. I picked up my screwdriver and tightened the screw. I picked up my
screwdriver and tightened the screw that was loose.

6. The student called the Records Office. <u>The student who had not</u>

   <u>received her transcript</u> called the Records Office.

7. The wineglass shattered. <u>The wineglass that sat on the countertop</u>

   shattered.

8. The lottery jackpot was one million dollars. <u>The lottery jackpot that I</u>

   <u>hoped to win</u> was one million dollars.

9. Jackie stepped on the thistle. <u>Jackie, who often walks barefoot,</u> stepped

   on the thistle.

10. The train crossed the bridge. <u>The train that was bound for San</u>

    <u>Francisco</u> crossed the bridge.

NEED TO KNOW

Modifiers

- Use *prepositional phrases* to show relationships of time, place, direction, or manner.
- Use *-ing phrases* to describe or modify a noun or pronoun.
- Use *relative clauses* (who, which, and that) to add detail by showing relationships.
- Be sure to check the punctuation of each of these phrases and clauses.

EXERCISE 7-12 ▶ Expand the following sentences by adding prepositional phrases, -ing phrases, and relative clauses. Underline the phrases and clauses that you add.

EXAMPLE: The sportscaster reported the game.

EXPANDED: The sportscaster, <u>who was wearing a really wild tie,</u> reported the game <u>with great enthusiasm.</u>

1. Randall will graduate. <u>Randall will graduate from Niagara University in</u>

   <u>May with a degree in biology.</u>

   _____

2. The race began. <u>The race that is one of the city's most popular</u> began at

   eleven o'clock.

   _____

3. The Smiths are remodeling. <u>Working on weekends, the Smiths are</u> <u>remodeling their house in the country.</u>

4. Hillary walked alone. <u>Having lost her car keys, Hillary, who seldom</u> <u>loses anything, walked alone to the bus stop.</u>

5. Manuel repairs appliances. <u>Manuel, who works for Orville's, repairs</u> <u>appliances during the evening.</u>

6. The motorcycle was loud. <u>The motorcycle that sped through the town</u> <u>was loud.</u>

7. My term paper is due Tuesday. <u>My term paper on misleading advertis-</u> <u>ing is due on Tuesday unless I request an extention.</u>

8. I opened my umbrella. <u>Leaving the building, I opened my umbrella</u> <u>underneath the awning.</u>

9. Austin built a garage. <u>Planning to resell his house, Austin built a two-car</u> <u>garage even though he owns only one car.</u>

10. Lucas climbs mountains. <u>Lucas, who is a strength and agility trainer,</u> <u>climbs mountains in Colorado.</u>

EXERCISE 7-13 Write a paragraph describing what you think is happening in the photograph on page 175. To make your writing vivid, use adjectives and adverbs, prepositional phrases, *-ing* phrases, and relative clauses.

STUDENT ESSAY

In this student essay, Darlene Livergood uses prepositional phrases, -*ing* phrases, and relative clauses to add
detail to her writing. As you read, highlight those that
you notice.

Army National Guard
Darlene Livergood

One afternoon my son, who was seventeen at the time, told his   1
father and me that he wanted to join the Army National Guard.
We discussed it over a period of time. On April 6, 1995, we
took our son to enlist at the local recruitment office that is located in
Niagara Falls. On the way my husband, Neil, stopped four times. He
asked Aaron if he was really sure that he wanted to do this. Each time
without hesitation, Aaron said yes. Pulling into the parking lot, Neil
asked Aaron once again, and he said yes.

So we proceeded to enter the building and met the recruiter.   2
Listening to the recruiter explain all the options, Aaron never seemed
hesitant or unsure of his decision. Before Aaron signed, his father asked
him for the final time. Aaron stated, yes, this was what he wanted to

do. Finally Aaron signed papers that would affect his life for the next several years.

Two months later Aaron left for Fort Jackson, South Carolina. This was his first time away from home for any length of time. Before he left, his father said, "Remember, I've been through this, but your mother hasn't, so go easy on her." I didn't understand what he meant, but he said I would understand later. Neil also gave Aaron a pep talk that seemed to boost his self-confidence.   3

When Aaron left on June 25, 1995, he was able to make one phone call to let me know he was there, and that he was okay. Before he called, my husband told me, "Don't ask him how he is. It will make him feel homesick."   4

One week after Aaron left, he called again. I tried to keep myself from crying because this was the first time Aaron had been away from home for any amount of time. But I started to cry, and he did likewise. He cried for only a few seconds, and then composed himself. It took me a little longer, but I managed.   5

During the eight weeks that Aaron was in basic training, I felt as if I were going through what he was, getting up at 4:30 A.M. and going through a full day of activities. During the eight weeks that Aaron was gone, I talked to him eight times and received five letters. The day Aaron was coming home, he called about ten times. His flight arrived around 11 P.M. Waiting for the plane to arrive, I wondered whether he had changed. All the passengers were getting off the plane and Aaron, of course, was the last one to get off. Confidently and proudly, Aaron walked off the plane and into the terminal. After not seeing my son for eight weeks, I was in shock. He was nearly bald and had lost at least twenty-five pounds, but he was still my son. It was a reunion of joy; his father and I were overwhelmed to have him home.   6

Over the next two weeks, it took Aaron a while to adjust to being back home. We were so glad to have him back, though. It was an experience I will never forget.   7

Evaluating the Essay

1. Evaluate the structure and content of the essay.
   a. Does the essay follow a logical plan? Describe its organization.
   b. What is the author's thesis statement?
   c. In what ways does the writer support her thesis?
   d. Evaluate the effectiveness of the title, introduction, and conclusion.

2. How well does the author use modifiers to add detail?

   a. Locate and underline at least four prepositional phrases.

   b. Locate and underline at least three *-ing* phrases.

   c. Locate and underline at least three relative clauses.

WRITING ABOUT A READING

Thinking before Reading

The following reading describes the life of an alcoholic before he quit drinking. As you read, you'll notice numerous prepositional phrases and relative clauses that enhance sentence meaning.

   Before you read:

1. Preview the reading, using the steps provided on page 20.

2. After you have done your preview, connect the reading to your own experience by answering the following questions:

   a. Do you know or have you heard about anyone who is (or was) an alcoholic? How has the disease affected this person's life?

   b. Why do you think some people use alcohol in excess?

READING

The Thirsty Animal
Brian Manning

I was very young, but I still vividly remember how my father fascinated my brothers and me at the dinner table by running his finger around the rim of his wineglass. He sent a wonderful, crystal tone wafting through the room, and we loved it. When we laughed too raucously, he would stop, swirl the red liquid in his glass and take a sip.

   There was a wine cellar in the basement of the house we moved into when I was eleven. My father put a few cases of Bordeaux[1] down there

1. A French wine

in the dark. We played there with other boys in the neighborhood, hid there, made a secret place. It was musty and cool and private. We wrote things and stuck them in among the bottles and imagined someone way in the future baffled by our message from the past.

Many years later, the very first time I drank, I had far too much. But I found I was suddenly able to tell a girl at my high school that I was mad about her.   3

When I drank in college with the men in my class, I was trying to define a self-image I could feel comfortable with. I wanted to be "an Irishman," I decided, a man who could drink a lot of liquor and hold it. My favorite play was Eugene O'Neill's *Long Day's Journey into Night,* my model the drunken Jamie Tyrone.   4

I got out of college, into the real world, and the drunk on weekends started to slip into the weekdays. Often I didn't know when one drunk ended and another began. The years were measured in hangovers. It took a long time to accept, and then to let the idea sink in, that I was an alcoholic.   5

It took even longer to do anything about it. I didn't want to believe it, and I didn't want to deny myself the exciting, brotherly feeling I had whenever I went boozing with my friends. For a long time, in my relationships with women, I could only feel comfortable with a woman who drank as much as I did. So I didn't meet many women and spent my time with men in dark barrooms, trying to be like them and hoping I'd be accepted.   6

It is now two years since I quit drinking, and that, as all alcoholics know who have come to grips with their problem, is not long ago at all. The urge to have "just one" includes a genuine longing for all the accouterments of drink: the popping of a cork, the color of Scotch through a glass, the warmth creeping over my shoulders with the third glass of stout. Those were joys. Ever since I gave them up I remember them as delicious.   7

I go to parties now and start off fine, but I have difficulty dealing with the changing rhythms as the night wears on. Everyone around me seems to be having a better time the more they drink, and I, not they, become awkward. I feel like a kid with a broken chain when everyone else has bicycled around the corner out of sight. I fight against feeling sorry for myself.   8

What were the things I was looking for and needed when I drank? I often find that what I am looking for when I want a drink is not really the alcohol, but the memories and laughter that seemed possible only with a glass in my hand. In a restaurant, I see the bottle of vintage port   9 on the shelf, and imagine lolling in my chair, swirling the liquid around in the glass, inhaling those marvelous fumes. I think of my neighbor, Eileen, the funniest woman I ever got smashed with, and I want to get up on a bar stool next to her to hear again the wonderful stories she told. She could drink any man under the table, she claimed, and I wanted to be one of those men who tried. She always won, but it made me feel I belonged when I staggered out of the bar, her delighted laughter following me.

I had found a world to cling to, a way of belonging, and it still attracts me. I pass by the gin mills and pubs now and glance in at the men lined up inside, and I don't see them as suckers or fools. I remember how I felt sitting there after work, or watching a Sunday afternoon ball game, and I long for the smell of the barroom and that ease—toasts and songs, jokes and equality. I have to keep reminding myself of the wasting hangovers, the lost money, the days down the drain.

I imagine my problem as an animal living inside me, demanding a drink before it dies of thirst. That's what it says, but it will never die of thirst. The fact an alcoholic faces is that this animal breathes and waits. It is incapable of death and will spring back to lustful, consuming life with even one drop of sustenance.

When I was eighteen and my drinking began in earnest, I didn't play in the wine cellar at home anymore; I stole there. I sneaked bottles to my room, sat in the window and drank alone while my parents were away. I hated the taste of it, but I kept drinking it, without the kids from the neighborhood, without any thought that I was feeding the animal. And one day, I found one of those old notes we had hidden down there years before. It fell to the ground when I pulled a bottle from its cubbyhole. I read it with bleary eyes, then put the paper back into the rack. "Beware," it said, above a childish skull and crossbones, "all ye who enter here." A child, wiser than I was that day, had written that note.

I did a lot of stupid, disastrous, sometimes mean things in the years that followed, and remembering them is enough to snap me out of the memories and back to the reality that I quit just in time. I've done something I had to do, something difficult and necessary, and that gives me satisfaction and the strength to stay on the wagon. I'm very lucky so far. I don't get mad that I can't drink anymore; I can handle the self-pity that overwhelmed me in my early days of sobriety. From time to time, I daydream about summer afternoons and cold beer. I know such dreams will never go away. The thirsty animal is still there, getting a little fainter every day. It will never die. A lot of my life now is all about keeping it in a very lonely cage.

From the *New York Times.*

Getting Ready to Write

Strengthening Your Vocabulary

Write a brief definition for each of the following words from the preceding reading. If you cannot figure out the meaning of a word from the way it is used in the reading, look the word up in a dictionary.

1. wafting (paragraph 1)   drifting, floating

2. raucously (paragraph 1)   roughly, uncontrollably

3. accouterments (paragraph 7)   accompaniments

4. lolling (paragraph 9)   relaxing

5. sustenance (paragraph 11)   food that sustains life

Reviewing the Reading Using an Idea Map

Review the reading by completing the missing pieces of the idea map shown below.

BRIAN MANNING IS ALCOHOLIC

> **How it began**
>
> > When child: fascinated by father drinking wine
> >
> > As a boy, played in wine cellar
> >
> > High school: drinking gave him courage
> >
> > College: drank for self-esteem
>
> **How it developed**
>
> > After college, drinking increased
> >
> > Drunk daily

Realized he was an alcoholic

Took long time to do something about it

Alcoholism acknowledged

Quit two years ago

Still finds it difficult

Why he drank

Memories of jokes and laughter

Feeling of belonging

How he is doing now

Knows he quit just in time

Satisfaction and strength from staying on wagon

Doesn't get mad at and pity himself anymore

Still fights to keep "thirsty animal" locked up

Examining the Reading

1. What kinds of experiences does Manning associate with drinking alcohol?

2. Why did he use alcohol?

3. Describe his personality.

4. Why did he quit drinking?

5. Why does he refer to his desire to drink as a "thirsty animal"?

Reacting to and Discussing Ideas

Get ready to write about the reading by discussing the following questions:

1. Do you think Manning will be able to keep "the thirsty animal" caged?

2. How did becoming an alcoholic affect his life?

3. Does he regret his experiences?

4. What image (stereotype) of college students does he reinforce in paragraph 4?

Writing about the Reading

The Paragraph Option

1. In paragraph 8, Manning describes himself as a "kid with a broken chain when everyone else has bicycled around the corner out of sight." Write a paragraph explaining how Manning felt, or one describing a situation in which you felt the same way.

2. Parties are difficult for Manning, as they are for many people. Write a paragraph describing how you handle parties.

The Essay Option

To overcome the urge to drink, Manning has to use a great deal of self-control. Write an essay describing a situation in which you had to use a great deal of self-control. Be sure to describe how you felt after the situation was over, as Manning does in his essay.

WRITING SUCCESS TIP 7

Avoiding Slang Expressions

Slang refers to informal, casual expressions used by specific groups to identify themselves as a group. Teenagers, for example, have numerous slang expressions that create an in-group feeling. Slang changes rapidly and is not widely understood by those outside its group of origin. People generally use slang when they are certain the person they are speaking to will understand it or when they want to make an outsider feel even more like an outsider.

Slang can interfere with effective communication. If your reader is unfamiliar with the slang, confusion or misunderstanding can occur. Also, the use of slang suggests a casualness or familiarity that may be inappropriate for your reader.

In each of the following examples, the Standard English version provides more complete and detailed information.

SLANG:	I told Joe to *call the shots.*
STANDARD ENGLISH:	I told Joe to select a movie and check the times.
SLANG:	I *rattled my sister's cage* about our weekend trip.
STANDARD ENGLISH:	I urged my sister to finalize the plans for our weekend trip.
SLANG:	I was *up* for the job interview.
STANDARD ENGLISH:	I was optimistic about and prepared for the job interview.

Sometimes it is difficult to know whether a word you commonly use in speech is considered slang. If you are uncertain of a word or phrase, check your dictionary. If you do not find the term in your dictionary, do not use it. If the word is listed, but its definition is preceded by the label *Slang* or the abbreviation *Sl.*, you will know the word is inappropriate to use in formal writing.

SKILLS CHECK

Paragraph 1

Revise the following student paragraph by supplying adjectives and adverbs and by adding prepositional phrases, *-ing* phrases, or relative clauses.

many young

One of the major problems facing college students today is

generously

the ease and enthusiasm with which credit-card companies

large amounts of   unsuspecting

offer credit to college students. The reason the companies do

n inordinately

this, of course, is to charge students a high interest rate.

Students are often inexperienced in the world of finance. What

who are inexperienced
in the world of finance   very quickly

often happens is that students fall into debt. Although they

innocent   fully

may be only teenagers, they are still responsible for paying

many

their debts, and records may follow them for years to come.

acutely   severe financial   unsuspecting

Companies are aware of the danger in which they place these

students. Still, it is legal for these companies to issue credit

cards to students, even if they do not have established credit,

freely   ,   ing

as long as the students sign up for the cards. They must signify

their agreement to accept the responsibilities involved.

SKILLS CHECK CONTINUED

Paragraph 2

Revise the following paragraph by supplying adjectives and adverbs and by adding prepositional phrases, *-ing* phrases, or relative clauses.

My grandmother, *who* lives in an antique-filled house. She is *extremely* picky about her furniture. Because of this, nobody puts his or her feet on chairs or sits on beds. When we were little, one of my cousins used to think he could ignore her *strict* rules. We would sleep over at Gram's often. Each time, Eric would turn off the lights and swan dive into the bed. This would shove the mattress sideways. *which* It would knock nearly every slat out of place. Of course, Gram *invariably* noticed and always *firmly* asked him to stop being so *needlessly* rough on the bed. Anyone else would have *surely* changed his or her ways, but Eric thought he was different. My grandmother decided that he needed a *memorable* lesson. During the next sleepover, when everyone was *snugly* in bed, we heard a *loud* crash from Eric's room. We *frantically* rushed to his room. When we got there, we were surprised to see *a startled* Eric and the mattress flat on the floor! Gram had fine-tuned the slats in her *precious* bed. *teaching* She taught Eric a*n unforgettable* lesson. He now *wisely* restricts his diving to beaches and pools.

COMMON SENTENCE PROBLEMS AND HOW TO AVOID THEM

Revising Confusing and Inconsistent Sentences

CHAPTER OBJECTIVES

In this chapter you will learn to

1. use pronouns clearly and correctly

2. avoid shifts in person, number, and verb tense.

3. avoid misplaced and dangling modifiers.

4. use parallelism.

In a book entitled *Anguished English,* writer Richard Lederer has collected wacky examples of ways the English language is misused. Read the following lines Lederer found in commercial and classified ads, and see if you find anything wrong with them.

We do not tear your clothing with machinery. We do it carefully by hand.

Have several very old dresses from grandmother in beautiful condition.

Tired of cleaning yourself? Let me do it.

Mt. Kilimanjaro, the breathtaking backdrop for the Serena Lodge. Swim in the lovely pool while you drink it all in.

Sometimes sentence errors create unintentional humor, as in Lederer's examples. Most often, though, they distract or confuse your reader. They may also convey the impression that you have not taken time to check and polish your work. In this chapter you will learn to avoid several common types of sentence errors.

WRITING

Using Pronouns Clearly and Correctly

A **pronoun** is a word that substitutes for or refers to a noun or another pronoun. *I, you, he, she, it, we, they, his, mine, yours, who,* and *whom* are all examples of pronouns. The noun or pronoun to which a pronoun refers is called the pronoun's **antecedent.** To use pronouns correctly, you need to make sure that the antecedent of the pronoun (your pronoun reference) is clear to your reader and that the pronoun and antecedent agree in number (singular or plural).

Pronoun Reference

If your pronoun reference is unclear, your sentence may be confusing and difficult to follow. Note the confusing nature of the following sentences.

The aerobics instructor told the student that *she* made a mistake. [Who made the mistake?]

They told Kevin that he was eligible for a Visa card. [Who told Kevin?]

Aaron bought a bowling ball at the garage sale *that* he enjoyed. [Did Aaron enjoy the garage sale or the bowling ball?]

The following suggestions will help you make sure that all your pronoun references are clear.

1. Make sure there is only one possible *antecedent* for each pronoun. The antecedent (the word to which the pronoun refers) comes before the pronoun (*ante* means "before") in the sentence. The reader should not be left wondering what the antecedent of any given pronoun is.

UNCLEAR: The father told the child that *he* was sunburned.
REVISED: The father told the child, "I am sunburned."

2. Avoid using vague pronouns that lack an antecedent. *They* and *it* are often mistakenly used this way.

UNCLEAR: *They* told me my loan application needs a cosigner.
REVISED: The loan officer told me my loan application needs a cosigner.

3. Eliminate unnecessary pronouns. If a sentence is clear without a pronoun, delete the pronoun.

UNCLEAR: The manager, *he* says that the store will close at midnight.
REVISED: The manager says that the store will close at midnight.

4. Always place the pronoun as close as possible to its antecedent.

UNCLEAR: Lucia saw a dress at the mall *that* she wanted.
REVISED: At the mall, Lucia saw a dress that she wanted.

5. Use the pronoun *you* only if you are directly addressing the reader.

UNCLEAR: *You* need daily exercise to keep physically fit.
REVISED: Everyone needs daily exercise to keep physically fit.

EXERCISE 8-1 ▶ | Revise each of the following sentences to correct problems in pronoun reference.

> EXAMPLE: The glass/ ~~it~~ was filled to the rim.

Everyone
1. ~~You~~ should try to be honest at all times.

the sales clerk
2. When I bought the shirt, I told ~~him~~ that I would pay with my credit card.

, "I   "
3. Bert told Rob ~~he had~~ received an A in the course.

4. James ~~talked with Bill because he~~ did not know anyone else at the party/ , so he talked with Bill.

the teachers
5. The teachers told the school-board members that ~~they~~ needed more preparation time.

6. The board of directors/ ~~they~~ decided that the company would have to go bankrupt.

7. The gallery owner hung a painting on the wall. ⟨that was blue⟩

The registrar
8. ~~They~~ sent our grades at the end of the semester.

everyone has
9. The Constitution says ~~you have~~ the right to bear arms.

Antique cars
10. ~~They~~ filled the parking lot on Sunday.

EXERCISE 8-2 ▶ | Revise each of the following sentences to correct problems in pronoun reference. If a sentence contains no errors, write *Correct* beside it.

> *The professor's note*
> EXAMPLE: ~~It~~ said that the grades would be posted on Tuesday.

A notice on
1. ~~On~~ the bulletin board says there will be a fire drill today.

2. Laverne and Louise they ~~pooled~~ their money to buy a new CD player.

The reporter
3. ~~They~~ said on the news that the naval base will be shut down.

Correct
4. The street that was recently widened is where I used to live.

5. Ivan sat on the couch (in the living room) that he had bought yesterday.

Correct
6. You should underline in your textbooks for better comprehension.

Christina
7. Christina handed Maggie the plate ~~she~~ had bought at the flea market.

8. Bridget found the cake mix (in the aisle with the baking supplies) that she needed for tonight's dessert.

"I   "
9. Rick told Larry, ~~he~~ was right.

According to   ,
10. ~~It said in~~ the letter ~~that~~ my payment was late.

EXERCISE 8-3 Write a paragraph on one of the following topics. After you have written your first draft, reread to be certain your pronoun references are clear. Make corrections if needed.

1. a recent clothing fad
2. advice columns
3. horoscopes
4. remembering names
5. an extreme weather condition (heat wave, storm, snow, flood) that you lived through

Pronoun-Antecedent Agreement

A pronoun must "agree" with its antecedent—that is, a pronoun must have the same number (singular or plural) as the noun or pronoun it refers to or replaces. Singular nouns and pronouns refer to one person, place, or thing; plural nouns and pronouns refer to more than one.

Always check your sentences for pronoun-antecedent agreement.

plural   singular
↓   ↓
UNCLEAR: The dogs are in its kennels.
CLEAR: The dogs are in their kennels.

plural   singular

UNCLEAR: Marcia and Megan called all her friends about the party.

CLEAR: Marcia and Megan called all their friends about the party.

Use the following guidelines to make sure your pronouns agree with their antecedents.

1. Use singular pronouns with singular nouns.

singular noun   singular pronoun

Marsha sold her bicycle.

2. Use plural pronouns with plural nouns.

plural noun   plural pronoun

The neighbors always shovel their walks when it snows.

3. Use a plural pronoun to refer to a compound antecedent joined by *and,* unless both parts of the compound refer to the same person, place, or thing.

plural antecedent   plural pronoun

Mark and Keith bought their concert tickets.

singular antecedent   singular pronoun

The pitcher and team captain broke her ankle.

4. When antecedents are joined by *or, nor, either . . . or, neither . . . nor, not . . . but,* or *not only . . . but also,* the pronoun agrees in number with the nearer antecedent.

plural noun   plural pronoun

Either the professor or the students will present their views.

Note: When one antecedent is singular and the other is plural, avoid awkwardness by placing the plural antecedent second in the sentence.

AWKARD: Neither the salespersons nor the manager has received his check.

REVISED: Neither the manager nor the salespersons have received their checks.

5. Avoid using *he, him,* or *his* to refer to general singular words such as *child, person, everyone.* These words exclude females. Use *he or she, him or her,* or *his or hers,* or rewrite your sentence to use a plural antecedent and a plural pronoun that do not indicate gender.

INCORRECT: A <u>person</u> should not deceive <u>his</u> friends.

REVISED: A <u>person</u> should not deceive <u>his or her</u> friends.

BETTER: <u>People</u> should not deceive <u>their</u> friends.

6. With collective nouns (words that refer to a group of people, such as *army, class, congregation, audience*), use a singular pronoun to refer to the noun when the group acts as a unit.

The <u>audience</u> showed <u>its</u> approval by applauding.

The <u>team</u> chose <u>its</u> captain.

Use a plural pronoun to refer to the noun when each member of the group acts individually.

The <u>family</u> exchanged <u>their</u> gifts.

The <u>team</u> changed <u>their</u> uniforms.

EXERCISE 8-4 Revise each of the following sentences to correct errors in pronoun-antecedent agreement.

EXAMPLE: Usually when a driver has been caught speeding, ~~they~~ *he or she* readily admit the mistake.

1. Each gas station in town raised ~~their~~ *its* prices in the past week.

2. Neither the waitresses nor the hostess received ~~their~~ *her* paycheck from the restaurant.

3. The committee put ~~his or her~~ *their* signatures on the document.

4. An infant recognizes ~~their~~ *his or her* parents within the first few weeks of life.

5. The Harris family lives by ~~his or her~~ *their* own rules.

6. Lonnie and Jack should put ~~his~~ *their* ideas together and come up with a plan of action.

7. An employee taking an unpaid leave of absence may choose to make ~~their~~ *his or her* own health-insurance payments.

8. The amount of time a student spends researching a topic depends, in part, on ~~their~~ *his or her* familiarity with the topic.

their

9. Alex and Susana lost ~~her~~ way while driving through the suburbs of Philadelphia.

10. Neither the attorney nor the protesters were willing to expose ~~himself~~ to public criticism.

themselves

Agreement with Indefinite Pronouns

Indefinite pronouns (such as *some, everyone, any, each*) are pronouns without specific antecedents. They refer to people, places, or things in general. When an indefinite pronoun is an antecedent for another pronoun, mistakes in pronoun agreement often result. Use the following guidelines to make your pronouns agree with indefinite pronoun antecedents.

1. Use singular pronouns to refer to indefinite pronouns that are singular in meaning.

another	either	nobody	other
anybody	everybody	no one	somebody
anyone	everyone	nothing	someone
anything	everything	one	something
each	neither		

singular   singular
antecedent   pronoun

<u>Someone</u> left <u>his</u> dress shirt in the locker room.

singular antecedent   singular compound pronoun

<u>Everyone</u> in the office must pick up <u>his or her</u> paycheck.

Note: To avoid the awkwardness of *his or her*, use plural antecedents and pronouns.

plural antecedent   plural pronoun

Office <u>workers</u> must pick up <u>their</u> paychecks.

2. Use a plural pronoun to refer to indefinite pronouns that are plural in meaning.

both   few   many   more   several

plural antecedent   plural pronoun

<u>Both</u> of the policemen said that, as far as <u>they</u> could tell, no traffic violations had occurred.

3. The indefinite pronouns *all, any, more, most,* **and** *some* **can be singular or plural, depending on how they are used.** If the indefinite pronoun refers to something that cannot be counted, use a singular pronoun to refer to it. If the indefinite pronoun refers to two or more of something that can be counted, use a plural pronoun to refer to it.

<u>Most</u> of the students feel <u>they</u> can succeed.

<u>Most</u> of the air on airplanes is recycled repeatedly, so <u>it</u> becomes stale.

EXERCISE 8-5 ▶ Revise each of the following sentences to correct errors in pronoun-antecedent agreement.

  EXAMPLE: No one could remember their student number.
  REVISED: No one could remember his or her student number.
  BETTER: The students could not remember their student numbers.

1. Someone left ~~their~~ jacket in the car.
   his or her

2. Everything Todd said was true, but I did not like the way he said ~~them.~~

3. In my math class, everyone works at ~~their~~ own pace.
   it   *his or her*

4. When someone exercises, ~~they~~ should drink plenty of liquids.
   he or she

5. No one should be forced into a curriculum that ~~they~~ do not want.
   he or she es

6. No one will receive ~~their~~ exam grades before Friday.
   his or her

7. Many of the club members do not pay ~~his or her~~ dues on time.
   their

8. Both of the cooks used ~~her~~ own secret recipe.
   their

9. No one was successful on ~~their~~ first attempt to run the race in less than two hours.
   his or her

10. Each of the workers brought ~~their~~ own tools.
    his or her

EXERCISE 8-6 ▶ Revise the sentences below that contain agreement errors. If a sentence contains no errors, write *Correct* beside it.

  EXAMPLE: Somebody dropped ~~their~~ ring down the drain.
                        his or her

1. Many of ~~the residents of the~~ neighborhood*s* have had their homes
   [*our* above "the residents of the"] [*s* above "neighborhood"]
   tested for radon.

2. Each college instructor established ~~their~~ own grading policies.
   [*his or her* above "their"]

3. The apple*s* fell from its tree.

4. Anyone may enter ~~their~~ painting in the contest.
   [*his or her* above "their"]

   [*Correct*]
5. All the engines manufactured at the plant have their vehicle-
   identification numbers stamped on.

6. No one requested that the clerk gift-wrap ~~their~~ package.
   [*his or her* above "their"]

7. Either Professor Judith Marcos or her assistant, Maria, graded the
   exams, writing ~~their~~ comments in the margins.
   [*her* above "their"]

8. James or his parents sail*s* the boat every weekend.

9. Most classes were not canceled because of the snowstorm; ~~it~~ met as
   regularly scheduled.
   [*they* above "it"]

10. Not only Ricky but also the Carters will take ~~his~~ children to
    Disneyland this summer.
    [*their* above "his"]

EXERCISE 8-7 ▶ Reread the paragraph you wrote for Exercise 8-3 to be certain that there
are no errors in pronoun-antecedent agreement. Revise as needed.

NEED TO KNOW

Pronouns

- **Pronouns** substitute for or refer to nouns or other pronouns.
- The noun or pronoun to which a pronoun refers is called its **antecedent.**
- Make sure that it is always clear to which noun or pronoun a pronoun refers.
- A pronoun must agree with its antecedent in number (singular or plural).
  Singular nouns and pronouns refer to one thing; plural nouns and pronouns
  refer to more than one.
- **Indefinite pronouns** are pronouns without specific antecedents. Follow the
  rules given in this chapter to make indefinite pronouns agree with their
  antecedents.

Avoiding Shifts in Person, Number, and Verb Tense

The parts of a sentence should be consistent. Shifts within a sentence in person, number, or verb tense make the sentence confusing and difficult to read.

Shifts in Person

Person is the grammatical term used to identify the speaker or writer (**first person:** *I, we*), the person spoken to (**second person:** *you*), and the person or thing spoken about (**third person:** *he, she, it, they,* or any noun, such as *Joan, children*). Be sure to refer to yourself, your audience (or readers), and people you are writing about in a consistent way throughout your sentence or paragraph.

In the following paragraph, note how the writer shifts back and forth when addressing her audience:

> A <u>person</u> should know how to cook. <u>You</u> can save a lot of money if <u>you</u> make <u>your</u> own meals instead of eating out. <u>One</u> can also eat more healthily at home if <u>one</u> cooks according to principles of good nutrition.

Here the writer shifts from sentence to sentence, first using the indefinite phrase *a person*, then the more personal *you*, then the more formal *one*.

In the next paragraph, the writer shifts when referring to himself.

> Florida has many advantages for year-round living, so <u>I</u> am hoping to move there when <u>I</u> graduate. One reason <u>I</u> want to live in Florida is that <u>you</u> never need to shovel snow.

In this paragraph, the writer shifts from the direct and personal *I* to the indirect and more general *you*.

To avoid making shifts in references to yourself and others, decide before you begin to write how you will refer to yourself, to your audience, and to those you are writing about. Base your decision on whether you want your paragraph to be direct and personal or more formal. In academic writing, most instructors prefer that you avoid using the personal pronoun *I* and try to write in a more formal style.

PERSONAL:	I want to live in Florida for a number of reasons.
MORE FORMAL:	Living in Florida is attractive for a number of reasons.
PERSONAL:	I have difficulty balancing school and a part-time job.
MORE FORMAL:	Balancing school and a part-time job is difficult.

Shifts in Number

Number distinguishes between singular and plural. A pronoun must agree in number with its antecedent. Related nouns within a sentence must also agree in number.

SHIFT: All the <u>women</u> wore a <u>dress</u>.
CONSISTENT: All the <u>women</u> wore <u>dresses</u>.

EXERCISE ▶ 8-8 Revise each of the following sentences to correct shifts in person or number.

me
EXAMPLE: I perform better on exams if the professor doesn't hover over ~~you~~.

Students have
1. ~~Each student has~~ to plan their schedules for the semester.

she has
2. Eva said she doesn't want to go to the wedding because ~~you have~~ to bring a gift.

3. In some states, continuing education is required for doctors or
they   they
lawyers; after ~~you~~ pass the board or bar exam, ~~you~~ are required to take a specified number of credits per year in brush-up courses.

s
4. Construction workers must wear a hard hat.

I
5. I swim with a life vest on because ~~you~~ could drown.

G   s are
6. ~~A~~ good friend ~~is~~ always there when you most need them.

their
7. The first and second relay racers discussed ~~his~~ strategies.

myself
8. I always tell ~~yourself~~ to think before acting.

they
9. Patients often expect their doctors to have all the answers, but ~~you~~ should realize doctors are not miracle workers.

The   s   s
10. ~~Each~~ giraffe stretched their neck to reach the leaves in the trees.

Shifts in Verb Tense

Use the same verb tense (past, present, future) throughout a sentence and paragraph unless meaning requires you to make a shift.

present   future

REQUIRED SHIFT: After the moon rises, we will go for a moonlight swim.

Incorrect shifts in verb tense can make a sentence confusing. One of the most common incorrect shifts is between present and past tenses.

past   present

INCORRECT: After Marguerite joined the food co-op, she seems healthier.

past   past

CORRECT: After Marguerite joined the food co-op, she seemed healthier.

EXERCISE 8-9 ▶ Revise each of the following sentences to correct shifts in verb tense.

             waited

EXAMPLE: I ~~was waiting~~ for the hailstorm to end, and then I dashed into the restaurant.

1. The factory workers punch in in the morning, but they ~~have~~ [do] not ~~punched~~ out at night.

2. José looked muscular; then he joined a gym and look~~s~~ [ed] even more muscular.

3. I ~~run~~ [ran] two miles, and then I rested.

4. Quinne call~~ed~~ [s] me but hangs up on my answering machine.

5. Until I took physics, I ~~will~~ [did] not understand the laws of aerodynamics.

6. While the rain fell, the campers ~~take~~ [took] shelter in their tent.

7. Because the moon will be full, the tide ~~was~~ [will be] high.

8. Katie drives me to work, and I work~~ed~~ until 9:30 P.M.

9. Richard went to the mall because he need [ed] to buy a suit for his job interview.

10. The speaker ~~stands~~ [stood] at the podium and cleared his throat.

> **NEED TO KNOW**
>
> **Shifts in Person, Number, and Verb Tense**
>
> • **Person** is a term used to identify the speaker or writer (**first person:** *I, we*), the person spoken to, **second person:** *you*), and the person or thing spoken about (**third person:** *he, she, it, they,* or any noun, such as *desk* or *Robert*).
>
> • Be sure to use a consistent person throughout a piece of writing.
>
> • **Number** distinguishes between singular and plural. A pronoun must agree in number with its antecedent.
>
> • **Verb tense** is the form of a verb that indicates whether the action or state of being that the verb tells about occurs in the past, present, or future. Unless there is a specific reason to switch tenses, be sure to use a consistent tense throughout a piece of writing.

EXERCISE 8-10 ▶ Revise each of the following sentences to correct errors in shift of person, number, or verb tense. If a sentence contains no errors, write Correct beside it.

EXAMPLE: Boats along the river were tied to their dock.

1. When people receive a gift, you should be gracious and polite.

2. When we arrived at the inn, the lights are on and a fire is burning in the fireplace.

3. Before Trey drove to the cabin, he packs a picnic lunch.

Correct
4. The artist paints portraits and weaves baskets.

5. The lobsterman goes out on his boat each day and will check his lobster traps.

6. All the cars Honest Bob sells have a new transmission.

7. Rosa ran the 100-meter race and throws the discus at the track meet.

8. Public schools in Florida have an air-conditioning system.

9. Office workers sat on the benches downtown and are eating their lunches outside.

         s   they

10. Before ~~a~~ scuba diver go underwater, ~~you~~ must check and recheck
  ~~your~~ breathing equipment.
  their

EXERCISE 8-11 ▶   Reread the paragraph you wrote for Exercise 8-3. Check for shifts in person, number, and verb tense. Make necessary revisions.

Avoiding Misplaced and Dangling Modifiers

A **modifier** is a word, phrase, or clause that describes, qualifies, or limits the meaning of another word. Modifiers that are not correctly placed can confuse your reader.

Types of Modifiers

The following list will help you review the main types of modifiers.

1. Adjectives modify nouns and pronouns.

It is an interesting photograph.

She is very kind.

2. Adverbs modify verbs, adjectives, or other adverbs.

I walked quickly.

The cake tasted very good.

The flowers are very beautifully arranged.

3. Prepositional phrases modify nouns, adjectives, verbs, or adverbs.

The woman in the green dress is stunning.

They walked into the store to buy milk.

4. *-ing* phrases modify nouns or pronouns.

Waiting for the bus, Joe studied his history notes.

5. Dependent clauses modify nouns, adjectives, verbs, or adverbs. (A dependent clause has a subject and verb but is incomplete in meaning.)

After I left campus, I went shopping.

I left because classes were canceled.

The kitten that I found in the bushes was frightened.

Misplaced Modifiers

Placement of a modifier in a sentence affects meaning:

I need <u>only</u> to buy Marcos a gift.

<u>Only</u> I need to buy Marcos a gift.

I need to buy <u>only</u> Marcos a gift.

If a modifier is placed so that it does not convey the meaning you intend, it is called a **misplaced modifier.** Misplaced modifiers can make a sentence confusing.

MISPLACED: Anthony found a necklace at the mall <u>that was sparkling and glittering</u>. [Which was sparkling and glittering—the mall or the necklace?]

MISPLACED: The president announced that the club picnic would be held on August 2 <u>at the beginning of the meeting</u>. [Is the picnic being held at the beginning of the meeting on August 2, or did the president make the announcement at the beginning of the meeting?]

You can avoid a misplaced modifier if you make sure that the modifier immediately precedes or follows the word it modifies.

CORRECT: Anthony found a necklace <u>that was sparkling and glittering</u> at the mall.

CORRECT: The club president announced <u>at the beginning of the meeting</u> that the picnic would be held on August 2.

Dangling Modifiers

Dangling modifiers are words or phrases that do not clearly describe or explain any part of the sentence. Dangling modifiers create confusion and sometimes unintentional humor. To avoid dangling modifiers, make sure that each modifying phrase or clause has a clear antecedent.

DANGLING: <u>Uncertain of which street to follow</u>, the <u>map</u> indicated we should turn left. [The opening modifier suggests that the map was uncertain of which street to follow.]

CORRECT: <u>Uncertain of which street to follow</u>, <u>we</u> checked a map, which indicated we should turn left.

DANGLING: My <u>shoes</u> got wet <u>walking across the street</u>. [The modifier suggests that the shoes were walking across the street.]

CORRECT: My shoes got wet <u>as I crossed the street</u>.

DANGLING: To pass the test, careful review is essential. [Who will pass the test?]

CORRECT: To pass the test, I must review carefully.

There are two common ways to revise dangling modifiers.

1. Add a word or words that the modifier clearly describes. Place the new material immediately after the modifier, and rearrange other parts of the sentence as necessary.

DANGLING: While walking in the garden, gunfire sounded. [The opening modifier implies that the gunfire was walking in the garden.]

CORRECT: While walking in the garden, Carol heard gunfire.

2. Change the dangling modifier to a dependent clause. (See pages 64–65.) You may need to change the verb form in the modifier.

DANGLING: While watching television, the cake burned.

CORRECT: While Pat was watching television, the cake burned.

EXERCISE 8-12 ▶ | Revise each of the following sentences to correct misplaced or dangling modifiers.

EXAMPLE: Jerome mailed a bill at the post office that was long overdue.

REVISED: At the post office, Jerome mailed a bill that was long overdue.

1. Running at top speed, dirt was kicked up by the horse. _____

   Running at top speed, the horse kicked up dirt.

2. Swimming to shore, my arms got tired. While I was swimming

   to shore, my arms got tired.

3. The helmet on the soldier's head with a red circle represented his

   nationality. The helmet with a red circle on the soldier's head represented

   his nationality.

4. In order to answer your phone, the receiver must be lifted.

   In order to answer your phone, you must lift the receiver.

   _____

5. Walking up the stairs, the book dropped and tumbled down.

   As I walked up the stairs, the book dropped and tumbled down.

   _____

6. Twenty-five band members picked their instruments up from chairs which were gleaming and began to play. <u>Twenty-five band members</u>

<u>picked up their gleaming instruments from their chairs and began to play.</u>

7. Laughing, the cat chased the girl. <u>The cat chased the laughing girl.</u>

_____

8. When skating, ice-skate blades must be kept sharp. <u>When you are</u>

<u>skating, you must keep your ice-skate blades sharp.</u>

9. The ball bounced off the roof that was round and red. _____

<u>The ball that was round and red bounced off the roof.</u>

10. Ducking, the snowball hit Andy on the head. <u>As Andy ducked, the</u>

<u>snowball hit him on the head.</u>

EXERCISE ▶ 8-13 ▶ Revise each of the following sentences to correct misplaced or dangling modifiers.

EXAMPLE: Deciding which flavor of ice cream to order, another customer cut in front of Roger.

REVISED: While Roger was deciding which flavor of ice cream to order, another customer cut in front of him.

1. Tricia saw an animal at the zoo that had black fur and long claws.

<u>At the zoo Tricia saw an animal that had black fur and long claws.</u>

2. Before answering the door, the phone rang. <u>Before I answered the</u>

<u>the door, the phone rang.</u>

3. I could see large snowflakes falling from the bedroom window.

<u>From the bedroom window I could see large snowflakes falling.</u>

4. Honking, Felicia walked in front of the car. <u>Felicia walked in front</u>

<u>of the honking car.</u>

5. After leaving the classroom, the door automatically locked.

<u>After we left the classroom, the door automatically locked.</u>

6. Applauding and cheering, the band returned for an encore.

<u>As the audience applauded and cheered, the band returned for an encore.</u>

7. The waiter brought a birthday cake to our table that had twenty-
   four candles. <u>The waiter brought to our table a birthday cake that had</u>

   <u>twenty-four candles.</u>

8. Books lined the library shelves about every imaginable subject.

   <u>Books about every imaginable subject lined the library shelves.</u>

9. While sobbing, the sad movie ended and the lights came on.

   <u>While everyone was sobbing, the sad movie ended and the lights came on.</u>

10. Turning the page, the book's binding cracked. <u>As I turned the page,</u>

    <u>the book's binding cracked.</u>

EXERCISE ▶ 8-14 | Reread the paragraph you wrote for Exercise 8-3. Check for dangling or misplaced modifiers. Revise as needed.

NEED TO KNOW

Misplaced and Dangling Modifiers

- A **modifier** is a word, phrase, or clause that describes, qualifies, or limits the meaning of another word.
- A **misplaced modifier** is placed so that it does not convey the intended meaning.
- To avoid misplaced modifiers, be sure that you place the modifier immediately before or after the word it modifies.
- A **dangling modifier** is a word or phrase that does not clearly describe or explain any part of the sentence.
- To revise a dangling modifier you can add a word or words that the modifier clearly describes, or change the dangling modifier to a dependent clause.

Using Parallelism

Study the following pairs of sentences. Which sentence in each pair reads more smoothly?

1. Seth, a long-distance biker, enjoys swimming and drag races cars.
2. Seth enjoys long-distance biking, swimming, and drag racing.
3. The dog was large, had a beautiful coat, and it was friendly.
4. The dog was large, beautiful, and friendly.

Do sentences 2 and 4 sound better than 1 and 3? Sentences 2 and 4 have balance. Similar words have similar grammatical form. In sentence 2, *biking, swimming,* and *drag racing* are all nouns ending in *-ing*. In sentence 4, *large, beautiful,* and *friendly* are all adjectives. The method of balancing similar elements within a sentence is called **parallelism**. Parallelism adds smoothness to your writing and makes your ideas easier to follow.

EXERCISE 8-15   In each group of words, circle the element that is not parallel.

> EXAMPLE: walking, running, (to jog,) dancing

1. intelligent, successful, (responsibly,) mature
2. happily, quickly, hurriedly, (hungry)
3. wrote, (answering,) worked, typed
4. to fly, (parachutes,) to skydive, to drive
5. were painting, (drew,) were carving, were coloring
6. sat in the sun, played cards, (scuba diving,) ate lobster
7. thoughtful, (honestly,) humorous, quick tempered
8. (rewrote my résumé,) arranging interviews, buying a new suit, getting a haircut
9. buy stamps, cash check, (dry cleaning,) return library books
10. eating sensibly, (8 hours of sleep,) exercising, drinking lots of water

What Should Be Parallel?

When you write, be sure to keep each of the following elements parallel.

1. Nouns in a series.

NOT PARALLEL: The callers on the talk show included a teenager, a man who worked in construction, and a flight attendant.

PARALLEL: The callers on the talk show included a teenager, a construction worker, and a flight attendant.

2. Adjectives in a series.

NOT PARALLEL: The students in the class seemed tired and not paying attention.

PARALLEL: The students in the class seemed <u>tired</u> and <u>bored</u>.

     adjective   adjective

3. Verbs in a series. (They should have the same tense.)

    simple past   past progressive

NOT PARALLEL: The couple <u>danced</u> and <u>were joking</u>.

    simple past   simple past

PARALLEL: The couple <u>danced</u> and <u>joked</u>.

4. Clauses within sentences.

    prepositional phrase

NOT PARALLEL: The students were angry <u>about the parking difficulties</u> and <u>that no one is concerned</u>.

    dependent clause

    dependent clause

PARALLEL: The students were angry <u>that it is difficult to park</u> and <u>that no one is concerned</u>.

    dependent clause

5. Items being compared or contrasted.

    noun   infinitive phrase

NOT PARALLEL: <u>Honesty</u> is better than <u>to be dishonest</u>.

    infinitive phrase   infinitive phrase

PARALLEL: It is better <u>to be honest</u> than <u>to be dishonest</u>.

    noun   pronoun

NOT PARALLEL: The students wanted <u>parking spaces</u>, not <u>someone to feel sorry for them</u>.

    infinitive phrase

    noun   noun

PARALLEL: The students wanted <u>parking spaces</u>, not <u>sympathy</u>.

EXERCISE 8-16 Revise each of the following sentences to correct errors in parallel structure.

    demanded hard work

EXAMPLE: The instructor ~~was demanding~~ and insisted on high standards.

1. Accuracy is more important than ~~being~~ speedy.

2. The teller counted and recounts the money. *(ed)*

3. Newspapers are blowing away and ~~scattered~~ on the sidewalk. *(ing)*

4. Judith was pleased when she graduated and ~~that she~~ received an honors diploma.

5. Thrilled and exhaus~~ting,~~ the runners crossed the finish line. *(ed)*

6. Our guest speakers for the semester are a radiologist, a student ~~studying medicine~~, and a hospital administrator. *(medical)*

7. Students shouted and were hollering at the basketball game. *(ed)*

8. We enjoyed seeing the Grand Canyon, riding a mule, and photography. *(taking)* *(s)*

9. Laughing and relax~~ed,~~ the co-workers enjoyed lunch at the Mexican restaurant. *(ing)*

10. Professor Higuera is well known for his humor, clear lecturing, and scholarship. *(es)*

EXERCISE ▶ 8-17 ▶ Revise each of the following sentences to achieve parallelism.

> EXAMPLE: Rosa has decided to study nursing instead of ~~going into~~ accounting.

1. The priest baptized the baby and congratulates the new parents. *(d)*

2. We ordered a platter of fried clams, a platter of corn on the cob, and fried shrimp. *(a platter of)*

3. Lucy entered the dance contest, but the dance ~~was watched by June~~ from the side. *(June watched)*

4. Léon purchased the ratchet set at the garage sale and ~~buying~~ the drill bits there too. *(bought)*

5. The exterminator told Brandon the house needed to be fumigated and spray~~ing~~ to eliminate the termites. *(ed)*

6. The bus swerved and hit the dump truck, which swerve~~s~~ [d] and hit the station wagon, which swerved and hit the bicycle.

7. Channel 2 covered the bank robbery, but [Channel 7 covered] a python that had escaped from the zoo ~~was reported by Channel 7~~.

8. Sal was born while Nixon was president, and [Rob was born while] ~~Johnson was president when Rob was born.~~
[Johnson was president.]

9. The pediatrician spent the morning [looking at] ~~with~~ sore throats, answering questions about immunizations, and treating bumps and bruises.

10. Belinda prefers to study in the library, but her brother Marcus [prefers to] ~~studies~~ at home.

EXERCISE **8-18** Reread the paragraph you wrote for Exercise 8-3. Correct any sentences that lack parallelism.

NEED TO KNOW

Parallelism

- **Parallelism** is a method of balancing similar elements within a sentence.
- The following elements of a sentence should be parallel: nouns in a series, adjectives in a series, verbs in a series, clauses within a sentence, and items being compared or contrasted.

EXERCISE **8-19** Now that you have learned about common errors that produce confusing or inconsistent sentences, turn back to the humorous sentences used to introduce the chapter on page 188. Identify each error, and revise the sentence so it conveys the intended meaning.

EXERCISE **8-20** Revise this student paragraph by correcting all instances of misplaced or dangling modifiers, shifts in verb tense, and faulty parallelism.

Robert Burns said that the dog is "man's best friend." To a large extent, this statement may be more true than we think. What makes dogs so special to humans is their unending loyalty

and ~~that they love~~ unconditionally. Dogs have been known to
[their] [love]

cross the entire United States to return home. Unlike people,

dogs never ~~made~~ fun of you or criticize you. They never throw
[make]

fits, and they seem happy always to see you. This may not nec-

essarily be true of your family, friends, and ~~those who live near~~
[neighbors]

~~you~~. A dog never lies to you, never betrays your confidences,

and never stayed angry with you for more than five minutes.
[s]

Best of all, he never expects more than the basics from you of

food and shelter and a simple pat on the head in return for his

devotion. The world would be a better place if only people could

be more like their dogs.

WRITING ABOUT A READING

Thinking before Reading

The following reading, "Job-Getting Techniques," is taken from a business communications textbook. It offers practical advice on finding a job. Note the author's carefully written, well-constructed sentences. In particular, notice the parallel structure used in sentences presenting items in a series.

Before you read:

1. Preview the reading using the steps provided on page 20.

2. After you have done your preview, connect the reading to your own experience by answering the following questions:

   a. What strategies have you already used in finding part-time or full-time jobs?

   b. Which strategies were successful? Why?

READING

Job-Getting Techniques
Scott Ober

Do not depend on any single technique for landing the ideal job. Instead, use every technique at your disposal that you feel can benefit you. Some of the more popular ones are networking, using professional employment services, and answering advertisements.   1

NETWORKING

In the job-getting process, networking refers to developing a group of acquaintances who might provide job leads and career guidance. The term has been used so much recently that it has perhaps become a buzz-word, but it is still an important job-getting tool. Everyone—from the most recent college graduate to the president of a Fortune 500 firm—has a network on which to draw in searching for a job.   2

Your initial network might include friends, family, professors, former employers, social acquaintances, college alumni, your dentist, family doctor, insurance agent, local businesspeople, your minister or rabbi—in short, everyone you know who might be able to help. Ideally, your network will combine both personal and professional connections. That's one benefit of belonging to professional associations, and college isn't too early to start. Most professional organizations either have student chapters of their associations or provide reduced-rate student memberships in the parent organization.   3

Certainly, you don't develop a network of acquaintances purely for personal gain; the friendships gained through such contacts can last a lifetime. But don't forget to seek the advice and help of everyone who can be of assistance in this important endeavor.   4

PROFESSIONAL EMPLOYMENT SERVICES

Professional employment services include your college placement office, the state employment service, private employment agencies, and private career consulting services. The college placement office is generally the first, the most effective, and often the only source of help used by most graduating students. Such offices typically provide career information, critique student résumés, and arrange interviews with campus recruiters.   5

Your state employment service can provide information on job   6
vacancies, job requirements, training programs available, and local economic conditions. For a fee, private employment agencies seek to match
vacancies at a firm with qualified applicants. Their primary allegiance is
to whoever pays their fee; the fee is sometimes paid by the applicant and
sometimes by the employer. Career consultants charge a fee for the service of helping people identify and promote their own strengths; their
services range from helping with résumé writing, to administering interest and aptitude tests, to career counseling.

ANSWERING ADVERTISEMENTS

Any large daily newspaper contains hundreds of classified ads of job   7
openings, and you would be wise to scan them. Often you can pick up
important words and phrases that will help you describe yourself appro-
priately in your résumé and application letter.

Be aware, however, that most jobs are not filled through want ads;   8
in fact, only 14% are. The methods by which all jobs are typically filled
are shown here as percentages of the whole:

Networking or personal contacts	70%
Help-wanted ads	14
Executive search firms	11
Mass mailing of résumés	5
	100%

For hiring new college graduates, on-campus interviewing is the   9
major source of jobs, accounting for 42% of all selections, with
responses from help-wanted ads accounting for 8%.

If you use want ads, don't rely on them exclusively; follow other   10
leads as well. In addition, to increase your chances respond as soon as
you see a suitable position advertised.

Many newspaper ads are "blind" ads; that is, instead of listing a   11
company name and address, they simply provide a box number for
responding to the ad. Although most such ads are legitimate, a word of
caution is in order. There have been instances of people submitting their
résumés in response to these blind ads who have been victimized as a
result of harassing phone calls, burglary, or even bodily harm. After all,
your résumé often contains your home address, home phone number,
and perhaps even the hours when you're most likely to be at home.
Anyone expecting to make heavy use of newspaper ads would be well
advised to rent a post-office box for this purpose.

From Scott Ober, *Contemporary Business Communication.*

Getting Ready to Write

Strengthening Your Vocabulary

Write a brief definition for each of the following words from the preceding reading. If you cannot figure out the meaning of a word from the way it is used in the reading, look the word up in a dictionary.

1. disposal (paragraph 1)   command, power to organize

2. network (paragraph 3)   collection of people with common interests

3. critique (paragraph 5)   evaluate, suggest how to improve

4. allegiance (paragraph 6)   loyalty

5. promote (paragraph 6)   sell or advertise

6. legitimate (paragraph 11)   authentic, genuine

7. harassing (paragraph 11)   irritating, annoying

Reviewing the Reading Using an Idea Map

Review the reading be completing the missing pieces of the idea map shown below.

USE A NUMBER OF JOB-GETTING TECHNIQUES
TO LAND THE IDEAL JOB.

Networking

Acquaintances who provide job leads and career guidance

Network combines personal and professional connections

Professional organizations; student chapters; memberships

Can lead to lifetime friendships

Professional employment services

College placement office

| State employment service |
| Private employment agencies |
| Career consultants |

| Answering advertisements |
| Scan classified ads in daily newspaper |
| Only 14% of jobs filled through want ads |
| Don't rely on just ads; follow other leads |
| Respond to ads immediately |
| Beware of "blind" ads |
| If use ads heavily, rent post-office box |

Examining the Reading

1. In what order does the author present the three job-finding techniques? Why?

2. How can networking help you find a job?

3. Which of the professional employment services is most effective in helping you locate a job?

4. What is the major source of jobs for new college graduates?

Reacting to and Discussing Ideas

Get ready to write about the reading by discussing the following questions:

1. Make a list of contact people you could include in a job-seeking network; include their relationship to you. Compare your list with other students' lists.

2. Review the want ads in your local newspaper. Are "blind" ads included? Why would a company run a "blind" ad?

3. Have you ever contacted your state employment service? If so, evaluate its effectiveness.

Writing about the Reading

The Paragraph Option

1. Write a paragraph explaining how you found a part- or full-time job or how you would go about finding a new job.

2. Imagine you have applied for a job and have been asked to describe in writing your strongest personal asset. Write a paragraph response.

The Essay Option

Write an essay describing someone you would include in your job-search network. Explain how he or she might be useful in helping you find a job.

WRITING SUCCESS TIP 8

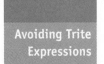

Avoiding Trite Expressions

Trite expressions, also known as **clichés,** are tired words and phrases that have been used so often they have become stale. They hurt your writing by making it seem lazy and bland.

The following list of trite expressions probably includes some you hear and use frequently:

add insult to injury	heavy as lead
all work and no play	hit the nail on the head
better late than never	ladder of success
beyond a shadow of a doubt	singing the blues
drop in the bucket	strong as an ox
easier said than done	tried and true
face the music	work like a dog

Trite expressions like these take the place of original, specific, meaningful descriptions in your writing. When you use a trite expression, you have lost a chance to convey a fresh, precise impression. Meaning suffers. Notice, in the sets of sentences below, that the revised version gives you much more precise and complete information.

TRITE: I worked like a dog to finish my term paper.

REVISED: I worked until midnight every night last week to finish my term paper.

TRITE: He smokes like a chimney.

REVISED: He smokes two packs of Camel cigarettes a day.

TRITE: My favorite restaurant is a hop, skip, and jump from my apartment.

REVISED: My favorite restaurant is a safe, easy, five-minute walk from my apartment, all downhill.

TRITE: I huffed and puffed into work thinking "better late than never" but I knew I would have to face the music.

REVISED: I jogged to work and was only a half hour late, but I knew I would get an angry lecture from my manager.

Whenever you find yourself using a trite expression, stop and take the time to reword it into an original, detailed description.

Using Verbs Correctly

9

Verbs are an important part of any language because they express action: *swim, walk, dance, eat.* Using them correctly is essential.

CHAPTER OBJECTIVES

In this chapter you will learn to

1. use verb tenses correctly.

2. use irregular verbs correctly.

3. avoid subject-verb agreement errors.

4. use active instead of passive voice.

WRITING

Using Verb Tenses Correctly

The primary function of verbs is to express action. However, verbs also indicate time. **Verb tenses** tell us whether an action takes place in the present, past, or future.

The three basic verb tenses are the **simple present, simple past,** and **simple future.** In this chapter we will concentrate on using these three tenses correctly. There are also nine other verb tenses in English. To review these tenses, see Part IX, "Reviewing the Basics," pages 447–507. Using verb tenses consistently (avoiding shifts in tense) is discussed in Chapter 8, on pages 198–199.

There are two types of verbs: *regular* and *irregular.* The forms of **regular verbs** follow a standard pattern of endings; the forms of irregular verbs do not. The English language contains many more regular verbs than irregular verbs. In this section we will focus on forming verb tenses with regular verbs. Later in the chapter we will look at forming verb tenses with irregular verbs.

The Simple Present Tense

The **present tense** indicates action that is occurring at the time of speaking or describes regular, habitual action.

217

Action at time of speaking: I see a rabbit in the lawn.

Habitual action: Maria works hard.

The ending of a verb in the **simple present tense** must agree with the subject of the verb. If the verb has one subject, use a singular ending. If the verb has two or more subjects, you must use a plural ending. (For more on subjects, see pages 472–473.)

Simple Present Tense

Singular		Plural	
Subject	**Verb**	**Subject**	**Verb**
I	like	we	like
you	like	you	like
he, she, it	likes	they	like
Sam	likes	Sam and Brenda	like

In speech we often use nonstandard verb forms, and these are perfectly acceptable in informal conversation. However, these nonstandard forms are *not* used in college writing or in career writing.

In the example below, note the nonstandard forms of the verb *lift* and the way these forms differ from the correct standard forms that you should use in writing.

Nonstandard Present	*Standard Present*
Singular	*Singular*
I lifts	I lift
you lifts	you lift
she (he) lift	she (he) lifts
Plural	*Plural*
we lifts	we lift
you lifts	you lift
they lifts	they lift

EXERCISE ▶ 9-1 ▶ The sentences below are in the simple present tense. First, underline the subject or subjects in each sentence. Then circle the correct verb form.

EXAMPLE: Sal (pick, picks) apples.

1. Planes (take, takes) off from the runway every five minutes.
2. I (enjoy, enjoys) sailing.
3. She (own, owns) a pet bird.
4. We (climb, climbs) the ladder to paint the house.
5. Engines (roar, roars) as the race begins.
6. They always (answer, answers) the phone on the first ring.
7. That elephant (walk, walks) very slowly.
8. You (speak, speaks) Spanish fluently.
9. He (say, says) his name is Luis.
10. Dinosaur movies (scare, scares) me.

EXERCISE ▶ 9-2 ▶ For each of the following verbs, write a sentence using the simple present tense. Use a noun or *he, she, it,* or *they* as the subject of the sentence.

EXAMPLE: prefer   Art prefers to sit in the front.

1. call   Mark calls 800 numbers frequently.

2. request   Sam requests an answer by tomorrow.

3. laugh   They laugh together, and they cry together.

4. grow   Yolanda grows a vegetable garden each summer.

5. hide   My son hides under the table.

The Simple Past Tense

The **past tense** refers to action that was completed in the past. To form the **simple past tense** of regular verbs, add *-d* or *-ed* to the verb. Note that with the simple past tense, the verb form does not change with person or number.

Simple Past Tense

Singular		Plural	
Subject	*Verb*	*Subject*	*Verb*
I	worked	we	worked
you	worked	you	worked
he, she, it	worked	they	worked
Sam	worked	Sam and Brenda	worked

In nonstandard English, the *-d* or *-ed* is often dropped. You may hear "Last night I work all night" instead of "Last night I work*ed* all night." In written English, be sure to include the *-d* or *-ed* ending.

The Simple Future Tense

The **future tense** refers to action that *will* happen in the future. Form the **simple future tense** by adding the helping verb *will* before the verb. Note that the verb form does not change with person or number.

Simple Future Tense

Singular		Plural	
Subject	*Verb*	*Subject*	*Verb*
I	will work	we	will work
you	will work	you	will work
he, she, it	will work	they	will work
Sam	will work	Sam and Brenda	will work

EXERCISE 9-3 For each of the following verbs, write a sentence using the simple past tense and one using the simple future tense.

EXAMPLE: overcook   The chef overcooked my steak.

I know he will overcook my steak.

1. dance   I danced until midnight.

We will dance until midnight.

2. hunt   My uncle hunted elk in Canada.

My uncle will hunt elk in Canada.

3. joke   The professor joked with the class.

The professor will joke with the class.

4. watch	We watched the sunset.
	We will watch the sunset.
5. photograph	We photographed the sunset.
	We will photograph the sunset.

EXERCISE 9-4 Write a paragraph on one of the following topics, using either the simple past tense or the simple future tense.

1. selecting a movie to rent
2. cleaning the attic or garage
3. selecting courses for next semester
4. buying groceries
5. caring for a three-year-old child

NEED TO KNOW

Verb Tense

- **Verb tense** indicates whether an action takes place in the present, past, or future.

- There are three basic verb tenses: **simple present, simple past, and simple future.**

- The **simple present tense** indicates action that is occurring at the time of speaking. It can also describe regular, habitual action. The ending of a simple present tense verb must agree with the subject of the verb.

- The **simple past tense** refers to action that was completed in the past. For regular verbs, the simple past tense is formed by adding -*d* or -*ed*.

- The **simple future tense** refers to action that will happen in the future. The simple future tense is formed by adding the helping verb *will* before the verb.

Using Irregular Verbs Correctly

Errors in verb tense can occur easily with irregular verbs. Irregular verbs do not form the simple past tense according to the pattern we have studied. A regular verb forms the simple past tense by adding -*d* or -*ed*. An irregular verb forms the simple past tense by changing its spelling internally (for example, "I feed" becomes "I fed") or by not changing at all (for example, "I cut" remains "I cut").

Three Troublesome Irregular Verbs

The verbs *be, do,* and *have* can be especially troublesome. You should master the correct forms of these verbs in both the present tense and the past tense since they are used so often.

Irregular Verb: Be

	Present	*Past*
Singular	I am	I was
	you are	you were
	he, she, it is	he, she, it was
Plural	we are	we were
	you are	you were
	they are	they were

It is nonstandard to use *be* for all present tense forms.

INCORRECT: I be finished.
CORRECT: I am finished.

INCORRECT: They be surprised.
CORRECT: They are surprised.

Another error is to use *was* instead of *were* for plural past tenses or with *you.*

INCORRECT: We was late.
CORRECT: We were late.

INCORRECT: You was wrong.
CORRECT: You were wrong.

Irregular Verb: Do

	Present	*Past*
Singular	I do	I did
	you do	you did
	he, she, it does	he, she, it did
Plural	we do	we did
	you do	you did
	they do	they did

A common error is to use *does* instead of *do* for present plural forms.

INCORRECT: We does our best.
CORRECT: We do our best.

INCORRECT: They <u>doesn't</u> know the answer.
CORRECT: They <u>don't</u> know the answer.

Another error is to use *done* instead of *did* for past plural forms.

INCORRECT: We <u>done</u> everything.   You <u>done</u> finish.
CORRECT: We <u>did</u> everything.   You <u>did</u> finish.

Irregular Verb: Have

	Present	*Past*
Singular	I have	I had
	you have	you had
	he, she, it has	he, she, it had
Plural	we have	we had
	you have	you had
	they have	they had

A common nonstandard form uses *has* instead of *have* for the present plural.

INCORRECT: We <u>has</u> enough.   They <u>has</u> a good reason.
CORRECT: We <u>have</u> enough.   They <u>have</u> a good reason.

Another error occurs in the past singular.

INCORRECT: I <u>has</u> nothing to give you.   You <u>has</u> a bad day.
CORRECT: I <u>had</u> nothing to give you.   You <u>had</u> a bad day.

EXERCISE 9-5 ▶ Circle the correct, standard form of the verb in each of the following sentences.

EXAMPLE: Last April Anne ((was), were) in Nevada.

1. After I watched the news, I (does, (did)) my homework.
2. You (be, (were)) lucky to win the raffle.
3. The electrician (have, (has)) enough time to complete the job.
4. When I am reading about the Civil War, I ((am), be) captivated.
5. All the waitresses I know ((have), has) sore feet.
6. We (was, (were)) at the grocery store yesterday.
7. He (do, (does)) his studying at the library.
8. We ((did), done) the jigsaw puzzle while it rained.
9. Alice Walker (be, (is)) a favorite author of mine.
10. You (was, (were)) in the audience when the trophy was awarded.

EXERCISE 9-6 | Write a sentence for each irregular verb. Use a singular subject: *I, you, he, she, it,* or a singular noun.

> EXAMPLE: am   I am going to the Bulls game tonight.
>
> be   Will you be at home tonight?

1. do — Do you know the answer?

    does — Tammy does know the answer.

2. was — Ellen was late for class.

    were — Were you late for class?

3. is — Is class cancelled?

    be — When will you be out of class?

4. do — Do you know where I live?

    did — Did you lose your parking spot?

5. am — I am going bowling.

    was — Was the exam difficult?

EXERCISE 9-7 | Write a sentence for each pair of irregular verbs. Use a plural subject: *we, you, they,* or a plural noun.

> EXAMPLE: be   We will be at my dad's house.
>
> were   They were happy to see us.

1. do — We do not want to be overcharged.

    did — We did not attend the lecture.

2. are — We are leaving at two o'clock.

    be — Sam and Andy will be late for dinner.

3. have — Students often have specific career goals.

    had — Maria and John had planned to leave campus at noon.

4. are — The leaves are falling.

    were — The leaves were falling yesterday.

5. be — We will be late for the movie.

    were — Sal and Anthony were planning to be home for dinner, but their plans changed.

EXERCISE 9-8 ▶ Read the following student paragraph and correct all verb errors.

                                         are

Sometimes first impressions of people ~~is~~ very inaccurate and

                                          ed

can lead to problems. My brother, Larry, learn∧this the hard way.

                                      were

When he was seventeen, Larry and I ~~was~~ driving to the mall.

                                      ed

Larry decided to pick up a hitchhiker because he looks∧safe and

                                      d

trustworthy. After the man got in the car, we notice∧that he was

                                      told

wearing a knife. A few miles later, the man suddenly ~~tell~~ us to

take him to Canada. So my brother said we'd have to stop for

                                      got

gas and explained that he did not have any money. The man ~~get~~

                                      went

out of the car to pump the gas. When he ~~goes~~ up to the atten-

                                      did

dant to pay for the gas, we took off. We ~~do~~ not stop until we

        ed   *told*

reach∧the police station, where we ~~tell~~ the officer in charge what

     ed

happens∧ The police caught the man several miles from the gas

        was

station. He ~~be~~ serving time in prison for burglary and had

escaped over the weekend. Later, Larry said, "I was lucky that

                      were

my first impressions ~~was~~ not my last!"

Other Irregular Verbs

Among the other verbs that form the past tense in irregular ways are
become (*became*), *drive* (*drove*), *hide* (*hid*), *stand* (*stood*), and *wear*
(*wore*). For a list of the past-tense forms of other common irregular verbs,
see Part IX, page 467. If you have a question about the form of a verb,
consult this list or your dictionary.

Confusing Pairs of Irregular Verbs

Two particularly confusing pairs of irregular verbs are *lie/lay* and *sit/set*.

Lie/Lay

Lie means to recline. *Lay* means to put something down. The past tense of *lie* is *lay*. The past tense of *lay* is *laid*.

Simple Present	*Simple Past*
Command the dog to <u>lie</u> down.	The dog <u>lay</u> down.
<u>Lay</u> the boards over here.	The carpenter <u>laid</u> the boards over there.

Sit/Set

Sit means to be seated. *Set* means to put something down. The past tense of *sit* is *sat*. The past tense of *set* is *set*.

Simple Present	*Simple Past*
Please <u>sit</u> over here.	We <u>sat</u> over here.
<u>Set</u> the books on the table.	He <u>set</u> the books on the table.

EXERCISE 9-9 ▶ Circle the correct verb in each of the following sentences.

EXAMPLE: Eric plans to (lay, (lie)) in bed all day.

1. The chef (sat, (set)) the mixer on "high" to beat the eggs.
2. I prefer to ((lie), lay) on the hammock rather than on a chaise.
3. The students ((sit), set) in rows to take the exam.
4. After putting up the wallboard, James (lay, (laid)) the hammer on the floor.
5. Bags of grain (set, (sat)) on the truck.
6. I'm going to ((lie), lay) down and take a short nap.
7. Because we came late, we ((sat), set) in the last row.
8. The kitten ((lay), laid) asleep in the laundry basket.
9. Bob (sat, (set)) the groceries on the counter.
10. Completely exhausted, Shawna ((lay), laid) on the sofa.

NEED TO KNOW

Irregular Verbs

- An **irregular verb** does not form the simple past tense with *-d* or *-ed*.
- Three particularly troublesome irregular verbs are *be*, *do*, and *have*.
- Two confusing pairs of verbs are *lie/lay* and *sit/set*. Each has a unique meaning.

Avoiding Subject-Verb Agreement Errors

A subject and its verb must agree (be consistent) in person (first, second, third) and in number (singular, plural). (See page 452 for pronoun forms and page 351 for verb forms in all persons and numbers.)

The most common problems with subject-verb agreement occur with third-person present-tense verbs, which are formed for most verbs by adding -s or -es. (See pages 221–226 for the present-tense and past-tense forms of certain irregular verbs.)

Agreement Rules

1. For a singular subject (one person, place, thing, or idea), use a singular form of the verb.

Singular Subject	Verb	Singular Subject	Verb
I	talk	it	talks
you	talk	Sally	talks
he	talks	a boy	talks
she	talks		

2. For a plural subject (more than one person, place, thing, or idea), use a plural form of the verb.

Plural Subject	Verb	Plural Subject	Verb
we	talk	Sally and James	talk
you	talk	boys	talk
they	talk		

Common Errors

The following circumstances often lead to errors in subject-verb agreement.

1. Third-person singular. A common error is to omit the -s or -es in a third-person singular verb in the present tense. The subjects *he, she,* and *it* or a noun that could be replaced with *he, she,* or *it* all take a third-person singular verb.

INCORRECT: She act like a professional.
CORRECT: She acts like a professional.

INCORRECT: Professor Simmons pace while he lectures.
CORRECT: Professor Simmons paces while he lectures.

2. Verbs before subjects. When a verb comes before its subject, as in sentences beginning with *Here* or *There,* it is easy to make an agreement error. *Here* and *there* are never subjects of a sentence and do not determine the correct form of the verb. Look for the subject *after* the verb, and, depending on its number, choose a singular or plural verb.

singular verb   singular subject

There is a pebble in my shoe.

plural verb   plural subject

There are two pebbles in my shoe.

3. Words between subject and verb. Words, phrases, and clauses coming between the subject and verb do not change the fact that the verb must agree with the subject. To check that the verb is correct, mentally cancel everything between the subject and its verb and make sure that the verb agrees in number with its subject.

singular subject   singular verb

A list of course offerings is posted on the bulletin board.

plural subject   plural verb

Details of the accident were not released.

Note: Phrases beginning with prepositions such as *along with, as well as,* and *in addition to* are not part of the subject and should not be considered in determining the number of the verb.

singular subject   singular verb

The stereo, together with the radios, televisions, and lights, goes dead during electrical storms.

Note: Using contractions such as *here's* and *there's* leads to mistakes because you cannot "hear" the mistake. "Here's two pens" does not sound incorrect, but "Here is two pens" does.

4. Compound subjects. Two or more subjects joined by the coordinating conjunction *and* require a plural verb, even if one or both of the subjects are singular.

INCORRECT: Anita and Mark plays cards.
CORRECT: Anita and Mark play cards.

When a compound subject is joined by the conjunction *or, nor, either . . . or, neither . . . nor, not . . . but,* or *not only . . . but also,* the verb should agree with the subject nearer to it.

<u>Neither</u> the <u>book</u> <u>nor</u> the <u>article</u> <u>was</u> helpful to my research.

<u>Sarah</u> <u>or</u> the <u>boys</u> <u>are</u> coming tomorrow.

EXERCISE 9-10 ▶ Circle the verb that correctly completes each sentence.

EXAMPLE: The newspapers (is, **are**) on the desk.

1. The hubcaps that fell off the car (was, **were**) expensive to replace.
2. The conductor and orchestra members (**ride**, rides) a bus to their concerts.
3. A Little League team (practice, **practices**) across the street each Tuesday.
4. Here (**is**, are) the computer disk I borrowed.
5. Not only the news reporters but also the weather forecaster (are broadcasting, **is broadcasting**) live from the circus tonight.
6. Nobody older than twelve (ride, **rides**) the merry-go-round.
7. The discussion panel (**offer**, offers) their separate opinions after the debate.
8. Terry's green shorts (**hang**, hangs) in his gym locker.
9. Several of the cookies (**taste**, tastes) stale.
10. A mime usually (wear, **wears**) all-black or all-white clothing.

EXERCISE 9-11 ▶ Circle the verb that correctly completes each sentence.

EXAMPLE: Everybody (like, **likes**) doughnuts for breakfast.

1. Physics (**is**, are) a required course for an engineering degree.
2. Most of my courses last semester (was, **were**) in the morning.
3. The orchestra members who (is, **are**) carrying their instruments will be able to board the plane first.
4. Suzanne (sing, **sings**) a touching version of "America the Beautiful."
5. Here (is, **are**) the performers who juggle plates.
6. Kin Lee and his parents (**travel**, travels) to Ohio tomorrow.
7. A box of old and valuable stamps (**is**, are) in the safety-deposit box at the bank.
8. The family (sit, **sits**) together in church each week.
9. Judith and Erin (**arrive**, arrives) at the train station at eleven o'clock.
10. Directions for the recipe (is, **are**) on the box.

EXERCISE 9-12 ▶ Revise any sentences that contain subject-verb agreement errors.

has
Los Angeles ~~have~~ some very interesting and unusual build-

are
ings. There ~~is~~ the Victorian houses on Carroll Avenue, for exam-

ple. The gingerbread-style trimmings and decorated architecture

make~~s~~ those houses attractive to tourists and photographers.

were
The Bradbury Building and the Oviatt Building ~~was~~ both part of

were
the nineteenth-century skyline. They ~~was~~ restored as office

buildings, which now house~~s~~ twentieth-century businesses.

s
Some of the architecture in Los Angeles seem to disguise a

is
building's function. One of the most startling sights ~~are~~ a build-

s
ing that look like a huge ship.

NEED TO KNOW

Subject-Verb Agreement

- A **subject** of a sentence must agree (be consistent) with the **verb** in person (first, second, or third) and in number (singular or plural).
- Watch for errors when using the third-person singular, placing verbs before their subjects, using compound subjects, and adding words, phrases, or clauses between the subject and the verb.

Using Active Instead of Passive Voice

When a verb is in the active voice, the subject performs the action of the verb.

subject   active-voice verb
ACTIVE VOICE: Mr. Holt opened his briefcase.

When a verb is in the **passive voice,** the subject is the receiver of the action of the verb.

subject   passive-voice verb

PASSIVE VOICE: The briefcase was opened.

This passive-voice sentence does not name the person who opened the briefcase. Passive-voice sentences seem indirect, as if the writer were purposefully avoiding giving information the reader might need or want.

PASSIVE VOICE: The fingerprints had been carefully wiped away.

PASSIVE VOICE: The vase had been broken.

Both active and passive sentence arrangements are grammatically correct. However, the active voice is usually more effective because it is simpler, more informative, and more direct. Use the active rather than the passive voice unless

1. you do not know who or what performs the action of the verb.

PASSIVE: The broken window had been wiped clean of fingerprints.

2. you want to emphasize the object of the action rather than the person who or thing that performs the action.

PASSIVE: The poem "The Chicago Defender Sends a Man to Little Rock" by Gwendolyn Brooks was discussed in class. [Here, exactly who discussed the poem is less important than what poem was discussed.]

As a general rule, try to avoid writing passive-voice sentences. Get in the habit of putting the subject—the person or thing performing the action—at the beginning of each sentence. If you do this, you will usually avoid the passive voice.

EXERCISE 9-13 Revise each of the following sentences by changing the verb from passive to active voice.

EXAMPLE: The china cups and saucers were painted carefully by Lois and her friends.

REVISED: Lois and her friends carefully painted the china cups and saucers.

1. *Good Night Moon* was read by the mother to her daughter. _____
   The mother read *Good Night Moon* to her daughter.

2. The maple tree was trimmed by the telephone company. _____
   The telephone company trimmed the maple tree.

3. The vacuum cleaner was repaired by Mr. Fernandez. Mr. Fernandez
   repaired the vacuum cleaner.

4. Many bags of flour were donated by the fraternity <u>The fraternity</u>
   <u>donated many bags of flour.</u>

5. Six quarts of strawberries were made into jam by Alice. <u>Alice made</u>
   <u>six quarts of strawberries into jam.</u>

6. Cornrows were braided into Pam's hair by Felicia. <u>Felicia braided</u>
   <u>cornrows into Pam's hair.</u>

7. Tanya was driven to Weston City by Janice. <u>Janice drove Tanya to</u>
   <u>Weston City.</u>

8. The transmission was repaired by Mike. <u>Mike repaired the</u>
   <u>transmission.</u>

9. Potholes were filled by the city employees. <u>The city employees filled</u>
   <u>the potholes.</u>

10. Grapes were pressed into juice by the winemaker. <u>The winemaker</u>
    <u>pressed grapes into juice.</u>

EXERCISE 9-14 ▶ Revise each of the following sentences by changing the verb from passive to active voice.

EXAMPLE: The patient was operated on by an experienced surgeon.

REVISED: <u>An experienced surgeon operated on the patient.</u>

1. The coin collection was inherited by Roderick from his grandfather.
   <u>Roderick inherited the coin collection from his grandfather.</u>

2. A large bunch of roses was cut by my sister. <u>My sister cut a large</u>
   <u>bunch of roses.</u>

3. The president's advisers were relied on by the president. <u>The</u>
   <u>president relied upon his advisers.</u>

4. Ice cream was served to the children at the birthday party by one of
   the adults. <u>One of the adults served ice cream to the children at the</u>
   <u>birthday party.</u>

5. Tools were packed in a box by Terry. <u>Terry packed the tools in a box.</u>

6. Scuba-diving equipment was handed to the students by the licensed instructor. The licensed instructor handed scuba-diving equipment to the students.

7. Alaska was visited by my parents last fall. My parents visited Alaska last fall.

8. A large rock bass was caught by James. James caught a large rock bass.

9. The newspaper was delivered by a twelve-year-old girl on her bike. A twelve-year-old girl on her bike delivered the newspaper.

10. Trash was collected and disposed of by the picnickers before they left for home. The picnickers collected and disposed of trash before they left for home.

EXERCISE 9-15 ▷ Reread the paragraph you wrote in Exercise 9-4. Check for subject-verb agreement errors and for sentences written in the passive voice. Revise as necessary.

NEED TO KNOW

Active and Passive Voices
- When a verb is in the **active voice,** the subject performs the action.
- When a verb is in the **passive voice,** the subject receives the action.
- Because the active voice is straightforward and direct, use it unless you do not know who or what performed the action or want to emphasize the object of the action rather than who or what performed it.

WRITING ABOUT A READING

Thinking before Reading

Have you ever thought about what it would be like to attend an Ivy League school like Harvard University? In the following reading, the author offers some valuable insights into how prestigious universities compare to community colleges. As you read, notice that most of her story is told in the past tense. However, when the author compares her community college with Harvard, she switches to the present tense.

Before you read:

1. Preview the reading using the steps provided on page 20.

2. After you have done your preview, connect the reading to your own experience by answering the following questions:

   a. If you were given the choice, would you attend a prestigious university or a community college? Why one instead of the other?

   b. Do you see a community college as an extension of high school? Why?

READING

Why I Took a Chance on Learning
Cynthia G. Inda

During my first semester at Santa Barbara City College in 1993, my classes included aerobics, typing and remedial math. Who would have guessed that after spending three years there, I would be attending Harvard University?   1

Without the opportunity to study at my local community college, I probably wouldn't have gone to college at all. My high school grades would have sufficed to get me into a decent university, but I didn't consider myself college material. After all, none of my six brothers and sisters had attended college; most didn't even finish high school. My parents have the equivalent of a second-grade education. Mexican immigrants who do not speak English, my mother worked as a maid and my father as a dishwasher. Considering my resources, I thought the convenience and limited cost of a community college made it my most viable option.   2

But enrolling in a community college was also one of the smartest decisions I ever made. Despite my slow start, I learned the skills I needed to move ahead academically. By my third semester, I was taking honors courses and had become a member of Phi Theta Kappa, an honorary society for community college students. I also began to explore educational alternatives. And transferring to a reputable four-year university became my most important goal. I specifically wanted to transfer   3 to an Ivy League university because I thought that would open more doors for me. I would need to spend an extra year to earn the credits.

People often ask me if I felt prepared for Harvard. The answer is yes—mostly.   4

Sure, I suffered my first semester there. Many of my classmates had attended preparatory schools and considered Harvard less difficult. For me, Harvard was definitely not a breeze. There were nights when I thought I would not finish my homework until the sun rose. And then I'd have to do the same thing the next night. And the next. I was overwhelmed.   5

Then I learned how to budget my time, how to take short cuts (I realized, for instance, that one does not have to do all of the required reading) and how to choose courses and professors. By the second semester, I felt confident about the work I was handing in.   6

Most important, the difficulties I encountered when I first transferred to Harvard were those I would have faced at any four-year institution. City College prepared me for the quality of academic work Harvard required, if not the quantity, and it also saved me thousands of dollars in tuition. Through City College, I also earned outstanding scholarships to continue my undergraduate education.   7

Community college, however, does have its drawbacks. Class selection is limited. For example, City College didn't have courses on Foucault, Nietzsche or Dostoyevsky. There is also a lack of camaraderie because community college students do not live on campus, and many are older adults with children, or have to work full time. And by attending a commuter school, I missed out on some of the social experiences so vital to college—from late-night rap sessions about exciting theorists to the dances and parties. But the hardest part about attending a community college was people's reactions.   8

There is a marked difference in others' responses when I say I attend Harvard rather than City College. Now people ask me what I'm doing when I graduate. Now they ask me what my major is. Now they take more of an interest in me. Yet I'm the same person, with the same work ethic, the same intelligence and the same aspirations.   9

There seems to be a common misconception that those who attend community college can't hack it anywhere else, didn't have any other choices or "aren't going anywhere." Sure, community colleges have an open admissions policy, and thus attract students of varied academic abilities—but that does not necessarily signal anything about those students' commitment to their education or about the level of success they will have in the future. One of the reasons that students of such diverse backgrounds and talents are able to succeed is the quality of instruction they receive at community college.   10

In fact, I preferred many of my professors at City College to those 11
at Harvard. At City College I received more personal attention and had
smaller classes and a better classroom experience, because community
colleges are focused on teaching. Universities, on the other hand, are
research institutions where the emphasis is not on the professors' ability
to teach but on their scholarship and the number of their publications.
One academic at Harvard even told me that it is considered "bad" for
the professors to focus too much attention on students and teaching,
because it means that they aren't working hard enough on their
research. I quickly learned that within some great scholars lurk
mediocre lecturers.

I do not mean to imply that one receives the same education at a 12
community college as at an Ivy League university. Nevertheless, at community college one can learn the skills necessary to succeed at any institution—even an Ivy.

Some criticize community colleges as merely a continuation of high 13
school. They have a point, considering the extensive number of remedial
courses they offer, but so what? For me, those remedial courses were
what I needed to move on to the next level, and I always gave my studies the serious attention that "real" college courses merit. Like most
endeavors, community colleges give back to you what you put into them.

From the *New York Times*

Getting Ready to Write

Strengthening Your Vocabulary

Write a brief definition for each of the following words used in the preceding reading. If you can't figure out the meaning of a word from the
way it is used in the reading, look the word up in the dictionary.

1. sufficed (paragraph 2)   been good enough, been satisfactory

2. viable (paragraph 2)   acceptable, doable, sensible

3. reputable (paragraph 3)   well respected, well known

4. encountered (paragraph 7)   came up against, faced

5. camaraderie (paragraph 8)   togetherness, fellowship

6. aspirations (paragraph 9)   hopes, plans, goals

7. misconception (paragraph 10)   wrong or mistaken idea

8. diverse (paragraph 10)   widely different

9. mediocre (paragraph 11)   average, dull, not very skillful

10. endeavors (paragraph 13)   tasks, efforts, undertakings

Reviewing the Reading Using an Idea Map

Review the reading by completing the missing pieces of the idea map shown below.

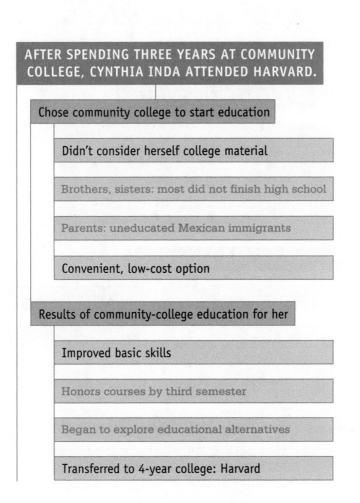

AFTER SPENDING THREE YEARS AT COMMUNITY COLLEGE, CYNTHIA INDA ATTENDED HARVARD.

Chose community college to start education

Didn't consider herself college material

Brothers, sisters: most did not finish high school

Parents: uneducated Mexican immigrants

Convenient, low-cost option

Results of community-college education for her

Improved basic skills

Honors courses by third semester

Began to explore educational alternatives

Transferred to 4-year college: Harvard

PERFORMANCE AT HARVARD

First semester difficult

Learned to budget time, to take shortcuts

Confident of work by second semester

ADVANTAGES OF STARTING AT COMMUNITY COLLEGE

Prepared her for university work

Saved money

Earned scholarships

DISADVANTAGES OF COMMUNITY COLLEGE

Limited course offerings

Lacking in social experiences

Public's misconceptions about community college

COMMUNITY COLLEGE VS. UNIVERSITY

Personal Attention	Research institutions
Smaller classes	Scholarship and publications
Focus on teaching	Emphasis not on teaching

REMEDIAL COURSES COMMUNITY COLLEGE'S STRENGTH

Provide skills for next educational level

Examining the Reading

1. Why didn't Cynthia Inda go to a four-year college first?

2. Why was she able to feel more confident by her second semester at Harvard?

3. Compare people's responses to Inda's attending Harvard University compared to their responses to her attending Santa Barbara City College.

4. What does Inda cite as some of the differences between a university and a community college?

5. What did she prefer about the community college?

Reacting to and Discussing Ideas

Get ready to write about the reading by discussing the following questions:

1. In what ways might it be difficult for a student from a working-class background to fit in at a prestigious university such as Harvard?

2. Inda says she "quickly learned that within some great scholars lurk mediocre lecturers." Discuss how this may or may not be true.

3. Given the positive and negative qualities of both Ivy League universities and community colleges, which would you prefer to attend and why?

Writing about the Reading

The Paragraph Option

1. Write a paragraph on the advantages of attending a community college.

2. Write a paragraph on the advantages of attending an Ivy League university.

3. Write a paragraph on your image of the "ideal" instructor at any college or university.

The Essay Option

Write an essay describing the "ideal" college experience. Include such factors as teachers, friends, classmates, grades, and living accommodations.

WRITING SUCCESS TIP 9

Wordiness results when you use more words than necessary to convey a message:

The rushed and pressured <u>nature</u> of nursing <u>is due to the fact that</u> hospitals lack adequate staff.

This sentence can be shortened:

Nurses are rushed and pressured because hospitals lack adequate staff.

To eliminate wordiness:

1. **Look for words that do not add meaning, and eliminate them.** You may need to rearrange the words in your sentence, as in the above example.

2. **Eliminate empty words and phrases and make substitutions.**

Wordy Phrase	*Substitute*
spell out in detail	detail, explain
the only difference being that	except
it is clear that	clearly
in the vicinity of	near
on the grounds that	because
at this point in time	now

3. **Use strong verbs that carry full meaning.** Replace weak verbs such as *is, has, makes.*

WEAK VERB: The workers <u>made</u> slow progress.
REVISED: The workers <u>progressed</u> slowly.

4. **Avoid saying the same thing twice in two different ways (redundancy).**

Redundant	*Clear*
square in shape	square [square is a shape]
mental attitude	attitude [the only type of attitude is a mental one]
the year of 1999	1999 [1999 is a year]

SKILLS CHECK

Paragraph 1

The following student paragraph has been revised to correct all errors except for those in subject-verb agreement and shifts in person and number. Complete the revision by correcting all such problems.

Now that the fascination with exercise has been in full

is

swing for a full decade, the public are starting to get tired of

our nation's overemphasis on fitness. It seems as though every

we

time you turn on the TV or pick up a newspaper or talk with a

friend, all we hear about is how we don't exercise enough. The

are

benefits of exercise is clear, but do we really need to have them

repeated to us in sermonlike fashion every time we turn

is

around? Each of us are at a point now where we are made to

feel almost guilty if we haven't joined a health club or, at the

very least, participated in some heavy-duty exercise every day.

we   *are*

It may be time you realized that there's better ways to get

exercise than these. Americans might be better off just exercis-

ing in a more natural way. Taking a walk or playing a sport

s

usually fit in better with our daily routines and needn't be so

strenuous. It could even be that our obsession with extreme

forms of exercise may be less healthy than not exercising at all.

SKILLS CHECK   CONTINUED

Paragraph 2

Revise the following paragraph so that all words or phrases in a series, independent clauses joined by a coordinating conjunction, and items being compared are parallel. Write your corrections above the lines.

The first practical pair of roller skates was made in Belgium

                             was

in 1759 and ~~is~~ designed like ice skates. The skates had two

wheels instead of ~~being made with~~ four wheels as they are

today. The wheels were aligned down the center of the skate,

              contained

but ~~were containing~~ no ball bearings. The skates had a life of

their own. Without ball bearings, they resisted turning, then

turned   d

~~were turning~~ abruptly, and then refuse to stop. Finally, they

jammed to a halt on their own. Until 1884, when ball bearings

were introduced, roller-skating was unpopular, difficult, and ~~it~~

~~was dangerous~~ for people to do. However, when skating tech-

                          ing

nology improved, roller-~~skates~~ began to compete with ice-

skating. Later, an American made roller skates with sets of

                                placed

wheels placed side-by-side rather than ~~by placing~~ them behind

one another, and that design lasted until recently. Since 1980,

however, many companies have been manufacturing skates

based on the older design. In other words, in-line skates are

SKILLS CHECK CONTINUED

back, and more and more people are discovering rollerblading

joys and ~~that it benefits their health.~~ *health benefits*

Paragraph 3

Revise any sentences in the following paragraph that contain pronoun-antecedent agreement errors.

The Smithsonian Institution has recently received the

largest single cash donation in ~~their~~ history. *its* The Mashantucket

Pequots have presented a ten-million-dollar gift to the

Smithsonian to help build the National Museum of the

American Indian. That small Connecticut tribe wants to share

the riches from ~~their~~ giant casino and bingo complex. *its* The

Pequots have given donations to many causes; for example, ~~it~~ *they*

gave two million dollars to the Special Olympics World Games

held in New Haven, Connecticut, in 1995. Most of the money

for the museum will come from the federal government, but pri-

vate organizations and individuals also are donating ~~his or her~~ *their*

share of the construction costs. The museum is scheduled to

open ~~their~~ doors at the National Mall in Washington, D.C., in *its*

the year 2001.

Adapted from the *Cape Cod Times,* October 25, 1994.

PARAGRAPH BASICS

10 Planning and Organizing

CHAPTER OBJECTIVES

In this chapter you will learn to

1. choose a topic.
2. keep your reader in mind as you write.
3. generate ideas.
4. organize your ideas.

Suppose today is your lucky day. In a sweepstakes drawing you have just won a free, all-expenses-paid trip for two to a city of your choice. After your initial shock and excitement, you think seriously about the trip. You consider various cities you have dreamed of visiting. After a great deal of thought and research, you finally choose one. Then you begin to plan and organize your trip. You decide what attractions to visit, where to stay, when to go, and what to pack. Finally, it is your departure day. As you step on the plane, you realize that you've spent hours, days, and weeks planning and organizing your special dream vacation.

Like planning a dream vacation, writing also requires planning and organization. First, you have to choose a topic, just as you had to choose a destination. Next, you have to plan and organize the ideas you'll write about, just as you had to arrange the details of your trip. Finally, planning and organizing your paragraph or paper help ensure its success, just as planning and organizing made your vacation dreams come true.

WRITING

Choosing a Topic

Many times, your instructor will assign a topic to write about. Other times, however, instructors will ask you to write a paragraph or essay on a topic of your own choice. The topic you choose often determines how successful your writing will be. The following tips will help you choose a workable topic:

1. **Look for an idea, not just for a topic.** An idea makes a point or states an opinion about a topic. For example, instead of deciding to write about children, start with an idea: "Children often reflect their parents' attitudes." Or "Children need their own personal space." Or, instead of trying to write about computers, start with the idea that computers are becoming more and more important in everyone's life. Start with an idea!

2. **Look for familiar topics and ideas.** It is easier to think of ideas about topics that you know a lot about. Therefore, examine your own experiences and areas of knowledge.

3. **Look for topics and ideas that interest you.** What subjects or problems grab your attention? What current events or issues spark your interest? You will feel more like writing and will write more successfully if you focus on something interesting and important to you.

4. **Keep an ongoing list of topics.** If a topic doesn't work for one assignment, it may be right for another.

Sources of Ideas

As long as you are aware of and interacting with the world around you, you will have ideas to write about. Never think that your ideas are unimportant or worthless. Very simple, ordinary ideas can be developed into interesting, effective paragraphs and essays. Here is a list of some good sources of ideas:

Sources of Ideas	*What to Look For*
daily or weekly activities	likes, dislikes, problems; best, worst, unexpected, exciting events
your physical surroundings	surprising, beautiful, ugly, unusual objects or places
local, national, or world events	memorable, shocking, surprising, interesting, tragic, happy, or amusing occurrences
people (family, friends)	predictable or unpredictable behavior, personalities, actions, histories, insights gained from acquaintances
television or other media	news events, documentaries, trends in programming or advertising, likes, dislikes

"Write about dogs!"

EXERCISE 10-1 ▶ Make a list of five to ten topics or ideas that you know about and are interested in. _____

_____

_____

_____

_____

_____

_____

_____

Chapter 10 • Planning and Organizing   **249**

_____

_____

_____

_____

Choosing a Manageable Topic

If your topic is either too broad or too narrow, you will have difficulty writing an effective paragraph or essay. If it is too broad, you will have too much to say. If your topic is too narrow, you won't have enough to say. Some warning signals for each situation are as follows:

A Topic May Be Too Broad If	*A Topic May Be Too Narrow If*
you don't know where to start writing.	you end up repeating ideas.
you don't know where to stop.	your paragraph is too short and you have nothing to add.
you feel as if you are going in circles.	you find yourself focusing again and again on small details.
the topics seems overwhelming.	the topic seems unimportant.

Narrowing a Topic

If your topic is too broad, try to divide it into smaller topics. Just as a large house can be divided into apartments, so a large topic can be divided into smaller, more manageable topics.

Let's return to the idea of a dream trip: Suppose you chose New Orleans as your destination and have decided to write a paragraph about your choice. Most likely you would not be able to cover the reasons for your choice in a single paragraph. Because the topic is too broad, you need to divide it into smaller parts. Try to think in terms of ideas, not topics, as shown in the following diagram:

Topic	*Ideas*
Reasons for visiting New Orleans	climate is mild
	historic sights are numerous
	French Quarter is exciting

Instead of writing about all of your reasons, you could limit your paragraph to any one of the above reasons.

The diagram below gives you a few other examples of ways to divide large topics into smaller, more manageable ones. Remember to think in terms of *ideas*.

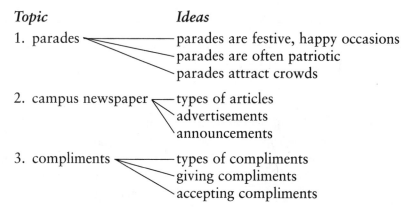

Topic   *Ideas*

1. parades ————————— parades are festive, happy occasions
                         parades are often patriotic
                         parades attract crowds

2. campus newspaper ——— types of articles
                         advertisements
                         announcements

3. compliments ————————— types of compliments
                         giving compliments
                         accepting compliments

For each topic you consider, think to yourself, "What are the various angles on this subject?" This will help you find *ideas* about the topic. Sometimes more than one narrowing is necessary. Note that the divisions for topics 2 and 3 above are still *topics,* not *ideas,* and that some of them are still too broad to be covered in a single paragraph. For example, in topic 2, "advertisements" (one division of "campus newspaper") is still a topic, not an idea, and is still very broad. The diagram below shows how you can narrow this topic down still further using ideas.

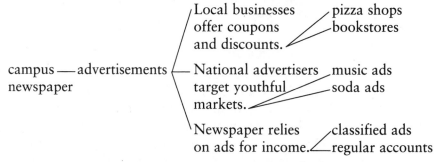

campus — advertisements — Local businesses offer coupons and discounts. — pizza shops, bookstores

National advertisers target youthful markets. — music ads, soda ads

Newspaper relies on ads for income. — classified ads, regular accounts

In the above diagram, the first narrowing of the topic "advertisements" yields ideas about the topic (for example, "National advertisers target youthful markets"). Note that each idea is further broken down into topics that act as examples to support the idea (for instance, "soda ads" and "music ads" are examples of ads that target youthful markets). You'll be working more with supporting your ideas in Chapter 12.

EXERCISE 10-2 ▷ Divide each of the following topics into at least three smaller topics or ideas. Then, choose one division and narrow it further until you've produced an idea that seems manageable to cover in one paragraph.

1. child-care problems
2. the importance of holidays
3. the value of friends

Keeping Your Reader in Mind

Whenever you speak, you are addressing a specific person or group of people. Usually you have some knowledge about whom you are addressing. You may know your listeners personally—for example, friends or family. Other times you know your listeners, but in a more distant way. According to your level of familiarity with your listeners and your knowledge about them, you automatically adjust both what you say and how you say it. You speak differently with friends than with your instructors, for example. Suppose the following people made the following comments to you. What would you say to each person? Write your response in the space provided.

Person	*Comment*	*Your Response*
parent or guardian	"Don't you think you should take a course in psychology?"	_____ _____ _____
employer	"Have you taken a psychology course yet? If not, you should."	_____ _____ _____
college instructor	"I advise you to register for a psychology course."	_____ _____ _____
close friend	"Why don't you take a psych. class?"	_____ _____ _____

Now analyze your responses. Did you choose different words? Did you express and arrange your ideas differently? Did your tone change? Were some responses casual and others more formal?

Your reaction to each person was different because you took into account who the speaker was as well as what each one said. In writing, your readers are your listeners. They are called your **audience**. As you write, keep your audience in mind. What you write about and how you explain your ideas must match the needs of your audience. Through your language and word choice, as well as through the details you include in your paragraphs, you can communicate effectively with your audience.

Remember, your audience cannot see you when you write. Listeners can understand what you say by seeing your gestures, posture, and facial expressions. When you write, all these nonverbal clues are missing, so you must make up for them. You need to be clear, direct, and specific to be sure you communicate your intended meaning.

EXERCISE 10-3 ▶ Select two people from the list below. For each, write an explanation of why you decided to attend college.

1. your best friend
2. your English instructor
3. your employer

Do not label which explanation is for which person. In class, exchange papers with a classmate. Ask your classmate to identify the intended audience of each explanation. When you've finished, discuss how the two pieces of writing differ. Next, decide whether each piece of writing is appropriate for its intended audience.

Generating Ideas

Once you have a topic and audience in mind, the next step is to generate ideas that you can use to write about that topic. This section describes three techniques for generating ideas.

1. brainstorming
2. freewriting
3. branching

These techniques can be used for both essay and paragraph writing, and they can help you narrow your topic if it is too broad or expand it if it is too narrow. If you are writing an essay, these techniques will help you break your general topic down into paragraphs. In paragraph writing, you can use these techniques for generating details that will fill out your paragraphs and support your main ideas.

Brainstorming

To do **brainstorming**, make a list of everything you can think of about your topic. Include facts, ideas, examples, questions, or feelings. Do not stop to decide if your ideas are good or bad; write down *all* of them. Concentrate on generating *ideas*, not topics. Don't worry about grammar or correctness. Give yourself a time limit. You can brainstorm alone or with another person. After you finish brainstorming, read through your list and mark usable ideas. If you have trouble getting ideas down on paper, consider tape recording your ideas or discussing ideas with a friend or classmate. The following is a list of ideas a student came up with while brainstorming on a topic.

Sample Brainstorming

Radio talk shows

lots of them
some focus on sports
some deal with issues of the day
some hosts are rude
don't let callers finish talking
some crazy callers, though!
some lack knowledge
some get angry
can learn a lot
get other viewpoints
sometimes hosts get too opinionated
fun to listen to
some topics too controversial
overkill on some issues

The topic of radio talk shows is too broad for a single paragraph. This student's brainstorming produced several paragraph-sized ideas:

characteristics of callers

characteristics of hosts

characteristics of topics covered on radio talk shows

EXERCISE 10-4 | Select a topic you listed in Exercise 10-1, or choose one of the following topics. Brainstorm for about five minutes. When you finish, review your work and mark ideas you could use in writing a paragraph.

1. your dream vacation
2. physical-education courses
3. street gangs
4. photographs
5. magazines

Freewriting

Freewriting is a way to generate ideas on a topic by writing nonstop for a specified period. Here's how it works:

1. Write whatever comes to your mind, regardless of whether it is about the topic. If you cannot think of anything to write, rewrite your last interesting phrase or idea until a new idea comes to mind.

2. Don't worry about complete sentences, grammar, punctuation, or spelling. Just record ideas as they come to mind. Don't even worry if they make sense.

3. The most important things are to keep writing and to write fast.

4. Give yourself a time limit: three to five minutes is reasonable.

5. After you have finished, underline or highlight ideas that might be usable in your paragraph.

Below is a sample of student freewriting on the topic of visiting the zoo.

Sample Freewriting

Pat and I went to the zoo Sunday. Great weather. Sunny. Warm. Warm . . . warm . . . warm . . . Oh! I know what I want to say. I didn't have as much fun as I thought I would. I used to love to go to the zoo as a kid. My parents would take us and we'd have a picnic. But I still could get cotton candy at the refreshment stand. It was a really big treat. My dad would carry me on his shoulders and my mother would be pushing my baby brother in the stroller. I loved the giraffes with their long necks and spots. And the tigers. But this time the animals looked so sad. The tiger was in an enclosed area, and he'd worn a path around the edges. He paces constantly. It was awful.

Notice that this sample contains numerous errors, including sentence fragments; this student was focusing on ideas, not correctness. Notice, too, that the student repeats the word *warm,* probably because she was stuck and needed to get her ideas flowing.

This freewriting contains two possible topics:

a childhood memory of the zoo

the quality of life for animals in a zoo

Once you have selected a topic, it may be helpful to freewrite again to generate more ideas.

EXERCISE 10-5 ▶ | Freewrite for five minutes on two of the following topics. Be sure to write without stopping. When you finish, underline or highlight any ideas that might be usable in writing a paragraph on that topic.

1. movies
2. cigarette smoke
3. common sense
4. bad motorists
5. hitchhikers

Branching

Branching uses freestyle diagrams to generate ideas. Branching begins with a trunk—that is, with a general topic. Related ideas branch out from the trunk like limbs on a tree. As on a tree, branches also can branch from other branches. To do branching, just follow these simple steps:

1. Write your general topic in the center of a full sheet of $8\frac{1}{2}$-by-11-inch paper. Draw a circle around the topic.

2. As you think of ideas related to the topic, write them down around the center circle. Draw a line connecting each idea to the central circle. In the following diagram, a student has used branching to generate ideas on the topic of homeless people.

First Branching Diagram

3. Now begin to think of ideas that relate to the branches. Write them down near the appropriate branch. You don't need to work with each branch. Choose only one or two to develop further. You may need to

use separate sheets of paper to give yourself room to develop each branch, as in the second branching diagram shown below. Here the student chose to develop further the idea of shelters for the homeless.

4. Continue to draw branches until you are satisfied you have enough for the assignment at hand. The student who made the second branching diagram decided to write about one of the experiences she had when she volunteered to serve food in a shelter for the homeless.

Second Branching Diagram

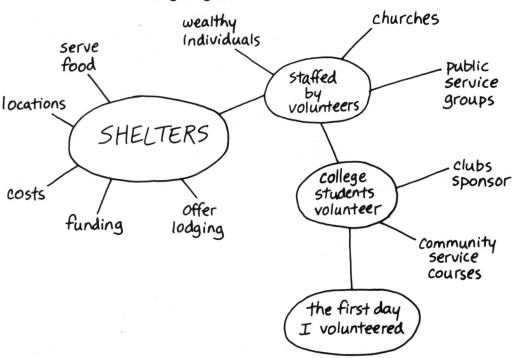

EXERCISE 10-6 ▶ Use branching to develop two of the following topics:

1. car-safety devices
2. noise
3. borrowing money
4. sales tax
5. convenience food stores

Choosing a Technique That Works

Now that you have tried these techniques, you may have a sense that one of them works best for you.

NEED TO KNOW

Techniques for Generating Ideas

Technique	*Description*
Brainstorming	1. List all ideas about your topic. 2. Use words and phrases. 3. Give yourself a time limit.
Freewriting	1. Write nonstop about your topic. 2. Write whatever comes to mind. 3. Give yourself a time limit.
Branching	1. Write down and circle your topic in the middle of your page. 2. As you think of related ideas, write them down around the center circle. Connect with lines. 3. Draw additional branches as needed.

However, don't judge the techniques too quickly. Try each three or four times. As you continue working with them, another preference may develop. You will also find that for certain topics, one technique may work better than another. For example, suppose you are writing a paragraph about snowmobiling. You may find that freewriting about it does not yield as many fresh ideas as branching. Or if you're describing a close friend, you may find that branching doesn't work as well as brainstorming or freewriting.

Identifying Usable Ideas

Brainstorming, freewriting, and branching each produce a large assortment of ideas. Your job is to decide which ideas are useful for the writing assignment at hand. Don't feel as if you have to use them all. Sometimes you might select just one idea and develop it further by doing a second freewriting, branching, or brainstorming. For example, suppose you brainstormed on the topic of radio talk shows and selected from your brainstorming list the subtopic of sports talk shows; then you might generate more ideas about sports talk shows by further brainstorming. Your goal is to produce ideas that you can use to develop a paragraph on your selected topic.

EXERCISE 10-7 ▸ | Select one of the topics listed below. Try brainstorming, freewriting, and branching to generate ideas on it. When you have finished, mark the usable ideas in each and compare your results. Then answer the questions below.

1. the value of exercise
2. dressing stylishly
3. choosing an apartment
4. managing money
5. amusement parks

1. Which technique worked best this time? Why?

_____

_____

2. Which technique was least successful this time? Why?

_____

_____

Organizing Your Ideas

After you have developed usable ideas to include in your paragraph or essay, the next step is to decide how to organize them. Ideas should flow logically from one to another. There are many ways to group or arrange ideas in both paragraphs and essays so that they are clear and easy to follow. The following list describes three of the most common types of organization:

1. Least/most arrangement. Arrange your ideas from most to least or least to most, according to some standard. For example, you might arrange ideas from most to least important, likeable, interesting, controversial, serious, or familiar.

2. Time sequence. Arrange events in the order in which they happened. Whatever happened first is placed first in the paragraph. Whatever occurred last is placed last. A time-sequence organization would be good to use if, for example, you wanted to describe events at a surprise party. This type of organization is also what you would use to describe a process, such as how to change a flat tire.

3. Spatial arrangement. Arrange descriptions of persons, places, or things according to their position in space. You could describe your topic from outside to inside, right to left, or top to bottom. For example, you might use a left-to-right organization to describe your psychology classroom, or you might use a front-to-back organization to describe your friend's pickup truck.

These methods of organization are discussed in more detail in Chapter 12.

NEED TO KNOW

Planning and Organizing

Planning and organizing contribute to successful writing. Be sure to

- Focus on ideas, not general topics
- Use events, activities, physical surroundings, media, and people around you as sources of ideas.
- Make sure your topic is manageable—neither too broad nor too narrow.
- Choose a topic that is well suited to your audience.
- Use brainstorming, freewriting, and branching to generate ideas.
- Organize your ideas using a logical method. Three common methods are least/most arrangements, time sequence, and spatial arrangement.

STUDENT ESSAY

In order to write the following essay, Heather Stopa brainstormed, producing a list of ideas about test anxiety. She listed her experiences with test anxiety, her symptoms of test anxiety, and her ways of controlling it. She decided to focus her essay on controlling test anxiety. As you read her essay, try to discover how it is organized.

Controlling Test Anxiety
Heather Stopa

When I take exams, I get terrible test anxiety. For me, test anxiety means I get really nervous and upset. Over the years I've discovered a number of ways to control these feelings. 1

First, I often don't sleep the night before a test. I get so worried and 2 nervous about how well I am going to do on the test that it is all I can think about the night before. I know this will happen, so one of the most important things to do is to get enough sleep several nights before so that I am not really tired the day of the test.

It is also helpful if I study a couple days before the test. If I study for   3
the test for several days, then all of the material is really fresh in my
mind. If I studied for the test only the day before, it would do me no
good. I would forget everything if I studied only the night before a test
because I'd be worrying, not studying.

Also when I study for a test I don't have as much anxiety if I   4
categorize what I need to learn for this test. Doing this helps me calm
down a lot. By categorizing the material when I go to review it, I break
it down little by little instead of learning and reviewing it all at once.

What I also find helpful for creating less test anxiety is making up a   5
set of flash cards. That way by making flash cards I can study the information any time I want or anywhere I want to. With flash cards I can
also have other people help me study. They can give me a little test to
see how much I know.

I like it when I have people helping me study because it makes it   6
more interesting than just studying all alone. Sometimes when other
people help you they might know things about the material that you
don't know, and you might know things that they don't know. Then,
by helping each other learn all of the material, you can be pretty certain
that you will do very well on the test.

Another way that I deal with test anxiety is by just telling and con-   7
vincing myself that I am going to do just fine on this test. If I keep convincing and telling myself that I will be fine, then I usually end up
passing the test. It also helps if you have people around you telling you
that you are going to do well on the test.

It also helps if you take a test on a full stomach. I was always told   8
to eat something before I took a test. It is good to do that because then
you can concentrate on the test instead of thinking about what you are
going to have to eat after you have finished the test.

Finally, you also have an even better chance of passing a test if you   9
are well and feeling healthy. A lot of times when I am sick and I have a
test to take, I don't do as well as I want to. If I am sick, I try to stay at
home because it isn't going to do me any good to be in school if I cannot concentrate as well as I normally would. All in all, taking tests is
something I am learning to manage, but I have to keep working on it.

Evaluating the Essay

1. Evaluate the structure and content of the essay.

   a. Does the essay follow a logical plan? Describe its organization.
   b. What is Stopa's thesis?
   c. In what ways does she support her thesis?
   d. Evaluate the effectiveness of the title, introduction, and conclusion.

2. In what sections do you feel more information, detail, or examples are needed?

3. Evaluate Stopa's sentence structure. Does she write interesting and varied sentences? Which ones would you expand or combine?

4. Evaluate Stopa's use of adjectives, adverbs, and other modifiers to add detail to her writing.

WRITING ABOUT A READING

Thinking before Reading

The following reading, "Toys," describes the frustration experienced by an African American mother when she shops for toys for her infant son. Notice that Bray's writing focuses on the single topic of lack of racial diversity in toys and that she organizes her ideas using time sequence. Her essay may cause you to think that she wrote it in one sitting, but you can be sure that Bray generated many ideas, selected the usable ones and organized them before writing.

1. Preview the reading using the steps provided on page 20.

2. After you have done your preview, connect the reading to your own experience by answering the following questions:

   a. How many toys have you seen that represent races other than white?
   b. Do you think the racial identity of dolls and toys matters to children?

READING

Toys
Rosemary Bray

Before I became a mother myself, I used to laugh at women who dressed their babies in excessively cute outfits. So who was it last year who started combing the stores in October, looking for a Santa suit for her 4-month-old? True, Allen was too young to under-

stand the season, but it was such fun to have him all dressed up like Santa for our Christmas party. And he did look adorable.

I'm not sure how much fun this holiday season will be, though. I've had a year to watch my son's budding consciousness, a year to read about the ways he comes to know that the little boy he grins at in the mirror is him. And I've had a year to shop for him in both massive toy-store chains and small stores, seeking out the kind of playthings that will help him enjoy himself and learn about the world. But in my travels up and down store aisles, I have been troubled and frustrated by what Allen will learn: that he and other black children are invisible and expendable.

I recently spent an hour in a Detroit toy store, hunting in vain for a single plaything that personified anything but white mothers, white fathers, and white babies. It's not just the overwhelming number of white dolls and action figures. Even the dinosaurs, stuffed rabbits, bop bags, rattles, and talking gadgets come in packaging decorated with photos of rosy-cheeked children with blond hair.

I resent my lack of choices and the people who tell me it doesn't matter, because infants don't know color. Maybe that's true, but babies begin to figure it out sooner than we realize. Besides, if color were as irrelevant as some claim, there would be far more products and packaging reflecting ethnic diversity. And toy chests across America would be filled by parents of all races with a mix of such toys. ⁴

The fact is, it does matter: Market research shows that white parents rarely purchase toys that reflect an ethnicity different from their own. Yet what effect will it have on my son's self-esteem and sense of self if, by default, he plays with toys that mostly ignore his heritage, that imply that only white children exist or are worthwhile? ⁵

These may seem like harsh claims. But we must guard and protect not only our children's bodies but their minds and hearts as well. My husband and I take great pride in being Americans of African descent. We think it's vital to our son's future that we raise him with that same pride. With that in mind, I wrote letters to several toy manufacturers. I reminded them that children of African, Hispanic, and Asian descent are people too—and let them know that I wouldn't spend anymore money on companies that ignored people of color. (I'm still waiting for an answer.) ⁶

I have also discovered several small mail-order companies—most of them started by other African American parents—that offer an array of toys and games that any child can enjoy, but that understand the importance of broadening children's awareness of other races and cultures in the real world (as opposed to the world of mainstream toy stores). ⁷

In the world I have in mind, Allen would have dolls with a rainbow of faces to gaze upon as he played. Although his most important lessons about his identity will come from his family, it would be a lot easier, and a lot more reassuring for the future of this country, if the toymakers of America got real. ⁸

From *Redbook* magazine

Getting Ready to Write

Strengthening Your Vocabulary

Write a brief definition for each of the following words from the preceding reading. If you can't figure out the meaning of a word from the way it is used in the reading, look the word up in the dictionary.

1. combing (paragraph 1) searching, looking everywhere

2. expendable (paragraph 2) unimportant, not needed

3. personified (paragraph 3) pictured, represented

4. irrelevant (paragraph 4) beside the point, off the subject

5. ethnic diversity (paragraph 4) variety, difference

6. default (paragraph 5) having no choice, being overlooked

7. vital (paragraph 6) essential, of great importance

8. array (paragraph 7) wide selection, range

Reviewing the Reading Using an Idea Map

Review the reading by completing the missing pieces of the idea map shown below.

ROSEMARY BRAY TRIES TO BUY SUITABLE TOYS FOR SON

Last Christmas, son too young to notice toys

This Christmas he will be more aware

Problem: toys represent whites

Dolls, action figures all white

Even packaging depicts whites

What she thinks of this

Resents lack of choices and lack of concern about it

Afraid of effect on son

Vital that son have pride in his heritage

What she did about it
Wrote manufacturers about problem
Discovered some mail-order sources

Wishes for a world where diversity is reflected in son's toys

Examining the Reading

1. What problem does Bray focus on in this article?

2. How does she feel about her lack of choices when shopping for toys?

3. How do she and her husband feel about their African American heritage?

4. When she wrote to toy companies about her problem, what was the result?

5. What does she think would be an ideal gift for her son? What further meaning does this gift have?

Reacting to and Discussing Ideas

Get ready to write about the reading by discussing the following questions:

1. Why do you think most toy packaging shows white children only?

2. Bray states that "market research shows that while parents rarely purchase toys that reflect an ethnicity different from their own." What do you think is the reason for this?

3. Bray implies that her son's self-esteem will be affected if he always sees packaging displaying children with an ethnicity different from his own. Do you agree or disagree? Why?

Writing about the Reading

The Paragraph Option

1. Write a paragraph on how you would deal with this racial problem if you were a toy manufacturer.

2. Pretend you are an important executive at Fisher-Price. Write a one-paragraph letter to Bray responding to her letter.

The Essay Option

Write an essay on your favorite childhood toy in which you describe how you would advertise it to all ethnicities.

WRITING SUCCESS TIP 10

Using the Computer to Generate Ideas

1. Use a computer in the same way you brainstorm or freewrite on paper. Sometimes just using a different medium makes a difference.
2. Try brainstorming or freewriting with your screen switched off (just turn down the brightness). This frees you to write without looking at what you've already written and criticizing it.
3. You can also branch on the computer. Put your general topic in large print. Put your first set of branches in bold. Then go back and add more branches in regular type.
4. Try talking about your topic with a friend on the Internet.
5. Make a list of questions that start with "who," "what," "when," "where," "why," and "how," and answer them.

Drafting and Revising

Advertisements often begin with a general announcement that catches your interest and suggests what the ad is about. This is called a *headline statement.* In the ad on page 268, the headline, "Joey, Katie and Todd will be performing your bypass," catches your attention and suggests the message the ad is trying to get across. The remainder of the ad, called the *body copy,* offers more information about the headline. Ads often end with either a *close* or a *tagline* intended to create a final, lasting impression or to urge action.

Paragraphs follow a similar structure. First, a paragraph must have a sentence that is similar to a headline statement. This sentence identifies the topic of the paragraph, indicates a main point (idea) about the topic, and catches the reader's interest. This sentence is called a **topic sentence.** Writers often place the topic sentence at the beginning of the paragraph. Paragraphs must also have details that support and explain the topic sentence. Finally, like ads, paragraphs need to draw to a close. Usually one or more sentences serve this function. The conclusion of a paragraph makes a strong statement. It leaves the reader with a summary of the paragraph's main point or a point related to what has come before.

In paragraph form, the Ad Council ad would look like this:

To handle tomorrow's good jobs, more kids need to take more challenging academic courses. Standards must be raised in America's schools. Joey, Katie, and Todd are good examples. Today they are children, but before you know it, they will be old enough to perform your bypass surgery. These kids and many like them will become doctors, nurses, and medical technicians. To perform these jobs, they will need technical knowledge and skills. They will need an excellent grasp of laser technology, advanced computing, and molecular genetics, for example. Unfortunately, very few American children are being prepared to master such sophisticated subjects. The Ad

Topic sentence

details

CHAPTER OBJECTIVES

In this chapter you will learn to

1. choose a manageable topic.
2. write topic sentences.
3. develop paragraphs using supporting details.
4. revise paragraphs.

Council is working toward raising academic standards. To find out how you can help, call 1-800-96-PROMISE. } closing sentence

From the above paragraph you can see that a topic sentence states the main point. The remainder of the paragraph contains details that support the main point. In this chapter you will learn how to write topic sentences and develop details to support them. You will also learn how to revise paragraphs to make them more effective.

EXERCISE 11-1

1. Find an advertisement in a newspaper or magazine. Identify the headline statement, body copy, and close. Rewrite the ad so that it is in paragraph form.
2. Select a product you commonly purchase. Write an advertisement for that product, including a headline statement, body copy, and a close. Exchange papers with a classmate. Rewrite your classmate's ad so that it is in paragraph form.

WRITING

Choosing a Manageable Topic

The topic you choose for a paragraph must not be too broad or too narrow. It must be the right size to cover in a single paragraph. If you choose a topic that is too big, you will have too much to say. Your paragraph will wander and seem unfocused. If you choose a topic that is too narrow (too small), you will not have enough to say. Your paragraph will seem skimpy.

Suppose you want to write a paragraph about pollution. You write the following topic sentence:

Pollution is everywhere.

Clearly, the topic of global pollution is too broad to cover in a single paragraph. Pollution has numerous types, causes, effects, and potential solutions. Would you write about causes? If so, could you write about all possible causes in one paragraph? What about effects? Are you concerned with immediate effects? Long-term effects? You can see that the topic of widespread global pollution is not a manageable one for a single paragraph. You could make this topic more manageable by limiting it to a specific pollutant, the immediate source or effect, and a particular place. Your revised topic sentence might read

Fuel emissions from poorly maintained cars greatly increase air pollution in the United States.

This topic may still prove too broad to cover in a single paragraph. You could narrow it further by limiting the topic to a particular city in the United States, or even a particular type of fuel emission.

A few more examples of topics that are too broad follow. Each has been revised to be more specific.

TOO BROAD: water conservation
REVISED: lawn-watering restrictions

TOO BROAD: effects of water shortages
REVISED: sinkholes caused by water shortages

TOO BROAD: crop irrigation
REVISED: a system for allocating water for crop irrigation in the San Joaquin Valley

If your topic is too narrow, you will run out of things to say in your paragraph. You run the risk, too, of straying from your topic as you search for ideas to include. Suppose you want to write a paragraph about environmental waste. You write the following topic sentence:

Each year Americans discard two billion disposable razors.

This sentence is too specific. It could work as a detail, but it is too narrow to be a topic sentence. To turn this statement into a good topic sentence, try to make your topic more general. Your revised topic sentence could be

Each year Americans fill landfills with convenient but environmentally damaging products.

You then could develop a paragraph such as the following:

Sample Paragraph

Each year Americans strain their landfills with convenient but environmentally damaging products. For example, Americans discard billions of disposable razors. Disposable diapers are another popular product. Parents use mountains of them on their children instead of washable cloth diapers. Milk, which used to come in reusable glass bottles, is now sold mainly in plastic or cardboard cartons that can only be used once. Other items, such as Styrofoam cups, aluminum cans, disposable cameras, and ballpoint pens, add to the solid-waste problem in this country. Eventually people will need to realize it's not OK to "use it once, then throw it away."

Here are a few other examples of topic sentences that are too narrow. Each has been revised to be more specific.

TOO NARROW:	Americans discard 250 million used tires per year.
REVISED:	Several companies are tackling the problem of what to do with used tires.
TOO NARROW:	Less than 4 percent of plastics are recycled.
REVISED:	Consumers need to take recycling more seriously.
TOO NARROW:	Americans in some states are paid five cents per can to recycle aluminum cans.
REVISED:	Money motivates many consumers to recycle.

EXERCISE 11-2 In each of the following pairs of topic sentences, place a check mark in the blank before the sentence that is more effective (neither too broad nor too narrow):

1. _____ a. Power tools can be dangerous.
   ___✓___ b. To avoid injury, users of power saws should follow several safety precautions.
2. _____ a. A Barbie doll from the 1950s recently sold for $3,000.
   ___✓___ b. Barbie dolls from the 1950s are valued by collectors.
3. _____ a. Parachuting is a sport.
   ___✓___ b. Parachuting is a sport that requires skill and self-confidence.
4. ___✓___ a. Learning keyboarding skills requires regular practice.
   _____ b. Learning a new skill is difficult.
5. _____ a. Children's toys should be fun.
   ___✓___ b. A toy should stimulate a child's imagination.

EXERCISE 11-3 Choose three of the following topics, and narrow each to a topic manageable in a single paragraph. Use branching (page 255) to help you.

1. packaging of products
2. the value of parks and "green spaces"
3. garbage
4. water pollution or conservation
5. building environmental awareness
6. recycling

Writing Topic Sentences

An effective **topic sentence** must

1. identify what the paragraph is about (the topic).
2. make a point (an idea) about that topic.

Suppose your topic is acid rain. You could make a number of different points about acid rain. Each of the following is a possible topic sentence:

1. Acid rain has caused conflict between America and Canada.
2. Acid rain could be reduced by controlling factory emissions.
3. Acid rain has affected the population of fish in our lakes.

Each of the above sentences identifies acid rain as the topic, but each expresses a different point about acid rain. Each would lead to a different paragraph and be supported by different details.

Think of your topic sentence as a headline; it states what your paragraph will contain. You can also think of a topic sentence as a promise. Your topic sentence promises your reader what you will deliver in the paragraph.

What does each of the following topic sentences promise the reader?

1. There are three basic ways to dispose of sewage sludge.
2. Each year we discard valuable raw materials into landfills.
3. Many people do not understand how easy composting is.

Sentence 1 promises to explain three ways to dispose of sewage sludge. Sentence 2 promises to tell what valuable resources we discard. Sentence 3 promises to explain how easy composting is.

Your topic sentence must be a clear and direct statement of what the paragraph will be about. Use the following suggestions to write effective topic sentences:

1. Be sure your topic sentence is a complete thought. If your sentence is a fragment, run-on sentence, or comma splice, your meaning will be unclear or incomplete.

FRAGMENT: People who don't throw their litter in the bin.

RUN-ON SENTENCE: The audience was captivated by the speaker no one spoke or moved.

COMMA SPLICE: Many children's games copy adult behavior, playing nurse or doctor is an example.

Chapters 3 and 4 discuss how to spot and correct these errors.

2. Place your topic sentence first in the paragraph. You *may* place your topic sentence anywhere in the paragraph, but you will find it easier to develop your paragraph around the topic sentence if you put it first.

3. Avoid direct announcements or statements of intent. Avoid sentences that sound like formal announcements, such as the following examples:

ANNOUNCEMENT: In this paragraph I will show that the average American is unaware of the dangers of smog.

REVISED: The average American is unaware of the dangers of smog.

ANNOUNCEMENT: This paragraph will explain why carbon monoxide is a dangerous air pollutant.

REVISED: There are three primary reasons why carbon monoxide is a dangerous air pollutant.

EXERCISE 11-4 ▶ Write a topic sentence for each of the three topics that you selected in Exercise 11-3.

Developing the Paragraph

Once you've written a preliminary topic sentence, your next step is to write details that support your sentence. Just as an advertiser provides facts and information that support the headline, so must you provide details that support your topic sentence. Let's look at another advertisement—this time about visiting Mexico.

In this ad, the headline states that visiting Mexico is an endless experience. Now study the body copy. What kinds of information are provided? Notice that only information that supports the headline is included: all the details are about experiences that Mexico has to offer. These are called **relevant details.** *Relevant* means that the details directly relate to or explain the headline. The ad does not mention other reasons for visiting Mexico. Notice, too, that a reasonable number of facts are included—enough to make the headline believable and convincing. In other words, a **sufficient** number of **details** are provided to make the headline effective. When you select details to support a topic sentence, they, too, must be *relevant* and *sufficient.* Even a detail that is interesting and true must be left out if it does not support the topic sentence, and you must provide a sufficient number of details to make your topic sentence understandable and convincing.

Choosing Relevant Details

Relevant details directly support the topic sentence, which is shaded. The following paragraph contains two details that do not support the topic sentence. Can you spot them?

Sample Paragraph

(1)Corporations are beginning to recognize the importance of recycling. (2)Our landfills are getting too full, and we are running out of room for our garbage. (3)Many companies are selling products with reusable containers. (4)Tide laundry soap and Jergens hand cream, for example, sell refills. (5)It bothers me that some manufacturers charge the same for refills as for the original containers, or even more. (6)I believe all cities and towns should have recycle bins to make it easy for individuals to recycle. (7)By recycling tin, glass, plastic, and paper, companies can save valuable natural resources. (8)Some corporations recycle plastic and paper bags to conserve energy and natural resources. (9)Through these methods corporations are helping save our environment.

Sentence 5 is not relevant because what companies charge for reusable containers does not relate to the importance of recycling. Sentence 6 is not relevant because it is about towns and individuals, not corporations.

Come to Mexico today. The experience is endless.

Explore the mysteries of our ancient Mayan ruins at Chichén Itzá, midway between the colonial city of Mérida and our beautiful Caribbean.

Come to Mexico today and discover the perfect place to relax, discover and enjoy your vacation. Spend some time strolling the cobblestone streets of our magnificent colonial cities. Enjoy the peaceful atmosphere and beauty of our stunning beaches, or play golf at our many world class courses. Enjoy our restful pace, our friendly people and our endless places to discover. Come discover the endless experience that is Mexico. Come today, while now, more than ever before, you get so much more for your money. Come to Mexico and begin an endless journey.

For more information, call: 1-800-44-MEXICO or http://mexico-travel.com

Experience the unmistakable warmth and hospitality of our people during your visit.

Mexico.
An Endless Journey.
Come discover it.

MEXICO

EXERCISE 11-5 ▶ Each of the topic sentences listed below is followed by a set of details. Place a check mark in the blank before those statements that are relevant supporting details.

1. TOPIC SENTENCE: People should take safety precautions when outside temperatures reach ninety-five degrees or above.

   DETAILS: ____✓____ a. It is important to drink plenty of fluids.

   _____ b. If you are exposed to extreme cold or dampness, you should take precautions.

    ✓   c. To prevent heat exhaustion, reduce physical activity.

    ✓   d. Infants and elderly people are particularly at risk for heat exhaustion.

2. TOPIC SENTENCE: Cuba is one of the last nations with a communist government.

   DETAILS:

    ✓   a. Cuba is an island nation and thus is able to keep other views and opponents out.

           b. Cuba makes high revenues from cigar sales despite the U.S. boycott against Cuba.

           c. Fidel Castro was chosen by the people, not imposed upon them.

    ✓   d. The movement to overthrow communism in Cuba is centered in Miami and thus is not very effective within Cuba itself.

3. TOPIC SENTENCE: Freedom of speech, the first amendment to the United States Constitution, does not give everyone the right to say anything at any time.

   DETAILS:

           a. The Constitution also protects the freedom of religion.

           b. The freedom of speech is a right that citizens of most Western countries take for granted.

    ✓   c. Freedom of speech is restricted by the libel and slander laws, which prohibit the speaking or publishing of harmful, deliberate lies about people.

           d. Citizens may sue if they feel their freedom of speech has been unfairly restricted.

4. TOPIC SENTENCE: Family violence against women is a growing problem that is difficult to control or prevent.

   DETAILS:

    ✓   a. Abusive partners will often ignore restraining orders.

    ✓   b. Violence shown on television may encourage violence at home.

_____ c. New laws make it easier for observers of child abuse to report the violence.

___✓___ d. Battered women frequently do not tell anyone that they have been battered because they are ashamed.

_____ e. Violence against the elderly is increasing at a dramatic rate.

Including Sufficient Details

Including **sufficient details** means including _enough_ details to make your topic sentence believable and convincing. Your details should be as exact and specific as possible. The following paragraph lacks sufficient detail:

Sample Paragraph

Recycling has a lot of positive sides. When you recycle, you receive money if you return used containers. When you recycle, you clean up the earth, and you also save the environment. Less waste and more space are our goals.

Notice that the paragraph is very general. It does not describe any specific benefits of recycling, nor does it explain how recycling saves the environment or creates more space.

Below is a revised version. Notice the addition of numerous details and the more focused topic sentence.

Revised Paragraph

Recycling offers benefits for consumers and manufacturers, as well as for the environment. Consumers benefit from recycling in several ways. Recycling generates revenue, which should, in the long run, reduce costs of products. Soda bottles and cans returned to the store produce immediate return for cash. Manufacturers benefit, too, since their costs are reduced. For example, soda bottles are refillable, and the only cost involved is for handling and cleaning. Most important, however, are benefits to the environment. Recycling reduces landfills. It also produces cleaner air by reducing manufacturing. Finally, recycling paper saves trees.

If you have difficulty thinking of enough details to include in a paragraph, try brainstorming, freewriting, or branching. Also, try to draft a more focused topic sentence, as the writer did in the above paragraph. You may then find it easier to develop supporting details. If you are still unable to generate additional details, your topic may be too narrow or you may need to do some additional reading or research on your topic.

If you use information from printed sources, be sure to give the author credit by using a citation. Indicate the author, title, place of publication, publisher, and year.

EXERCISE 11-6 ▷ Write a paragraph developing one of the topic sentences you wrote in Exercise 11-4. Then, check to see if you can improve your topic sentence by making it more focused. Make the necessary changes. Finally, be sure you have included relevant and sufficient details in the rest of your paragraph.

NEED TO KNOW

Drafting Paragraphs

To draft effective paragraphs, be sure to

- Choose a manageable **topic.** Your topic should be neither too broad nor too narrow.

- Write a clear **topic sentence.** Your topic sentence should identify the topic and make a point about that topic.

- Develop your paragraph by providing **relevant** and **sufficient details.** Relevant details are those that directly support the topic. Including sufficient details means including enough details to make your topic sentence believable and convincing.

Revising Paragraphs

Did you know that it takes an advertising agency months to develop and write a successful ad? Copy writers and editors work through many drafts until they decide on a final version of the ad. Often, too, an agency may test an ad on a sample group of consumers. Then, working from consumer responses, the agency makes further changes in the ad.

To produce an effective paragraph, you will need to revise and test your work. Revision is a process of examining and rethinking your ideas. It involves adding text, deleting text, and changing both *what* you have said and *how* you have said it.

When to Revise

It is usually best to wait a day before beginning to revise. You will have a fresh outlook on your topic and will find that it is easier to see what needs changing.

How to Revise

Sometimes it is difficult to know how to improve your own writing. Simply rereading your own work may not help you discover flaws, weaknesses, or needed changes. This section presents two aids to revision that will help you identify what and how to revise: (1) a **revision map** and (2) a **revision checklist**.

Using Revision Maps

A **revision map** is a visual display of your ideas in a paragraph or essay. It is similar to an idea map (see page 36). While an idea map shows how ideas in someone else's writing are related, a revision map will show you how ideas in your writing fit together. A revision map will also help you identify ideas that do not fit and those that need further explanation. The diagram below is a sample revision map.

To draw a revision map of a paragraph, follow these steps:

1. Write a shortened topic sentence at the top of your paper, as in the sample revision map on page 279. Be sure your topic sentence has both a subject and a verb and expresses an *idea*. Do *not* simply write the topic of your paragraph.

2. Work through your paragraph sentence by sentence. On your revision map, list underneath the topic sentence each detail that directly supports the topic sentence.

3. If you spot a detail that is an example or a further explanation of a detail already listed, write it underneath the first detail and indent it.

4. If you spot a detail that does not seem to support anything you've written, write it to the right of your list, as in the sample revision map below.

Sample Revision Map

TOPIC SENTENCE

Detail

Detail

   Example

   Further explanation

Detail

Unrelated details

1. _____

2. _____

3. _____

The following paragraph is a first draft written by a student named Eric. His revision map follows the paragraph.

Sample First Draft

Pizza is a surprisingly nutritional food. It has cheese, tomato sauce, and crust. Each of these is part of a basic food group. However, nutritionists now talk about the food pyramid instead of food groups. Toppings such as mushrooms and peppers also add to its nutritional value. Pepperoni, sausage, and anchovies provide protein. Pizza is high in calories, though, and everyone is counting calories. But pizza does provide a wide variety of nutrients from vegetables, dairy products, meats, and carbohydrates. And the best part is that it is tasty, as well as nutritious.

Sample Revision Map

PIZZA IS NUTRITIONAL.

Cheese, sauce, crust all in food groups

Toppings add nutrition

Pepperoni, sausage, anchovies add protein

Wide variety of nutrients

Vegetables, dairy meat, and carbohydrates

Tasty as well as nutritious

Unrelated details

1. Nutritionists talk about pyramid

2. Pizza high in calories

Eric's map is a picture of his paragraph. The map reduces his ideas to a brief, skeletonlike form that allows him to concentrate on the ideas themselves. He is not distracted by other revision matters, such as wording, spelling, and punctuation, which come later in the revision process. The map showed Eric that two of his details—the ones about the food pyramid and the number of calories—do not belong in the paragraph.

EXERCISE 11-7 ▶ Draw a revision map of the sample paragraph on page 270.

EXERCISE 11-8 ▶ Draw a revision map of the paragraph you wrote in Exercise 11-6.

Using Revision Checklists

Focused questions can help you evaluate a piece of writing. The Revision Checklist is a list of questions in checklist form to help you look closely and critically at your writing and to identify parts that need improvement. It will also help you confirm that you have mastered certain skills. The Revision Checklist is divided into two parts: Paragraph Development and Sentence Development. The Sentence Development section covers what you learned in Chapters 1 through 9. As you learn more about writing paragraphs in later chapters, we will add items to the Paragraph Development section.

REVISION CHECKLIST

		YES	NO
Paragraph Development	1. Is your topic manageable (neither too broad nor too narrow)?	☐	☐
	2. Is your paragraph written with your reader in mind?	☐	☐
	3. Does your topic sentence identify your topic?	☐	☐
	4. Does your topic sentence make a point about your topic?	☐	☐
	5. Does each remaining sentence support the topic sentence?	☐	☐
	6. Did you include sufficient detail?	☐	☐
Sentence Development	7. Have you avoided writing sentence fragments, run-on sentences, and comma splices?	☐	☐
	8. Have you combined ideas to produce more effective sentences?	☐	☐
	9. Have you used adjectives and adverbs to make your sentences vivid and interesting?	☐	☐
	10. Have you used prepositional phrases, -ing phrases, and relative clauses to add detail?	☐	☐
	11. Have you used pronouns correctly and consistently?	☐	☐
	12. Have you avoided shifts in person, number, and verb tense?	☐	☐
	13. Have you placed modifiers correctly?	☐	☐
	14. Are elements within each sentence parallel?	☐	☐
	15. Have you used correct verb tenses and correct verb forms?	☐	☐

If you have checked any *no*s, go back to your paper and make the necessary changes.

Now let's apply the questions from the Paragraph Development section of the checklist to a sample student paragraph. Read the paragraph, and then answer the questions in the space provided.

Sample Paragraph

The world is experiencing a steady decline in water quality and availability. About 75 percent of the world's rural population and 20 percent of its urban population have no ready access to uncontaminated water. Many states have a limited water supply, and others waste water. Bans on lawn sprinkling and laws restricting water use would help solve the problem. Building more reservoirs would also help.

Revision Checklist

Paragraph Development

1. Is the topic manageable (neither too broad nor too narrow)?

   No—the topic is too broad.

2. Is the paragraph written with the reader in mind?

   It is unclear for whom the paragraph was written.

3. Does the topic sentence identify the topic? (What is the topic?)

   Yes—the topic is water quality and availability throughout the world.

4. Does the topic sentence make a point about the topic? (What is the point?)

   Water quality and availability are declining.

5. Does each remaining sentence explain the topic sentence? (List any that do not.)

   No—the last two sentences deal with solutions to the problem.

6. Is there sufficient detail?

No. _____

_____

7. Is there a sentence at the end that brings the paragraph to a close? (What is it?)

No. _____

_____

The topic of this paragraph—water quality and availability through-out the world—is too broad. Water quality and water availability are two separate topics, and both vary greatly throughout the world. To revise this paragraph the writer first narrowed the topic to one idea. Choosing the topic of increasing water availability in the United States, he wrote the following revised paragraph:

Revised Paragraph

> There are several easy-to-take actions that could increase water availability in the United States. First, lawn-sprinkling bans would reduce nonessential use of water in areas in which water is in short supply. Second, laws limiting the total amount of water a household could use would require people to cut down on their water use at home. Increasing the cost of water to households is a third way to restrict its use. Each of these actions could produce an immediate increase in water availability.

EXERCISE 11-9 ▷ Apply all the questions in the Revision Checklist—both about sentences and paragraphs—to the paragraph you wrote in Exercise 11-6.

NEED TO KNOW

Revising Paragraphs

Revision is a process of examining and rethinking your ideas. It involves adding text, deleting text, and changing both what you say and how you say it. To know what to revise, do the following:

- Draw a **revision map.** A revision map is similar to an idea map. It shows how your ideas relate to one another.

- Use a **revision checklist.** The revision checklist offers focused questions that will help you evaluate your writing.

STUDENT ESSAY

This essay by Tracy Burgio illustrates the process of discovering and narrowing a topic, writing a first draft, and revising. As you read through
Burgio's drafts, pay particular attention to the changes she makes.

Topic Selection:

beach
Illuminations
Holiday Inn Grand Island, modeling
Pleasure Island—Planet Hollywood
view from the window
Dinner at Grand Floridian Beach Resort
(Washington, D. C.)
Wash., D.C., changing of the guards

Narrowing a Topic:

Washington, D. C.
Capitol
Lincoln Memorial
visit to White House   — why it was created
(Vietnam Memorial) ◄————— (my reaction to it)
The Mall   — response of others
Smithsonian Museum   — construction and location
Georgetown University

First Draft

The Emotional Wall
Tracy Burgio

This is one of the trips that I went on, that I'll never for-
get. The place was the Vietnam Memorial in Washington, D. C., about 6:30 p.m. and
the sun was going down. ~~That means that the sunset was~~ So there was a beautiful sunset.
~~beautiful.~~

What colors?—add

~~I was standing at the beginning of the wall, of the Vietnam Memorial.~~ It was the perfect time to be there/ because all of a sudden, I felt very emotional ~~next to~~ *exactly right behind* the Memorial. The Washington Monument is there, and after that/ ~~its~~ *is* the Capit*o*al. Straight in front of the Vietnam Memorial is the Lincoln Memorial. The way that the sunset was going down, it lit up the whole sky, and the colors were just beautiful from reflecting on the Memorials, and the Capit*o*al.

As I started walking passed the wall, ~~I had a very~~ *certain things started to change.* ~~strange feeling~~. The wall became larger and larger‚ *and taller than me and seemed as* and all of a sudden, I felt very emotional. I couldn't get over how big *if it were 20–25 feet tall* the wall became. ~~On~~ *As I looked at* the wall, they had all the names of all the men who had died in the Vietnam War. As soon as ~~you~~ I start*ed* to look at all the names, ~~you~~ I automatically (became)

in what way? (emotional)‚ *as if I were going to cry. I felt sorry for all the men who died in the Vietnam War.* A lady standing next to me was crying ~~and~~ she put flowers in front of the wall on the ground. I ~~decided~~ *as realized* that it was okay to be emotional at that time and at that place.

After a little while, I wanted to touch the wall, to see what it *what did it feel like?* was like, ~~and my friend took a picture of me.~~ *and as soon as I did, I had more feelings about it. It felt very smooth, and the names were engraved on the wall.*

Finally I finished walking and the wall became smaller and smaller, ~~as it was in the beginning, which was a little higher above my ankles.~~ *as it was in the beginning, which was a little higher above my ankles.*

I realized that I'm never going to forget that moment in

my life. The scenery was beautiful and the moment was sad,

but the view was spectacular. It's something that ~~you don't~~ *I won't*

want to forget, in fact ~~you will want~~ *I will* to treasure it!

Second Draft

The Emotional Wall
Tracy Burgio

~~This is one of the trips that I went on that~~ I'll never for-

get, ~~The place was the Vietnam~~ *my trip to the* Memorial in Washington,

D. C./ *It was* ~~about~~ 6:30 p.m. and the sun was going down, so there

was a beautiful sunset! It was the perfect time to be there

because exactly right behind the Memorial/ *is* the Washington

Monument ~~is there,~~ and after that is the Capitol. Straight in

front of the Vietnam Memorial is the Lincoln Memorial. ~~The~~

~~way that~~ the sun~~set was going down, it~~ lit up the whole sky,

and the colors were just be*au*atiful/ ~~the way~~ they reflected on

the memorials and the Capitol/ ~~Such as~~ pink, purple, yellow

and green.

As I started walking ~~passed~~ *past* the wall, ~~certain things~~

~~started to change.~~ *+* The wall became larger and larger, proba-

bly 20 to 25 feet taller than ~~me and the width would be~~ *I.*

~~about 30 inches.~~ All of a sudden, I felt very emotional. I
couldn't get over how big the wall became. As I looked on
the wall, [I saw] ~~were~~ all the names of all the men [and women] who had died
in the Vietnam War. As soon as I started to look at it, I
automatically became emotional, [a] ~~A~~s if I were going to cry,
~~because~~ I felt very sorry for the men and women who died in
the war. A lady standing next to me was crying as she put
flowers ⌐in front of the wall⌐ on the ground. I realized that it
was okay to be emotional at that time and that place. ¶After a
little while, I wanted to touch the wall, to see what it was
like, and as soon as I [di]~~need~~, I had more feelings about it. It
felt very smooth and the names were engraved on the wall.
Finally, [as] I finished walking, ~~and~~ the wall became smaller and
smaller as it was ~~in the beginning which was a little higher~~ [when I first saw it.]
~~above my ankles.~~

~~I realized that~~ I'm never going to forget that moment in my
life. The scenery was beautiful and the moment was sad, but
the view was spectacular. ~~It's something that I won't want~~
~~to forget,~~ [I]n fact I will [always] treasure it!

Final Version

The Emotional Wall
Tracy Burgio

I'll never forget my trip to the Vietnam Memorial in Washington, D. C. It was about 6:30 p.m. and the sun was going down, so there was a beautiful sunset! It was the perfect time to be there because exactly right behind the Memorial is the Washington Monument, and after that is the Capitol. Straight in front of the Vietnam Memorial is the Lincoln Memorial. The sun lit up the whole sky, and the colors were just beautiful; they reflected on the memorials and the Capitol, pink, purple, yellow and green.

As I started walking past the wall, the wall became larger and larger, probably 20 to 25 feet taller than I. All of a sudden, I felt very emotional. I couldn't get over how big the wall became. As I looked on the wall, I saw all the names of all the men and women who had died in the Vietnam War. As soon as I started to look at it, I automatically became emotional, as if I were going to cry. I felt very sorry for the men and women who died in the war. A lady standing next to me was crying as she put flowers on the ground in front of the wall. I realized that it was okay to be emotional at that time and that place.

After a little while, I wanted to touch the wall, to see what it was like, and as soon as I did, I had more feelings about it. It felt very smooth and the names were engraved on the wall. Finally, as I finished walking, the wall became smaller and smaller as it was when I first saw it.

I'm never going to forget that moment in my life. The scenery was beautiful and the moment was sad, but the view was spectacular. In fact I will always treasure it!

Evaluating the Essay

1. Evaluate the structure and content of the essay.

   a. Does the essay follow a logical plan? Describe its organization.
   b. What is Burgio's thesis?
   c. In what ways does she support her thesis?
   d. Evaluate the effectiveness of the title, introduction, and conclusion.

2. Study the changes Burgio made in her revision. What kinds of changes did she make?

3. What further revisions would you suggest?

WRITING ABOUT A READING

Thinking before Reading

In the following reading, "Superstitious Minds," a woman reminisces about her mother by describing her mother's superstitions. As you read, notice that each paragraph focuses on and develops a single idea, and that the rich descriptions provide relevant and sufficient details for each topic sentence.

1. Preview the reading using the steps provided on page 20.

2. After you have done your preview, connect the reading to your own experience by answering the following questions:

   a. Do you or anyone you know perform any superstitious rituals?
   b. Do you think there is any truth to common superstitions?

READING

Superstitious Minds
Letty Cottin Pogrebin

I am a very rational person. I tend to trust reason more than feeling.   1
But I also happen to be superstitious—in my fashion. Black cats
and rabbits' feet hold no power for me. My superstitions are my
mother's superstitions, the amulets and incantations she learned from
her mother and taught me.

I don't mean to suggest that I grew up in an occult atmosphere. On the contrary, my mother desperately wanted me to rise above her immigrant ways and become an educated American. She tried to hide her superstitions, but I came to know them all: Slap a girl's cheeks when she first gets her period. Never take a picture of a pregnant woman. Knock on wood when speaking about your good fortune. Eat the ends of bread if you want to have a boy. Don't leave a bride alone on her wedding day.

2

When I was growing up, my mother often would tiptoe in after I seemed to be asleep and kiss my forehead three times, making odd noises that sounded like a cross between sucking and spitting. One night I opened my eyes and demanded an explanation. Embarrassed, she told me she was excising the "Evil Eye"—in case I had attracted its attention that day by being especially wonderful. She believed her kisses could suck out any envy or ill will that those less fortunate may have directed at her child.

3

By the time I was in my teens, I was almost on speaking terms with the Evil Eye, a jealous spirit that kept track of those who had "too much" happiness and zapped them with sickness and misery to even the score. To guard against this mischief, my mother practiced rituals of interference, evasion, deference, and above all, avoidance of situations where the Evil Eye might feel at home.

4

This is why I wasn't allowed to attend funerals. This is also why my mother hated to mend my clothes while I was wearing them. The only garment one should properly get sewn *into* is a shroud. To ensure that the Evil Eye did not confuse my pinafore with a burial outfit, my mother insisted that I chew a thread while she sewed, thus proving

5

myself very much alive. Outwitting the Evil Eye also accounted for her closing the window shades above my bed whenever there was a full moon. The moon should only shine on cemeteries, you see; the living need protection from the spirits.

Because we were dealing with a deadly force, I also wasn't supposed to say any words associated with mortality. This was hard for a twelve-year-old who punctuated every anecdote with the verb "to die," as in "You'll die when you hear this!" or "If I don't get home by ten, I'm dead." I managed to avoid using such expressions in the presence of my mother until the day my parents brought home a painting I hated and we were arguing about whether it should be displayed on our walls. Unthinking, I pressed my point with a melodramatic idiom: "That picture will hang over my dead body!" Without a word, my mother grabbed a knife and slashed the canvas to shreds.   6

I understand all this now. My mother emigrated in 1907 from a small Hungarian village. The oldest of seven children, she had to go out to work before she finished the eighth grade. Experience taught her that life was unpredictable and often incomprehensible. Just as an athlete keeps wearing the same T-shirt in every game to prolong a winning streak, my mother's superstitions gave her a means of imposing order on a chaotic system. Her desire to control the fates sprung from the same helplessness that makes the San Francisco 49ers' defensive more superstitious than its offensive team. Psychologists speculate this is because the defense has less control; they don't have the ball.   7

Women like my mother never had the ball. She died when I was 15, leaving me with deep regrets for what she might have been—and a growing understanding of who she was. *Superstitious* is one of the things she was. I wish I had a million sharp recollections of her, but when you don't expect someone to die, you don't store up enough memories. Ironically, her mystical practices are among the clearest impressions she left behind. In honor of this matrilineal heritage—and to symbolize my mother's effort to control her life as I in my way try to find order in mine—I knock on wood and I do not let the moon shine on those I love. My children laugh at me, but they understand that these tiny rituals have helped keep my mother alive in my mind.   8

A year ago, I awoke in the night and realized that my son's window blinds had been removed for repair. Smiling at my own compulsion, I got a bed sheet to tack up against the moonlight and I opened his bedroom door. What I saw brought tears to my eyes. There, hopelessly askew, was a blanket my son, then 18, had taped to his window like a curtain.   9

My mother never lived to know David, but he knew she would not want the moon to shine upon him as he slept.   10

From *Ms.* magazine

Getting Ready to Write

Strengthening Your Vocabulary

Write a brief definition for each of the following words from the preceding reading. If you can't figure out the meaning of a word from the way it is used in the reading, look the word up in the dictionary.

1. amulets (paragraph 1)   *lucky charms*

2. incantations (paragraph 1)   *magic words or spells*

3. occult (paragraph 2)   *having to do with the supernatural or magical*

4. deference (paragraph 4)   *polite respect*

5. shroud (paragraph 5)   *burial cloth or sheet*

6. pinafore (paragraph 5)   *apronlike dress worn by young girls, jumper*

7. incomprehensible (paragraph 7)   *not able to be understood*

8. imposing (paragraph 7)   *applying, placing*

9. ironically (paragraph 8)   *opposite of what one would expect*

10. matrilineal (paragraph 8)   *passed on from mother to daughter*

11. compulsion (paragraph 9)   *unusually strong urge or impulse*

Reviewing the Reading Using an Idea Map

Review the reading by completing the missing pieces of the idea map shown below.

> **LETTY INHERITED HER SUPERSTITIONS FROM HER MOTHER**
>
> She tried to hide them: Letty learned anyway
>
> Most serious one: Evil Eye
>
> 3 kisses at night to suck out evil

Letty couldn't attend funerals
She would not mend clothes while Letty was wearing them
She closed window shades when moon full
Letty could not use words about dying

Letty understands why now

Mother's life unpredictable and confusing
Superstitions: way to feel in control

Letty practices them to keep mother alive for her

Even her son carries it on

Examining the Reading

1. What were some of the superstitions of Pogrebin's mother?

2. As a child, why couldn't Pogrebin use the words "dead" or "die" in front of her mother?

3. Pogrebin claims she is rational; however, she practices her mother's superstitions. What is her real reason for doing this?

4. Do you think Pogrebin's mother really believed in the Evil Eye? Why or why not?

5. Why did the son, who never met his grandmother and who laughed at his mother's superstitions, tape a blanket to his bedroom window to keep out the full moon?

Reacting to and Discussing Ideas

Get ready to write about the reading by discussing the following questions:

1. Why do you think people believe in superstitions?

2. Do you think there can be any harm in being superstitious? Explain.

3. How widespread do you think superstitions are? Explain.

Writing about the Reading

The Paragraph Option

1. Write a paragraph describing a particular superstition.

2. Write a paragraph describing superstitions you don't believe in, explaining why.

The Essay Option

Write an essay describing a ritual you perform or family tradition you carry on that connects you with your parents or grandparents.

Use this Revision Checklist for the paragraph or essay you wrote as a result of reading "Suspicious Minds."

REVISION CHECKLIST

		YES	NO
Paragraph Development	1. Is your topic manageable (neither too broad nor too narrow)?	☐	☐
	2. Is your paragraph written with your reader in mind?	☐	☐
	3. Does your topic sentence identify your topic?	☐	☐
	4. Does your topic sentence make a point about your topic?	☐	☐
	5. Does each remaining sentence support the topic sentence?	☐	☐
	6. Did you include sufficient detail?	☐	☐
Sentence Development	7. Have you avoided writing sentence fragments, run-on sentences, and comma splices?	☐	☐
	8. Have you combined ideas to produce more effective sentences?	☐	☐
	9. Have you used adjectives and adverbs to make your sentences vivid and interesting?	☐	☐
	10. Have you used prepositional phrases, -ing phrases, and relative clauses to add detail?	☐	☐
	11. Have you used pronouns correctly and consistently?	☐	☐
	12. Have you avoided shifts in person, number, and verb tense?	☐	☐

REVISION CHECKLIST (CONTINUED)

	YES	NO
13. Have you placed modifiers correctly?	☐	☐
14. Are elements within each sentence parallel?	☐	☐
15. Have you used correct verb tenses and correct verb forms?	☐	☐

If you have checked any *no*s, go back to your paper and make the necessary changes.

WRITING SUCCESS TIP 11

Using Nonsexist Language

The words you choose when you write or speak can be unintentionally sexist. By using certain expressions and personal pronouns you might make unfair references to males or females, or you may fail to include both sexes in a particular group.

SEXIST: A student will get good grades if *he* knows how to take lecture notes. (This statement fails to recognize that some students are women.)

NONSEXIST: A student will get good grades if *he* or *she* knows how to take lecture notes.
or
Students will get good grades if *they* know how to take lecture notes.

SEXIST: The *girl* at the customer service desk was helpful and efficient. (The term *girl* implies childishness or immaturity.)

NONSEXIST: The *woman* at the customer service desk was helpful and efficient.
or
The *customer service representative* was helpful and efficient.

SEXIST: The *male nurse* gave my grandmother the prescribed medication. (This statement makes an unnecessary distinction between male and female nurses.)

NONSEXIST: The nurse gave my grandmother the prescribed medication.

Here are a few guidelines to follow in avoiding sexist language:

1. When referring to people in general, use "he or she" rather than "he."

SEXIST: A writer should proofread *his* paper.
NONSEXIST: A writer should proofread *his or her* paper.

2. When "he or she" seems awkward or wordy, rewrite your sentence using plural nouns and pronouns.

NONSEXIST: *Writers* should proofread *their* papers.

3. Avoid using the words "man" or "mankind" to refer to people in general; avoid occupational terms ending in *-man*.

Sexist	*Nonsexist*
Any man who gives . . .	Anyone who gives . . .
policeman	police officer
salesman	sales person

4. Avoid expressions that make unfair or negative references to men or women.

Sexist	*Nonsexist*
career gal	career woman
my old man	my husband

5. Refer to a woman by her own name, not by her husband's name.

SEXIST: Mrs. Samuel Goldstein was named Educator of the Year.
NONSEXIST: Rita Goldstein was named Educator of the Year.

SKILLS CHECK

See Selected
Answer Key on
p. 515.

Paragraph 1

The following paragraph describing how fog forms is confusing
because it is disorganized. Revise it so that it reflects a time-sequence
arrangement of the details.

Fog is caused by the natural movements of air from one
place to another. When this moist air that was picked up over
warm water moves to cool land or from warmer to cooler water,
it cools down. As these warm winds pass over the water, they
pick up moisture. When these water molecules condense into a
liquid near the ground, fog forms. Warm winds pass over the
ocean or another large body of water. As the moist air cools
down, the molecules in the water move more slowly and begin
to stick together rather than to bounce off each other when
they collide.

Paragraph 2

The following student paragraph begins with a topic sentence that is
too broad. Revise this topic sentence to make it more specific.

College is different from high school. In high school, there
were almost no papers assigned. When we were given writing
assignments, we were not expected to type them out on a
word processor. It was acceptable to write papers using pencil

and paper. My instructors at college not only expected me to type my papers neatly, but to write papers that provided objective support for an opinion. My first semester, I spent nearly all of my time at the library trying to figure out how to write an objective paper instead of a paper with just my opinion. It didn't take me long to figure out that the requirements for college papers are very different from those assigned in high school. Furthermore, my high school teachers would take class time to help students review for exams and even small tests. As a result, I did very little studying on my own. In addition, most high school tests were objective tests, and essay questions were found only on final exams. College instructors expect students to prepare themselves for exams, and only rarely are these exams objective ones. It was a real struggle for me to learn how to prepare for college exams and to write good essays, but now that I have two semesters' experience, I think I am on the right track.

SKILLS CHECK   CONTINUED

Paragraph 3

The following paragraph is a description of a bedroom. It is a weak description because it lacks detail. Revise it by adding details that help the reader to visualize this room.

My favorite room in the house is my bedroom. My room is a shade of blue that contrasts with its white drapes and bedspread. The bed and dressers are made of pine. Plants hang in the windows. The room is always quiet because it is in the back of the house and overlooks the yard.

PARAGRAPH DEVELOPMENT

Developing, Arranging, and Connecting Details

Read the Buster® FoodCube ad on page 301, which describes how a dog named Samson learned to enjoy the FoodCube and feels much smarter as time goes by. Now reread the ad, paying particular attention to the details and how they are arranged. You no doubt notice that the ad contains many specific details: Samson's first reaction, his visit to the dog across the street and so forth. You also see that the details are arranged in the order in which they happened. This arrangement is called **time sequence**. Next, look at how the copy writer connected details to one another. Notice words and phrases such as *so now* and *the other day*. These words and phrases are called **transitions**. They lead the reader from one step to another.

Your writing, like this advertising copy, will improve when you use specific details to make your material come alive. Details make writing more interesting and lively. They convey information about your topic, too. In this chapter you will learn how to use specific details to develop your paragraph. You will use the three methods of arranging ideas (time sequence, spatial arrangement, and least/most arrangement) and transitions to make your paragraphs clear and effective.

WRITING

Developing a Paragraph Using Specific Details

Read the following pairs of statements. For each pair, place a check mark in the blank before the statement that is more vivid and that contains more information.

1. _____ a. Professor Valquez gives a lot of homework.
   _____✓_____ b. Professor Valquez assigns twenty problems each class and requires us to read two chapters per week.

2. _____ a. In Korea, people figure age differently.
   _____✓_____ b. In Korea, people are considered to be one year old at birth.

3. _____ a. It was really hot Tuesday.
   _____✓_____ b. On Tuesday the temperature in New Haven reached ninety-seven degrees.

These pairs of sentences illustrate the difference between vague statements and specific statements. The first statement in each pair conveys little information and also lacks interest and appeal. The second statement offers specific, detailed information and, as a result, is more interesting.

As you generate ideas and draft paragraphs, try to include as many specific details as possible. These details (called **supporting details** because they support your topic sentence) make your writing more interesting and your ideas more convincing.

The sample paragraph below lacks detail. Compare it with the revised paragraph that follows it. Notice how the revision has produced a much more lively, informative, and convincing paragraph.

Sample Paragraph

Being a waiter or waitress is a more complicated job than most people think. First of all, you must have a friendly personality. You must be able to maintain a smile no matter what your inner feelings may be. Proper attire and good hygiene are also essential. You have to be good at memorizing who wants what and make sure each order is made to their specifications. If you are friendly, neat, and attentive to your customers, you will be successful.

Revised Paragraph

Being a waitress is a more complicated job than the average customer thinks. First of all, a friendly, outgoing personality is important. No one wants to be greeted by a waitress who has an angry, indifferent, or "I'm bored with this job" expression on her face. A waitress should try to smile, regardless of the circumstances. When a screaming child hurls a plate of french fries across the table, smile and wipe up the ketchup. Proper attire and good hygiene are important, too. A waitress in a dirty dress and with hair hanging down into the food does not please customers. Finally, attentiveness to customers' orders is important. Be certain that each person gets the correct order and that the food is prepared according to specifications. Pay particular attention when serving salads and steaks since different dressings and degrees of rareness are easily confused. Following these suggestions will lead to happy customers as well as larger tips.

In this revision, the writer added examples, included more descriptive words, and made all details more concrete and specific.

Here are a few suggestions for how to include more specific details:

1. Add names, numbers, times, and places.

VAGUE: I bought a new used car.

MORE SPECIFIC: Yesterday afternoon I bought a 1996 two-door red Toyota Tercel at the new "Toy-a-Rama" dealership.

2. Add more facts and explanation.

VAGUE: My fax machine works well.

MORE SPECIFIC: My fax machine allows me to send letters and documents through a phone line in seconds and at minimal cost.

3. Use examples.

VAGUE: Dogs learn their owners' habits.

MORE SPECIFIC: As soon as I reach for my wire garden basket, my golden retriever knows this means I'm going outside and rushes to the back door.

4. Draw from your personal experience.

VAGUE: People sometimes eat to calm down.

MORE SPECIFIC: My sister relaxes every evening with a bowl of popcorn.

Depending on your topic, you may need to do research to get more specific details. Dictionaries, encyclopedias, and magazine articles are often good sources. Think of research as interesting detective work and a chance to learn. For example, if you are writing a paragraph about the safety of air bags in cars, you may need to locate some current facts and statistics. Your college library will be one good source; a car dealership and a mechanic may be two others. (Refer to Chapter 14, page 346, to learn more about doing research and to Writing Success Tip 14, "Avoiding Plagiarism and Citing Sources" to learn more about telling your reader where you got your information.)

EXERCISE ▶ 12-1 Revise each of the following statements to make it more specific.

EXAMPLE: Biology is a difficult course.

Biology involves memorizing scientific terms and learning some of life's complex processes.

1. I rode the train. On Tuesday I took the Red Line train to Cambridge to visit my cousin.

2. Pizza is easy to prepare. <u>Making pizza involves three simple steps:</u>

   <u>stretching prepared dough, adding toppings, and baking.</u>

3. The Fourth of July is a holiday. <u>The Fourth of July is fun because</u>

   <u>my town has a big parade and picnic.</u>

4. I bought a lawnmower. <u>I bought a used ten-horsepower John Deere</u>

   <u>lawnmower from Drake's Garden Shop.</u>

5. The van broke down.
   <u>My brother's 1976 Chevy van blew a gasket.</u>

EXERCISE **12-2** Write a paragraph on one of the following topics. Develop a topic sentence that expresses one main point about the topic. Then develop your paragraph using specific details.

1. your favorite food (or junk food)
2. how pets help people
3. why shopping is (or is not) fun
4. a sport (or hobby) you would like to take up
5. an annoying habit

Methods of Arranging Details

Your paragraph can have many good details in it, but if they are arranged in a jumbled fashion, your writing will lack impact. You must arrange your details logically within each paragraph. Let us look at three common ways of arranging details:

1. time sequence
2. spatial arrangement
3. least/most arrangement

Time Sequence

When you are describing an event or series of events, it is often easiest to arrange them in the order in which they happened. This arrangement is called **time sequence**. For example, in the Buster® FoodCube advertisement on page 301, Samson describes the series of events that he experienced with the FoodCube. The following time-sequence map will help you visualize this arrangement.

Time-Sequence Map

HERE IS HOW TO BUILD A LOW-FAT DELI SELECT SANDWICH:

Start with a portion of Low Fat Honey Ham and double it.

Add Fat Free Smoked Chicken Breast.

Using your mouth to measure, add Low Fat Pastrami.

Add 2 pounds of Fat Free Smoked Turkey Breast.

Add slices of Fat Free Mesquite Smoked Turkey Breast.

You can also use time sequence to explain how events happened or to tell a story. For example, you can explain how you ended up living in Cleveland or tell a story about a haunted house. This is called a narrative and is discussed in more detail in Chapter 13, page 321. In the following sample paragraph, the student has arranged details in time sequence. Read the paragraph, and then fill in the blanks in the time-sequence map that follows it.

Sample Time-Sequence Paragraph

Driving a standard-shift vehicle is easy if you follow these steps. First, push the clutch pedal down. The clutch is the pedal on the left. Then start the car. Next, move the gearshift into first gear. On most cars this is the straight-up position. Next, give the car some gas, and slowly release the clutch pedal until you start moving. Finally, be ready to shift into higher gears—second, third, and so on—depending on the make of car. A diagram of where to find each gear usually appears on the gearshift knob. With practice, you will learn to start up smoothly and shift without the car making grinding noises or lurching.

Time-Sequence Map

Fill in the blanks in the following time-sequence map using the information in the sample paragraph above. List the information in the same sequence in which it appears in the paragraph.

DRIVING A STANDARD-SHIFT VEHICLE IS EASY.

Make sure clutch pedal is pushed in.

Start the car.

Shift car into first gear.

Give some gas, and slowly let out clutch.

Once moving, shift into higher gear.

Practice.

This last sample paragraph was clear and easy to follow because the events were described in the order in which they occurred.

Time-Sequence Transitions

Look again at the sample paragraph above. Notice that transitions are used to lead you from one step to another. Try to pick them out; underline those that you find. Did you underline *first, then, next,* and *finally*? Using transitions like those listed below will help you to link details in a time-sequence paragraph.

NEED TO KNOW		
Common Time-Sequence Transitions		
first	next	before
second	during	now
third	at the same time	later
in the beginning	following	at last
then	after	finally

EXERCISE 12-3 ▶ Arrange in time sequence the supporting-detail sentences that follow the topic sentence below. Place a "1" in the blank before the detail that should appear first in the paragraph, a "2" before the detail that should appear second, and so on.

TOPIC SENTENCE: Registration for college classes requires planning and patience.

Supporting-Detail Sentences

_____3_____ a. Find out which courses that you need are being offered that particular semester.

_____1_____ b. Study your degree requirements, and figure out which courses you need to take before you can take others.

_____4_____ c. Then start working out a schedule.

_____2_____ d. For example, a math course may have to be taken before an accounting or a science course.

_____6_____ e. Then, when you register, if one course or section is closed, you will have others in mind that will work with your schedule.

_____5_____ f. Select alternative courses that you can take if all sections of one of your first-choice courses are closed.

EXERCISE 12-4 | Write a paragraph on one of the following topics. First, write a topic sentence that identifies your topic and expresses your main point about it. Then arrange your supporting-detail sentences in order. Be sure to use transitions to connect your ideas. When you have finished, draw a time-sequence map of your paragraph (see page 305 for a model). Use your map to check that you have included sufficient details and that you have presented your details in the correct sequence.

1. making up for lost time
2. closing (or beginning) a chapter of your life
3. getting more (or less) out of an experience than you expected
4. having an adventure
5. having an experience that made you feel like saying, "Look who's talking!"

Spatial Arrangement

Suppose you are asked to describe a car you have just purchased. You want your reader, who has never seen the car, to visualize it. How would you organize your description? You could describe the car from bottom to top or from top to bottom, or from front to back. This method of presentation is called **spatial arrangement.** For other objects, you might arrange your details from inside to outside, from near to far, or from east to west. Notice how, in the following paragraph, the details are arranged from top to bottom.

Sample Spatial-Arrangement Paragraph

My dream house will have a three-level outdoor deck that will be ideal for relaxing on after a hard day's work. The top level of the deck will be connected by sliding glass doors to the family room. On this level there will be a hot tub, a large picnic table with benches, and a comfortable padded chaise. On the middle level there will be a suntanning area, a hammock, and two built-in planters for a mini-herb garden. The lowest level, which will meet the lawn, will have a built-in stone barbeque pit for big cookouts and a gas grill for everyday use.

Can you visualize the deck?

Spatial-Arrangement Transitions

In spatial-arrangement paragraphs, transitions are particularly important since they often reveal placement or position of objects or parts. Using transitions like those listed in the Need to Know box below will help you to link details in a spatial-arrangement paragraph.

NEED TO KNOW

Common Spatial-Arrangement Transitions

above	next to	nearby
below	inside	on the other side
beside	outside	beneath
in front of	behind	to the west (or other direction)

EXERCISE 12-5 Use spatial arrangement to order the supporting-detail sentences that follow the topic sentence below. Place a "1" in the blank before the detail that should appear first in the paragraph, a "2" before the detail that should appear second, and so on.

TOPIC SENTENCE: My beautiful cousin Audry always looks as if she has dressed quickly and given her appearance little thought.

Supporting-Detail Sentences

_____3_____ a. She usually wears an oversized baggy sweater, either black or blue-black, with the sleeves pushed up.

_____6_____ b. Black slip-on sandals complete the look; she wears them in every season.

_____5_____ c. On her feet she wears mismatched socks.

_____1_____ d. Her short, reddish hair is usually wind-blown, hanging every which way from her face.

_____2_____ e. She puts her makeup on unevenly, if at all.

_____4_____ f. The sweater covers most of her casual, rumpled skirt.

EXERCISE 12-6 ▶ Write a paragraph on one of the following topics. First, write a topic sentence that identifies your topic and expresses your main point about it. Then use spatial arrangement to develop your supporting details.

1. the room you are in now
2. the building where you live
3. a photograph or painting that you like
4. your dream car
5. your favorite chair or place

Least/Most Arrangement

Another method of arranging details is to present them in order from least to most or most to least according to some quality or characteristic. For example, you might choose least to most important, serious, frightening, or humorous. In writing a paragraph explaining your reasons for attending college, you might arrange them from most to least important. In writing about an exciting evening, you might arrange your details from most to least exciting.

As you read the following paragraph, note how the writer has arranged details in a logical way.

Sample Least/Most Paragraph

This week has been filled with good news. One night when balancing my checkbook, I discovered a $155 error in my checking account—in my favor, for once! I was even happier when I finally found a buyer for my Chevy Blazer, which I had been trying to sell all winter. Then my boss told me he was submitting my name for a fifty-cent hourly raise; I certainly didn't expect that. Best of all, I learned that I'd been accepted into the Radiology curriculum for next fall.

In this paragraph, the details are arranged from least to most important.

Least/Most Transitions

In least/most paragraphs, transitions help your reader to follow your train of thought. Using transitions like those listed below will help you link details in a least/most paragraph.

NEED TO KNOW

Common Least/Most Transitions

most important	particularly important	moreover
above all	even more	in addition
especially	best of all	not only . . . but also

EXERCISE **12-7**

Write a paragraph on one of the following topics. First, write a topic sentence that identifies your topic and expresses your main point about it. Then use a least/most arrangement to order your details. When you have finished, draw a map of your paragraph. Use your map to check that you have included sufficient details and that you have arranged your details in least/most order.

1. your reasons for choosing the college you are attending
2. changes in your life since you began college
3. three commercials you saw on television recently
4. why you liked a certain book or movie
5. good (or bad) things that have happened to you recently

EXERCISE **12-8**

Write a topic sentence for each of the following topics. Then indicate what method (time sequence, spatial, or least/most) you would use to arrange supporting details.

TOPIC: relationship with a friend

TOPIC SENTENCE: Whenever George and I get together, he always takes over the conversation.

METHOD OF ARRANGEMENT: Time sequence

1. TOPIC: animals that have humanlike behaviors

TOPIC SENTENCE: My golden retriever and my two-year-old granddaughter react in similar ways to household happenings.

METHOD OF ARRANGEMENT: Least/most

2. TOPIC: a difficulty that I faced

   TOPIC SENTENCE: I was going to drop my math class, but instead I met
   with my teacher and she helped me line up a tutor.

   METHOD OF ARRANGEMENT: Time sequence

3. TOPIC: feeling under pressure

   TOPIC SENTENCE: Recently a number of mishaps have increased my
   level of stress.

   METHOD OF ARRANGEMENT: Time sequence or least/most

4. TOPIC: a favorite dinner menu

   TOPIC SENTENCE: For Thanksgiving dinner I served broccoli soup, roast
   turkey with chestnut stuffing, and pecan pie.

   METHOD OF ARRANGEMENT: Time sequence

5. TOPIC: an exciting sporting event

   TOPIC SENTENCE: The Superbowl is an annual event in which two
   championship teams display their talents.

   METHOD OF ARRANGEMENT: Least/most

EXERCISE 12-9 ▶ Find several magazine or newspaper ads. Working in a group, identify the method of arrangement of the advertising copy.

NEED TO KNOW

Developing, Arranging, and Connecting Details

Be sure to use interesting and lively **details** to support your topic sentence.

- Choose details that are specific and concrete.
- Within your paragraphs, arrange details in a **logical order.** Three techniques for arranging details are
  — time sequence—information is presented in the order in which it happened.
  — spatial arrangement—descriptive details are arranged according to their position in space.
  — least/most arrangement—ideas are arranged from least to most or most to least according to some quality or characteristic.
- Use transitions to help your reader move easily from one key detail to the next.

The following essay was written by Maya Prestwich, a student at Northwestern University, and was published in the college newspaper, *The Daily Northwestern*. This essay is a good example of the use of concrete details to support a thesis. As you read, highlight particularly informative or interesting details.

Halloween: Fun Without Cultural Guilt
Maya Prestwich

W hat are you gonna be?" That's the question circulating around school yards this week. I overheard a group of children talking about Halloween costumes as I walked by the school three blocks from my house.   1

The lone girl of the group was going as a ballerina, and the boys were fighting it out over who could be Batman. All feelings about feminism and gender stereotypes aside, the whole scene made me smile. I'd forgotten how much children love Halloween and how much I love it too. Years of being immersed in campus life had left me feeling as if Halloween really was just another day, but moving off-campus has allowed me to rediscover it.   2

What is it about Halloween that seems to put everyone in a happier, more adventurous mood? There's that feeling in the air (beneath the chill), a festive feeling, a primitive feeling, a pagan feeling. October 31 is really the only time when we allow ourselves to freely embrace that aspect of our humanity.   3

It's also a very rare chance for everyone, children and adults, to reinvent themselves a little. School teachers get to be witches, little boys and girls can be superheroes. Country farm girls who listen to Garth Brooks pretend to be punk rock fans and for one night, I can pretend to be a confident, indifferent, dangerous black cat. It seems sort of ridiculous on the surface, but it's important to me to have this day when coloring outside the lines is acceptable. I believe it is crucial that we help our children learn that doing things they wouldn't normally do can be fun and exhilarating and liberating.   4

For grown-ups, and us almost-grown-ups, it's important to remember on Halloween that you can change what you are "going to be" if you know you made the wrong decision. Being a cat or a ghost or a   5 globe or a Power Ranger is a decision I would agonize over for a full month, but it was still just a decision. A different costume could easily be thrown together or an old one dragged out of the closet, and I could take the evening in a different direction.

Similarly, all of those big adult things that we agonize over, what career to choose, which job to go for, whom to marry, they are still just decisions.   6

Reinventing yourself, changing your life. It's not quite as simple as changing your costume, but it's not quite as difficult as we make it out to be either.   7

There's another pretty spiffy thing about Halloween, and that's the way that it unifies us. Catholic, Jewish or unaffiliated, rich or middle class, city or country, believers in one god, believers in many gods, believers in no gods. We can share this one holiday without having to go through sensitivity training. Every kid gets dressed up and hopes for a good haul, everyone who can leaves the porch light on and answers the doorbell bearing Tootsie Rolls and every mom decides that a crime wave is going to hit their small town and participates in the ritual "inspecting of the candy."   8

Halloween is freer of culture clash than even Independence or Columbus days. Face it, it is a really awesome holiday, a day for fun and spontaneity without any of the ramifications of cultural guilt, and that is cause for celebration. Or at least the consumption of candy.   9

Evaluating the Essay

1. Evaluate the structure and content of the essay.
   a. Does the essay follow a logical plan? Describe its organization.
   b. What is Prestwich's thesis?
   c. In what ways does she support her thesis?
   d. Evaluate the effectiveness of the title, introduction, and conclusion.

2. Evaluate Prestwich's use of detail.
   a. What types does she use?
   b. Identify five details that make her essay vivid and interesting.
   c. Do you feel further detail is needed? If so, suggest which paragraphs need more detail.

WRITING ABOUT A READING

Thinking before Reading

The following reading, "A Brother's Murder," explains how a man feels about the circumstances surrounding the death of his street-smart, younger brother. As you read this selection, notice that Brent Staples uses specific details to make his essay vivid and real. Also notice that he arranges his details logically, mainly using the time-sequence pattern.

1. Preview the reading using the steps provided on page 20.

2. After you have done your preview, connect the reading to your own experience by answering the following questions:

   a. If you have grown up in a neighborhood filled with crime, run-down buildings, and hopelessness, would you remain part of the community or move away from it?

   b. What could you say or do to help a relative or friend headed for trouble?

READING

A Brother's Murder
Brent Staples

It has been more than two years since my telephone rang with the news that my younger brother Blake—just 22 years old—had been murdered. The young man who killed him was only 24. Wearing a ski mask, he emerged from a car, fired six times at close range with a massive .44 Magnum, then fled. The two had once been inseparable friends. A senseless rivalry—beginning, I think, with an argument over a girlfriend—escalated from posturing, to threats, to violence, to murder. The way the two were living, death could have come to either of them from anywhere. In fact, the assailant had already survived multiple gun-shot wounds from an incident much like the one in which my brother lost his life.

I left the East Coast after college, spent the mid- and late-1970's in Chicago as a graduate student, taught for a time, then became a journalist. Within 10 years of leaving my hometown, I was overeducated and "upwardly mobile," ensconced on a quiet, tree-lined street where voices

1

2

raised in anger were scarcely ever heard. The telephone, like some grim umbilical, kept me connected to the old world with news of deaths, imprisonings, and misfortune. I felt emotionally beaten up. Perhaps to protect myself, I added a psychological dimension to the physical distance I had already achieved. I rarely visited my hometown. I shut it out.

As I fled the past, so Blake embraced it. On Christmas of 1983, I traveled from Chicago to a black section of Roanoke, Virginia, where he then lived. The desolate public housing projects, the hopeless, idle young men crashing against one another—these reminded me of the embittered town we'd grown up in. It was a place where once I would have been comfortable, or at least sure of myself. Now, hearing of my brother's forays into crime, his scrapes with police and street thugs, I was scared, unsteady on foreign terrain.

I saw that Blake's romance with the street life and the hustler image had flowered dangerously. One evening that late December, standing in some Roanoke dive among drug dealers and grim, hair-trigger losers, I told him I feared for his life. He had affected the image of the tough he wanted to be. But behind the dark glasses and the swagger, I glimpsed the baby-faced toddler I'd once watched over. I nearly wept. I wanted desperately for him to live. The young think themselves immortal, and a dangerous light shone in his eyes as he spoke laughingly, of making fools of the policemen who had raided his apartment looking for drugs. He cried out as I took his right hand. A line of stitches lay between the thumb and index finger. Kickback from a shotgun, he explained, nothing serious. Gunplay had become part of his life.

I lacked the language simply to say: Thousands have lived this for you and died. I fought the urge to lift him bodily and shake him. This place and the way you are living smells of death to me, I said. Take some time away, I said. Let's go downtown tomorrow and buy a plane ticket anywhere, take a bus trip, anything to get away and cool things off. He took my alarm casually. We arranged to meet the following night—an appointment he would not keep. We embraced as though through glass. I drove away.

As I stood in my apartment in Chicago holding the receiver that evening in February 1984, I felt as though part of my soul had been cut away. I questioned myself then, and I still do. Did I not reach back soon or earnestly enough for him? For weeks I awoke crying from a recurrent dream in which I chased him, urgently trying to get him to read a document I had, as though reading it would protect him from what had happened in waking life. His eyes shining like black diamonds, he smiled and danced just beyond my grasp. When I reached for him, I caught only the space where he had been.

From Bearing Witness.

Getting Ready to Write

Strengthening Your Vocabulary

Write a brief definition for each of the following words from the preceding reading. If you can't figure out the meaning of a word from the way it is used in the reading, look the word up in the dictionary.

1. rivalry (paragraph 1)   competition, attempts to outdo each other

2. escalated (paragraph 1)   increased in intensity and seriousness

3. posturing (paragraph 1)   putting on an attitude, posing

4. ensconced (paragraph 2)   settled in comfortably

5. umbilical (paragraph 2)   connecting cord

6. desolate (paragraph 3)   grim, dreary, uninhabitable

7. forays (paragraph 3)   raids, sudden entries

8. terrain (paragraph 3)   territory, turf

9. swagger (paragraph 4)   boastful show of fearlessness

10. recurrent (paragraph 6)   returning, repeating

Reviewing the Reading Using an Idea Map

Review the reading by completing the missing pieces of the idea map shown below.

BRENT STAPLES'S BROTHER BLAKE MURDERED AT AGE 22

- Staples left hometown after college

  - Went to graduate school, taught, became journalist

  - 10 years after leaving, lived different lifestyle

  - Rarely visited home; only phoned

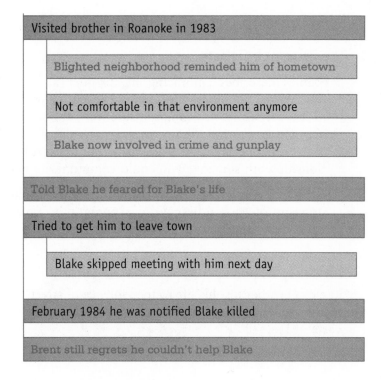

Examining the Reading

1. How and why did Blake, Staples's younger brother, die?

2. Why was Staples so worried about Blake?

3. Describe Staples's attempts to help Blake when he visited him in 1983 in Roanoke, Virginia.

4. What effects did Blake's death have on Staples?

Reacting to and Discussing Ideas

Get ready to write about the reading by discussing the following questions:

1. Why did Staples rarely visit his hometown?

2. Staples wonders whether or not he could have done more to protect and rescue his brother. Do you think there was more he could or should have done? Explain.

3. Why do you think Staples keeps dreaming about his brother? What does his dream mean?

Writing about the Reading

The Paragraph Option

1. Staples describes embracing his brother as if through glass. This description and others throughout the reading suggest that Staples and his brother could not communicate well, although they seemed to care about one another. Write a paragraph describing your relationship with someone you had difficulty communicating with or your relationship with someone you could communicate with easily.

2. Members of the same family often are very different, sometimes the opposite of each other. Write a paragraph explaining how you are either very similar to or very different from a member of your family.

The Essay Option

Staples's brother lost his life to the violence of street crime. Write an essay describing what you feel can or should be done to avoid such a tragic waste of life.

Use this Revision Checklist for the paragraph or essay you wrote as a result of reading "A Brother's Murder."

REVISION CHECKLIST

Paragraph Development		YES	NO
	1. Is your topic manageable (neither too broad nor too narrow)?	☐	☐
	2. Is your paragraph written with your reader in mind?	☐	☐
	3. Does your topic sentence identify your topic?	☐	☐
	4. Does your topic sentence make a point about your topic?	☐	☐
	5. Does each remaining sentence support the topic sentence?	☐	☐
	6. Did you include sufficient detail?	☐	☐
	7. Are your details arranged logically?	☐	☐
	8. Have you used transitions to connect your details?	☐	☐
	9. Is there a sentence at the end that brings the paragraph to a close?	☐	☐

REVISION CHECKLIST (CONTINUED)

Sentence Development		YES	NO
	10. Have you avoided writing sentence fragments, run-on sentences, and comma splices?	☐	☐
	11. Have you combined ideas to produce more effective sentences?	☐	☐
	12. Have you used adjectives and adverbs to make your sentences vivid and interesting?	☐	☐
	13. Have you used prepositional phrases, *-ing* phrases, and relative clauses to add detail?	☐	☐
	14. Have you used pronouns correctly and consistently?	☐	☐
	15. Have you avoided shifts in person, number, and verb tense?	☐	☐
	16. Have you placed modifiers correctly?	☐	☐
	17. Are elements within each sentence parallel?	☐	☐
	18. Have you used correct verb tenses and correct verb forms?	☐	☐

If you have checked any *no*s, go back to your paper and make the necessary changes.

WRITING SUCCESS TIP 12

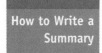
How to Write a Summary

In many college courses you will be asked to write a summary of a reading. A summary is a very short restatement of the ideas and major supporting details. It does not include all information in the reading. The following tips will help you gather and organize the material you need to write a clear summary:

1. Be sure you understand the reading and have identified the writer's major points.

2. Reread the material and underline each major idea, or draw a revision map of the reading.

3. Write one sentence that states the writer's overall concern or most important idea. To do this, ask yourself, "What one topic is the material about?" Then ask, "What point is the writer trying to make about that topic?" This sentence will be the topic sentence of your summary.

4. Be sure to use your own words rather than those of the author.

5. Review the major supporting information that you underlined. Select key details to include in your summary. The amount of detail you include will depend on your purpose for writing the summary.

6. Present ideas in the summary in the same order in which they appear in the reading.

7. If the writer presents a clear opinion on or expresses an attitude toward the subject matter, include it in your summary.

Writing Descriptive and Narrative Paragraphs

Suppose you are writing an advertisement for a new fat-free line of ice creams. You could develop your ad in a number of ways. For example, you could describe the ice creams by their delicious taste, texture, and flavors. Another choice might be to tell the story of someone who tried the ice creams and enjoyed them. If you described the taste, appearance, or feel of the ice cream, you would be using a method of development called **description.** If you told a story about someone enjoying the ice creams, you would be using a method called **narration.** This chapter will concentrate on these two methods of development.

The descriptive method often involves an element of personal opinion, since people's tastes and impressions vary. Another possible way to write the ice cream ad would be to present factual information that goes beyond personal impressions and opinions. For example, you might write about the calories, ingredients, and preparation of the ice cream. These are qualities that are provable and not open to debate. With this approach, you would be using the **informative** method of development. You'll learn more about this method in the next chapter.

CHAPTER OBJECTIVES

In this chapter you will learn to

1. write descriptive paragraphs.
2. write narrative paragraphs.

WRITING

Writing Descriptive Paragraphs

The following Starbucks coffee advertisement uses the **descriptive** method of development. By providing details about the flavor, aroma, and effects of coffee, the advertisement enables you to imagine what the product tastes like and what mood it produces. After reading the

advertisement, you are left with the overall impression that drinking Starbucks coffee is comforting and relaxing.

Descriptive paragraphs work the same way. You use details that appeal to the senses—taste, touch, smell, sight, hearing—to help your reader imagine an object, person, place, or experience. Your details should also leave your reader with an overall impression of what you are describing.

Creating an Overall Impression

The **overall impression** in a descriptive paragraph is the *one* central idea you want to present to your reader. It is the one main point that all of your details prove or support. For example, if you are writing a paragraph about your math instructor's sense of humor, then all of your details should be about amusing things he or she has said or done.

Your overall impression should be expressed in your topic sentence. Usually it is best to place your topic sentence at the beginning of the paragraph. Notice that each of the following topic sentences expresses a different overall impression of Niagara Falls. Each would lead to a different descriptive paragraph because each would need different supporting details.

1. Niagara Falls is stunningly beautiful and majestic.

2. The beauty of Niagara Falls is hidden by its tourist-oriented commercial surroundings.

3. Niagara Falls would be beautiful to visit if I could be there alone, without the crowds of tourists.

EXERCISE 13-1 Select four products that you buy and use (for example, soap, shampoo, aspirin, cereal, soda). For each product, write a sentence that expresses your overall impression of the particular brand that you buy.

PRODUCT: Great Grains cereal

OVERALL IMPRESSION: Great Grains cereal is tasty and nutritious.

1. L'Oreal hair spray provides control without damaging the hair.

_____

2. Dannon yogurt is a healthy, low-fat dairy product.

_____

3. Land o' Lakes butter has a pure, authentic butter taste.

_____

4. Kraft fat-free salad dressings are surprisingly tasty.

_____

Your overall impression is often your first reaction to a topic. Suppose you are writing about your college snack bar. Think of a word or two that sums up how you feel about it. Is it noisy? Smelly? Relaxing? Messy? You could develop any one of these descriptive words into a paragraph. For example, your topic sentence might be

The snack bar is a noisy place that I try to avoid.

The details that follow would then describe the noise—the clatter of plates, loud conversations, chairs scraping the floor, and music blaring.

If you have difficulty thinking of an overall impression of a topic, quickly jot down a list of your observations and reactions. Use the prewriting techniques discussed in Chapter 10 (pages 252–258) to generate ideas.

EXERCISE Write a few words that sum up your reaction to each of the following topics. Then develop each into a topic sentence that expresses an overall impression that could lead to a descriptive paragraph.

TOPIC: a parent or guardian

REACTION: Dad: loving, accepting, smart, helpful, calm, generous

_____

TOPIC SENTENCE: My whole life, my father has been generous and

helpful in the way he let me be me.

1. TOPIC: a library or gym that you have used

   REACTION: Gold's Gym: well-equipped, fitness programs,

   TOPIC SENTENCE: Gold's Gym is famous for its state-of-the-art equipment,

   fine fitness programs, and helpful, knowledgeable trainers.

2. TOPIC: a part-time job, past or present

REACTION: life guard—a lot of benefits

TOPIC SENTENCE: My job as a lifeguard has many benefits: good pay, flexible

hours, and the chance to meet new friends.

3. TOPIC: **a small shop or a shopkeeper that you know**

REACTION: Louie's Deli: fabulous take-out foods

TOPIC SENTENCE: Louie's Deli has the best take-out foods in town including

freshly baked pizza, homemade salads, and delicious

Italian desserts.

4. TOPIC: **a music video, movie, or song**

REACTION: Movie: *As Good As It Gets*: popular, crowd-pleaser

TOPIC SENTENCE: The recent crowd-pleaser, *As Good As It Gets*, starring

Jack Nicholson and Helen Hunt, is popular with many

different age groups.

5. TOPIC: **a person in the news**

REACTION: Bill Gates: one of the world's richest people

TOPIC SENTENCE: Bill Gates, one of the world's richest people, founded

Microsoft Corporation when he dropped out of college to

pursue his childhood interest in computers.

Selecting Descriptive Details

All the details in a descriptive paragraph must support your overall impression. Begin by brainstorming details that describe your topic or relate to your overall impression. Try to imagine the person, place, thing, or experience. Depending on what your topic is, write down what you see, hear, smell, taste, or feel. Here's a student's list of details describing a popular ocean beach:

waves crashing   sunburns
smell of suntan oil   police patroling in
joggers splashing in   all-terrain vehicles
   the waves   refreshment-stand lines
skimpy bikinis   large group parties
kids running & screaming   Frisbee games
volleyball   not enough bathrooms
radios blaring   airplanes overhead

If you do not have an overall impression, just list all details that in any way describe your topic. Then reread your list. What feeling or impression do many of them suggest? In the above list, many of the details suggest that the beach was an unpleasantly crowded, noisy, busy scene. Once you've chosen an overall impression, eliminate those details that do not relate to it.

Using the above list of details, a student wrote the following paragraph to describe an ocean beach. Notice that all of the details directly support the overall impression expressed in the first sentence. After reading the paragraph, complete the map of the paragraph by filling in what details and examples the writer uses. The topic sentence and the main supporting points are already filled in for you.

Sample Descriptive Paragraph

It is a mystery to me why anyone spends the day at Mercury Beach; this place is one of the most crowded and commercialized beaches I have ever visited. I find it impossible to enjoy the shoreline's natural beauty. Radios blare, police patrol in ATVs, airplanes fly overhead carrying banners, and large group parties create distraction. Swimming is nearly impossible. The swimming area is filled with kids running, screaming, and splashing. Volleyball and Frisbee games make walking along the water's edge difficult. Crowds create numerous inconveniences, too. There are long lines at the refreshment stands and even longer lines at the restrooms. The parking lot is filled by eleven o'clock every day. Thanks, but no thanks, for a day at Mercury Beach!

Idea Map

MERCURY BEACH IS CROWDED AND COMMERCIALIZED.

Cannot enjoy natural beauty

radios blaring

police patroling in ATVs

airplanes carrying banners

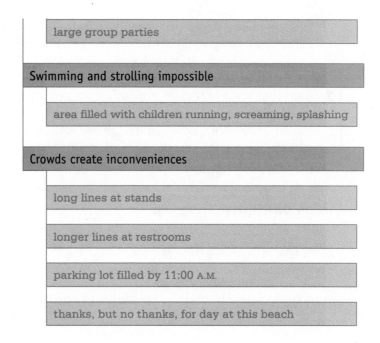

large group parties

Swimming and strolling impossible

area filled with children running, screaming, splashing

Crowds create inconveniences

long lines at stands

longer lines at restrooms

parking lot filled by 11:00 A.M.

thanks, but no thanks, for day at this beach

EXERCISE 13-3 ▶ | Select one of the topics listed in Exercise 13-2. Brainstorm details that support your overall impression.

Organizing Your Details

How you arrange details in a descriptive paragraph is determined by the topic you choose and the overall impression you want to convey. Two common methods of ordering details in descriptive writing are spatial arrangement and least/most arrangement. In **spatial arrangement,** you organize details according to their physical location (see Chapter 12, pages 307–309, for a discussion of this method). For example, you could describe a favorite newsstand by arranging your details from right to left or from front to back.

In **least/most arrangement,** you organize details in increasing or decreasing order according to some quality or characteristic, such as importance. (See Chapter 12, pages 309–310.) Suppose your overall impression of a person is that she is disorganized. You might start with some minor traits (she never can find a pen) and move to more serious and important characteristics of disorganization (she misses classes and forgets appointments).

Whatever method you choose to arrange your details, you will want to use good transitional words and phrases between details. Transitions allow your reader to connect easily the various points in your description.

(See Chapter 12, pages 308 and 310, for a discussion of transitions in paragraphs using spatial and least/most arrangements.)

EXERCISE 13-4 | Using the details you developed in Exercise 13-3, write a paragraph. Assume that your reader is someone from another country who is unfamiliar with what you are describing. Organize your paragraph using a spatial or least/most arrangement. Then draw a revision map of your paragraph. Use it to check that all your details support your overall impression and that you have included sufficient detail.

Using Descriptive Language

Unlike advertising copy (as in the Starbucks advertisement on page 322), your paragraphs are not accompanied by photographs, which add color, interest, and appeal. Consequently, you must supply these features in other ways. By using descriptive words that help your reader imagine your topic, you can make it exciting and appealing.

Consider the following sentences. The first is dull and lifeless; the second describes what the writer sees and feels.

NONDESCRIPTIVE: The beach was crowded with people.
DESCRIPTIVE: The beach was overrun with teenage bodies in neon Lycra suits, slicked with sweet-smelling oil.

Making your details more descriptive is not difficult. Keep in mind these four simple guidelines:

NEED TO KNOW

Using Descriptive Details

1. Use verbs that help your reader picture the action.

NONDESCRIPTIVE: The boy walked down the beach.
DESCRIPTIVE: The boy <u>ambled</u> down the beach.

2. Use exact names. Include the names of people, places, brands, animals, flowers, stores, streets, products—whatever will make your description more precise.

NONDESCRIPTIVE: Kevin parked his car near the deserted beach.
DESCRIPTIVE: Kevin parked his <u>maroon</u> Saturn <u>convertible</u> at Burke's Garage next to the deserted beach.

3. Use adjectives to describe. Adjectives are words that describe nouns. Place them before or after nouns to add detail.

(continued on next page)

NONDESCRIPTIVE: The beach was deserted.
DESCRIPTIVE: The remote, rocky, windswept beach was deserted.

4. Use words that appeal to the senses. Use words that convey touch, taste, smell, sound, and sight.

NONDESCRIPTIVE: I saw big waves roll on the beach.
DESCRIPTIVE: Immense black waves rammed the shore, releasing with each crash the salty, fishy smell of the deep ocean.

EXERCISE 13-5 ▶ Revise each of the following sentences to make it more descriptive.

NONDESCRIPTIVE: The radio talk show host answered calls from his listeners.

REVISED: The rude, insensitive radio talk show host repeatedly insulted and dismissed his naive, polite callers.

1. The child played in the water. The red-haired three-year-old splashed noisily in the plastic backyard pool.

2. The birds flew away. Startled by my sudden arrival in the square, the pigeons took flight, their wings nearly brushing my hair.

3. The lifeguard watched the swimmers. The sunburned lifeguard watched the synchronized-swimming class at the new YMCA.

4. Teenagers played a game. Three teenagers wearing baseball caps played a game in the video game room.

5. A cliff overhung the path. A dangerous, rocky cliff overhung the narrow path.

6. The couple took a walk. The young couple took a leisurely walk through the rose garden at midnight.

7. A trail led to the lake. An overgrown hiking trail led to the crystal-clear, unspoiled lake.

8. The hiker was tired. The inexperienced hiker was too tired to set up camp for the night.

9. Snow made the city street look different. Eighteen inches of fresh snow blanketed the city street, making it look like a pasture.

10. The train stopped. <u>For no apparent reason, the E train screeched to a</u>

<u>sudden stop in the dark tunnel.</u>

EXERCISE 13-6 ▶ Revise the paragraph you wrote in Exercise 13-4 by adding descriptive details and effective transitions.

Writing Narrative Paragraphs

The technique of making a point by telling a story is called **narration.** Narration is *not* simply listing a series of events—"this happened; then that happened." Narration shapes and interprets events to make a point. Notice the difference between the two paragraphs below.

Paragraph 1

Last Sunday we visited the National Zoo in Washington, D.C. As we entered, we decided to see the panda bear, elephants, and giraffes. All were outside enjoying the springlike weather. Then we visited the bat cave. I was amazed at how closely bats pack together in a small space. Finally, we went into the monkey house. There we spent time watching the giant apes watch us.

Paragraph 2

Last Sunday's visit to the National Zoo in Washington, D.C., was a lesson to me about animals in captivity. First we visited the panda, elephants, and giraffes. All seemed slow moving and locked into a dull routine—pacing around their yards. Then we watched the seals. Their trainer had them perform stunts for their food; they would never do these stunts in the wild. Finally, we stopped at the monkey house, where sad old apes stared at us and watched kids point at them. The animals did not seem happy or content with their lives.

The first paragraph retells events in the order in which they happened, but with no shaping of the story. The second paragraph, a narrative, uses the events to make a point: animals kept in captivity are unhappy. All details and all events thus work together to support that point.

Selecting a Topic and Generating Ideas

When selecting a topic for a narrative paragraph, use the following guidelines:

1. Use your personal experience as your source of ideas. What has happened recently that made an impression on you?

2. Choose an event or experience about which you have a definite feeling or opinion. Your feeling or opinion can be the point you make by telling the story. For example, did an event reveal a friend's true character? Did an experience help you decide on a career or eliminate one that you were considering? Did a chance meeting have good (or bad) consequences?

3. Choose a single event or experience. Do not try to cover an entire weekend or several recent experiences at work in a single paragraph. Instead, choose one weekend activity or one particularly revealing event at work.

Once you have selected a topic, make a list of events that occurred. In your margin, record any reactions or feelings you have. These may be useful in writing your topic sentence.

EXERCISE 13-7 ▶ Think of an experience that falls into one of the following categories, and make a list of events that occurred.

1. a big mistake or hasty decision
2. a childhood or family story
3. a new experience
4. a funny situation
5. a visit to a new place

Writing Your Topic Sentence

Your topic sentence should accomplish two things:

1. It should identify your topic.
2. It should reveal your attitude toward your topic.

For example, suppose you are writing about visiting a zoo. Your topic sentence could take your narrative in a variety of directions, each of which would reveal a very different attitude.

1. During my recent visit to the zoo, I was saddened by the animals' behavior in captivity.

2. A recent visit to the zoo gave my children a lesson in geography.

3. My recent visit to the zoo taught me more about human nature than about animals.

EXERCISE 13-8 ▶ Complete three of the following topic sentences by adding information that reveals your attitude toward the topic.

EXAMPLE: My first date was   <u>an experience I would rather forget.</u>

1. Holidays are   <u>memorable family celebrations.</u>

2. Soap operas appeal <u>to people who enjoy romance stories.</u>

3. My first day on campus was <u>overwhelming.</u>

4. The college bookstore is <u>a miniature library.</u>

5. My advisor <u>is helpful and thoughtful.</u>

EXERCISE 13-9 ▶ Write a topic sentence for the experience you chose in Exercise 13-7. Be sure your topic sentence identifies the experience you are writing about and reveals your attitude toward it.

Developing and Organizing Your Details

The events in a narrative are usually arranged in the order in which they happened. This method of organization is called **time-sequence arrangement.** (See Chapter 12, pages 304–307, for a discussion of this method.)

The following map will help you visualize the organization of a narrative paragraph.

Narrative-Organization Map

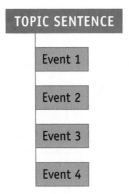

Before you draft your paragraph, review your list of events to make sure they are in the correct order, numbering them if they are not.

A narrative paragraph should include enough detail to allow your reader to understand fully the experience you are writing about. Be sure you have answered most of the following questions.

- *What* events occurred?
- *Where* did they happen?
- *When* did they happen?

- *Who* was involved?
- *Why* did they happen?
- *How* did they happen?

Following is a sample narrative paragraph a student wrote about ordering an unusual dish in a restaurant. Notice that it includes only details relevant to the topic. It also includes a sufficient number of details to make the experience real and believable. Read the paragraph, and then underline and label the parts that answer each of the above questions.

Sample Narrative Paragraph

I don't usually take risks, especially when it comes to food, but last Saturday I took a bold step and ordered tripe at Trivoli, a local Italian restaurant. When I ordered, the waiter told me there would be a fifteen-minute wait. I tried to convince myself, "Well, it *must* be worth waiting for!" When fifteen minutes became twenty-five, I called the waiter. He apologized and said the kitchen was short-handed and that it would be another ten minutes! As I waited, I really got nervous. I wondered if I had made a mistake. Would I hate it? Would I be able to eat it? Finally my long-awaited tripe arrived. Once I tasted tripe, a dish made from the stomach lining of beef, I was delighted. It was well worth the risk and the long wait. I wonder what new food I should try next!

Notice, too, in the above paragraph that the writer used transitions to connect details. Refer to page 306 for a list of transitions used to link one event to the next in a time-sequence arrangement. Then, in the above paragraph, highlight each transition.

> ### NEED TO KNOW
>
> #### Narrative Paragraphs
>
> Narration is a method of making a point by relating a series of events. To write effective narrative paragraphs, be sure to
>
> - Choose a single event about which you have a definite feeling or opinion.
> - Write a topic sentence that identifies your topic and reveals your attitude toward it.
> - Organize your details in time-sequence arrangement.

EXERCISE 13-10 | Write a narrative paragraph using the topic sentence you wrote in Exercise 13-9. Be sure to include relevant and sufficient details. Use transitions to connect your ideas. Then draw a revision map of your paragraph. Use it to check whether your details are relevant and whether you have arranged them in correct sequence.

STUDENT ESSAY

This essay was written by Darlene Gallardo, a college student who lives near the U.S.–Mexican border, and was published in *Hispanic* magazine. In this essay she shares her thoughts on her Mexican heritage and relates her experience with folklorico (Mexican folk dancing). As you read the essay, notice both the sequence of events and her use of descriptive language.

What My Culture Means to Me
Darlene Gallardo

Culture is a term used to define a person's way of life. Cultures differ   1
from one part of the world to another. Most people accept the culture in which they were brought up and are proud of it. Others, on the other hand, are not. I consider myself lucky to live in a border city. This way I am exposed to two different cultures, American and Mexican.

When I was about five and a half years old, my parents enrolled me   2
in dance classes. Walking into class with my older sister on our first day, I was amazed at what I saw. I had never seen Mexican folklorico dance before. The dance was very graceful and full of expression. I did not quite understand why the girls were wearing high shoes and long, heavy skirts. As I grew older, I learned what folklorico was and why costumes were important. This was one of the few symbols of the Mexican culture.

Folklorico dancing brings joy to those who watch it. It is performed   3
with great passion. The stomping of the feet accompanied by the dancers' yells sends chills down your spine. The reactions and compliments given to me by the audience after a performance give me a feeling I try to hold on to until the next performance.

I have been dancing for fourteen years with various groups. When   4
I started high school, I decided to take time off and concentrate on

school. This was a hard choice to make, but in my heart of hearts I knew school came first. During high school, I would go to many performances given by folklorico groups. It was all too strange for me. Now I was in the audience. Watching the dancers perform made me want to get up there and dance. That is why I joined Ballet Folklorico Paso Del Norte in February of 1993.

Our practices are long and hard, and we have performances every weekend and sometimes on weekdays. There are times when we perform three to four times a day. To me it's worth it. The group has been presented many awards and has been invited to many cities. Last summer we were invited to perform in Oklahoma. It was a very emotional experience for everyone. People came up and took photographs with us. Many had never seen this type of dancing before. I couldn't help but wonder if the Mexican culture was lost.   5

I was very honored to think that I had presented something to the people that they enjoyed and would remember forever. It made me realize that when I am dancing, I am not just dancing for myself but for people of different races and backgrounds. It also brought to my attention that the Mexican culture is not lost; it just isn't acknowledged as much. There are many Hispanics who are very successful and proud, and many who are waiting for an opportunity.   6

I have just now completed my first year of college at the University of Texas at El Paso. I'm still dancing and plan to do so for as long as I can. I never thought that a simple thing like dancing would be an important symbol of my background. I am trying to pass this down to younger generations by teaching folklorico at a community center. My advice to young Hispanics is to never deny where you come from. I know I will become successful. The confidence that I have within me comes from being proud to be who I am.   7

Evaluating the Essay

1. Evaluate the structure and content of the essay.
   a. Does the essay follow a logical plan? Describe its organization.
   b. What is Gallardo's thesis?
   c. In what ways does she support her thesis?
   d. Evaluate the effectiveness of the title, introduction, and conclusion.

2. Draw a map that shows the sequence of events described in the essay.

3. Underline four examples of the use of descriptive language. In which paragraphs of the essay do you think more description could have been included?

WRITING ABOUT A READING

Thinking before Reading

The following reading, "Born in the U.S.A." by Abel Salas, is a good example of both narrative and descriptive writing. A reporter, the author tells how he conducted a test to determine how different people are treated by customs officials at the U.S.–Mexican border. In telling his story, Salas provides vivid descriptions of people he met and of his changes in appearance. As you read, pay attention to the sequence of events and the descriptive language used. Although in this chapter you learned narration and description as separate writing techniques, you will discover that they often overlap, as in this reading.

1. Preview the reading using the steps provided on page 20.

2. After you have done your preview, connect the reading to your own experience by answering the following questions:
   a. Have you or anyone you know ever been stopped by customs officials?
   b. What are some of the reasons a border patrol or customs official might detain you?

READING

Born in the U.S.A.
Abel Salas

The Rio Grande, or Rio Bravo for those from the opposite bank, winds its way down from the Rockies, cutting a path that twists and bends for hundreds of miles through deserts, hills, and valleys. Dammed up at several points along its meandering route to the sea, the river is no more than a small stream by the time it reaches Brownsville, Texas, the southernmost city along its trajectory. Through Laredo, the Rio Grande is still recognizable as a river, although national and international attention has shifted to its role as a border.   1

Every day, the undeniable ebb and flow of human traffic moves briskly back and forth across south Texas bridges in Nuevo Laredo/Laredo, Reynosa/McAllen, Matamoros/Brownsville. To ensure   2 that our borders are respected, the Immigration and Naturalization Service (INS), with the support of Congress and President Clinton, keeps vigil at the gates.

Stepping up funds and manpower to stem the flow of illegal immigration, the Clinton Administration has tacitly acknowledged a concern that unchecked immigration along the U.S.–Mexico border will rip the fabric of our society, that the flood of Mexicans is a complex problem. By contrast, what are the fears, concerns, and worries that preoccupy those civilians from either side who are forced—for whatever reason—to cross the river regularly? It was at these gateways that I decided to test a theory. I wondered what the impact would be on locals, campesinos,[1] and tourists with the increased focus on illegal immigration, and how the U.S. Border Patrol would behave. Unfortunately, the performance exceeded my expectations.

3

For the first border entry in Brownsville, I wore extremely baggy pants in the homeboy or modern cholo[2] tradition. With a pair of thick-soled sneakers and a coat modeled on the jail-house blues uniform, I chose not to add the knit cap or even a bright bandanna for fear of overdoing the costume.

4

On return from a reception in Matamoros with a Mexican friend and an Anglo kid who had moved to Brownsville from Austin several months before, I reached the turnstile inside the customs check building first. There I was asked by a severe looking Mexican American whether I was a citizen and what I was bringing back.

5

"Nada," I said, raising my empty hands. Hardly hesitating, the officer proceeded to frisk me, checking my pockets physically and finding a pair of sunglasses along with a nearly empty pack of Mexican filterless cigarettes. Opening up the package of smokes, he lifted it to his nose, apparently checking for drugs. Talk about personal discomfort. Both of my companions came through immediately afterward with no trouble whatsoever. A response to my appearance? More than likely.

6

The confrontation I was most unprepared for was the next one. "U.S. citizen," I said, in response to the predictable question you get at any gate that separates the U.S. and Mexico. Dressed in silver-tipped cowboy boots, a black western shirt, black jeans, and a white hat similar to those worn by leading Tejano[3] musicians and patterned on a style long popular in northern Mexico, I carried a cloth briefcase and a plastic shopping bag containing a change of clothes.

7

1. farmers, peasants, or small landowners
2. teenage members of a street gang
3. a style of music similar to American country music.

The federal agent, a slight Hispanic with hair in an early Beatles   8
bang cut, offered me a steely-eyed stare and followed with the expected
question, "Where are you coming from?"

"Mocambo's," I replied, naming a well-known seafood restaurant   9
one block across the border in Matamoros. With no hint of recognition,
he sized me up warily.

"Where's your ID?" he asked. "In my bag—it's a press pass," I   10
answered. "Step over there," he ordered curtly, pointing to a table in a
small room immediately beyond the turnstile, which would, with a click,
record my passage. Following me into the cubicle, he proceeded to
empty my bags and spread their contents across the table, poring over
them with care.

Examining a press credential complete with my photo and signature   11
issued by the local daily for free-lance assignments, he fired away his
next round of questions, giving me barely enough time to respond,
rephrasing and repeating some of the same questions to see if I could be
confused into changing my answers.

"Where's your birth certificate? What do you do? Where do you   12
work? Where do you live? What were you doing in Mexico? Where are
you going? Where were you born? How did you get to the interior of
Mexico without proper documents?"

Welcome to the United States of America. So much for a hassle-   13
free lunch break, I thought, retracing my steps over the bridge that
spans what has become little more than a creekbed, a border that has
given the little man behind the table the authority to make me feel like
a three-year-old, babbling uncomfortably while being informed that I
was responsible for proving my right to be within the U.S. territorial
boundaries.

Of the laminated press badge, he scoffed, "Anybody can get one of   14
these. And can you tell me the name of the head honcho over at the
Herald, the guy in charge? . . . because I know who he is. And so far
you haven't given me any reason to let you in."

Still unconvinced and perhaps to add to the insult, he handed me a   15
yellow slip of paper and ordered me into an office where more-thorough
ID checks are run by computer and travel permits are issued to those
seeking to visit places in the U.S. more than 25 miles from the border.

For my third entry, I gave myself a meticulous shave before boarding   16
the bus. During the bus ride back to Matamoros, I donned a spare set of
clothes, aiming for the licenciado,[4] or young professional, effect.
Sporting a white double-breasted blazer, a tie, and slip-on loafers, I
approached the familiar customs check just over the bridge, where I

4. Literally meaning "licensed," this term refers to people holding
   college degrees. It is similar to the term "yuppie."

went unrecognized. In addition to the cowboy clothing, which I'd transferred to several small plastic shopping bags, I carried two carton-sized packages of Delicados, a brand of Mexican cigarettes, one extra than the one carton allowed by immigration officials.

Clean-shaven and neatly attired, I was met with a friendly smile. 17
Once I declared my citizenship, the officer simply asked about the contents of my shopping bags. When I mentioned cigarettes, he waved me through and said simply, "Next time just bring one carton of cigarettes, okay?"

Why was I singled out while elderly winter Texans in Bermuda shorts 18
and Hawaiian-print shirts waltzed merrily through the turnstile? What were the criteria used by the Border Patrol to establish an individual's citizenship? What exactly is it that they check for when trying to spot an illegal immigrant? Falsified documents? An accent? These were all considerations as I crossed the border into the United States, changing my appearance in several significant ways and entering at various intervals.

The variables along the border and at the gates are numerous and 19
often change, but in my experience, it's apparent that looks are important and that U.S. Latinos are targeted for scrutiny. I might also suggest that if you don't have obviously Anglo or European features, you might consider getting yourself a green card before making that quaint border-town excursion you've always planned. Otherwise, they might not let you back in.

From *Hispanic*

Getting Ready to Write

Strengthening Your Vocabulary

Write a brief definition for each of the following words from the preceding reading. If you can't figure out the meaning of a word from the way it is used in the reading, look the word up in the dictionary.

1. meandering (paragraph 1)   winding, turning frequently

2. trajectory (paragraph 1)   course, path

3. vigil (paragraph 2)   watch

4. stem (paragraph 3)   stop

5. tacitly (paragraph 3)   silently, not openly, expressed or suggested

6. poring (paragraph 10)   examining closely

7. credential (paragraph 11)   identification paper or card

8. donned (paragraph 16)   put on

9. scrutiny (paragraph 19)   close inspection

10. excursion (paragraph 19)   trip

Reviewing the Reading Using an Idea Map

Review the reading by completing the missing pieces of the idea map shown below.

ABEL SALAS WANTS TO TEST THEORY AT U.S.–MEXICO BORDER PATROL

How different customs officials act at border

How different people are treated

CROSSES BORDER DRESSED IN DIFFERENT OUTFITS

First: Homeboy, modern cholo

Questioned briefly

Frisked, pockets examined

Cigarette pack examined for drugs

Friends went through easily

Second: Mexican cowboy

Pulled aside

Bags emptied, searched

Interrogated intensively

Press I.D. rejected by official

Computer I.D. checked

Third: Young professional

Friendly treatment

Bags inquired about

Let through with extra carton of cigarettes

CONCLUDES LOOKS ARE IMPORTANT AND U.S. LATINOS ARE TARGETED

Examining the Reading

1. What happened when Salas tried to cross the U.S.–Mexican border wearing a cowboy outfit?

2. How was he viewed by U.S. customs when he was dressed in conventional clothing for a U.S. citizen?

3. Why wasn't he assumed to be a U.S. citizen when he displayed a press pass?

4. Why, on his first trip across the border, was he stopped and frisked by an officer while his two friends went through without a problem?

5. Why was he stopped at the border when he was carrying less than a pack of cigarettes, but was let through when he carried two cartons of cigarettes?

Reacting to and Discussing Ideas

Get ready to write about the reading by discussing the following questions:

1. How much difference do you think personal appearance makes to people who don't know you?

2. Do you think people are treated equally when they enter the United States? Why or why not?

3. Do you think physical appearance makes a big difference in the business world? If so, in what way?

Writing about the Reading

The Paragraph Option

1. Write a paragraph describing an experience crossing a border between the United States and another country. It can be real or imaginary.

2. Write a paragraph describing how you would feel about being stopped and detained at customs by officials who didn't believe you were a U.S. citizen.

The Essay Option

Write an essay explaining how appearance alone can determine what other people think of you.

Use this Revision Checklist for the paragraph or essay you wrote on "Born in the U.S.A."

REVISION CHECKLIST

Paragraph Development		YES	NO
	1. Is your topic manageable (neither too broad nor too narrow)?	☐	☐
	2. Is your paragraph written with your reader in mind?	☐	☐
	3. Does your topic sentence identify your topic?	☐	☐
	4. Does your topic sentence make a point about your topic?	☐	☐
	5. Does each remaining sentence support the topic sentence?	☐	☐
	6. Did you include sufficient detail?	☐	☐
	7. Are your details arranged logically?	☐	☐
	8. Have you used transitions to connect your details?	☐	☐
	9. Is there a sentence at the end that brings the paragraph to a close?	☐	☐

REVISION CHECKLIST (CONTINUED)

		YES	NO
For DESCRIPTIVE Paragraphs	10. Have you created an overall impression?	☐	☐
	11. Do your details support that impression?	☐	☐
	12. Have you used descriptive language?	☐	☐
For NARRATIVE Paragraphs	13. Have you made a point with your narrative?	☐	☐
	14. Are the events arranged in the order in which they occurred?	☐	☐
	15. Have you used transitions to help your reader follow events?	☐	☐
Sentence Development	16. Have you avoided writing sentence fragments, run-on sentences, and comma splices?	☐	☐
	17. Have you combined ideas to produce more effective sentences?	☐	☐
	18. Have you used adjectives and adverbs to make your sentences vivid and interesting?	☐	☐
	19. Have you used prepositional phrases, *-ing* phrases, and relative clauses to add detail?	☐	☐
	20. Have you used pronouns correctly and consistently?	☐	☐
	21. Have you avoided shifts in person, number, and verb tense?	☐	☐
	22. Have you placed modifiers correctly?	☐	☐
	23. Are elements within each sentence parallel?	☐	☐
	24. Have you used correct verb tenses and correct verb forms?	☐	☐

If you have checked any *nos*, go back to your paper and make the necessary changes.

**Writing Essay
Exam Answers**

WRITING SUCCESS TIP 13

You can master the art of writing good essay-exam answers. The following suggestions and strategies will help.

1. **Read the directions carefully.** They may, for example, tell you to answer only two out of four questions.

2. **Plan your time.** For example, if you have to answer two essay questions in a fifty-minute class session, give yourself twenty to twenty-five minutes for each one.

3. **Answer the easiest question first.** Doing so may take you less time than you budgeted, and consequently, you can spend additional time on harder questions.

4. **Analyze each question.** Look for words that tell you what to write about and how to organize your answer. If an exam question says, "Trace the history of advertising in the United States," the word *trace* tells you to organize your essay using a time-sequence arrangement. The question also identifies the topic—the history of advertising.

5. **Plan your answer.** On the back of the exam or on a separate sheet of paper that you will not turn in, jot down ideas you will include in your essay. Arrange your ideas to follow the method of development suggested in the question.

6. **Write your thesis statement.** A thesis statement is like a topic sentence. It announces what your essay will be about. Thesis statements in essay-exam answers should be simple and straightforward. Start by rewording the question.

Sample Essay Question	*Sample Thesis Statement*
1. Describe the psychological factors that may affect a person's decision to change jobs.	There are five psychological factors that may affect a person's decision to change jobs.
2. Define and give an example of age discrimination.	Age discrimination takes place whenever people are mistreated or unfairly judged simply because of how old they are.

7. **Present adequate supporting details.** Write a separate paragraph for each major supporting detail. Begin each paragraph with a topic sentence that introduces each new point. Each paragraph should provide relevant and sufficient support for the topic sentence.

8. **Proofread your answer.** Be sure to leave enough time to proofread your answer. Check for errors in spelling, punctuation, and grammar.

9. **If you run out of time . . .** If you run out of time before you have finished answering the last question, don't panic. Take the last minute or two to make a list or outline of the other points you planned to cover. Some instructors will give you partial credit for this outline.

14 Writing Informative Paragraphs

CHAPTER OBJECTIVES

In this chapter you will learn to

1. write paragraphs that present information.
2. use logical methods of organization.

S ome advertisements are primarily informative. They seek to educate the consumer about a product or service. The following advertisement for State Farm Insurance offers information about a language-arts class that State Farm presented with its Good Neighbor Award. The advertisement presents factual information about the class and the award it was given.

Much of what you will read and write in college and on the job is **informative**. That is, it is written to present *factual information*—to *explain*. Informative writing presents facts rather than personal impressions or opinions. Textbooks, some newspaper and magazine articles, term papers, and essay exams use informative writing. The main goal of most reports, memos, business letters, and summaries is to explain something. In each, the writer presents information to make the topic clear and understandable to the reader. In this chapter you will learn to write paragraphs that explain. You will learn how to obtain correct and complete information and how to organize and develop your paragraph.

WRITING

Obtaining Correct and Complete Information

When you write informative paragraphs, you are responsible for presenting *correct* and *complete* information. Your information must be clear and understandable to your reader.

Analyzing Your Reader

The first step, then, in developing an informative paragraph is to analyze your reader. How much information will he or she need to grasp your ideas? For example, suppose you are writing a paragraph to explain a specific play in football, such as the flea flicker. If your reader is familiar with the game of football, you will not need to provide explanations of the various types of players and their positions on the field at the beginning of the play. If, however, your reader has little or no knowledge of football, you will need to provide background information on the game's players, positions, and rules.

EXERCISE ▶ 14-1

Think of a task you can perform well, or select one from the list below. Write a paragraph explaining how to perform the task; your reader is someone who is familiar with your topic. Then revise your paragraph, adding information for a reader who is unfamiliar with your topic. Exchange papers with a classmate for peer review. Try to find two reviewers—one who is familiar with your topic and one who is not. Ask each reviewer to evaluate your paper. Your reviewers should consider the following questions:

- Is necessary background information provided?
- Is the explanation complete?
- Is the explanation understandable?
- Are the steps of the task in the correct order?

1. shopping for _____
2. fishing for _____
3. cooking _____
4. fixing _____
5. attending _____

Obtaining Additional Information

Once you have analyzed how much information your reader needs, the next step is to be sure you have enough information. If you are writing about a familiar topic, you need only to check your first draft to be sure you have not omitted important or necessary information. If the topic is less familiar, you may need to obtain additional information. Following is a quick review of useful sources of information.

The College Library

Your college library is usually the best source of additional information. It is also one of the easiest and fastest sources to use. If you have trouble finding information, a librarian can help you locate what you need quickly. Be sure to keep track of the sources you use and the information from each source. For further information on crediting your sources, see Writing Success Tip 14, "Avoiding Plagiarism and Citing Sources," at the end of this chapter.

Experts

Depending on your topic, it may be helpful to consult someone who is an expert in the field you are writing about. Suppose you are writing about leasing and renting apartments. If your sister-in-law is a real-estate agent, she may be able to provide all the information you need or direct you to appropriate sources. You could also talk to a superintendent or a landlord. Prepare a list of questions to ask your expert. As you talk to or interview the person, be sure to take detailed notes.

News Media

If you are writing about a current news topic, you will find that magazines, newspapers, radio and television news shows, documentary programs, and videos provide a wealth of information. If you want to write a paragraph on graffiti artists, for example, you can find articles on this topic in your library's media collection.

EXERCISE 14-2 | Working with another student, select one of the following topics. Use the college library to locate information for a paragraph on your topic. List the information you might include in your paragraph. Also list the source of your information, including the page number(s) on which you found it. You can either take notes or make photocopies of the page(s).

1. how the United States deals with the used-tire problem
2. how the Chinese calendar works
3. how smoke alarms work
4. how to use biofeedback to control test anxiety
5. how drivers are tested for blood alcohol levels

Using a Logical Method of Explaining

Suppose you have to explain what your part-time job involves. Your topic sentence is

Working construction in the summer is exhausting.

You can back up that statement and explain the job in a number of ways. You can recount particular events in the order they happened on a certain day or over the course of the summer. You can give reasons why the job is demanding or exhausting, such as the heat, the pace, and the hours. You can compare the job with other jobs you have held, or you can give examples of demanding and tiring tasks. You can also use combinations of all these methods.

Although you can develop a topic in a variety of ways, one approach may work better than another, depending on the topic or the readers for whom you are writing. You have already learned three ways to develop and arrange details logically: time sequence, spatial arrangement, and least/most important arrangement (see Chapter 12). In this section you will be given a brief overview of three other common methods of development:

1. process
2. comparison and contrast
3. cause and effect

Process

A **process** paragraph explains how to do something by describing a sequence of steps. One student was writing a paragraph on how to find a reliable day-care center, which is a **process** because it involves a sequence of steps. In developing ideas for her paragraph, the student made a list of the tasks or steps involved, then rearranged and numbered them to show the order in which she would do them:

1. decide qualifications/requirements
2. ask friends for recommendations
3. call college for possible list
4. check yellow pages for nearby centers
5. select centers to visit
6. call for appointments
7. meet directors
8. observe children in centers
9. make final choice

A process paragraph is similar to a straightforward narrative paragraph. Both describe events or steps in the order in which they occur. Both present information in chronological, or time-sequence, order. The following map will help you visualize the arrangement of a process paragraph.

Process Map

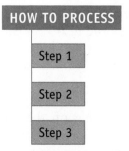

Follow these suggestions to write effective process paragraphs:

1. Choose a topic with which you are familiar.

2. Write a topic sentence that identifies the process or procedure you will explain. Your topic sentence also should indicate *why* your reader should learn about the process. You might give a reason why the process is important or state what can be accomplished by using the process. It is usually best to place your topic sentence first in the paragraph. In this position it gives your reader a purpose for reading.

Because charcoal grilling makes meats tastier, every cook should know how to light a charcoal fire.

Homemade chili is an inexpensive, healthy, and easy meal to prepare.

Your cat will be more comfortable this summer if you can prevent or get rid of the flea problem.

3. Develop your details. Imagine yourself performing the whole process from start to finish. Ask yourself which are the essential, necessary steps, and include only those when you write. Be sure to define unfamiliar terms and identify clearly any specialized tools, procedures, or objects.

4. Use transitions to lead your reader step-by-step through the process. Using transitions like those listed below will help you link the details in your process. Note that these are the same transitions listed on page 306 for the time-sequence arrangement. A process is a series of steps performed over time.

NEED TO KNOW

Common Process Transitions

first	next	before
second	during	at last
third	at the same time	finally
in the beginning	following	later
then	after	now

Here is a sample process paragraph. After reading the paragraph, complete the map following it and underline the transitions used in the paragraph.

Sample Process Paragraph

If you have ever been asked a rude question, then you will be glad to learn that there are ways of not answering it. Suppose someone asks you, "How much did you pay for that suit?" First, pause before saying anything—maybe as long as five to ten seconds. Sometimes the person will feel uncomfortable or embarrassed and say something to fill the gap. Then you're off the hook. Unfortunately, this ploy does not usually work. Rude people ask rude questions, and rude people are not easily embarrassed. Next, try to avoid the question by answering, "More than it should have!" "Too much!" or "You don't really want to know!" If the person persists, a direct, honest response is best: "I really would rather not say," or "That question embarrasses me," or "I'm not comfortable answering your question." Whatever you do, don't give in and answer!

Process Map

HOW TO AVOID A RUDE QUESTION
Pause before answering
Avoid the question by giving a vague answer
Give honest response

EXERCISE 14-3 ▶ Write a process paragraph on one of the following topics. Assume that your reader has no familiarity with your topic. After making a list of steps in the process, use time-sequence arrangement to organize your details. Then draw a revision map of your paragraph to check that your details are relevant and arranged correctly. Make necessary revisions, and underline your transitions.

1. how to select _____
2. how to be smart about _____
3. how to stay fit for _____
4. how to plan a _____
5. how to spot a _____

Comparison and Contrast

A **comparison-and-contrast** paragraph gives information by showing how two objects, people, or ideas are similar or different. When you consider similarities, you are *comparing*. When you consider differences, you are *contrasting*. Sometimes you may want to do both.

Following are some suggestions for writing comparison or contrast paragraphs:

1. Use a two-column list to brainstorm. Suppose you want to write about two jobs by comparing and contrasting your present job at Speedy Car Wash with your old one at Burger King. Divide a piece of paper into two columns. Write "Speedy Car Wash" at the top of one column and "Burger King" at the top of the other. In each column list all the characteristics, features, and details of each job. When you have finished, match up items that deal with the same feature or characteristic, as shown below.

Sample Two-Column List

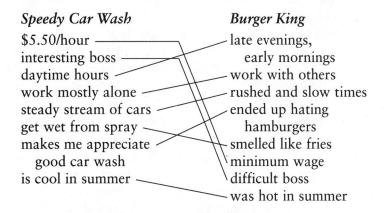

Speedy Car Wash

$5.50/hour
interesting boss
daytime hours
work mostly alone
steady stream of cars
get wet from spray
makes me appreciate
    good car wash
is cool in summer

Burger King

late evenings,
    early mornings
work with others
rushed and slow times
ended up hating
    hamburgers
smelled like fries
minimum wage
difficult boss
was hot in summer

If you have a characteristic in one column but not in the other, try to add what is missing. For example, if you mention your supervisor in one column, also do so in the second.

EXERCISE Make a two-column list of similarities and differences for one of the following topics. Match up items that deal with the same characteristic.

1. two movies or books
2. two musicians or artists
3. two foods or restaurants
4. two friends or relatives
5. two seasons

2. Decide whether to compare or contrast. It is usually best to focus on either similarities or differences when writing a single paragraph. In longer pieces of writing, you may discuss both similarities and differences.

3. Write your topic sentence. Your topic sentence should (a) identify the two subjects and (b) indicate whether you will focus on similarities or differences.

The number of similarities between racquetball and tennis is striking.

Hockey and golf players tend to be very different types of people.

Football and baseball fans behave quite differently while watching a game.

4. Organize your details. There are two basic methods of organizing a comparison-and-contrast paragraph:

a. subject by subject
b. point by point

In **subject-by-subject** organization, you are comparing or contrasting two subjects. In this method, first you write about one of your subjects and then you switch to the second. For example, if you wanted to use this method to write about your jobs at Speedy Car Wash and Burger King, you would first describe the Speedy job and then the Burger King one.

One student used subject-by-subject organization to write the following paragraph contrasting stock-car and drag racing. After reading the paragraph, fill in the organization map that follows it.

Sample Subject-by-Subject Comparison Paragraph

subjects

The two most popular car races are stock-car and drag racing. Stock-car races consist of three classes of cars: street stock, modifieds, and premodifieds. Stock cars race on oval blacktop or dirt tracks. The cars run a number of laps with anywhere from ten to twenty other cars. In contrast, drag races consist of four classes of cars: street, pro, superpro, and supergas. Drag races are run on one-eighth- or one-quarter-mile straight tracks. Each driver runs against only one opponent at a time. Personally, I prefer drag racing to stock-car racing because I enjoy the one-on-one competition.

Subject-by-Subject Comparison Map

CAR RACING

Stock-car races

three classes

oval tracks

compete with 10–20 cars

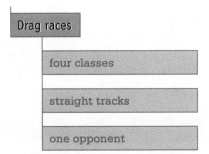

In **point-by-point** organization, you discuss both of your subjects according to each point of comparison. For example, using the Speedy Car Wash/Burger King list, you might write about the wages at both places—first at Speedy, then at Burger King. Then you might write about the hours at both places—first at Speedy, then at Burger King. For each remaining point of comparison on your list, you would continue the same order—first Speedy, then Burger King.

Let us look at how the sample student paragraph on the previous page could be organized using the point-by-point method. After reading the paragraph below, fill in the organization map that follows.

Sample Point-by-Point Comparison Paragraph

points

> The two most popular car races are stock-car and drag racing. Stock-car races usually have three classes of cars: street stock, modified, and premodifieds. In contrast, drag races have four classes of cars: street, pro, superpro, and super-gas. Stock cars race only on oval tracks, either black-top or dirt, whereas drag races are held on one-eighth- or one-quarter-mile straight tracks. Stock cars run a certain number of laps around the track, with anywhere from ten to twenty opponents, but drag cars run against only one other opponent in the same class. Personally, I prefer drag racing to stock-car racing because I enjoy the one-on-one competition.

Point-by-Point Comparison Map

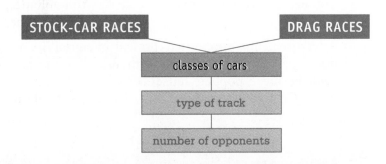

5. Use transitions. Using transition words like those listed below will help you show your reader the relationship between items you want to compare or contrast. After studying the list, go back and underline the transitions used in the two comparison-and-contrast paragraphs on pages 354 and 355.

NEED TO KNOW

Common Comparison/Contrast Transitions

Comparison	*Contrast*
likewise	however
similarly	on the contrary
too	unlike
also	on the other hand
in the same way	in contrast
in comparison	whereas
	but

EXERCISE 14-5 For the topic you chose in Exercise 14-4, write a comparison or contrast paragraph. Assume that your reader is a classmate who is not familiar with your topic. Use either the subject-by-subject or point-by-point method to organize your details. Then draw a revision map to check that your details are relevant, sufficient, and clearly organized. Revise as necessary, and underline your transitions.

Cause and Effect

Cause and effect is a very common relationship between events. Many of our daily experiences are related in this way:

Cause	*Effect*
You forgot to put the milk away.	It spoiled.
You spilled your coffee.	It stained your shirt.
You lost ten pounds.	Your clothes don't fit.
You needed work experience.	You volunteered to work for a local charity.

Advertisements, too, often present material in a cause-and-effect relationship. Whiten your teeth with Brand X toothpaste (cause), and you will be more popular (effect). Buy Car Y, and you will feel safer or sexier. Go to Restaurant Z for a bargain special, and you will save money and be glad. Of course, a wise consumer will question how true these cause-and-effect relationships are, but advertisers count on their persuasive power.

In using cause-and-effect organization in your writing, sometimes you may want to start with a *cause* (you want to take a summer trip to Mexico) and explain its effects (you took a part-time job in a Mexican restaurant, started a special savings account, cut down on expenses, and are taking a Spanish course). Other times, you may want to start with an *effect* (you are working in a Mexican restaurant) and explain its causes (you want to earn money and practice your Spanish for a summer trip to Mexico). It is usually best to focus on either the causes or the effects of something when writing a single paragraph. In longer pieces of writing, you may discuss both causes and effects.

The following maps will help you visualize the organization of the two kinds of cause-and-effect paragraphs.

Cause-and-Effect Maps

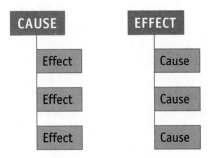

Follow these suggestions to write effective cause-and-effect paragraphs:

1. Discover ideas. Brainstorm or freewrite to discover all possible causes or effects. Select the ideas you will use, and number them in the order you will use them in your paragraph.

2. Write a topic sentence. Your topic sentence should identify your topic and make it clear whether you will focus on causes or effects.

FOCUS ON EFFECTS: Watching too much television can have negative effects on a child's behavior.

FOCUS ON CAUSES: There are several reasons why starting your own business is a high-risk venture.

FOCUS ON CAUSES: There are several causes of migraine headaches.

3. **Use details to explain your causes or effects.** Suppose you are writing to explain why you are attending college. One reason may be to get a better-paying job. To explain the connection between going to college and getting a better-paying job, however, you will need to include more information. Use relevant facts, such as why you need a college education for the job you want and how much you expect to earn if you get it.

4. **Use transitions.** Using transitions like those listed on the following page will help you show your reader the connection between your causes or effects.

Following is a sample cause-and-effect paragraph. After reading the paragraph, fill in the map below it and underline the cause-and-effect transitions used in the paragraph.

Sample Cause-and-Effect Paragraph

My attending college has resulted in a major change in my home life. At first it was tough trying to juggle all my responsibilities, my children, home, husband, and homework. I felt as if my world were upside down. Therefore, one night after school, during dinner, I had a talk with my family. I explained to them that I needed help now in running the house, especially with cleaning, cooking, laundry, and taking care of the animals. As far as everybody wanting to go here and there after school every night, it was all going to stop. I was running myself ragged. The talk I had with my family paid off. As a result, now when I get home at night, dinner is cooking, the chores are done, the house is clean, and I don't have to go anywhere.

Cause-and-Effect Map

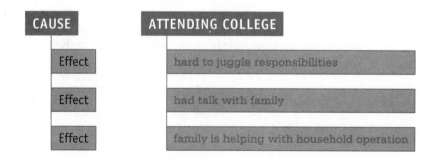

CAUSE	ATTENDING COLLEGE
Effect	hard to juggle responsibilities
Effect	had talk with family
Effect	family is helping with household operation

> ### NEED TO KNOW
>
> **Common Cause-and-Effect Transitions**
>
> | *Cause* | *Effect* |
> |---------|----------|
> | because | consequently |
> | since | as a result |
> | one cause is | thus |
> | for | one result is |
> | first | another effect is |
> | second | therefore |

EXERCISE 14-6

Choose one of the following topics and think of it as an *effect*. Then write a paragraph focusing on the *causes* of the topic. Be sure your topic sentence indicates that you will focus on causes. When you have finished writing, draw a revision map to check that you have explained the effect and its causes in a clear way. Revise your paragraph as needed, and underline your transitions.

1. a major change in lifestyle
2. attending college
3. choosing a career or major
4. the popularity of _____
5. arguments between _____

EXERCISE 14-7

Choose one of the following topics and think of it as a *cause*. Then write a paragraph focusing on the *effects* of the topic. Be sure your topic sentence indicates that you will focus on effects. When you have finished writing, draw a revision map to check that you have explained the cause and its effects in a clear way. Revise your paragraph as needed, and underline your transitions.

1. a kind word or good deed
2. a good sense of humor
3. a heart-to-heart talk
4. an important decision
5. an important phone call

> **N E E D   T O   K N O W**
>
> Informative writing presents facts; it does not present personal opinion or reaction. To make informative writing clear, be sure to
>
> - Analyze your audience and consider what they need to know to understand your topic
> - Obtain necessary information through research and consultation
> - Use a logical method of development to organize your details. Three common methods are:
>
>   **process**—arranging details in a step-by-step sequence.
>
>   **comparison and contrast**—showing how two objects, people, or ideas are similar to or different from one another.
>
>   **cause and effect**—explaining the cause or the result of something.

S T U D E N T   E S S A Y

The following essay was written by Todd Maxwell, a college student who is also a professional magician. In this informative essay, Maxwell explores the definition and popularity of magic.

Magic: Is It a Trick or Is It an Illusion?
Todd Maxwell

I am a magician, and I do magic because it is what I know best. It is true; I am one of those who work with water, fire, bright lights, fans, and the mysterious and spooky clouds of fog rolling from off the stage. I fight the laws of gravity and matter simply because I love proving the impossible can be done. Some people say magic is just a trick, and others will call it an illusion. Whether magic is a trick or an illusion, it is a popular form of entertainment.

A magic trick is a crafty or underhanded device, maneuver, or strategy intended to deceive the everyday person. A magician will tell you a magic trick is something that amazes the general public in an entertaining way, but cannot be proven by science. For example, card tricks are magic tricks. A magician like me brings out a deck of cards, asks you to pick a card of your free choice, and asks you to sign it. Then, magically I make it disappear from the deck and into your wallet. That is a magic trick. How it is done is known only to those of us who are magicians. Of course, we all know that a magician will never tell his secrets. This is the first rule in magic.

Other people may say that magic is one great big illusion. So, what is an illusion? An illusion is something that deceives by producing a false or misleading impression of reality. A magician, however, will tell you that an illusion is something that you see, and that you misinterpret as something else. A good example of an illusion is the sawing-a-person-in-half trick. Here's how it works. The magician is on stage with his assistant. The magician puts the assistant into a box and takes giant blades and shoves them through the box. Then he separates the box in half, showing that she has been cut in half. At this point, the audience does not believe it, so the magician makes her wiggle her toes and move her head. The magician also will open the sides of the box so the audience can see her arms and legs are really still there and moving. Finally, the magician puts the box back together, and she comes out of the box without injury or scratches and walks away as if nothing ever happened. I won't tell you how it is done, but, as you already know, there are many ideas about how it is done. Time and time again, though, the magician will prove your theories wrong.

Magic, then, is both a trick and an illusion, and it is one of the most dynamic forms of entertainment. Magic is usually performed live, unlike movies and videos. It is performed in front of your face. A magician faces many of the same risks that a stunt devil faces in a movie, but with only one difference. He faces them live and without a second chance. Magicians keep proving that they can outwit gravity because they love proving the impossible can be done.

You are probably wondering why magicians never release their secrets. If you knew how that card trick described above was done, would you be as amazed as you were the first time you saw it? The answer is no. Once you know how something is done, you are not as fascinated because you can go out and perform it yourself. A trick, once understood, is no longer amazing.

Will magic ever cease to be magical? It is true that there are a lot of books out there that are available to everyone and that you can pick up one of these books and learn how tricks are done. Even with people taking advantage of that fact, the magician will still prove that he can do magic. You may know how to make a hanky disappear, but only a real magician can do the trick and amaze people, for one reason: a magician has style.

Evaluating the Essay

1. Evaluate the structure and content of the essay.
    a. Does the essay follow a logical plan? Describe its organization.
    b. What is Maxwell's thesis?
    c. In what ways does he support his thesis?
    d. Evaluate the effectiveness of the title, introduction, and conclusion.
2. Evaluate the effectiveness of this informative essay. What did you learn, and what, if anything, do you wish Maxwell had included?
3. For what audience is this essay intended?
4. Does Maxwell provide information appropriate for his audience?

WRITING ABOUT A READING

Thinking before Reading

The following reading, "The Waiting Game," by the director of a university psychology department, explains the benefits of procrastinating. Notice that the overall method of explaining is cause and effect and that the final paragraph is a good example of the process method. Before you read:

1. Preview the reading, using the steps provided on p. 20.
2. After you have done your preview, connect the reading to your own experience by answering the following questions:
    a. What do you think of people who procrastinate?
    b. Can you think of any advantages to procrastination?

READING

The Waiting Game
Kit Carman

People who procrastinate are lazy, undisciplined and just plain bad—that's the myth most of us grew up with. It's true, of course, that putting things off can get you into trouble (with friends, coworkers, the IRS)—and that chronic deadline-itis may signal serious

1

problems. But if you're a procrastinator who always—eventually—gets the job done, then your delaying tactics may actually serve a useful purpose.

When you can't acknowledge an uncomfortable feeling—anxiety or anger—it may surface as a behavior pattern such as procrastination. That was the case with Julie, a student at Golden Gate University in San Francisco, where I am director of the psychology department. Before she entered grad school, Julie had worked in corporate sales. Her position required her to write lengthy proposals for prospective accounts—and she would always put off writing them until she was down to the wire. This nerve-racking syndrome finally convinced her that it was time for a career change, so she decided to study psychology. If she hadn't procrastinated, she might never have gotten the message.

Procrastination may also tip you off to unconscious insecurities. If you put off routine chores, like cleaning the oven, the message probably isn't anything deeper than that you hate housework. But if you delay doing things you're excited about, you may be struggling with a lack of confidence. It could be that you're short on self-esteem, that you've overestimated the importance of the project or that you're a perfectionist. In any case, waiting until the last minute may be the only way to force yourself to perform.

If your habit of postponing projects isn't sending you secret signals, it may be your mind's way of buying you time to think or to iron out problems. Here's how the process works: Our conscious minds gather information and relate it to the world, but psychologists speculate that most of our important thought processes—solving problems, generating ideas—take place in our unconscious minds, which routinely make sense of massive quantities of information. Therefore, while it may seem that you're avoiding a task, the truth is, your brain could be grappling with it the best way it knows how.

Unfortunately, nobody can see what's going on in the unconscious— so our society places a greater value on "doing" rather than on "thinking." Imagine your boss walking into your office to find you sitting at your desk, staring into space. She asks what you're doing, and you reply, "Thinking." What will her response be? Probably something along the lines of "Get back to work!" So perhaps we justify our incubation time by engaging in various automatic activities (chatting on the phone, reshuffling the Rolodex) that disguise the real work that we're doing. (Remember: There's a difference between thumbing your nose at deadlines and taking a healthy, thought-provoking break. To procrastinate effectively, you must first collect facts and information about your project, so your mind will have something to work with.)

In a nutshell, here's how to make procrastination work for you: (1) Be sure you understand the parameters of the project you're putting

off. (2) Make a deal with yourself: You will gather preliminary informa- 6
tion now in exchange for delaying completion. (3) Gather data. Ask
questions about the project. Make an outline. (4) Relax! Have fun!
Engage in mindless activities! (Just keep a notepad handy so you can
write down any ideas that may pop into your head.) (5) Complete
the task and revel in your brilliance.

From *Mademoiselle*

Getting Ready to Write

Strengthening Your Vocabulary

Write a brief definition of each of the following words from the preceding reading. If you cannot figure out the meaning of a word from the way
it is used in the reading, look the word up in a dictionary.

1. procrastinate (paragraph 1) put off doing something

2. chronic (paragraph 1) continuing over a long period

3. prospective (paragraph 2) possible, potential

4. syndrome (paragraph 2) predictable series of events

5. perfectionist (paragraph 3) someone who wants everything exact and
correct, stickler

6. speculate (paragraph 4) think, believe, consider alternatives

7. massive (paragraph 4) very large, huge

8. grappling (paragraph 4) struggling or trying to cope with

9. incubation (paragraph 5) idea growth and development

10. parameters (paragraph 6) main characteristics or factors

11. preliminary (paragraph 6) beginning, basic

12. revel (paragraph 6) celebrate, rejoice, take delight in

Reviewing the Reading Using an Idea Map

Review the reading by completing the missing pieces of the idea map
shown on the next page.

PROCRASTINATION MAY HAVE USEFUL PURPOSES

Help you understand yourself

Recognize anxiety or anger

Tip you off to unconscious insecurity

Buy you time to think

Solve problems

Generate ideas

HOW TO MAKE PROCRASTINATING WORK

Understand the task

Gather preliminary information

Gather data, question, make an outline

Relax but keep notepad handy for ideas

Complete the task

Examining the Reading

1. In what ways can procrastination be helpful?

2. Explain how procrastinating can help you think about and solve problems.

3. Why does Carman say, "waiting until the last minute may be the only way to force yourself to perform"?

Reacting to and Discussing Ideas

1. Do you agree with the idea that people who procrastinate are taking time to allow their unconscious to work out a problem? Why or why not?

2. Do you think procrastinating is a good thing or a bad thing? Justify your position.

3. What do you think of Carman's steps for making procrastination work for you? If you follow these steps, are you procrastinating or just tricking yourself into starting the project?

4. If Carman hadn't included the last paragraph, do you think this article would still help procrastinators? Explain your answer.

Writing about the Reading

The Paragraph Option

1. Write a paragraph explaining why you or someone you know procrastinates.

2. Write a paragraph about the activity or job that most often makes you procrastinate.

The Essay Option

Write an essay about a person you know who procrastinates. Explain what he or she procrastinates about and why.

Use this Revision Checklist for the paragraph or essay you wrote on "The Waiting Game."

REVISION CHECKLIST

Paragraph Development		YES	NO
	1. Is your topic manageable (neither too broad nor too narrow)?	☐	☐
	2. Is your paragraph written with your reader in mind?	☐	☐
	3. Does your topic sentence identify your topic?	☐	☐
	4. Does your topic sentence make a point about your topic?	☐	☐
	5. Does each remaining sentence support the topic sentence?	☐	☐
	6. Did you include sufficient detail?	☐	☐

REVISION CHECKLIST (CONTINUED)

		YES	NO
	7. Are your details arranged logically?	☐	☐
	8. Have you used transitions to connect your details?	☐	☐
	9. Is there a sentence at the end that brings the paragraph to a close?	☐	☐
For INFORMATIVE paragraphs	1. Have you analyzed your reader's familiarity with your topic?	☐	☐
	2. Have you used correct and complete information?	☐	☐
Sentence Development	3. Have you avoided writing sentence fragments, run-on sentences, and comma splices?	☐	☐
	4. Have you combined ideas to produce more effective sentences?	☐	☐
	5. Have you used adjectives and adverbs to make your sentences vivid and interesting?	☐	☐
	6. Have you used prepositional phrases, *-ing* phrases, and relative clauses to add detail?	☐	☐
	7. Have you used pronouns correctly and consistently?	☐	☐
	8. Have you avoided shifts in person, number, and verb tense?	☐	☐
	9. Have you placed modifiers correctly?	☐	☐
	10. Are elements within each sentence parallel?	☐	☐
	11. Have you used correct verb tenses and correct verb forms?	☐	☐

If you have checked any *no*s, go back to your paper and make the necessary changes.

WRITING SUCCESS TIP 14

Avoiding Plagiarism and Citing Sources

Plagiarism is using another person's words or ideas without giving that person credit. (*Plagiarism* comes from a Latin word meaning "to kidnap.") An author's writing is considered legal property. To take an author's words or ideas and use them as your own is dishonest.

Avoiding Plagiarism and Citing Sources

1. It is not necessary to credit information that is common knowledge—the major facts of history, for example—or information that is available in many reference books.

2. You should credit unique ideas, little-known facts, interpretations of facts, and unique wording.

3. If you copy in your notes a phrase, sentence, or paragraph from a source, always put quotation marks around it. Then you'll never make the mistake of presenting it as your own. Following the quotation indicate the title of the source and the author's name.

4. When taking notes on someone else's unique ideas, place brackets around your notes to indicate that the information was taken from a source. Include information on the source.

How to Credit Sources

When you do use someone else's words or ideas, you must indicate from where and whom you took the information.

1. Be sure to record complete information on each source you use. On a 3-by-5-inch index card or on a photocopy of the source materials you have found, write the source's title and author and the page number of the quotation or other information you want to use. If the source is a book, include the publisher and the year and place of publication. If the source is a magazine article, include the volume and issue numbers and the beginning and ending page numbers of the article.

2. In your paper, use the documentation style that your instructor specifies. Two common documentation methods are the MLA (Modern Language Association) style and the APA (American Psychological Association) style. With both styles, you place a brief reference to the source within your paper, giving the author, the year of publication, and the page number for the material you used. You then give complete information on your sources in a list of references at the end of your paper.

3. To obtain further information about MLA and APA styles, consult the most recent edition of *The MLA Handbook for Writers of Research Papers* or *Publication Manual of the American Psychological Association*. Your library or bookstore will have copies. You may also find summaries of these styles in some writing handbooks.

SKILLS CHECK

Paragraph 1

The following paragraph lacks transitions to connect its details. Revise it by adding transitional words or phrases where useful.

Registering a used car with the Department of Motor Vehicles requires several steps. First, You should be sure you have proper proof of ownership. You must have the previous owner's signature on his "transfer of ownership" stub of the registration or on an ownership certificate to show that you purchased the car. Next, You also need a receipt for the amount you paid for the car. You should get proof that the vehicle is insured. You need to obtain forms from your insurance company showing you have the required amount of insurance. Third, You must have the car inspected if the old inspection sticker has expired. Finally, Take the previous owner's registration form or ownership certificate, insurance forms, and proof of inspection to the Department of Motor Vehicles office. Here you will fill out a new registration form and pay sales tax and a registration fee. Then you will be issued a temporary registration. Within two weeks, You will receive your official vehicle registration in the mail.

SKILLS CHECK   CONTINUED

See Selected
Answer Key on
p. 515.

Paragraph 2

The following narrative paragraph is weak because it lacks focus and only retells events. Revise it by filling out the details and focusing them so they make a point.

Last summer my family took a trip to the Canadian Rockies. We flew to Chicago and then to Calgary. Then we took a train into the mountains. We stopped at Banff first. The next part of the trip was long and very scenic. We crossed a number of rivers, rode along riverbanks, and went through tunnels. At the end of the first day, we stayed in Kamloops, British Columbia. The next day, we traveled down the mountains to Vancouver and arrived there in the afternoon. We were tired but we had fun.

See Selected
Answer Key on
p. 515.

Paragraph 3

The following informative paragraph comparing two types of skis is not organized logically. Revise this paragraph so that its main idea is developed logically.

Cross-country skis and downhill skis are different in many aspects. Cross-country skis are intended for gliding over fairly level terrain. Unlike cross-country skis, downhill skis have steel edges and the bindings keep the entire boot clamped to the ski. Downhill skis are broader and heavier, and they have a

SKILLS CHECK CONTINUED

flatter bottom. Cross-country skis are lightweight and very narrow, and the bottom is curved so the ski does not lie flat on the snow. Downhill skis are meant for skiing down steep slopes with frequent turns. The bindings on cross-country skis do not keep the heel clamped down, since the long running strides used in cross-country skiing depend on free movement of the heel.

COMMON PARAGRAPH PROBLEMS AND HOW TO AVOID THEM

15

Revising Underdeveloped Paragraphs

CHAPTER OBJECTIVES

In this chapter you will learn to

1. revise ineffective topic sentences.
2. revise underdeveloped paragraphs.

Advertisements often rely on a photograph to complete the message and make the advertisement meaningful. Think, for a moment, of how ineffective an advertisement would be without an accompanying photograph. Imagine the advertisement on page 301 for the Buster® FoodCube without the photograph of the dog at a computer, and without the photograph of the FoodCube. The advertisement would lose its interest and appeal, and its meaning would be incomplete. The photograph supplies the additional information and details you need to understand the advertisement.

Many ineffective paragraphs are like an ad without a photo. They leave the reader frustrated, confused, or bored, with an incomplete understanding of the writer's message. In this chapter you will learn how to recognize common paragraph problems and how to revise to correct them.

WRITING

Revising Ineffective Topic Sentences

Your topic sentence is the most important sentence in the paragraph. It promises what the remainder of the paragraph will deliver. A weak topic sentence usually produces a weak paragraph. Your topic sentence will be weak if it (1) lacks a viewpoint or attitude, (2) is too broad, or (3) is too narrow.

374

Topic Sentences That Lack a Point of View

A topic sentence should identify your topic *and* express an attitude or viewpoint. It must make a point about the topic.

If your topic is the old roller coaster at Starland Park, it is not enough to make a general statement of fact in your topic sentence.

LACKS POINT OF VIEW: There is an old roller coaster at Starland Park.

Your reader would rightly ask in this case, "So what?" A topic sentence needs to tell the reader what is important or interesting about your topic. It should state the point you are going to make in the rest of the paragraph. For every topic, you can find many points to make in a topic sentence. For example:

EXPRESSES POINT OF VIEW: The old roller coaster at Starland Park is unsafe and should be torn down.

The old roller coaster at Starland Park no longer seems as frightening as it did when I was young.

Three types of people go on the old roller coaster at Starland Park: the brave, the scared, and the stupid.

If you write a topic sentence that does not express a viewpoint, you will find you have very little or nothing to write about in the remainder of the paragraph. Look at these topic sentences:

LACKS POINT OF VIEW: Pete works at the YMCA.

EXPRESSES POINT OF VIEW: Pete got over his shyness by working at the YMCA.

If you used the first topic sentence, "Pete works at the YMCA," what else could you include in your paragraph? If you instead used the second topic sentence, you would have something to write about. You could describe Pete before and after he began working at the YMCA, discuss positive aspects of the job, or give examples of friends Pete has made through his work.

Notice how the following topic sentences have been revised to express a point of view.

LACKS POINT OF VIEW: Mark plays soccer.

REVISED: Mark's true personality comes out when he plays soccer. [Details can explain Mark's personality as revealed by his soccer game.]

LACKS POINT OF VIEW: Professor Cooke teaches accounting.

REVISED: Professor Cooke makes accounting practical. [Details can describe how Professor Cooke makes accounting skills relevant to everyday life.]

LACKS POINT OF VIEW: I read newspapers.

REVISED: I recommend reading newspapers from back to front. [Details can give reasons why this method is best.]

The following suggestions will help you revise your topic sentence if you discover that it lacks a point of view:

1. Use brainstorming, freewriting, or branching. Try to generate more ideas about your topic. Study your results to discover a way to approach your topic.

2. Ask yourself questions about your topic sentence. Specifically, ask, "Why," "How," "So what," or "Why is this important?" Answering your own questions will give you ideas for revising your topic sentence.

EXERCISE 15-1 The following topic sentences lack a point of view. Revise each to express an interesting view on the topic.

SENTENCE: I took a biology exam today.

REVISED: <u>The biology exam that I took today contained a number of surprises.</u>

1. I am taking a math course this semester.

    REVISED: <u>My math course this semester is more challenging than I expected it to be.</u>

2. I purchased a videocamera last week.

    REVISED: <u>The videocamera I bought last week will be used to preserve family memories.</u>

3. Soft rock was playing in the dentist's office.

    REVISED: <u>The soft rock playing in the dentist's office soothed some nervous patients but made me fish for my earplugs.</u>

4. Sam has three televisions and four radios in his household.

    REVISED: <u>Because his daily existence depends on news and weather, Sam has three televisions and four radios in his household.</u>

5. There is one tree on the street where I live.

   REVISED: <u>The one oak tree on my street provides a canopy for</u>

   <u>children's games and play.</u>

6. Many people wear headphones on their way to work.

   REVISED: <u>Many people wear headphones on their way to work to shut</u>

   <u>out surrounding noise and distractions.</u>

7. Our sociology professor will give three exams.

   REVISED: <u>The three exams our sociology professor will give us will force</u>

   <u>us to keep up with the reading assignments.</u>

8. The first hurricane of the season is predicted to strike land tomorrow.

   REVISED: <u>The first hurricane of the season is predicted to strike land</u>

   <u>tomorrow, and tourists are panicking.</u>

9. My four-year-old son has learned the alphabet.

   REVISED: <u>My four-year-old son has learned the alphabet, so he is</u>

   <u>eager to learn to read.</u>

10. Juanita enrolled her son in a day-care center.

    REVISED: <u>Juanita enrolled her son in a day-care center to encourage him</u>

    <u>to play cooperatively with other children.</u>

Topic Sentences That Are Too Broad

Some topic sentences express a point of view, but they cover too much information.

TOO BROAD: The death penalty is a crime against humanity.

This statement cannot be supported in a single paragraph. Lengthy essays, even entire books, have been written to argue this opinion.

A broad topic sentence promises more than you can reasonably deliver in a single paragraph. It leads to writing that is vague and rambling. With a broad topic sentence, you will end up with too many facts and ideas to cover or too many generalities (general statements) that do not sufficiently explain your topic sentence. In the following example, note the broad topic sentence and its effects on paragraph development.

Sample Paragraph

All kinds of violent crimes in the world today seem to be getting worse. Sometimes I wonder how people could possibly bring themselves to do such horrible things. One problem may be the violent acts shown on television programs. Some people think crime has a lot to do with horror movies and television programs. We have no heroes to identify with other than criminals. News reporting of crimes is too "real"; it shows too much. Kids watch these programs without their parents and don't know what to make of them. Parents should spend time with their children and supervise their play.

The topic sentence above promises more than a good paragraph can reasonably deliver: to discuss all violent crimes in the world today and their worsening nature. If you reread the paragraph, you will see that in the supporting sentences the author wanders from topic to topic. She first mentions violence on television, then moves to lack of heroes. Next she discusses news reporting that is too graphic, then switches to children watching programs alone. Finally, she ends with parental supervision of children. Each point about possible causes of violence or ways to prevent it seems underdeveloped.

An effective topic sentence needs to be more focused. For example, the topic sentence for a paragraph about crime might focus on one type of crime in one city and one reason for its increase.

FOCUSED: Home burglaries are increasing in Owensville because of increased drug usage.

Another effective topic sentence for a paragraph on crime could focus on one possible cause of rising violence in the workplace.

FOCUSED: The mass layoffs in the past few years have led to more attacks by desperate fired workers.

The topic sentence of the following paragraph is also too broad.

Sample Paragraph

People often forget the spirit and value of life and concentrate on worldly goods. These people buy things for show—nice cars, nice clothes, nice houses. These people are scraping their pennies together just to live well. They do not realize that things not from the store are just as nice.

Their health, their family, and people they care about are far more important than money. You can be rich and poor at the same time.

Because the topic was too broad, the writer continued to write general statements throughout the paragraph and to repeat the same or similar ideas. A more effective approach might be to select one worldly good and show how it affects one person.

FOCUSED: My sister is so concerned with dressing stylishly that she ignores everyone around her.

Now the writer can explain how an emphasis on clothing detracts from her sister's relationship with others.

Another effective topic sentence might focus the paragraph on not taking good health for granted:

FOCUSED: I used to think I could buy my way to happiness, but that was before I lost my good health.

The following suggestions will help you revise your topic sentence if you discover that it is too broad:

1. Narrow your topic. A topic that is too broad often produces a topic sentence that is too broad. Narrow your topic by subdividing it into smaller topics. Continue subdividing until you produce a topic that is manageable in a single paragraph.

2. Rewrite your topic sentence to focus on one aspect or part of your topic. Ask yourself, "What is the part of this topic that really interests me or that I care most about? What do I know most about and have the most to say about?" Then focus on *that* aspect of the topic.

3. Apply your topic sentence to a specific time and place. Ask yourself, "How does this broad topic that I'd like to write about relate to some particular time and place that I know about? How can I make the general topic come alive by using a well-defined example?"

4. Consider using one of your supporting sentences as a topic sentence. Reread your paragraph; look for a detail that could be developed or expanded.

EXERCISE 15-2 | Turn each of the following broad topic sentences into a well-focused topic sentence that could lead to an effective paragraph. Remember that your topic sentence must also include a point of view. Then compare your answers with your classmates' answers to see the variety of effective topic sentences that can come from a broad one.

TOO BROAD: Hunting is a worthwhile and beneficial sport.

FOCUSED: Hunting deer in overpopulated areas is beneficial to
the herd.

1. I would like to become more creative.

   REVISED: I would like to try writing songs as a way to express parts
   of myself most people never see.

2. Brazil is a beautiful country.

   REVISED: Brazil is an ideal vacation spot for people who like to relax
   and enjoy the scenery.

3. Pollution is a big problem.

   REVISED: Asbestos in older buildings is a serious health hazard for
   people who plan to remodel these buildings.

4. The space program is amazing.

   REVISED: The space program has enabled scientists to make
   technological advances that are useful to us in
   everyday life.

5. It is very important to learn Japanese.

   REVISED: Learning Japanese will be an asset to anyone who wants to
   work in international trade.

6. We must protect the environment.

   REVISED: To safeguard our drinking water, we must protect our lakes
   and rivers from industrial pollution.

7. Lani is a good mother.

   REVISED: Lani feels the most important things she can teach her
   daughter are self-control and independence.

8. The book was interesting.

   REVISED: The mystery novel *Decider,* by Dick Francis, contains many
   details of English horseracing that only a former jockey
   would know.

9. Lots of magazines are published.

REVISED: <u>Sports fans can find a magazine to satisfy their craving for</u>

<u>inside knowledge on almost any sport.</u>

10. Honesty is important.

REVISED: <u>Honesty with friends is important to maintain a</u>

<u>trusting relationship.</u>

Topic Sentences That Are Too Narrow

If your topic sentence is too narrow, you will realize it right away because you won't have enough to write about to complete your paragraph. Topic sentences that are too narrow also frequently lack a point of view.

TOO NARROW: My birdfeeder attracts yellow songbirds.
REVISED: Watching the different birds at our feeder is a pleasant diversion enjoyed by our entire family, including our cat.

TOO NARROW: My math instructor looks at his watch frequently.
REVISED: My math instructor has a number of nervous habits that detract from his lecture presentations.

The following suggestions will help you revise your topic sentence when it is too narrow:

1. Broaden your topic to include a wider group or range of items or ideas. For example, do not write about one nervous habit; write about several. Look for patterns and trends that could form the basis of a new, less narrow topic sentence.

2. Broaden your topic so that it takes in both causes and effects or makes comparisons or contrasts. For example, do not write only about how fast an instructor lectures. Also write about the effect of his lecture speed on students trying to take notes, or contrast that instructor with others who have different lecture styles.

3. Brainstorm and research; try to develop a more general point from your narrower one. Ask yourself, "What does this narrow point mean? What are its larger implications?" Suppose you've written the following topic sentence:

I wanted to buy a CD this week, but it was not in my budget.

You could expand this idea to discuss the importance or value of making and following a weekly budget.

NEED TO KNOW

Topic Sentences

Ineffective paragraphs may frustrate, confuse, or bore your reader. A weak topic sentence may

- lack a point of view or attitude toward the topic.
- be too broad.
- be too narrow.

To revise a topic sentence that lacks a point of view

- use brainstorming, freewriting, or branching.
- ask yourself questions about your topic sentence.

To narrow a topic sentence that is too broad, consider

- narrowing your topic.
- rewriting your topic sentence to focus on one aspect of your topic.
- applying your topic sentence to a specific time and place.
- using one of your supporting sentences as a topic sentence.

To broaden a topic sentence that is too narrow, consider.

- broadening your topic to make it more inclusive.
- broadening your topic to consider causes and effects or to make comparisons or contrasts.
- brainstorming and researching to develop a more general point.

EXERCISE 15-3

Turn each of the following narrow topic sentences into a broader, well-focused topic sentence that could lead to an effective paragraph. Remember that your topic sentence must also include a point of view. Then compare your answers with your classmates' answers to see the variety of effective topic sentences that can come from a narrow one.

TOO NARROW: Football players wear protective helmets.

REVISED: Football players wear several types of protective equipment to guard against injuries.

1. I planted a tomato plant in my garden.

REVISED: I planted enough vegetable plants in my garden to produce tasty salads throughout the summer.

2. The cafeteria served hot dogs and beans for lunch.

REVISED: The students complained that the cafeteria serves high-fat, calorie-laden foods.

3. Orlando sings in a low key.

   REVISED: Orlando's soulful singing is intended to appeal to his audience.
   _____

4. Suzanne bought a stapler for her desk.

   REVISED: Suzanne equipped her desk with supplies to enable her to
   work more efficiently.

5. Koala bears are really marsupials, not bears.

   REVISED: Koalas, marsupials from Australia, are lovable animals that
   have become popular attractions at zoos.

6. On our vacation, we stopped at a small town called Boothbay Harbor.

   REVISED: Boothbay Harbor is a picturesque New England coastal town
   that is ideal for a weekend vacation.

7. Homemade bread contains no preservatives.

   REVISED: Homemade bread is healthier than most commercially
   made loaves.

8. At Halloween, the girl dressed as a witch.

   REVISED: At Halloween, the girl dressed as a witch to frighten her
   younger brothers.

9. The comedian told a joke about dental floss.

   REVISED: The comedian told several jokes that made fun of the
   medical profession.

10. We had a family portrait taken for Christmas.

    REVISED: Each year, our family has a portrait taken for Christmas, which
    helps us trace our growth and change.

Revising Paragraphs to Add Supporting Details

The details in a paragraph should give your reader sufficient information to make your topic sentence believable. Paragraphs that lack necessary detail are called **underdeveloped paragraphs.** Underdeveloped paragraphs lack supporting sentences to prove or explain the point made in the topic sentence. As you read the following student paragraph, keep the topic sentence in mind and consider whether the rest of the sentences support it.

Sample Student Paragraph

> I am a very impatient person, and my impatience interferes with how easily I can get through a day. If I ask for something, I want it immediately. If I'm going somewhere and I'm ready and somebody else isn't, I get very upset. I hate driving behind someone who drives slowly when I cannot pass. I think that annoys me the most, and it never happens unless I am in a hurry. If I were less impatient, I would probably feel more relaxed and less pressured.

This paragraph begins with a topic sentence that is focused (it is neither too broad nor too narrow) and that includes a point of view. It promises to explain how the writer's impatience makes it difficult for him to get through a day. However, the rest of the paragraph does not fulfill this promise. Instead, the writer gives two very general examples of his impatience: (1) wanting something and (2) waiting for someone. The third example, driving behind a slow driver, is a little more specific, but it is not developed well. The last sentence suggests, but does not explain, that the writer's impatience makes him feel tense and pressured.

Taking into account the need for more supporting detail, the author revised his paragraph as follows.

Revised Paragraph

> I am a very impatient person, and my impatience interferes with how easily I can get through a day. For example, when I decide to buy something, such as a new CD, I *have* to have it right away—that day. I usually drop everything and run to the store. Of course, I shortchange myself on studying, and that hurts my grades. My impatience hurts me, too, when I'm waiting for someone, which I hate to do. If my friend Alex and I agree to meet at noon to work on his car, I get annoyed if he's even five minutes late. Then I usually end up saying something nasty or sarcastic like "Well, where *were* you?" which I regret later. Perhaps I am most impatient when I'm behind the steering wheel. If I get behind a slow

driver, I get annoyed and start honking and beeping my horn. I know this might fluster the other driver, and afterwards I feel guilty. I've tried talking to myself to calm down; sometimes it works, so I hope I'm overcoming this bad trait.

Did you notice that the writer became much more specific in the revised version? He gave an example of something he wanted—a CD—and he described his actions and their consequences. The example of waiting for someone was provided by the incident involving his friend Alex. Finally, the writer explained the driving example in more detail and stated its consequences. With the extra details and supporting examples, the paragraph is more interesting and effective.

The following suggestions will help you revise an underdeveloped paragraph:

1. **Analyze your paragraph sentence by sentence.** If a sentence does not add new, specific information to your paragraph, delete it or add to it so that it becomes relevant.

2. **Think of specific situations, facts, or examples that illustrate or support your topic.** Often you can make a general sentence more specific.

3. **Brainstorm, freewrite, or branch.** To come up with additional details or examples to use in your paragraph, try some prewriting techniques. If necessary, start fresh with a new approach and new set of ideas.

4. **Reexamine your topic sentence.** If you are having trouble generating details, your topic sentence may be the problem. Consider changing the approach.

> EXAMPLE: Rainy days make me feel depressed.
>
> REVISED: Rainy days, although depressing, give me a chance to catch up on household chores.

5. **Consider changing your topic.** If a paragraph remains troublesome, look for a new topic and start over.

EXERCISE ▶ 15-4 The following paragraph is poorly developed. What suggestions would you make to the writer to improve the paragraph? Write them in the space provided. Be specific. Which sentences are weak? How could each be improved?

I am attending college to improve myself. By attending college, I am getting an education to improve the skills that I'll need for a good career in broadcasting. Then after a successful career, I'll be able to get the things that I need to be happy in my life. People will also respect me more.

_____Make the topic sentence more specific; focus on one or several aspects of_____

_____self-improvement. Add detail. Name and describe the skills needed for_____

_____broadcasting. Indicate how a general education or specific courses will pro-_____

_____vide those skills. Revise and combine the last two sentences to draw the_____

_____paragraph to a close._____

EXERCISE **15-5**   Evaluate the following paragraph by answering the questions that follow it.

> One of the best ways to keep people happy and occupied is to entertain them. Every day people are being entertained, whether it is by a friend for a split second or by a Broadway play for several hours. Entertainment is probably one of the nation's biggest businesses. Entertainment has come a long way from the past; it has gone from plays in the park to films in eight-screen movie theaters.

1. Evaluate the topic sentence. What is wrong with it? How could it be revised?   _The topic sentence is too general. Focus on one kind of_ _entertainment and discuss its benefits._

2. Write a more effective topic sentence on the topic of entertainment. _Television entertainment keeps viewers occupied and happy._

   _____

3. Evaluate the supporting details. What is wrong with them? _They need to be more specific._

   _____

   What should the writer do to develop her paragraph? _Add descriptive and relevant detail._

   _____

4. Use the topic sentence you wrote in question #2 above to develop a paragraph about entertainment.

EXERCISE **15-6**   Develop one of the topic sentences you wrote in Exercise 15-2 into a paragraph that uses good supporting details. Then, draw an idea map of your paragraph, and revise your paragraph as needed.

NEED TO KNOW

Adding Supporting Details

To revise an underdeveloped paragraph,

- analyze your paragraph sentence by sentence.
- think of specific situations, facts, or examples that illustrate or support your main point
- use brainstorming, freewriting, or branching.
- reexamine your topic sentence.
- consider changing your topic.

STUDENT ESSAY

The following essay was written by Tom Ford, a student athlete who is now a member of a collegiate baseball team. The two drafts illustrate the types of changes in both content and organization that revision usually involves.

As you read the first draft, notice that the essay does not develop the thesis introduced in the first paragraph and that the paragraphs lack effective topic sentences. Paragraph 2 describes Ford's little-league experiences, the types of players he observed, and his discovery that he is a competitive player. Paragraph 3 lacks a topic sentence. It discusses both aggressive and timid players, but does not make a point about either type. Paragraph 4 does have a topic sentence, but does not clearly support Ford's thesis that there are many different types of players. Instead, it discusses viewers' responses to aggressive behavior.

First Draft

Athletes and Their Emotions
Tom Ford

When I was growing up, I played many different sports and played with many different kinds of people. I played with laid-back, timid people and with aggressive and competitive people. I witnessed many problems due to players' different emotions. 1

The first time I witnessed players' emotions was when I played little- league baseball at about age six. We had a good team and we were 2 going to the championship game. It was then that I first noticed differences among the players on my team. Some players just lopped around and seemed not to care. Others never said anything and seemed to be afraid, and then there were players who were so violent that they had to be removed from the game. A fourth group included players like me who yelled, cheered, and did everything they could to win. I classify myself as a competitive player. I hate to lose and I'll do everything I can to win. Years later I came to understand these differences much better by watching games on TV and by playing sports in school.

A good example of a player who shows his violent or aggressive side 3 is Dennis Rodman from the Chicago Bulls. This man has a temper, but is a good basketball player. Rodman is so violent that when a photographer took a picture of him he kicked the photographer right in the groin. Another aggressive player I witnessed on the field and the court was Jeff Jordan who was on my football, basketball, and baseball teams during high school. If he didn't get his way he would become violent. An athlete I know who represents a laid-back type of player is Tim Round. Tim is the kicker/punter for the Sweet Home Football Team. He's a great kicker, who doesn't show much emotion on the field, but he gets the job done! I don't consider players like this to be timid, because they are not afraid to express their emotions. They just don't like to become very excited or emotional when they play.

I feel that the different attitudes and emotions of athletes probably 4 attract T.V. viewers because the variety makes sports more interesting to watch. For example, many people watch hockey because of the fighting and aggressive behavior. If all players showed just one kind of emotion, sports would not be as interesting. That, at least, is my point of view. I must admit, my friends and I like seeing aggressive behavior in sports, but it depends on the sport. In a basketball game, I don't think its right if a player is going up for a lay-up and a player from the opposing team tackles him from behind. I feel that would be wrong. However, I do believe that physical contact is an important part of the game in hockey and football.

In conclusion, I am glad that athletes have different personalities and 5 emotions when they play. If this were not so, sports would probably not be as interesting to many people. Also, sports allow people to let their emotions out and release stress. I know that's my situation in sports.

As you read Ford's final draft, notice that he has clearly stated his thesis, rewritten paragraphs to focus on a single idea, and added detail to support each topic sentence. Specifically, Ford's thesis identifies four types of players; each type is then explained in the essay. Paragraph 2 provides background information and explains how Ford came to realize that the four types of players exist. Paragraphs 3 through 6 explain each of the four types of players in the order they were mentioned in the thesis statement. Notice that each paragraph begins with a focused topic sentence that identifies the type of player to be described in the paragraph. Paragraph 7 returns to the thesis by suggesting why different types of players are important in sports.

Final Draft

Athletes and Their Emotions
Tom Ford

When I was growing up, I played many different sports and played with many different kinds of people. From these experiences I have come to recognize four basic types of athletes, each with a different emotional style. Athletes tend to be violent, aggressive players, timid players, laid-back players, or competitive players. These different styles taken together help to make sports interesting and fun to both play and watch.

The first time I became aware of players' emotional styles was when I played little-league baseball at about six years of age. We had a good team, and we were going to the championship game. It was then that I first noticed the differences among the players on our team. Some players were so mean they had to be removed from the game. Others were very quiet and seemed to be afraid. Some players just lopped around and seemed not to care. A fourth group included players like me who yelled, cheered, and did everything they could to win. Years later I came to understand these types of players much better by watching games on television and by playing organized sports in school.

The first type of athlete is the overly aggressive or violent kind of player. This kind of athlete is usually the toughest. He will do anything necessary to win, but he often loses control, gets caught, and is ejected from the game. Aggressive players can be good to have on a team, but also can cause some problems for their team. I have played against and with many aggressive players. I prefer playing against them because I can often cause them to do something stupid or to react violently. An example of a violent player is Dennis Rodman of the Chicago Bulls. This man is essentially a good basketball player, but he has an uncontrollable temper. During a game, Rodman once became so angry when a photographer took a picture of him that he kicked the photographer. This is an example of how aggressiveness can cross the line into violence. Another aggressive player I witnessed on the field and on the court is Jeff Jordan. If he did not get his way he would turn violent, shouting and threatening other players.

A second type of athlete is the timid player. This athlete usually has   4
plenty of talent, but does not show enough of an outgoing attitude. This is the type of player who is afraid of speaking out and expressing opinions. I think the timid type is afraid of what people might think if he berates his teammates or objects to a bad call by an official. A good example of this kind of player is my younger brother. He is twelve years old and plays basketball well, but never opens his mouth on the court.

A third kind of athlete that is similar to the timid player is the low-   5
emotion player. A laid-back player is not afraid, but just doesn't get very excited when playing sports. This type of player controls his emotions during the game. Tim Rounds is an example of a laid-back player. Tim is the kicker/punter on the Sweet Home High School football team. He is very good, but doesn't show much emotion. Even when he broke the record for the longest field goal in Sweet Home history, he did not get excited.

The fourth type of athlete is the competitive player. This type of   6
player has the strongest desire to win and shows great enthusiasm for every sport he plays. Competitive players always try their hardest to win. I classify myself in this category of athletes. Once during a basketball game, I took a head-first dive into the bleachers to save the ball from going out of bounds. I jumped right back up on my feet and yelled, "Let's pick it up, team." I will do everything I can to win even if I must risk injury.

Overall, I feel that many athletes have different personalities and   7
emotions when they play, but if this were not true, playing or watching sports would not be as much fun. Sports are games in which people can release their emotions and reduce stress, even though they may do so in many different ways.

Evaluating the Essay

1. What are the most important changes that Ford made?
   a. How did Ford refocus his essay?
   b. How did he organize it?
   c. What information did he add?
   d. What information did he delete?

2. Evaluate the structure and content of the final draft.

   a. What is Ford's thesis?

   b. What plan of development did he use?

   c. Evaluate the effectiveness of the title, introduction, and conclusion.

3. What further revisions would you suggest?

WRITING ABOUT A READING

Thinking before Reading

The following reading, "The Lure of Gambling's 'Easy' Money," by Robert McClory, is a good example of writing that contains effective topic sentences and well-developed details. As you read, notice that each paragraph contains numerous facts, examples, statistics, and quotations that support the main point.

Before you read:

1. Preview the reading, using the steps provided on page 20.

2. After you have done your preview, connect the reading to your own experience by answering the following questions:

   a. Have you ever bought a lottery ticket, entered a raffle, or bet on a race? If not, why not? If so, why did you do it? Did you expect to win?

   b. What forms of gambling, other than lotteries, are popular? Why are they popular?

READING

The Lure of Gambling's "Easy" Money
Robert McClory

In the '60s it was marijuana, in the '70s heroin, in the '80s cocaine; and in the '90s the addiction of the decade is gambling. "It's already a major social and economic problem, and little is being done about it," says Valerie Lorenz, executive director of the Compulsive Gambling

Center in Baltimore, the only facility in the country devoted exclusively to research on, treatment of, and education about gambling abuse. "It's costing as much in financial terms as the current drug epidemic."

Gambling is a soaring industry in the United States: The total amount of money circulated through gambling activity in 1990 was $286 billion, according to *Gaming and Wagering Business* magazine. That's $34 billion more than in the previous year—more, in fact, than Americans spent on health insurance, dentists, shoes, foreign travel, and household appliances put together.

2

Paul Dworin, publisher of *Gaming and Wagering*, ascribes the steady rise to an "explosion" of new gambling facilities and state-run lotteries. Four years ago, he notes, only Nevada and New Jersey had legal casinos, while today some 12 states have them and others plan to follow. Casino growth has been stimulated in part by the Indian Gaming Act, passed by Congress in 1986, which allows Native American entrepreneurs[1] to open casinos, with table games and slot machines, on many reservations. Eleven such casinos are currently flourishing in Minnesota alone. Large cities like Chicago are planning major casinos, and some 34 states and the District of Columbia now sponsor lotteries. If it were not for the recession, says Dworin, gambling receipts would be growing at an even faster rate.

3

Lorenz contends that the recession is an impetus,[2] not a brake. "Studies show that as the economy goes bad," she says, "people look for quick solutions to their problems, especially the people who are hardest hit."

4

Studies also report that gambling activity is significantly higher among the poor, those most damaged by losing. In their book *Selling Hope: State Lotteries in America,* Charles T. Clotfelter and Philip J. Cook claim that 20 percent of lottery players account for 65 percent of lottery wagers, with poor blacks and Hispanics doing most of the gambling. A California study found that a 10 percent segment of the players—who were disproportionately poor—purchased more than 50 percent of the tickets. A survey in the Chicago area found that the per capita lottery purchase during a recent year was $76 in affluent communities, but $221 in neighborhoods with the lowest incomes and the highest reliance on public aid.

5

Clotfelter and Cook excoriate[3] state lotteries, charging that they use misleading advertising, offer terrible odds, generate revenues far less important to the states than people imagine, and, most importantly, make gamblers of millions of people who have never wagered before. The lottery, in their view, is a "powerful recruiting device," since legiti-

6

1. businesspersons
2. force or energy
3. criticize

mate civil authority puts its seal of approval on the practice, thus raising participation almost to the level of civic virtue.

"What if the state spent millions advertising cigarettes and vodka?" asks Lorenz. "Wouldn't responsible people react?" 7

Despite all the money that changes hands in state-sponsored gambling, the revenues targeted for various state-funded programs—most often education—are surprisingly minuscule. In Illinois, for example, raising the state income tax from 2.5 percent of personal income to 2.83 percent would raise the same revenues as the lottery. Betting is bally-hooed as the savior of public education, but in Illinois, as in most of the states that allot lottery revenues to schools, none of the money directly affects the schools' budgets. These budgets are fixed by the state legislature and remain unchanged no matter how much money the lottery brings in. Instead, the proceeds are scattered through programs that otherwise might have to be trimmed back during budget shortfalls. 8

Organizations like the National Council of Problem Gambling and Gamblers Anonymous agree with Lorenz that even if the fiscal benefits were enormous, "gaming's" terrifying social consequences would be enough to justify opposing it. A study by the National Institute of Mental Health indicated that the suicide rate among compulsive gamblers is the highest for any known addicted group. A three-year institute study concluded that 4.2 million Americans are addicted gamblers (36 9 percent of them women, 43 percent non-white, 38 percent under the age of 30, 60 percent with yearly incomes under $25,000). The biggest recent surge in addicts, says Lorenz, is among teenagers; many regularly bet sizable amounts on the lottery.

But Lorenz insists that gambling is not just one more addiction.   10
"Compulsive gamblers as a group are strongly attracted to risk-taking situations," she says. "They have an exceptionally low threshold of boredom and a peculiar dysfunction in their relationship with money. It's almost as if they've been brainwashed into thinking money can solve everything. They need special attention. We're just beginning to under- stand how this addiction works."

Some states are beginning to agree. Iowa, Texas, Wisconsin, and   11
Minnesota are among states that now allocate funds for treatment of prob- lem gamblers. But the amount spent on treatment in no way compares with the money spent for running and promoting the gambling industry.

Indeed, the whole issue of state-sponsored gambling is beset with   12
contradictions, none more glaring than this: An activity heralded[4] for its contribution to education is in fact teaching people that the easiest way to success is to hit it big in a game of chance.

4. announced

From *Utne Reader.*

Getting Ready to Write

Strengthening Your Vocabulary
Write a brief definition for each of the following words from the preced- ing reading. If you cannot figure out the meaning of a word from the way it is used in the reading, look the word up in a dictionary.

1. epidemic (paragraph 1)   <u>rapidly spreading occurrence</u>

2. ascribes (paragraph 3)   <u>identifies the cause of</u>

3. flourishing (paragraph 3)   <u>growing, doing well</u>

4. minuscule (paragraph 8)   <u>very small</u>

5. surge (paragraph 9)   <u>sudden, strong increase</u>

6. glaring (paragraph 12)   <u>noticeable, obvious</u>

Reviewing the Reading Using an Idea Map

Review the reading by completing the missing pieces of the idea map shown below.

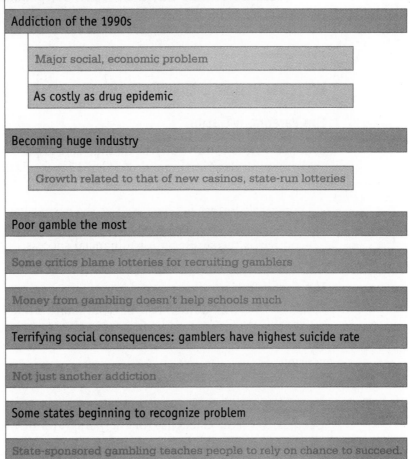

GAMBLING IS THE ADDICTION OF THE '90s AND IS A GROWING PROBLEM IN THE U. S.

Addiction of the 1990s

> Major social, economic problem

> As costly as drug epidemic

Becoming huge industry

> Growth related to that of new casinos, state-run lotteries

Poor gamble the most

Some critics blame lotteries for recruiting gamblers

Money from gambling doesn't help schools much

Terrifying social consequences: gamblers have highest suicide rate

Not just another addiction

Some states beginning to recognize problem

State-sponsored gambling teaches people to rely on chance to succeed.

Examining the Reading

1. List the reasons McClory gives for the increasing popularity of gambling.

2. According to the surveys he cites, who is doing the gambling?

3. What arguments does he present against state-run lotteries?

Reacting to and Discussing Ideas

1. Do you know anyone who is addicted to gambling? What behavior have you observed? Why is gambling appealing to him or her?

2. Evaluate ads for state lotteries or other forms of legalized gambling. What are their messages? To whom do they appeal?

3. Tobacco advertising has been restricted. Should lottery ads also be restricted? If so, how?

Writing about the Reading

The Paragraph Option

1. Gambling is a form of risk taking; that is part of its appeal. Write a paragraph describing a risk you have taken. Explain whether the outcome was worth the risk.

2. Winning a lottery is advertised as the easiest way to financial success. What are other routes to success? Write a paragraph describing what you feel is the surest path to financial success.

The Essay Option

Write a letter to a member of your state House of Representatives supporting one of the following positions: (1) lotteries should be illegal; (2) lotteries should be restricted; or (3) lotteries should be begun or continued.

Use this Revision Checklist for the paragraph or essay you wrote about "The Lure of Gambling."

REVISION CHECKLIST

Paragraph Development		YES	NO
	1. Is your topic manageable (neither too broad nor too narrow)?	☐	☐
	2. Is your paragraph written with your reader in mind?	☐	☐

REVISION CHECKLIST (CONTINUED)

	YES	NO
3. Does your topic sentence identify your topic?	❑	❑
4. Does your topic sentence make a point about your topic?	❑	❑
5. Is your topic sentence effective (neither too broad nor too narrow)?	❑	❑
6. Does each remaining sentence support the topic sentence?	❑	❑
7. Did you include sufficient detail?	❑	❑
8. Are your details arranged logically?	❑	❑
9. Have you used transitions to connect your details?	❑	❑
10. Is there a sentence at the end that brings the paragraph to a close?	❑	❑
11. Is your paragraph fully developed?	❑	❑

Sentence Development	12. Are there any fragments, run-on sentences, or comma splices?	❑	❑
	13. Are ideas combined to produce more effective sentences?	❑	❑
	14. Do adjectives and adverbs make the sentences vivid and interesting?	❑	❑
	15. Are prepositional phrases, *-ing* phrases, and relative clauses used to add detail?	❑	❑
	16. Are pronouns used correctly and consistently?	❑	❑
	17. Are there any shifts in person, number, or verb tense?	❑	❑
	18. Are modifiers correctly placed?	❑	❑
	19. Are elements within each sentence parallel?	❑	❑
	20. Are verb tenses and verb forms used correctly?	❑	❑

If you have checked any *no*s, go back to your paper and make the necessary changes.

WRITING SUCCESS TIP 15

When you send your résumé (a list of your qualifications for a job) to a prospective employer, you should enclose with it a letter of application (also known as a cover letter). Your letter introduces you and interests the employer in you. Employers pay careful attention to cover letters because they reveal much about an applicant's personality, style, and writing ability. Use the following tips to write a confident, convincing, effective cover letter.

1. **Length.** Your letter should be no more than one page long.

2. **Typing.** Type your letter, or keyboard it on a computer, using standard letter format.

3. **Address and salutation.** Address the letter to an individual rather than a company or department. Make a phone call, if necessary, to discover who is in charge of employment interviews. Use a standard salutation, such as "Dear Mr. _____" or "Dear Ms. _____."

4. **First paragraph.** The first paragraph should capture your reader's attention and state your purpose for writing. If someone has referred you to the company, mention his or her name. Indicate exactly what position you are applying for. Try to show that you know something about the company.

5. **Gimmicks.** Avoid gimmicks and cute beginnings; they are seldom effective.

6. **Body.** Highlight your qualifications in one or two paragraphs. Explain how you can contribute to the company.

7. **Last paragraph.** End your letter by requesting an interview. Indicate when you are available, and be sure to include your telephone number and e-mail address if you have one.

8. **Closing.** Use a standard closing, such as "Yours truly" or "Sincerely." Then type your full name, leaving enough space above it for your signature.

9. **Revise and proofread.** Be sure your letter is convincing, effective, and correct. Be sure it is free of grammar, punctuation, and spelling errors. Ask someone else to read it before you send it.

Using an Idea Map to Spot Revision Problems

16

Movie directors do numerous "takes" of each scene they are filming. They may ask actors and actresses to repeat a scene ten or fifteen times before they are satisfied with it. Advertisers review many drafts of an ad's copy before they select one that best achieves their goals. Writers also do several drafts of a paragraph or essay before they are satisfied with it and are confident that it meets their goals.

Some students find revision a troublesome step because it is difficult for them to see what is wrong with their own work. After working hard on a first draft, it is tempting to say to yourself that you've done a great job and to think, "This is fine." Other times, you may think you have explained and supported an idea clearly when actually you have not. In other words, you may be blind to your own paper's weaknesses. Almost all writing, however, needs and benefits from revision. An idea map can help you spot weaknesses and discover what you may not have done as well as you thought.

An idea map will show how each of your ideas fits with and relates to all of the other ideas in the paragraph or essay. When you draw an idea map, you reduce your ideas to a skeleton form that allows you to see and analyze them more easily.

In this chapter you will learn how to use an idea map to (1) discover problems in a paragraph and (2) guide your revision. This chapter will discuss five questions to help you identify weaknesses in your writing and suggest ways for revising your paragraphs to correct each weakness.

1. Does your paragraph stray from your topic?
2. Does every detail belong?
3. Are your details arranged and developed logically?
4. Is your paragraph balanced?
5. Is your paragraph repetitious?

CHAPTER OBJECTIVES

In this chapter you will learn to

1. use an idea map to identify problems in your paragraphs.
2. use an idea map to correct the problems you identify.

399

WRITING

Does Your Paragraph Stray From Your Topic?

When you are writing a first draft of a paragraph, it is easy to drift away from the topic. As you write, one idea triggers another, and that idea another, and eventually you end up with ideas that have little or nothing to do with your original topic, as in the following first-draft student paragraph.

Sample Student Paragraph

One Example of Toxic Waste

The disposal of toxic waste has caused serious health hazards. Love Canal is one of the many toxic dump sites that have caused serious health problems. This dump site in particular was used by a large number of nearby industries. The canal was named after a man named Love. Love Canal, in my opinion, was an eye-opener into toxic dump sites. It took about ten years to clean the dump site up to a livable condition. Many people living near Love Canal developed cancers. There were many miscarriages and birth defects. This dump site might have caused irreversible damage to our environment, so I am glad it has been cleaned up.

The following idea map shows the topic sentence of the paragraph and, underneath it, the supporting details that directly relate to the topic sentence. All the unrelated details are in a list to the right of the map. Note that the concluding sentence is also included in the map, since it is an important part of the paragraph.

Idea Map

DISPOSAL OF TOXIC WASTES CAUSES HEALTH HAZARDS.

Chemicals in Love Canal caused health problems.

Many people developed cancer.

There were many miscarriages and birth defects.

I am glad it has been cleaned up.

Unrelated details

1. Love Canal was used by many industries.

2. It was named after man named Love.

3. It was an eye-opener.

4. It took ten years to clean up.

In this paragraph the author began by supporting her topic sentence with the example of Love Canal. However, she began to drift when she explained how it was used by many industries and how Love Canal was named. To revise this paragraph the author could include more detailed information about Love Canal health hazards or examples of other disposal sites and their health hazards. You can use an idea map to spot where you begin to drift away from your topic. To do this, take the last idea in the map and compare it to your topic sentence.

LAST IDEA ⟵⟶ TOPIC SENTENCE

Does the last idea directly support your topic sentence? If not, you may have drifted from your topic. Check the second-to-last detail, going through the same comparison process. Working backwards, you'll see where you started to drift. This is the point at which to begin revising.

Use the following suggestions to revise your paragraph if it strays from your topic:

1. Locate the last sentence that does relate to your topic, and start again from there. What could you say next that *would* relate to the topic?

2. Consider expanding your existing ideas. If, after two or three details, you have strayed from your topic, consider expanding the details you have, rather than searching for additional details.

3. Reread your brainstorming, freewriting, or branching to find more details. Look for additional ideas that support your topic. Do more brainstorming if necessary.

4. Consider changing your topic. Drifting from your topic is not always a loss. Sometimes by drifting you discover a more interesting topic than your original one. If you decide to change topics, revise your entire paragraph. Begin by rewriting your topic sentence.

EXERCISE 16-1 Read the following first-draft paragraph. Then draw an idea map that includes the topic sentence, only those details that support the topic sentence, and the concluding sentence. List the unrelated details to the side of the map, as in the example on page 400. Identify where the writer began to stray from the topic, and make specific suggestions for revising this paragraph.

Junk food lacks nutrition and is high in calories. Junk food can be anything from candy and potato chips to ice cream and desserts. All of these are high in calories. But they are so tasty, they are addictive. Once a person is addicted to junk food, it is very hard to break the addiction. To break the habit, one must give up any form of sugar. And I have not gone back to my old lifestyle in over two weeks. So it is possible to break an addiction, but I still have the craving.

EXERCISE **16-2**   Write a paragraph on one of the following topics. Then draw an idea map. Use the same procedure you used in Exercise 16-1. If you have strayed from your topic, revise your paragraph, using the suggestions given above.

1. a memorable sight, or sound, or meal
2. city language or country language
3. trends in TV ads
4. a crowd you have watched or been a part of
5. the way that a certain friendship developed

Does Every Detail Belong?

Every detail in a paragraph must directly support the topic sentence or one of the other details. Unrelated information should not be included, a mistake one student made in the following first-draft paragraph.

Sample Student Paragraph

In a world where stress is an everyday occurrence, many people relieve stress through entertainment. There are many ways to entertain ourselves and relieve stress. Many people watch movies to take their minds off day-to-day problems. However, going to the movies costs a lot of money. Due to the cost, some people rent movies at video stores. Playing sports is another stress reliever. Exercise always helps to give people a positive attitude and keeps them in shape. Racquetball really keeps someone in shape because it is such a fast game. A third form of entertainment is going out with friends. With friends, people can talk about their problems and feel better about them. But some friends always talk and never listen, and such conversation creates stress instead of relieving it. So if you are under stress, be sure to reserve some time for entertainment.

The following idea map shows that this writer included four unrelated details.

Idea Map

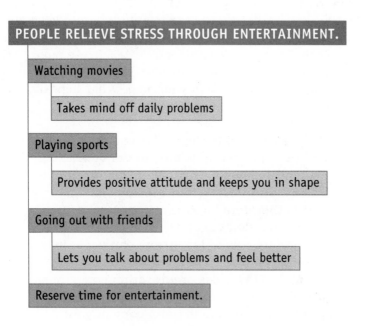

PEOPLE RELIEVE STRESS THROUGH ENTERTAINMENT.

Watching movies

Takes mind off daily problems

Playing sports

Provides positive attitude and keeps you in shape

Going out with friends

Lets you talk about problems and feel better

Reserve time for entertainment.

Unrelated details

1. Movies cost money.

2. People rent movies at video stores.

3. Racquetball is a fast game.

4. Some friends never listen.

To spot unrelated details, draw an idea map. To decide if a detail is unrelated, ask, "Does this detail directly explain the topic sentence or one of the other details?" If you are not sure, ask, "What happens if I take this out?" If meaning is lost or if confusion occurs, the detail is important. Include it in your map. If you can make your point just as well without the detail, mark it "unrelated."

In the sample student paragraph above, the high cost of movies and the low-cost alternative of renting videos do not directly explain how or why movies are entertaining. The racquetball detail does not explain how exercise relieves stress. The detail about friends not listening does not explain how talking to friends is helpful in reducing stress.

The following suggestions will help you use supporting details more effectively:

1. Add explanations to make the connections between your ideas clearer. Often a detail may not seem to relate to the topic because you have not explained *how* it relates. For example, health-care insurance may seem to have little to do with the prevention of breast-cancer deaths until you explain that mammograms, which are paid for by some health-care plans, can prevent deaths.

2. Add transitions. Transitions make it clearer to your reader how one detail relates to another.

3. Add new details. If you've deleted several inessential details, your paragraph may be too sketchy. Return to the prewriting step to generate more details you can include.

EXERCISE 16-3 ▸ Read the following paragraph, and draw an idea map. Underline any unrelated details and list them to the side of your map. What steps should the writer take to revise this paragraph?

> Your credit rating is a valuable thing that you should protect and watch over. A credit rating is a record of your loans, credit-card charges, and repayment history. If you pay a bill late or miss a payment, that information becomes part of your credit rating. It is therefore important to pay bills promptly. Some people just don't keep track of dates; some don't even know what date it is today. Errors can occur in your credit rating. Someone else's mistakes can be put on your record, for example. Why these credit-rating companies can't take more time and become more accurate is beyond my understanding. It is worthwhile to get a copy of your credit report and check it for errors. Time spent caring for your credit rating will be well spent.

EXERCISE 16-4 ▸ Study the paragraph and the idea map you produced for Exercise 16-2. Check for unrelated details. If you find any, revise your paragraph using the suggestions given above.

Are Your Details Arranged and Developed Logically?

Details in a paragraph should follow some logical order. As you write a first draft, you are often more concerned with expressing your ideas than with presenting them in the correct order. As you revise, however, you should make sure you have followed a logical arrangement. Chapter 12 discusses various methods of arranging and developing details. The following Need to Know box reviews these arrangements.

NEED TO KNOW

Methods of Arranging and Developing Details

Method	Description
1. time sequence	Arranges details in the order in which they happen.
2. least/most	Arranges details from least to most or from most to least according to some quality or characteristic.
3. spatial	Arranges details according to their physical location.

Chapters 13 and 14 discuss several methods of organizing and presenting material. The following Need to Know box reviews these arrangements.

NEED TO KNOW

Methods of Organizing and Presenting Material

Method	Description
1. description	Arranges descriptive details spatially or uses the least/most arrangement.
2. narration	Arranges events in the order in which they occurred.
3. process	Arranges steps in the order in which they are to be completed.
4. comparison and contrast	Explains an idea by comparing or contrasting it with another, usually more familiar, idea.
5. cause and effect	Explains why something happened or what happened as a result of a particular action.

Your ideas need a logical arrangement to make them easy to follow. Poor organization creates misunderstanding and confusion. After drafting the following paragraph, a student drew an idea map that showed her organization was haphazard.

Sample Student Paragraph

When I was pregnant with my son, I wondered if life would ever be normal again. There were the nights I couldn't sleep because of all the kicking and the baby moving up to my lungs so I couldn't breathe. That was when I really had it! Each month I got bigger and bigger, and after a while I was so big I couldn't bend over or see my feet. Then there was the morning sickness. I don't know why they call it that because you're sick all the time for the first two months. Then there were all those doctor visits during which she told me, "Not for another week or two." Of course, when I realized my clothes didn't fit, I broke down and cried. But all of a sudden everything started up, and I was at the hospital delivering the baby two weeks early and, it's like it happened so fast and it was all over, and I had the most beautiful baby in my arms and I knew it was worth all that pain and suffering.

Idea Map

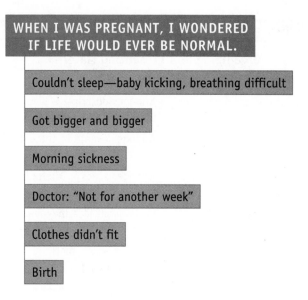

WHEN I WAS PREGNANT, I WONDERED IF LIFE WOULD EVER BE NORMAL.

Couldn't sleep—baby kicking, breathing difficult

Got bigger and bigger

Morning sickness

Doctor: "Not for another week"

Clothes didn't fit

Birth

An idea map lets you see quickly when a paragraph has no organization or when an idea is out of order. This student's map showed that her paragraph did not present the events of her pregnancy in the most logical arrangement: time sequence. She therefore reorganized the events in the order in which they happened and revised her paragraph as follows.

Revised Paragraph

When I was pregnant with my son, I wondered if life would ever be normal again. First there was the morning sickness. I don't know why they call it that because I was sick all the time for the first two months. Of course, when I realized my clothes didn't fit, I broke down and cried. Each month I got bigger and bigger, and finally I was so big I couldn't bend over or see my feet. Then there were the nights I couldn't sleep because of all the kicking and the baby moving up to my lungs so I couldn't breathe. That was when I really had it. Finally, there were all those doctor visits during which she told me, "Not for another week or two." But all of a sudden everything started to happen, and I was at the hospital delivering the baby two weeks early. Everything happened so fast, it was all over, and I had the most beautiful baby in my arms. Then I knew it was worth all that pain and suffering.

The following suggestions will help you revise your paragraph if it lacks organization:

1. Review the methods of arranging and developing details and of organizing and presenting material. (See the Need to Know boxes on page 407.) Will one of those arrangements work? If so, number the ideas in your idea map according to the arrangement you choose. Then begin revising your paragraph.

2. Look at your topic sentence again. If you are working with a new arrangement, you may need to revise your topic sentence to reflect that arrangement.

3. Check whether additional details are needed. Suppose, for example, you are writing about an exciting experience and you decide to use the time-sequence arrangement. Once you make that decision, you may need to add details to enable your reader to understand exactly how the experience happened.

4. Add transitions. Transitions help make your organization obvious and easy to follow.

If you find one or more details out of logical order in your paragraph, do the following:

1. Number the details in your idea map to indicate the correct order, and revise your paragraph accordingly.

2. Reread your revised paragraph, and draw another idea map.

3. Look to see if you've omitted necessary details. After you have placed your details in a logical order, you are more likely to recognize gaps.

EXERCISE 16-5 ▶ Read the following student paragraph, and draw an idea map. Evaluate the arrangement of ideas. What revisions would you suggest?

> The minimum wage is not an easily resolved problem; it has both advantages and disadvantages. Its primary advantage is that it does guarantee workers a minimum wage. It prevents abuse. Employers cannot take advantage of workers by paying them less than the minimum. Its primary disadvantage is that the minimum wage is not sufficient for older workers with families to support. For younger workers, such as teenagers, however, this minimum is fine. It provides them with spending money and freedom from their parents. Another disadvantage is that as long as someone, such as a teenager, is willing to work for the minimum, employers don't need to pay a higher wage. Thus the minimum prevents the experienced worker from getting more money. But the minimum wage does help our economy by requiring a certain level of income per worker.

EXERCISE 16-6 ▶ Review the paragraph and idea map you produced for Exercise 16-2. Evaluate the logical arrangement of your points and details, and revise if needed.

Is Your Paragraph Balanced?

An effective paragraph achieves a balance among its points. That is, each idea receives an appropriate amount of supporting detail and emphasis. The following student paragraph lacks balance, as its idea map shows.

Sample Student Paragraph

Waiting

> Waiting is very annoying, exhausting, and time consuming. Waiting to buy books at the college store is an example of a very long and tiresome task. I need to buy books, and so does everyone else. This causes the lines to be very long. Most of the time I find myself leaning against the wall daydreaming. Sometimes I will even leave the line and hope to come back when the store isn't extremely busy. But that never works because everyone else seems to get the same idea. So I finally realize that I just have to wait. Another

experience is waiting for a ride home from school or work. My ride always seems to be the last car to pull up in the parking lot. When I am waiting for my ride, I often wonder what it would be like to own a car or if I will ever make it home. Waiting in line at a fast-food restaurant is also annoying because, if it is fast, I shouldn't have to wait. Waiting for an elevator is also no fun. Waiting just seems to be a part of life, so I might as well accept it.

Idea Map

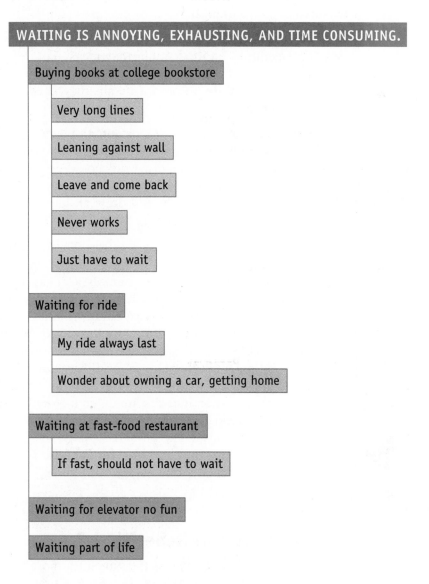

WAITING IS ANNOYING, EXHAUSTING, AND TIME CONSUMING.

Buying books at college bookstore

Very long lines

Leaning against wall

Leave and come back

Never works

Just have to wait

Waiting for ride

My ride always last

Wonder about owning a car, getting home

Waiting at fast-food restaurant

If fast, should not have to wait

Waiting for elevator no fun

Waiting part of life

As the idea map shows, a major portion of the paragraph is devoted to waiting in line to buy books. The second example, waiting for a ride, is not as thoroughly explained. The third example, waiting at a fast-food restaurant, is treated in even less detail, and the fourth, waiting for an elevator, in still less. To revise, the writer should expand the treatment of waiting for rides, fast food, and elevators and perhaps decrease the treatment of the bookstore experience. An alternative solution would be for the writer to expand the bookstore experience and eliminate the other examples. In this case, a new topic sentence would be needed.

The following suggestions will help you revise your paragraph for balance:

1. Not every point or example must have the *same* amount of explanation. For example, more complicated ideas require more explanation than simpler, more obvious ones. When you are using a least/most arrangement, the more important details may need more coverage than less important ones.

2. If two ideas are equally important and equally complicated, they should receive similar treatment. For instance, if you include an example or statistic in support of one idea, you should do so for the other.

EXERCISE 16-7 Read the following paragraph, and draw an idea map. Evaluate the balance of details, and indicate where more details are needed.

I am considering buying a puppy. There are four breeds I am looking at: golden retrievers, German shepherds, Newfoundlands, and cocker spaniels. Cocker spaniels are cute, but golden retrievers are cute *and* intelligent. Golden retrievers are very gentle with children, and I have two sons. They are also very loyal. But they have a lot of fur, and they shed, unlike German shepherds, which have short fur. Newfoundlands are very large, and they have dark-colored fur that would show up on my rug. Newfoundlands also drool a lot. My apartment is small, so a Newfoundland is probably just too big, furry, and clumsy.

EXERCISE 16-8 Review your paragraph and idea map for Exercise 16-2. Evaluate the balance of details, and revise if necessary.

Is Your Paragraph Repetitious?

In a first draft, you may express the same idea more than once, each time in a slightly different way. As you are writing a first draft, repetitive statements may help you stay on track. They keep you writing and help generate new ideas. However, it is important to eliminate repetition at the revision stage. Repetitive statements add nothing to your paragraph. They detract from its clarity. An idea map will bring repetition to your attention quickly because it makes it easy to spot two or more very similar items.

As you read the following first-draft student paragraph, see if you can spot the repetitive statements. Then notice how the idea map following the paragraph clearly identifies the repetition.

Sample Student Paragraph

Chemical waste dumping is an environmental concern that must be dealt with, not ignored. The big companies care nothing about the environment. They would just as soon dump waste in our backyards as not. This has finally become a big issue and is being dealt with and forcing the companies to clean up their own mess. It is incredible that large companies have the nerve to dump just about anywhere. The penalty should be steep. When the companies are caught, they should be forced to clean up their mess.

Idea Map

CHEMICAL WASTE DUMPING MUST BE DEALT WITH.

Big companies care nothing about environment

Just as soon dump in our backyards

Dumping has become big issue—companies forced to clean up own mess

Companies have nerve to dump just about anywhere

Penalty should be steep

The idea map shows that points 1, 2, and 4 say nearly the same thing—that big companies don't care about the environment and dump waste nearly anywhere. Because there is so much repetition, the paragraph lacks development. To revise, the writer first needs to eliminate the repetitious statements. Then she needs to generate more ideas that support her topic sentence and explain how or why chemical waste dumping must be dealt with.

The following suggestions will help you revise a paragraph with repetitive ideas:

1. Try to combine ideas. Select the better elements and wording of each idea to produce a revised sentence. Add more detail if needed.

2. Review places where you make deletions. When you delete a repetitious statement, check to see if the sentence before and the sentence after the deletion connect. Often a transition will be needed to help the paragraph flow easily.

3. Decide if additional details are needed. Often we write repetitious statements when we don't know what else to say. Thus, repetition often signals lack of development. Refer to Chapter 15 for specific suggestions on revising underdeveloped paragraphs.

4. Watch for statements that are only slightly more general or specific than one another. For example, although the first sentence below is general and the second is more specific, they repeat the same idea.

Ringing telephones can be distracting. The telephone that rang constantly throughout the evening distracted me.

(To make the second sentence a specific example of the idea in the first sentence, rather than just a repetition of it, the writer would need to add specific details about how the telephone ringing throughout the evening was a distraction.)

EXERCISE ▶ 16-9 | Read the following paragraph, and underline all repetitive statements. Make suggestions for revision.

> Children's misbehaving is an annoying problem in our society. I used to work as a waiter at Denny's, and I have seen many incidences in which parents allow their children to misbehave. Once I served a table at which the parents allowed their four-year-old to make his toy spider crawl up and down my pants as I tried to serve the food. The parents just laughed. Children have grown up being rewarded for their actions, regardless of whether they are good or bad. Whether the child does something the parents approve of or whether it is something they disapprove of, they react in similar ways. This is why a lot of toddlers and children continue to misbehave. Being rewarded will cause the child to do the same actions again to get the same reward.

> **NEED TO KNOW**
>
> **Using Idea Maps**
>
> An idea map is a visual display of the ideas in your paragraph. It allows you to see how ideas relate to one another and to identify weaknesses in your writing. You can use idea maps to answer five questions that will help you revise your paragraphs:
>
> • Does your paragraph stray from your topic?
>
> • Does every detail belong?
>
> • Are your points and details arranged and developed logically?
>
> • Is your paragraph balanced?
>
> • Is your paragraph repetitious?

EXERCISE 16-10 Review your paragraph and idea map for Exercise 16-2. Identify and revise any repetitive statements.

STUDENT ESSAY

The following essay drafts were written by Anjum Lokhat, a student who was born in India and now lives in western New York state. In this informative essay, Lokhat explains the role of superstition in her native country. Read her first draft, and then study the idea map drawn to help her revise. Also study the comments that follow it. Then read Lokhat's second draft, noting the changes made based on this idea map.

First Draft
Superstitions in India
Anjum Lokhat

Superstition is a kind of blind belief, and its believers believe in it even after knowing that the fact behind such superstitious belief is far away from reality. Believing in superstition is a kind of shameful act for its believers, who cannot get rid of it even at the end of the twentieth century when the world is so advanced that we have made many trips to the moon and are looking forward to going to Mars. Superstition is a belief which is beyond reality but it does exist in most parts of the world, affecting people in one way or another, from the

1

most developed countries to the least developed countries and from educated people to uneducated people. India is one of the countries which is
badly affected by superstition and its society has suffered a lot for it and
if they don't give up their superstition they will continue to suffer for
it. Superstition occurs in many fields and it has many ways in which it
affects people. In this essay, *Superstitions in India,* we are going to
analyze the fact that superstition arises due to our ignorance about
something beyond our understanding but it could be eliminated by
knowledge and education.

Firstly, superstition or blind belief does affect most people on a daily
basis in India. People sometimes do or don't do a particular thing just
because of their superstition. First, Indian people think it is very unlucky
if a cat crosses their path when they are going to do some important
thing, and if sometimes a cat does cross their path they will never try to
do that thing, predicting beforehand that because a cat crossed their
path they will not be successful. Contrary to this fact, American people
are fond of cats and cats are fond of most people here. And cats pass by
them thousands of times a day and never bring them bad luck, then how
come cats bring bad luck to Indians only?

According to Indian tradition one should never give a handkerchief as
a gift to anybody or put salt in a person's hand when they ask for it
because people think that if they do so that will bring conflict between
them. Some people think that when food is prepared it should never be
served to the eldest member of the family first, because they think that
this very act will limit their food and none will be left over for the others.

In Indian history there was a king named Chandra Gupta Maurya,
who used to believe so much in superstition he thought that when he
woke up the person his sight first fell upon would be lucky for him and
if someday something went wrong then he would have this person killed
thinking he was lucky no more and would replace him with another.

Not only Indians and uneducated people, but even some Americans,
who are educated are afflicted with the disease of superstition. Recently
a girl of nineteen, in NCC College announced in the campus cafeteria
that if two people enter the doorway at the same time it brings bad
luck. Many famous players even believe in superstition, like Mark
Woug, a famous English cricket player who always puts his right glove
on first then the left one. V. V. Richardson always throws his ball three
times against a wall before going to the pitch.

Among the colors, black is considered to be a very unlucky color,
and Hindu people never wear it on happy occasions. For example,
Hindu people never have even a bit of black color, not even a thread in
the stitches of their clothes when they go to get married, because they

think that black color will give them a bad start and that their marriage will not work, but they don't take into consideration that the black hair they have goes everywhere with them, and so their life should be a failure in every aspect. They need to be educated.

Many times superstitious beliefs bring physical and emotional 7
hurt, like in India when somebody is going for the first day to his job and if a cat passes by, his family members would not allow him to go to work or for an interview and the result would be he would not be hired for this situation of employment. They guy would have to give up the job.

Many times, if a person sees somebody else's face first early in the 8
morning and if anything turns out bad in the rest of the day then that person is considered as an unlucky person. In many cases, if a child is born and some family member dies on that same day, then that child is held responsible for it and this has a very bad effect on the child who grows up with the guilt that he killed a family member.

In India sometimes when somebody gets chicken pox or smallpox 9
people think that that is a sign that God has visited that particular person's body and then they will worship that person as God and not take him to the hospital and this results in a very serious injury to that person, sometimes even causing death.

A few generations ago, it was a belief that if a husband dies before 10
his wife then his spirit will not rest because he will be worried about his wife very much until she, too, is dead. So before the nineteenth century there was a tradition called Satiie, burning a woman alive on her husband's funeral pyre, [1] which was really a cruel and violent act of killing a human. Even today in Indian society widows are considered unlucky persons, so they can't participate in any religious or happy occasions neither are they given priority in anything. This is really hurtful; in order to console them, people hurt them very badly emotionally.

In conclusion, everything is equal in this world, everything is made 11
by God. If one is a good Christian or a good Muslim he will never believe in such superstitions, which are contrary to the faith that God made everything to do something. As the Bible says, "Every work has its time and so every time has some work." Nothing can bring good or bad luck to anything. Sometimes superstition can go more than its limit in causing a lot of emotional hurt and maybe even death. Society should try to eliminate it, education is the best way to eliminate superstition and even faith in God could eliminate such a thing. People in the twentieth century must be past such incredible beliefs.

1. A heap of wood used for burning a dead body as part of a funeral ritual.

INDIA IS BADLY AFFECTED BY SUPERSTITION

Peple have suffered because of it

Must give them up or continue to suffer

PARA. 1

SUPERSTITION IS BLIND BELIEF

It is far from reality

Believe even at end of twentieth century

World is very advanced

Have travelled to moon

Will travel to Mars

Exists in most of world

Most developed, least developed countries

Educated, uneducated

Unrelated details

1. Shameful act for believers.
2. Occurs in many fields.
3. Affects people in many ways.
4. In this essay... beyond our understanding.
5. ...but it could be eliminated by knowledge and education.

PARA. 2

AFFECTS MOST PEOPLE ON A DAILY BASIS IN INDIA

Cat crossing path predicts failure

Don't even try to do the thing

1. Americans are fond of cats.
2. Pass them daily.
3. Why do they bring bad luck only to Indians?

PARA. 3

?

Never give handkerchief as gift

Don't give another person salt

Never feed the eldest person first

When people call you back, not successful

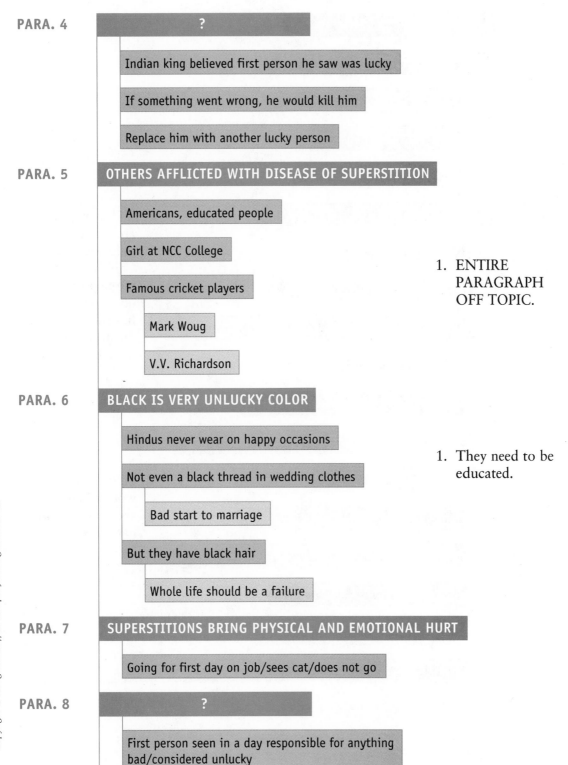

PARA. 4   **?**

Indian king believed first person he saw was lucky

If something went wrong, he would kill him

Replace him with another lucky person

PARA. 5   **OTHERS AFFLICTED WITH DISEASE OF SUPERSTITION**

Americans, educated people

Girl at NCC College

Famous cricket players

Mark Woug

V.V. Richardson

1. ENTIRE PARAGRAPH OFF TOPIC.

PARA. 6   **BLACK IS VERY UNLUCKY COLOR**

Hindus never wear on happy occasions

Not even a black thread in wedding clothes

Bad start to marriage

But they have black hair

Whole life should be a failure

1. They need to be educated.

PARA. 7   **SUPERSTITIONS BRING PHYSICAL AND EMOTIONAL HURT**

Going for first day on job/sees cat/does not go

PARA. 8   **?**

First person seen in a day responsible for anything bad/considered unlucky

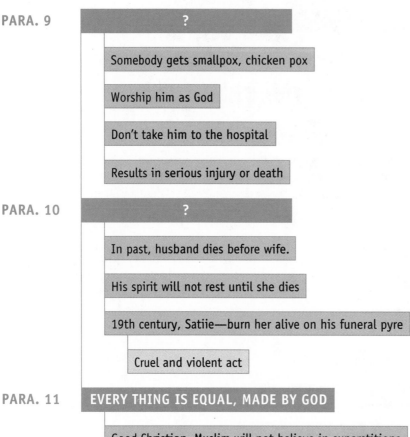

PARA. 9   **?**

Somebody gets smallpox, chicken pox

Worship him as God

Don't take him to the hospital

Results in serious injury or death

PARA. 10   **?**

In past, husband dies before wife.

His spirit will not rest until she dies

19th century, Satiie—burn her alive on his funeral pyre

Cruel and violent act

1. Today widows are considered unlucky.
2. Can't participate in religious occasions.
3. In order to console them, people hurt them emotionally.

PARA. 11   **EVERY THING IS EQUAL, MADE BY GOD**

Good Christian, Muslim will not believe in superstitions

Contrary to faith in God

Nothing can bring good or bad luck

Superstitions can cause emotional hurt or even death

Society should try to eliminate them

Education or faith in God best way

People in the twentieth century should be beyond it

1. Bible says, "Every work has its time and so every time has some work."

Evaluating the Idea Map

In paragraphs 1 and 2 Lokhat discovered she had included many irrelevant details. Notice that she eliminated these in her second draft.

In paragraphs 3 and 4 she discovered that she lacked topic sentences. The paragraphs contained examples but lacked sentences that stated the point the examples illustrated. Notice that in her revision Lokhat combined these two paragraphs with paragraph 2.

In paragraph 5 she realized that the entire paragraph did not support her thesis. She eliminated it in her next draft.

In paragraphs 8, 9, and 10 she discovered topic sentences were lacking. She combined paragraph 8 with the previous paragraph and wrote a topic sentence that allowed her to combine paragraphs 9 and 10.

Second Draft
Superstitions in India
Anjum Lokhat

Superstition is a kind of blind belief. People believe in superstitions even after knowing they are far away from reality. People believe in superstitions even at the end of the twentieth century, when the world is so advanced that we have made many trips to the moon and are looking forward to going to Mars. Superstitions exist in most parts of the world, affecting people from the most developed countries to the least developed countries and from educated people to uneducated people. India is one of the countries which is badly affected by superstition. It has suffered a lot for it, and, if the people don't give up their superstition, they will continue to suffer for it. 1

Superstition affects many people on a daily basis in India. People sometimes don't do a particular thing just because of their superstition. For example, Indian people think it is very unlucky if a cat passes their way when they are going to do some important thing. Sometimes they don't even do the thing because they predict beforehand that they will fail. According to Indian superstition, one should never give a handkerchief as a gift or give salt to a person when they ask for it because these things will bring conflict between them. Some people think that when food is prepared, it should never be served to the eldest member of the family first because then there will not be any food left over for others. Also, black is considered to be a very unlucky color, and Hindu people never wear it on happy occasions. For example, Hindu people never have even a bit of black color, not even a thread in the stitches of their clothes when they go to get married because they think then their 2 marriage will not work. But they don't take into consideration that the black hair they have goes everywhere with them, and so their life should be a failure in every aspect.

Superstitious beliefs often bring emotional hurt. In India, if somebody is going for a job interview and a cat passes by, he or she would not go for the interview and the result would be unemployment. If a child is born and some family member dies on that same day, the child is held responsible, which can have a very bad effect. The child grows up with the guilt that he killed that family member. Today in parts of Indian society, widows are considered unlucky, so they can't participate in any religious or happy occasion. This is really hurtful.   3

Sometimes superstitions can bring very serious physical harm. In India when sometimes somebody gets chicken pox or smallpox, people think it is a sign that God has visited that person's body. Then they will worship that person as God and not take him or her to the hospital. This results in very serious illness, sometimes even death. In Indian history there was a king named Chandra Gupta Maurya, who used to believe so much in superstition that when he woke up, the first person he saw was considered to be lucky for him. But if something went wrong, then he had this person killed, thinking he was no longer lucky and replaced him with another. Before the nineteenth century, there was a tradition called Satiie. If a husband died before the wife, it was believed that his spirit would be worried about his wife until she too was dead. So the woman would throw herself alive on her husband's funeral pyre and burn to death.   4

In conclusion, every thing is equal in this world, every thing is made by God. Believing in superstition is contrary to faith that God made everything. Nothing can bring good or bad luck to anything. Sometimes superstition can cause great emotional hurt or even death. Society should try to eliminate it. Education or faith in God are ways to eliminate superstition. People in the twentieth century should be beyond superstition.   5

Evaluating the Essay

1. What are the most important changes that Lokhat made?

2. Evaluate the structure and content of Lokhat's second draft.

3. What futher revisions are needed?

WRITING ABOUT A READING

Thinking before Reading

The following article, reprinted from the *Chicago Tribune*, discusses the chronically low turnout of voters in U. S. elections by examining the types of people who are nonvoters. You will notice that each paragraph focuses on the topic and that the main points and details are relevant, logically arranged, and balanced.

Before you read:

1. Preview the reading, using the steps provided on page 20.
2. After previewing, connect the reading to your own experience by answering the following questions:
   a. Why is voting important?
   b. Did you vote in the most recent election? Why or why not?

READING

How the Other Half Lives without Voting
Jack C. Doppelt and Ellen Shearer

When Henry Montoya walked into his neighborhood polling place in west Denver earlier this month, as he has for the past 10 years, he signed in to record that he was voting, went behind the curtain and pushed the exit button at the bottom, having deliberately voted for no one.   1

Montoya is unusual, but in him lie two distinct political species: Americans who vote and those who don't. Those who don't outnumber those who do. In presidential elections, it's a close call, with 51 percent of the voting-age population—about 100 million people—not voting in November 1996. In off-year elections, it's not even close.   2

Only 13.5 percent of registered voters turned out for the school and municipal elections in the six counties in and around Chicago.   3

In New York City, where Rudolph Giuliani won re-election for mayor, the *New York Times* reported that turnout was "among the lowest for any mayoral election in recent decades, with 38 percent of the registered voters casting ballots."   4

In New Jersey, where Christine Todd Whitman was narrowly re-elected governor in one of the nation's most hotly contested races, The Record in Bergen County reported that 54 percent of registered voters cast ballots, far lower than the 65 percent who turned out in 1993.   5

In Maine, the Portland Press Herald reported the highest turnout in   6
a "post-presidential year in Maine in at least a quarter of a century."
Yet, it was only 37 percent of the state's voting-age population.

In Colorado, where Montoya cast his symbolic ballot, The Denver   7
Post reported that turnout in the city was 20 percent among registered
voters.

The message is the same state by state and election by election. Non-   8
voting is a chronic phenomenon in the United States. The hardened core
of non-voters are not turned off by a particular candidate or a certain
election. They opted out long ago and generally are beyond the reach of
conventional measures to bring them back.

They may tell pollsters they don't vote because they don't like the   9
choice of candidates. What they mean, we have found, is they don't connect and aren't likely to connect enough with any political candidate or
party or with the electoral process to be involved.

Northwestern University's Medill School of Journalism surveyed   10
1,000 likely non-voters before the 1996 presidential election. We found
that non-voters tended to be younger, less educated, poorer and less
likely than voters to discuss politics or public affairs with either family
or friends. Beyond that, non-voters presented much like voters, and
spanned the spectrum of American society.

We identified five types of non-voters: Doers, Unpluggeds, Irritables,   11
Don't Knows and Alienateds. To go beneath the survey data, we inter-
viewed 30 in depth.

Doers, like Dr. Robert Wolkow, Claudine D'Orazio and Gene   12
Tencza, tend to be educated, financially secure, active and selectively
involved news consumers. Wolkow, who has voted twice in his life,
is offended by people who blithely vote for the lesser of two evils.
D'Orazio, who's in the thick of Savannah's thriving tourism and conven-
tion industry, feels she doesn't know enough about candidates. Tencza is
content to let those interested in politics carry the load while he exercises his right to pursue ordinary happiness.

Unpluggeds tend not to have much formal education and don't   13
interact much with their communities. There's jazz musician Jack
Daniels whose only interest in politics has been the heightened dramas
of President Kennedy's assassination and Watergate. Barbara Beth tends
bar and ignores discussions of politics, Iris Llamas tends to her nephew,
her job, bowling and movies, and Janet Shepherd tends to leave her
mobile home mostly to sit at the pub across the road. Politics never
enters the picture. They feel politicians don't tend to them and they
return the sentiment in kind.

Irritables are inclined to believe their vote doesn't matter no matter   14
who's running. Michael Keagan hasn't seen a politician yet who deserves
his vote. Melody Lewis, who sees them all as hollow faces on parade,

wishes she could be a fly on the government wall to see what they really do with their days.

Don't Knows know they don't know. George Perez watches televi-   15
sion news every night and realizes he doesn't know a Democrat from a Republican, a liberal from a conservative, or what Congress or his local government officials do. Erica Smith didn't know until the last minute that Hillary Clinton was coming to her son's school, and when she saw it with her own eyes, she just got mad.

Alienateds, like Kathy Smith, are possibly the hardest core of non-   16
voters. They've lost faith in the system, and no quick fixes are likely to move them. Though her father voted and was a lifelong Democrat, she's never voted, never registered to vote, and "never will be."

The mistake we made every election, as we did again in the after-   17
math of last Tuesday's off-year election, is to treat voter turnout as part of the political campaign awaiting the evening's returns.

Let's face it, the results are in, and for at least a generation to come,   18
a vast core of America shows no signs of opting in. Worse yet is that the political process—its candidates, parties and pollsters—and the media are unlikely to do anything about it. Their investment is tied more to the stuff of elections than to the disaffection beyond the vote.

Which brings us back to Henry Montoya. One Election Day years   19
ago, he walked into the booth, closed the curtain and looked at the list of candidates. "None of this is a value to me or anyone else," he recalls thinking. He pulled the lever on a blank ballot and walked out.

From *Chicago Tribune*

Getting Ready to Write

Strengthening Your Vocabulary

Write a brief definition for each of the following words from the preceding reading. If you can't figure out the meaning of a word from the way it is used in the reading, look the word up in the dictionary.

1. municipal (paragraph 3)   of the local government

2. chronic (paragraph 8)   occurring over a long period

3. phenomenon (paragraph 8)   happening, event

4. electoral process (paragraph 9)   the way people are voted into office

5. spectrum (paragraph 10)   whole range

6. blithely (paragraph 12)   gladly, happily

7   aftermath (paragraph 17)   events following, results, consequences

8. opting (paragraph 18)   choosing

9. pollsters (paragraph 18)   those who sample public opinion

10. disaffection (paragraph 18)   dissatisfaction, indifference

Reviewing the Reading Using an Idea Map

Review the reading by completing the missing pieces of the following idea map.

MANY AMERICANS DO NOT VOTE.

They outnumber those who do vote.

51 percent did not vote in 1996 presidential election

More do not vote in local and state elections.

General characteristics

Don't connect with party, candidate, process

Younger, less educated, poorer

Don't discuss politics, public affairs

Otherwise, much like voters

Five types

Doers: educated, well off, selectively involved news consumers

Unpluggeds: little education, don't interact with community

Irritables: believe their vote doesn't matter

Don't knows: know they don't know politics

Alienateds: lost faith in the system

No sign of change for at least a generation

Candidates, parties, pollsters won't do anything

Media won't either

Examining the Reading

1. In presidential elections, are there significantly more people who vote than people who don't or are they about the same? Where in the reading does it tell you this?

2. In general, how do nonvoters compare with those who vote?

3. What are the five types of voters identified by Northwestern University's survey?

4. Of these, which group believes its votes make no difference?

5. Which type of nonvoter is likely to be upset with people who vote for a particular candidate because he or she is not as bad as the opponent?

6. Which type is probably the hardest to convince to vote? Why?

Reacting to and Discussing Ideas

Get ready to write about the reading by discussing the following questions:

1. Do you vote regularly? If not, with which group of nonvoters do you most identify? Why?

2. According to the reading, "doers" are educated people. Why do you think educated people choose not to vote?

3. Do you think the trend of nonvoting will get better or worse in the future? Why?

4. Do you think your vote really matters? Why or why not?

5. Do you think the image of politicians as all talk and no action is justified? Why or why not?

Writing about the Reading

The Paragraph Option

1. Write a paragraph describing which type of nonvoter either you or someone you know is. Explain why you or that person doesn't vote.

2. Write a paragraph from the point of view of a nonvoter. Describe what it would take to make you vote: what kind of politician would motivate you to vote and why.

The Essay Option

1. Write an essay describing in detail the ideal politician. Explain what characteristics he or she should have and why you would vote for him or her.

2. Imagine yourself as a volunteer for a political campaign. Describe the jobs you would like to do as well as those you would not like. Identify those talents you have that could contribute to a candidate's election.

Use this Revision Checklist for the paragraph or essay you wrote about "How the Other Half Lives Without Voting."

REVISION CHECKLIST

Paragraph Development		YES	NO
	1. Is your topic manageable (neither too broad nor too narrow)?	☐	☐
	2. Is your paragraph written with your reader in mind?	☐	☐
	3. Does your topic sentence identify your topic?	☐	☐
	4. Does your topic sentence make a point about your topic?	☐	☐
	5. Is your topic sentence effective (niether too broad nor too narrow)?	☐	☐
	6. Does each remaining sentence support the topic sentence?	☐	☐
	7. Did you include sufficient detail?	☐	☐
	8. Are your details arranged logically?	☐	☐
	9. Have you used transitions to connect your details?	☐	☐

REVISION CHECKLIST (CONTINUED)

		YES	NO
	10. Is there a sentence at the end that brings the paragraph to a close?	☐	☐
	11. Is your paragraph fully developed?	☐	☐
	12. Have you corrected all problems identified by your idea map?	☐	☐
Sentence Development	13. Are there any fragments, run-ons, or comma splices?	☐	☐
	14. Are ideas combined to produce more effective sentences?	☐	☐
	15. Do adjectives and adverbs make the sentences vivid and interesting?	☐	☐
	16. Are prepositional phrases, *-ing* phrases, or relative clauses used to add detail?	☐	☐
	17. Are pronouns used correctly and consistently?	☐	☐
	18. Are there any shifts in person, number, or verb tense?	☐	☐
	19. Are modifiers correctly placed?	☐	☐
	20. Are elements within each sentence parallel?	☐	☐
	21. Are verb tenses and verb forms used correctly?	☐	☐

If you have checked any *no*s, go back to your paper and make the necessary changes.

WRITING SUCCESS TIP 16

Taking Writing Competency Tests

Some colleges require students to pass competency tests in writing. Competency tests are designed so that you will not be placed in courses that are too difficult or courses for which you are inadequately prepared. Think of them as readiness tests. Try your best, but don't be upset if you don't score at the required level. It is best to be certain you have the skills you need before tackling more difficult courses.

Preparing for Competency Tests

If your test requires that you write an essay, follow these suggestions:

1. **Study your error log** (see Writing Success Tip 3 on pages 76–77). If you haven't kept an error log, review papers your instructor has marked to identify your most common errors. Make a list of these common errors. As you revise and proofread your competency test answers, mentally check for each of these errors.

2. **Construct a mental revision checklist before you go into the exam.** Use the final revision checklist in this book as a guide. If time permits, jot your checklist down on scrap paper during the exam and use it to revise your essay.

3. **If your test is timed, plan how to divide your time.** Estimate how much time you will need for each step in the writing process. To find out, gauge your time on a practice test. Wear a watch to the exam, and check periodically to keep yourself on schedule.

4. **Take a practice test.** Ask a classmate to make up a topic or question for you to write about. It should be the same type of question that will be on the test. Give yourself the same time limit that the test will have. Then ask your classmate to evaluate your essay.

Taking Competency Tests

1. **If you are given a choice of topics to write about, choose the one you know the most about.** One of the most common mistakes students make on competency tests is failing to support their ideas with specific details. If you are familiar with a topic, you will be able to supply details more easily.

2. **If none of the topics seems familiar, spend a minute or two generating ideas on each topic before choosing one.** You will quickly see which will be the best choice.

3. **As you've learned throughout this book, be sure to follow the writing process step-by-step.** Generate and organize ideas before you write. If time permits, revise your essay, using your mental revision checklist, and proofread, checking for common errors.

SKILLS CHECK

Paragraph 1

The following paragraph contains a weak topic sentence. Revise this sentence to make it stronger.

Studying history can enrich your life in a number of ways.

It is good to study history. First, studying history gives you

a new way of looking at your own life. When you learn about

the past, you begin to see that your lifetime is only part of a

larger picture. Second, history can help you understand prob-

lems better. You begin to see why the world is as it is and

what events caused it to be this way. Finally, history allows

you to think of yourself in a different way. In looking at every-

thing that has happened before us, we as individuals seem

small and unimportant.

Paragraph 2

See Selected Answer Key on page 515 for sample revision.

The following first draft of a student's paragraph has a number of problems in paragraph development and organization. Draw an idea map for this paragraph, and then revise it using the map.

Students attend my college for financial, social, and acade-

mic reasons. The college I attend is a community college and

most of the students still live at home. Attending a community

college gives them the opportunity to experiment for a couple

of years before they decide about careers. Also, it is a state

SKILLS CHECK   CONTINUED

school, so the cost of tuition is more reasonable than it might be in a private college. The college is located in a beautiful setting in the countryside on the site of a former landscape nursery. Since the students commute to school and the student body is small, it is easy to get to know a lot of people. The commute takes most students less than thirty minutes. Most of the students come from a few local high schools, so there is not a long period of social adjustments. My college has an excellent reputation because of our sports teams which are usually in contention for a state title. Many of the students who attend my college are either committed to a particular vocational program, or they have not yet made up their minds about a career.

Paragraph 3

See Selected Answer Key on page 515 for sample revision.

The following paragraph is underdeveloped. Revise it by expanding on and adding to the details in order to support its main point.

The average American worker is worse off today than at any time in the past decade. There are fewer good jobs now. Living expenses and taxes have increased. Workers' salaries have declined. More families need both spouses to work. Clearly, we are worse off today.

Part

VIII

ADDITIONAL READINGS

What's in a Label: "Black" or "African-American"?
Zick Rubin, Letitia Anne Peplan, and Peter Salovey

Over the past three centuries, from the time they first arrived in America as slaves, African Americans have referred to themselves in a variety of ways. In the seventeenth and eighteenth centuries, the accepted term was "African." Later, "colored" and "Negro" came into common usage.

In the mid-1960s, the Black Power movement spearheaded a nation-wide shift from "Negro" to "black." This change was part of a consciousness-raising movement that gave many black people a new sense of pride. "Say it loud—I'm black and I'm proud!" was its rallying cry.

Today, many African Americans believe that the term "black" has outlived its usefulness and have urged adoption of "African American." Psychologist Kenneth L. Ghee (1990) is one of those African Americans who advocates this change in terminology, for several reasons:

"Black" has negative connotations.[1] In most languages, the term "black" is associated with dirt, wickedness (a "black soul"), and darkness. In Ghee's view, "thirty years of redefinition for political change [cannot] undo perhaps over 3,000 years of negative conceptual thinking associated with the concept of Blackness."

Racial groups should not be defined as opposites. The colors black and white are mutually exclusive opposites. Ghee believes that constant linguistic emphasis on the "oppositeness" of races cannot help race relations.

African Americans should celebrate their African heritage. Most racial and ethnic groups in America label themselves in ways that acknowledge their origins—Mexican Americans, Japanese Americans, Italian Americans, and so on. Only blacks describe themselves without reference to their geographical and cultural origins. Ghee believes that the label "black" conveys an unfortunate message: "Forget your ancestry; remember your skin color. Forget you are African; remember you are black."

Not all black Americans agree with Ghee's call for a new label. Many believe that the term "black" remains a powerful way to foster pride and positive self-definition, especially among black children.

Does the term we use to refer to a racial or ethnic group really make a difference? Psychological research suggests that it does. The words we use to refer to ourselves can have important effects on our self-concepts—our views of who we are and who we are striving to be.

From *Psychology* (5th edition).

1. associations

Reacting to and Discussing Ideas

1. Which term, *black* or *African American,* do you feel is more appropriate? Why?

2. What labels have been applied to you as a college student, if any? Do you regard them as positive or negative?

Writing about the Reading

The Paragraph Option

1. The authors state that the names we are called affect our self-concept. Have you ever been called a name that you disliked or have you been referred to in an unfavorable way? Write a paragraph describing your experience and your reaction to it.

2. Write a paragraph describing your ancestry.

The Essay Option

Many of us adopt or are given nicknames by friends and family. What effect do nicknames have? Write an essay explaining whether you think nicknames affect how people think of and respond to one another. Use your own experience, if possible, to support your ideas.

The Discovery of Coca-Cola
E. J. Kahn, Jr.

The man who invented Coca-Cola was not a native Atlantan, but   1
on the day of his funeral every drugstore in town testimonially shut up shop. He was John Styth Pemberton, born in 1833 in Knoxville, Georgia, eighty miles away. Sometimes known as Doctor, Pemberton was a pharmacist who, during the Civil War, led a cavalry troop under General Joe Wheeler. He settled in Atlanta in 1869, and soon began brewing such patent medicines as Triplex Liver Pills and Globe of Flower Cough Syrup. In 1885, he registered a trademark for something called French Wine Coca—Idea Nerve and Tonic Stimulant; a few months later he formed the Pemberton Chemical Company, and recruited the services of a bookkeeper named Frank M. Robinson, who

not only had a good head for figures but, attached to it, so exceptional a nose that he could audit the composition of a batch of syrup merely by sniffing it. In 1886—a year in which, as contemporary Coca-Cola officials like to point out, Conan Doyle unveiled Sherlock Holmes and France unveiled the Statue of Liberty—Pemberton unveiled a syrup that he called Coca-Cola. It was a modification of his French Wine Coca. He had taken out the wine and added a pinch of caffeine, and, when the end product tasted awful, had thrown in some extract of cola (or kola) nut and a few other oils, blending the mixture in a three-legged iron pot in his back yard and swishing it around with an oar. He distributed it to soda fountains in used beer bottles, and Robinson, with his flowing bookkeeper's script, presently devised a label, on which "Coca-Cola" was written in the fashion that is still employed. Pemberton looked upon his concoction less as a refreshment than as a headache cure, especially for people whose throbbing temples could be traced to overindulgence. On a morning late in 1886, one such victim of the night before dragged himself into an Atlanta drugstore and asked for a dollop of Coca-Cola. Druggists customarily stirred a teaspoonful of syrup into a glass of water, but in this instance the factotum on duty was too lazy to walk to the fresh-water tap, a couple of feet off. Instead, he mixed the syrup with some charged water, which was closer at hand. The suffering customer perked up almost at once, and word quickly spread that the best Coca-Cola was a fizzy one.

From The Big Drink: The Story of Coca-Cola.

Reacting to and Discussing Ideas

1. Why do you think drugstores in Atlanta closed for Pemberton's funeral?

2. Why is Coca-Cola still popular today?

3. Why does the Coca-Cola Company like to point out that Sherlock Holmes was introduced and the Statue of Liberty was unveiled the same year that Coca-Cola was invented?

Writing about the Reading

The Paragraph Option

1. Pemberton improved the taste of Coca-Cola by changing its original ingredients. Write a paragraph describing an improvement you made

in something. For example, you might describe a piece of furniture you refinished, a recipe you revised, or a room you remodeled.

2. Carbonated water was added to Coca-Cola accidentally, but it turned out to be a popular change. Write a paragraph describing an accidental happening that had a positive outcome.

The Essay Option

Although Pemberton's improvements to Coca-Cola were successful, they did not seem to be carefully planned or researched. Write an essay describing an event or situation that turned out well even though careful planning was not involved.

Music Lady
Vickie Sears

O n days of rain, when poetry often came to paper, I'd sneak   1
away from the orphanage, running to leg tautness and chest burn all the way to 15th and 65th streets to the record store. That's where the music lady lived. Where there were sounds that made my poetry seem brighter. Where the music lady smiled under high cheekbones, patted my head, and whispered words of encouragement.

It wasn't an ordinary record store, then or now. It had listening   2
booths and rows of deep wooden forest-green troughs filled with the faces of musicians and instruments. These were the instruments of the big band music my mother liked. Different from the flutes, bells, and drums of my father's family. Different, too, from the silence of the orphanage, except for the dinner bell. Here trumpets and cellos blared in silence from cardboard covers. Grownups strolled the aisles and flicked through the records, like playing cards, choosing their hand of music before taking it to one of the narrow rectangles, each equipped with turntable and speakers, to listen. The soundproofed booths created individual worlds of monophonic magic seeping through the glass doors.

It never really mattered much what was playing, although I began to   3
gravitate to jazz and playful Bach. Bach sounded of creek-skipping water and duck laughs. It was hard for me to understand how a man who dressed with lace edging his jacket and pants, and wearing such a

ponderous wig, could have so much fun. Still, I'd walk beside the
booths, spiral binder and pencil in hand, searching for just the right
music to write near. As casually as a walnut-colored nine-year-old
among the tall, mostly white adults could, I'd position myself against a
booth's doorjamb and lean an ear to sound. I'd close my eyes for filling,
follow the strings of music, and slip down into its colors. All other
sounds faded. My body, rain rhythm, and the music became all. After
awhile I could make a poem and slide back into the downpour, happy in
its beat. I felt special in the rainsong and slow walk home.

One afternoon as I wandered the aisles, a slim creamed-skinned lady   4
with rouge-circled cheeks motioned to me. As she crooked her finger,
my first thought was to apologize for entering this secret world supposed to be for adults. Yet she didn't seem really threatening.
Cautiously, I went toward the woman, noting the gray day through the
window framing her pale hazel hair and the openness of her arms held
still at either side of herself. She smelled of softness as she asked,
"Would you like to have a booth for yourself?"

Magic!   5

The only thing I could say was, "I can't buy no music!"   6

A soft smile spread as she slowly shook her head asking, "No? Well,   7
can you listen anyway?"

I jiggled an affirmative head. She said, "I'm Mrs. Smith, and this is   8
my store so you're welcome here anytime."

Feeling drained away from my body as she took the tips of my fin-   9
gers to lead me to a listening booth. There were no words as she bent
toward me, asking, "Is there something special you'd like to hear?"

"No, Ma'am," staggered out, but Mrs. Smith, undaunted by my   10
lacking, said, "Well, you wait here. I'll come back with something wonderful."

I wanted to run, but my legs weighed too heavy. An adult   11
approached the booth, saying, "Oh, excuse me," just as though I
belonged. I slid to floor, sitting down as I wrested my folded spiral
binder from my back pocket and my pencil from above my ear where
writers always carried them. Mrs. Smith returned to my show of calm
confidence and put on *Peter and the Wolf.* Story and music! How could
she have known? Grownups usually didn't understand about such
things. They often forgot their heart secrets. But the days that followed,
where I could pick anything I wanted to listen to, proved me wrong.
Billie Holiday sang sadness after I'd listen to tribal music and wonder
where my father was. Big Band sounds signaled tears of my missing
mother, but Scott Joplin had a "Maple Leaf Rag" that warmed.
Beethoven got mad and made thunderous rain. Haydn knew the calm of
a sunny Lake Washington.

Mrs. Smith asked what I was writing as though it were really impor-   12
tant and not merely an adult being tolerant. She let me read her poem
after poem without laughing or correcting the English or telling me not
to dream. She'd say, "You keep doing that," and patted my head. I'd
leave the music store with the feeling of being cuddled in sunlight, even
in the rain. It was really quite all right to be a cross-eyed funny Indian
kid who secretly scribbled poetry. Mrs. Smith said it was good. And all
those different people of all those colors and looks on all those records
knew it was too.

Many years later, when I was forty-five and in a cold early-spring-   13
drizzle mood, I went into Standard Records and Hi-Fi feeling the need
for some new music to match the time I wanted to spend writing. In one
of the floorworn aisles still narrow with record bins, I stopped for the
passage of an Elder. Her thin body, shoulder-stooped and year-wrinkled,
slipped sprightly past me. She smiled at my having slightly bowed with
hand gesturing for her to have right of way. A warm rush flooded over
me. I watched her bending toward a customer, her slight hands softly
bridging the width of a record as she placed it on a turntable. She had
not been in the store the other times I had come since growing up. I
waited until she was behind the counter again, then stood before her,
feeling shy.

Mrs. Smith asked me if there was anything else I wanted other than   14
the Billie Holliday I'd chosen. I took in deep air and said, "I want to
thank you for all the times you listened to my poetry as a kid and for
your patting my head."

A puzzled face turned up toward me, a broad smile cresting her   15
mouth. I told her about her gift. She grinned more widely and said,
"How nice that I could be there for you to save some beauty. The world
needs people like you in it. Well, I'll pat your head again."

From *Simple Songs*.

Reacting to and Discussing Ideas

1. Why do you think Mrs. Smith befriended Sears and allowed her to listen to music in her store?

2. Explain the statement, "They (adults) often forgot their heart secrets."

3. Why do you think Sears listens to music while she writes?

4. Describe Mrs. Smith's reaction upon meeting Sears as an adult.

Writing about the Reading

The Paragraph Option

1. Write a paragraph describing a memorable childhood experience.

2. Sears describes her responses to various types of music and composers. Write a paragraph describing your response to a particular song, composer, or artist.

The Essay Option

Mrs. Smith had a strong influence on Sears. Write an essay describing a person who has affected or influenced your life.

How to Put Off Doing a Job
Andy Rooney

February is one of the most difficult times of the year to put off doing some of the things you've been meaning to do. There's no vacation coming up, there are no long weekends scheduled in the immediate future; it's just this long, grim February. Don't tell me it's a short month. February is the longest by a week.

Because I have so many jobs that I don't like to do, I've been reviewing the notebook I keep with notes in it for how to put off doing a job. Let's see now, what could I use today?

—Go to the store to get something. This is one of my most dependable putter-offers. If I start a job and find I need some simple tool or a piece of hardware, I stop right there. I put on some better clothes, get in the car and drive to the store. If that store doesn't have what I'm looking for, I go to another. Often I'm attracted to some item that has nothing whatsoever to do with the job I was about to start and I buy that instead. For instance, if I go to the hardware store to buy a new snow shovel so I can clean out the driveway, but then I see a can of adhesive spray that will keep rugs in place on the floor, I'm apt to buy the adhesive spray. That ends the idea I had to shovel out the driveway.

—Tidy up the work area before starting a job. This has been useful to me over the years as a way of not getting started. Things are such a mess in my workshop, on my desk, in the kitchen and in the trunk of the car that I decide I've got to go through some of the junk before starting to work.

—Make those phone calls. There's no sense trying to do a job if you   5
have other things on your mind, so get them out of the way first. This is
a very effective way of not getting down to work. Call friends you've
been meaning to call, or the distant relative you've been out of touch
with. Even if someone is in California, Texas or Chicago and you're in
Florida, call. Paying for a long-distance call is still easier and less
unpleasant than actually getting down to work.

—Study the problem. It's foolish to jump right into a job before   6
you've thought it through. You might be doing the wrong thing. There
might be an easier way to accomplish what you want to do, so think it
over carefully from every angle. Perhaps someone has written a how-to
book about the job you have in front of you. Buy the book and then sit
down and read it. Ask friends who have had the same job for advice
about the best way to do it.

Once you've studied the problem from every angle, don't make a   7
quick decision. Sleep on it.

—Take a coffee break. Although the term "coffee break" assumes   8
that you are drinking coffee in an interim period between stretches of
solid work, this is not necessarily so. Don't be bound by old ideas about
when it's proper to take a coffee break. If taking it before you get
started is going to help keep you from doing the work, by all means
take your coffee break first.

—As a last resort before going to work, think this thing over. Is this   9
really what you want to do with your life? Philosophize. Nothing is better for putting off doing something than philosophizing. Are you a
machine, trapped in the same dull, day-after-day routine that everyone
else is in? Or are you a person who makes up his or her own mind
about things? Are you going to do these jobs because that's what's
expected of you, or are you going to break the mold and live the way
you feel like living?

Try these as ways for not getting down to work.   10

From Word for Word.

Reacting to and Discussing Ideas

1. Do you agree that February seems like the longest month of
   the year?

2. Rooney offers advice on how to get a job done by telling you
   how not to get a job done. Is this technique effective?

3. Rooney states that tidying up the work area is an avoidance technique. Do you agree? Can a messy work area interfere with your ability to work effectively?

Writing about the Reading

The Paragraph Option

1. Rooney states that "there's no sense trying to do a job if you have other things on your mind." Write a paragraph describing what you do to concentrate when you have other things on your mind.
2. Write a paragraph describing a strategy you have used to postpone or avoid doing an unpleasant task.

The Essay Option

Rooney gives advice about time management in a humorous way. Write an essay offering advice on how to perform a specific task. You may use Rooney's technique of explaining how not to accomplish the task if you wish.

A Day Away
Maya Angelou

We often think that our affairs, great or small, must be tended   1
continuously and in detail, or our world will disintegrate, and we will lose our places in the universe. That is not true, or if it is true, then our situations were so temporary that they would have collapsed anyway.

Once a year or so I give myself a day away. On the eve of my day   2
of absence, I begin to unwrap the bonds which hold me in harness. I inform housemates, my family and close friends that I will not be reachable for twenty-four hours; then I disengage the telephone. I turn the radio dial to an all-music station, preferably one which plays the soothing golden oldies. I sit for at least an hour in a very hot tub; then I lay out my clothes in preparation for my morning escape, and knowing that nothing will disturb me, I sleep the sleep of the just.

On the morning I wake naturally, for I will have set no clock, nor   3
informed my body timepiece when it should alarm. I dress in comfort-

able shoes and casual clothes and leave my house going no place. If I am living in a city, I wander streets, window-shop, or gaze at buildings. I enter and leave public parks, libraries, the lobbies of skyscrapers, and movie houses. I stay in no place for very long.

On the getaway day I try for amnesia. I do not want to know my name, where I live, or how many dire responsibilities rest on my shoulders. I detest encountering even the closest friend, for then I am reminded of who I am, and the circumstances of my life, which I want to forget for a while. 4

Every person needs to take one day away. A day in which one consciously separates the past from the future. Jobs, lovers, family, employers, and friends can exist one day without any one of us, and if our egos permit us to confess, they could exist eternally in our absence. 5

Each person deserves a day away in which no problems are confronted, no solutions searched for. Each of us needs to withdraw from the cares which will not withdraw from us. We need hours of aimless wandering or spates of time sitting on park benches, observing the mysterious world of ants and the canopy of treetops. 6

If we step away for a time, we are not, as many may think and some will accuse, being irresponsible, but rather we are preparing ourselves to more ably perform our duties and discharge our obligations. 7

When I return home, I am always surprised to find some questions I sought to evade had been answered and some entanglements I had hoped to flee had become unraveled in my absence. 8

A day away acts as a spring tonic. It can dispel rancor, transform indecision, and renew the spirit. 9

From Wouldn't Take Nothing for My Journey Now

Reacting to and Discussing Ideas

1. What do you think Angelou means by trying "for amnesia" on her day away?

2. Do you think she is irresponsible for taking a getaway day the way she does? Why or why not?

3. Why does she believe it is important to consciously separate "the past from the future" occasionally?

4. Have you ever noticed how problems sometimes seem easier to solve when you can get away from them for a while? Why do you think this is so?

Writing about the Reading

The Paragraph Option

1. Write a paragraph describing what you do to reduce tension and refresh yourself.

2. Angelou believes that a day away "acts as a spring tonic." Explain in one paragraph why it would be healthy for you to take a day away occasionally.

The Essay Option

Write an essay summarizing and evaluating Angelou's reasons for taking a day away. Provide additional justification of your own.

Sex in Advertising: Has It Gone Too Far?
William M. Pride, Robert J. Hughes, and Jack R. Kapoor

For years, advertising flirted with sexual innuendoes[1] but avoided being sexually explicit. Then, in a Calvin Klein jeans ad, actress Brooke Shields asked the question, "Want to know what comes between me and my Calvins?" The answer, "Nothing," raised eyebrows, sold jeans, and paved the way for a new generation of sexually provocative[2] advertising.

Ever since a beautiful woman first posed on the hood of a new model automobile, or a handsome man first rode his horse over a mountain and lit up a cigarette, advertisers have been satisfied that sex sells products. From coffee to clothing, advertising contains sexual innuendo. A series of Bugle Boy ads currently running on MTV shows more women dressed in bikinis and tight skirts than men wearing Bugle Boy jeans. In Maidenform underwear ads, women squirm and stuff their way into constricting underwear fashions from the past. Beer marketers are notorious for relying on sexy men and women to sell their product. When the "Swedish Bikini Team," a group of shapely blonds in skimpy bathing suits, joins a group of men drinking Old Milwaukee Beer, the implication is clear—drinking this brand of beer attracts beautiful

1. indirect suggestions
2. stimulating or suggestive

women. Although these ads range from humorous and inoffensive to obviously sexist, others cross the line into what many call crass, soft-core pornography. The epitome of advertising that provokes an uproar was Calvin Klein's explicit ad insert in *Vanity Fair* magazine. On 116 textless—and many say tasteless—pages of advertising that would make anyone's grandmother blush, readers saw naked bodies, tattoos, and motorcycles, but not many jeans.

For Calvin Klein's marketers, shocking and outraging some people is permissible if it means selling more jeans. Other advertising executives, however, ask themselves if it is ethical to offend for the sake of profit. To get expert advice and increase awareness, agencies are hiring consultants and holding seminars on sex in advertising. As a result, many sexist, exploitative, or degrading ads are disappearing. There are those, however, who argue that if the public really objected to this type of ad, the products they promote wouldn't sell. In addition, they insist, it's the role of advertisers to market products, not to serve as America's social conscience.

From *Business* (4th edition).

Reacting to and Discussing Ideas

1. Do you think restrictions or limitations should be placed on advertisers who run offensive ads?

2. Do you think advertising that uses sex as an appeal is effective in convincing consumers to buy a product?

Writing about the Reading

The Paragraph Option

1. The reading describes the way advertisers use sex as an appeal in advertising. What other types of appeals do advertisers use? Write a paragraph explaining and giving examples of another feature that makes some ads attractive and appealing. (Hint: Why do advertisers use movie stars and other famous people in their ads? Do some advertisers want you to think that people just like you buy their products?)

2. Locate an advertisement that uses sex as part of the advertising appeal. Write a paragraph describing the ad and explaining its appeal.

The Essay Option

Write an essay explaining your reaction to offensive advertising. Do you stop buying the product? Do you stop watching or reading the ad?

Can Self-Esteem Fight Poverty and Drugs?
Teo Furtado

The people at the Modello Housing Project—a poor, crime-infested   1
neighborhood in Miami that's among the worst in America—had never look or sound
like a crusader. Instead of talking about raising more money to rid the
neighborhood of its pimps and prostitutes, its hustlers and crack houses,
Mills talked about mental health. Instead of directing people to act, he
talked to them about changing the way they felt about themselves. To
Modello's residents, Mills' words sounded like the remote feel-good
mouthings of a man out of touch with the crude truths of the ghetto.

"Here's this white man coming in with his little ideas about, you   2
know, feeling good about yourself and all that crap," said Virene
McCreary when she first heard about Mills. What could he do in a
neighborhood where more than 65 percent of the families took or sold
drugs? Where 85 percent of the families were headed by a single parent,
where the school dropout rate was over 50 percent, and child abuse and
neglect were an everyday fact of life?

"I went to the first class he held, and here he was saying that regard-   3
less of what was happening in your unit, if your self-esteem is high then
it don't matter," McCreary continued. "And right away I said, well, he
ain't too bright and I ain't got time for what he's talking about."

But Mills won her over, along with most of the other residents. He   4
was nonjudgmental, but persistent. If one of the women could not
attend a meeting, Mills would volunteer to discuss his ideas at her
home. When another claimed not to be able to find a baby-sitter, no
problem, he told her. He'd be right over. The important thing was for
the residents to hear what he had to say. Once they heard it, he felt,
they'd recognize the truth of his message.

Mills did not work alone. He sought and got cooperation from the   5
local department of Housing and Urban Development (which rebuilt
120 housing units in the project), the Metro-Dade Team Police, and a
crime prevention organization. His approach was to offer community
leadership training classes, to invite parents and teachers to come

together in a PTA format, to form student workshops, to contact community service programs, and to keep on talking. The root of the problem, he told them, was their self-image.

"People's lives become what they think is possible," he said. "Only when the residents began to feel hope was there a possibility for change."   6

"Mental health is like a cork rising to the surface from under water," he said. "You can hold it under, but because it's buoyant it'll rise to the top once you let go."   7

The community responded to his message of confidence and hope. Within two years, school delinquency dropped by 80 percent. Severe child neglect decreased by 60 percent. Parent involvement in schools increased by 500 percent. More than half of the parents involved in the project began work toward a high school equivalency degree; another 21 percent decided to attend a job training program through Miami-Dade Community College. Drug trafficking dropped by 75 percent. "The changes were quite remarkable," says Curtis Ivy, chief of the Homestead Police Department, "especially in conjunction with the efforts of HUD and other local organizations."   8

Elsewhere in the country, psychology of mind therapists are claiming unrivaled success in dealing with a slew of different problems. In Minneapolis, for example, Mavis Karn and Joe Bailey use the approach to work with drug and alcohol dependency and sexual abuse. Just outside the city, the Second Chance Ranch applies psychology of mind to help so-called incorrigible kids. Eugenia Perez in San Francisco says her success with trauma patients illustrates what can be done using the approach. Educators in Florida, Colorado, and Minnesota have reported success in using psychology of mind techniques to improve students' grade point averages and attendance. If the reports are true, something significant is happening.   9

"The real answer to problems of deviance, school failure, truancy, delinquency, and welfare dependence is to teach people how they're using their thinking to keep themselves in an insecure pattern of thinking about their lives," Mills says. "Psychology of mind teaches them to become conscious of their inner power for self-esteem. Once they have that, the possibilities are limitless."   10

From *Utne Reader.*

Reacting to and Discussing Ideas

1. Why do you think Roger Mills's message of self-esteem was effective in reducing delinquency, child neglect, and drug trafficking?

2. Do you think that Mills's self-esteem message would be effective in reducing other types of crime, such as burglary or rape?

Writing about the Reading

The Paragraph Option

1. At first the residents of the Modello Housing Project were negative and skeptical about Mills, but eventually he won their trust and confidence. Write a paragraph about a person or idea that you were doubtful about at first but eventually came to trust and accept.

2. Mills's self-esteem project was intended to improve the quality of life in the Modello Housing Project. Write a paragraph describing something you have done to improve the quality of life within your family, neighborhood, or community.

The Essay Option

According to the reading, your attitude toward yourself affects how you behave and perform. Write an essay agreeing or disagreeing with this idea. Use examples from your own experience to support your position.

REVIEWING THE BASICS

GUIDE TO REVIEWING THE BASICS

Most of us know how to communicate in our language. When we talk or write, we put our thoughts into words, and, by and large, we make ourselves understood. But many of us do not know the specific terms and rules of grammar. Grammar is a system that describes how language is put together. Grammar must be learned, almost as if it is a foreign language.

Why is it important to study grammar, to understand grammatical terms like *verb, participle,* and *gerund* and concepts like *agreement* and *subordination*? There are several good reasons. Knowing grammar will allow you to

- **recognize an error in your writing and correct it.** Your papers will read more smoothly and communicate more effectively when they are error-free.
- **understand the comments of your teachers and peers.** People who read and critique your writing may point out a "fragment" or a "dangling modifier." You will be able to revise and correct the problems.
- **write with more impact.** Grammatically correct sentences are signs of clear thinking. Your readers will get your message without distraction or confusion.

As you will see in this section, "Reviewing the Basics," the different areas of grammatical study are highly interconnected. The sections on parts of speech, parts of sentences, punctuation, and mechanics and spelling fit together into a logical whole. To avoid errors in capitalization, for example, you need to know parts of speech *and* mechanics. In other words, grammar cannot be studied piecemeal, nor can it be studied superficially. If grammar is to help you in your writing, your knowledge of it must be thorough. As you review the following "basics," be alert to the interconnections that make language study so interesting.

Grammatical terms and rules demand your serious attention. Mastering them will pay handsome dividends: error-free papers, clear thinking, and effective writing.

Understanding the Parts of Speech

The eight parts of speech are **nouns, pronouns, verbs, adjectives, adverbs, conjunctions, prepositions,** and **interjections.** Each word in a sentence functions as one of these parts of speech. Being able to identify the parts of speech in sentences allows you to analyze and improve your writing and to understand grammatical principles discussed later in this book.

It is important to keep in mind that *how* a word functions in a sentence determines *what* part of speech it is. Thus, the same word can be a noun, a verb, or an adjective, depending on how it is used.

He needed some blue <u>wallpaper</u>. ⌐noun⌐

He will <u>wallpaper</u> the hall. ⌐verb⌐

He went to a <u>wallpaper</u> store. ⌐adjective⌐

A.1 Nouns

A **noun** names a person, place, thing, or idea.

People	*woman, winner, Maria Alvarez*
Places	*mall, hill, Indiana*
Things	*lamp, ship, air*
Ideas	*goodness, perfection, harmony*

The form of many nouns can change to express **number** (**singular** for one, **plural** for more than one): *one bird, two birds; one child, five children.* Most nouns can also be made **possessive** (to show ownership) by the addition of *-'s: city's, Norma's.*

Sometimes a noun is used to modify another noun:

450

noun modifying diploma

Her goal had always been to earn a college diploma.

Nouns are classified as **proper, common, collective, concrete, abstract, count,** and **noncount.**

1. Proper nouns name specific people, places, or things and are always capitalized: *Martin Luther King, Jr., East Lansing, Ford Taurus.* Days of the week and months are considered proper nouns and are capitalized.

proper noun proper noun   proper noun

In September Allen will attend Loyola University.

2. Common nouns name one or more of a general class or type of person, place, thing, or idea and are not capitalized: *president, city, car, wisdom.*

common noun common noun   common noun   common noun

Next fall the students will enter college to receive an education.

3. Collective nouns name a whole group or collection of people, places, or things: *committee, team, jury.* They are usually singular in form.

collective noun   collective noun

The flock of mallards is flying over the herd of bison.

4. Concrete nouns name tangible things that can be tasted, seen, touched, smelled, or heard: *sandwich, radio, pen.*

concrete noun   concrete noun

The frozen pizza was stuck in the freezer.

5. Abstract nouns name ideas, qualities, beliefs, and conditions: *honesty, goodness, poverty.*

abstract nouns   abstract noun

Their marriage was based on love, honor, and trust.

6. Count nouns name items that can be counted. Count nouns can be made plural, usually by adding *-s* or *-es: one river, three rivers; one box, ten boxes.* Some count nouns form their plural in an irregular way: *man, men; goose, geese.*

count noun   count noun   count noun

The children put the eggs in their baskets.

7. Noncount nouns name ideas or qualities that cannot be counted. Noncount nouns almost always have no plural form: *air, knowledge, unhappiness.*

noncount noun   noncount noun

As the r͞ai͞n pounded on the windows, she tried to find the c͞our͞age to walk home.

A.2 Pronouns

A **pronoun** is a word that substitutes for or refers to a noun or another pronoun. The noun or pronoun to which a pronoun refers is called the pronoun's **antecedent**. A pronoun must agree with its antecedent in person, number, and gender (these terms are defined below).

After the campers discovered the cave, they mapped it for the next group, which was arriving next week. [The pronoun *they* refers to its antecedent, *campers*; the pronoun *it* refers to its antecedent, *cave*; the pronoun *which* refers to its antecedent, *group*.]

The eight kinds of pronouns are **personal, demonstrative, reflexive, intensive, interrogative, relative, indefinite,** and **reciprocal**.

1. Personal pronouns take the place of nouns or pronouns that name people or things. A personal pronoun changes form to indicate **person, gender, number,** and **case.**

Person is the grammatical term used to distinguish the speaker (**first person:** *I, we*); the person spoken to (**second person:** *you*); and the person or thing spoken about (**third person:** *he, she, it, they*). **Gender** is the term used to classify pronouns as **masculine** *(he, him)*; **feminine** *(she, her)*; or **neuter** *(it)*. **Number** classifies pronouns as **singular** (one) or **plural** (more than one). Some personal pronouns also function as adjectives modifying nouns *(our house)*.

	Singular	*Plural*
First person	I, me, my, mine	we, us, our, ours
Second person	you, your, yours	you, your, yours
Third person		
Masculine	he, him, his	they, them, their, theirs
Feminine	she, her, hers	
Neuter	it, its	

1st person singular
1st person   (pronoun/   3rd person   3rd person
singular   adjective)   singular   plural

I called my mother about the twins. She wanted to know as soon as they took their first steps. "Your babies are talented," she said.

3rd person   2nd person   3rd person
plural   singular   singular
(pronoun/adjective) (pronoun/adjective)

A pronoun's **case** is determined by its function as a subject (**subjective** or **nominative case**) or an object (**objective case**) in a sentence. A pronoun that shows ownership is in the **possessive case**.

2. Demonstrative pronouns refer to particular people or things. The demonstrative pronouns are *this* and *that* (singular) and *these* and *those* (plural). (*This, that, these,* and *those* can also be demonstrative adjectives when they modify a noun. See page 463.)

This is more thorough than that.

The red shuttle buses stop here. These go to the airport every hour.

3. Reflexive pronouns indicate that the subject performs actions to, for, or upon itself. Reflexive pronouns end in *-self* or *-selves*.

	Singular	*Plural*
First person	myself	ourselves
Second person	yourself	yourselves
Third person	himself	
	herself	themselves
	itself	

We excused ourselves from the table and left.

4. An intensive pronoun emphasizes the word that comes before it in a sentence. Like reflexive pronouns, intensive pronouns end in *-self* or *-selves*.

The filmmaker herself could not explain the ending.

They themselves washed the floor.

Note: A reflexive or intensive pronoun should not be used as a subject of a sentence. An antecedent for the reflexive or intensive pronoun must appear in the same sentence.

INCORRECT: Myself create colorful sculpture.
CORRECT: I myself create colorful sculpture.

5. Interrogative pronouns are used to introduce questions: *who, whom, whoever, whomever, what, which, whose.* The correct use of *who* and *whom* depends on the role the interrogative pronoun plays in a sentence or clause. When the pronoun functions as the subject of the sentence or clause, use *who.* When the pronoun functions as an object in the sentence or clause, use *whom.*

What happened?

Which is your street?

Who wrote *Ragtime*? [*Who* is the subject of the sentence.]

Whom should I notify? [*Whom* is the object of the verb *notify: I should notify whom?*]

6. Relative pronouns relate groups of words to nouns or other pronouns and often introduce adjective clauses or noun clauses (see page 485). The relative pronouns that refer to people are *who, whom, whoever, whomever,* and *whose* and those that refer to things are *that, what, whatever,* and *which.*

In 1836 Charles Dickens met John Forster, who became his friend and biographer.

Don did not understand what the child said.

We read some articles that were written by former astronauts.

7. Indefinite pronouns are pronouns without specific antecedents. They refer to people, places, or things in general.

Someone has been rearranging my papers.

Many knew the woman, but few could say they knew her well.

Here are some frequently used indefinite pronouns:

Singular		Plural
another	nobody	all
anybody	none	both
anyone	no one	few
anything	nothing	many
each	one	more
either	other	most
everybody	somebody	others
everyone	someone	several
everything	something	some
neither		

8. The **reciprocal pronouns** *each other* and *one another* indicate a mutual relationship between two or more parts of a plural antecedent.

Bernie and Sharon congratulated each other on their high grades.

EXERCISE 1 ▶ In each of the following sentences (a) circle each noun and (b) underline each pronoun.

EXAMPLE: Mark parked his car in the lot that is reservd for commuters like him.

1. (Shakespeare) wrote many (plays) that have become famous and important.
2. Everyone who has visited (Disneyland) wishes to return.
3. (Jonathan) himself prepared the delicious (dinner) that the (guests) enjoyed.
4. That (hat) used to belong to my (great-grandmother)
5. (Aretha's) (integrity) was never questioned by her (coworkers).
6. The (class) always laughed at (Professor Wayne's) (jokes) even though they were usually corny.
7. When will (humankind) be able to live in outer (space) for long (periods)?
8. Whoever wins this (week's) (lottery) will become quite wealthy.
9. As the (plane) landed in the Atlanta (airport), many of the (passengers) began gathering their carry-on (luggage).
10. This (week) in physics (class) we are studying (gravity)

A.3 Verbs

Verbs express action or state of being. A grammatically complete sentence has at least one verb in it.

There are three kinds of verbs: **action verbs, linking verbs,** and **helping verbs** (also known as **auxiliary verbs**).

1. Action verbs express physical and mental activities.

Mr. Royce <u>dashed</u> for the bus.

The incinerator <u>burns</u> garbage at high temperatures.

I <u>think</u> that seat is taken.

The baby <u>slept</u> until 3:00 A.M.

Action verbs are either **transitive** or **intransitive.** The action of a **transitive verb** is directed toward someone or something, called the **direct object** of the verb. Direct objects receive the action of the verb. Transitive verbs require direct objects to complete the meaning of the sentence.

```
            transitive  direct
 subject      verb      object
Amalia       made      clocks.
```

An **intransitive verb** does not need a direct object to complete the meaning of the sentence.

subject — intransitive verb

The traffic stopped.

Some verbs can be both transitive and intransitive, depending on their meaning and use in a sentence.

INTRANSITIVE: The traffic stopped. [No direct object.]

TRANSITIVE: The driver stopped the bus at the corner.

2. A linking verb expresses a state of being or a condition. A linking verb connects a noun or pronoun to words that describe the noun or pronoun. Common linking verbs are forms of the verb *be* (*is, are, was, were, being, been*), *become, feel, grow, look, remain, seem, smell, sound, stay,* and *taste.*

Their child grew tall.

The boat smells fishy.

Mr. Davenport is our accountant.

3. A helping (auxiliary) verb helps another verb, called the **main verb,** to convey when the action occurred (through verb tense) and to form questions. One or more helping verbs and the main verb together form a **verb phrase.** Some helping verbs, called **modals,** are always helping verbs:

can, could	shall, should
may, might	will, would
must, ought to	

helping main verb verb

The cat will nap on that windowsill for hours.

helping verb / main verb

Will the cat nap through the noise of the vacuum cleaner?

The other helping verbs can sometimes function as main verbs as well:

am, are, be, been, being
did, do, does
had, has, have
is, was, were

The verb *be* is a very irregular verb, with eight forms instead of the usual five: *am, are, be, being, been, is, was, were.*

Forms of the Verb

All verbs except *be* have five forms: the **base form** (or dictionary form), the **past tense**, the **past participle**, the **present participle**, and the **-s form**. The first three forms are called the verb's **principal parts**. The infinitive consists of "to" plus a base form: *to go, to study, to talk*. For **regular verbs**, the past tense and past participle are formed by adding *-d* or *-ed* to the base form. **Irregular verbs** follow no set pattern to form their past tense and past participle.

	Regular	*Irregular*
Infinitive:	work	eat
Past tense:	worked	ate
Past participle:	worked	eaten
Present participle:	working	eating
-s form:	works	eats

Verbs change form to agree with their subjects in person and number (see page 227); to express the time of their action (**tense**); to express whether the action is a fact, command, or wish (**mood**); and to indicate whether the subject performs or receives the action (**voice**).

Principal Parts of Irregular Verbs

Consult the following list and your dictionary for the principal parts of irregular verbs.

Base Form	*Past Tense*	*Past Participle*
be	was	been
become	became	become
begin	began	begun
bite	bit	bitten
blow	blew	blown
burst	burst	burst
catch	caught	caught
choose	chose	chosen
come	came	come
dive	dived, dove	dived
do	did	done
draw	drew	drawn
drive	drove	driven
eat	ate	eaten
fall	fell	fallen
find	found	found

Base Form	*Past Tense*	*Past Participle*
fling	flung	flung
fly	flew	flown
get	got	gotten
give	gave	given
go	went	gone
grow	grew	grown
have	had	had
know	knew	known
lay	laid	laid
lead	led	led
leave	left	left
lie	lay	lain
lose	lost	lost
ride	rode	ridden
ring	rang	rung
rise	rose	risen
say	said	said
set	set	set
sit	sat	sat
speak	spoke	spoken
swear	swore	sworn
swim	swam	swum
tear	tore	torn
tell	told	told
throw	threw	thrown
wear	wore	worn
write	wrote	written

Tense

The **tenses** of a verb express time. They convey whether an action, process, or occurrence takes place in the present, past, or future.

The three **simple tenses** are **present, past,** and **future.** The **simple present** tense is the base form of the verb (and the *-s* form for third-person singular subjects; the **simple past** tense is the past-tense form; and the **simple future** tense consists of the helping verb *will* plus the base form.

	Regular	*Irregular*
Simple present	I talk	I go
Simple past	I talked	I went
Simple future	I will talk	I will go

The **perfect tenses,** which indicate completed action, are **present perfect, past perfect,** and **future perfect.** They are formed by adding the helping verbs *have* (or *has*), *had*, and *will have* to the past participle.

	Regular	*Irregular*
Present perfect	I have talked	I have gone
Past perfect	I had talked	I had gone
Future perfect	I will have talked	I will have gone

In addition to the simple and perfect tenses, there are six progressive tenses: the **simple progressive tenses** are the **present progressive,** the **past progressive,** and the **future progressive.** These progressive tenses are formed by adding the present, past, and future forms of the verb *be* to the present participle. The **perfect progressive tenses** are the **present perfect progressive,** the **past perfect progressive,** and the **future perfect progressive.** They are formed by adding the present perfect, past perfect, and future perfect forms of the verb *be* to the present participle.

	Regular	*Irregular*
Present progressive	I am talking	I am going
Past progressive	I was talking	I was going
Future progressive	I will be talking	I will be going
Present perfect progressive	I have been talking	I have been going
Past perfect progressive	I had been talking	I had been going
Future perfect progressive	I will have been talking	I will have been going

Mood

The mood of a verb indicates the writer's attitude toward the action. There are three moods in English: **indicative, imperative,** and **subjunctive.**

The **indicative mood** is used for ordinary statements of fact or questions.

The light <u>flashed</u> on and off all night.

<u>Did</u> you <u>check</u> the batteries?

The **imperative mood** is used for commands, suggestions, or directions. The subject of a verb in the imperative mood is *you,* though it is not always included.

Stop shouting!

Come to New York for a visit.

Turn right at the next corner.

The **subjunctive mood** is used for wishes, requirements, recommendations, and statements contrary to fact. For statements contrary to fact or for wishes, the past tense of the verb is used. For the verb *be,* only the past-tense form *were* is used.

If I had a million dollars, I'd take a trip around the world.

If my grandmother were younger, she could live by herself.

To express suggestions, recommendations, or requirements, the infinitive form is used for all verbs.

I recommend that the houses be sold after the landscaping is done.

The registrar required that Maureen pay her bill before attending class.

Voice

Transitive verbs (those that take objects) may be in either the active voice or the passive voice. (See page 230.) In an **active-voice** sentence, the subject does the action described by the verb; that is, the subject is the actor. In a **passive-voice** sentence, the subject is the receiver of the action. The passive voice of a verb is formed by using an appropriate form of the helping verb *be* and the past participle of the main verb.

subject is actor / active voice
Dr. Hillel delivered the report on global warming.

subject is receiver / passive voice
The report on global warming was delivered by Dr. Hillel.

EXERCISE 2 ▶ Revise the following sentences, changing each verb from the present tense to the tense indicated.

EXAMPLE: I know the right answer.

PAST TENSE: I knew the right answer.

1. The boy loses the ball in the water.

SIMPLE PAST: The boy lost the ball in the water.

2. Malcolm begins classes at the community college.

PAST PERFECT: Malcolm had begun classes at the community college.

3. The microscope <u>enlarges</u> the cell.

   PRESENT PERFECT: <u>The microscope has enlarged the cell.</u>

4. Sunflowers <u>follow</u> the sun's path.

   SIMPLE FUTURE: <u>Sunflowers will follow the sun's path.</u>

5. Meg Ryan <u>receives</u> excellent reviews.

   FUTURE PERFECT: <u>Meg Ryan will have received excellent reviews.</u>

6. Juanita <u>writes</u> a computer program.

   PRESENT PERFECT: <u>Juanita has written a computer program.</u>

7. The movie <u>stars</u> Whoopi Goldberg.

   SIMPLE FUTURE: <u>The movie will star Whoopi Goldberg.</u>

8. Dave <u>wins</u> a medal at the Special Olympics.

   SIMPLE PAST: <u>Dave won a medal at the Special Olympics.</u>

9. Many celebrities <u>donate</u> money to AIDS research.

   PRESENT PERFECT: <u>Many celebrities have donated money to AIDS research.</u>

10. My nephew <u>vacations</u> in Michigan's Upper Peninsula.

    PAST PERFECT: <u>My nephew had vacationed in Michigan's Upper Peninsula.</u>

A.4 Adjectives

Adjectives modify nouns and pronouns. That is, they describe, identify, qualify, or limit the meaning of nouns and pronouns. An adjective answers the question *Which one? What kind?* or *How many?* about the word it modifies.

WHICH ONE? The <u>twisted</u>, <u>torn</u> umbrella was of no use to its owner.
WHAT KIND? The <u>spotted</u> owl has caused <u>heated</u> arguments in the Northwest.
HOW MANY? <u>Many</u> people waited in line for <u>four</u> hours before the ticket office opened.

In form, adjectives can be **positive** (implying no comparison), **comparative** (comparing two items), or **superlative** (comparing three or more items). (See page 144 for more on the forms of adjectives.)

positive
The scissors are sharp.

comparative
Your scissors are sharper than mine.

superlative
These are the sharpest scissors I have ever used.

There are two general categories of adjectives. **Descriptive adjectives** name a quality of the person, place, thing, or idea they describe: *mysterious man*, *green pond*, *healthy complexion*. **Limiting adjectives** narrow the scope of the person, place, or thing they describe: *my hat*, *this tool*, *second try*.

Descriptive Adjectives

A **regular** (or **attributive**) adjective appears next to (usually before) the word it modifies. Several adjectives can modify the same word.

The enthusiastic new barber gave short, lopsided haircuts.

The wealthy dealer bought an immense blue vase.

Sometimes nouns function as adjectives modifying other nouns: *tree house*, *hamburger bun*.

A **predicate adjective** follows a linking verb and modifies or describes the subject of the sentence or clause (see page 475). (See page 483 on clauses.)

predicate adjective
The meeting was long. [Modifies the subject, *meeting*.]

Limiting Adjectives

The **definite article**, *the*, and the **indefinite articles**, *a* and *an*, are classified as adjectives. *A* and *an* are used when it is not important to specify a particular noun or when the object named is not known to the reader (*A radish adds color to a salad*). *The* is used when it is important to specify a particular noun or when the object named is known to the reader or has already been mentioned (*The radishes from the garden are on the table*).

A squirrel visited the feeder that I just built. The squirrel tried to eat some bird food.

When the possessive pronouns *my*, *your*, *his*, *her*, *its*, *our*, and *their* are used as modifiers before nouns, they are considered **possessive adjectives**.

Your friend borrowed <u>my</u> jacket for <u>his</u> wife.

When the demonstrative pronouns *this, that, these,* and *those* are used as modifiers before nouns, they are called **demonstrative adjectives.** (See page 453.) *This* and *these* modify nouns close to the writer; *that* and *those* modify nouns more distant from the writer.

Eat <u>these</u> sandwiches, not <u>those</u> sardines.

<u>This</u> freshman course is a prerequisite for <u>those</u> advanced courses.

Cardinal adjectives are words used in counting: *one, two, twenty,* and so on.

I read <u>four</u> biographies of Jack Kerouac and <u>seven</u> articles about his work.

Ordinal adjectives note position in a series.

The <u>first</u> biography was too sketchy, whereas the <u>second</u> one was too detailed.

Indefinite adjectives provide nonspecific, general information about the quantities of the nouns they modify. Some common indefinite adjectives are *another, any, enough, few, less, little, many, more, much, several,* and *some.*

<u>Several</u> people asked me if I had <u>enough</u> blankets or if I wanted the thermostat turned up a <u>few</u> degrees.

The **interrogative adjectives** *what, which,* and *whose* modify nouns and pronouns used in questions.

<u>Which</u> radio station do you like? <u>Whose</u> music do you prefer?

The words *which* and *what,* along with *whichever* and *whatever,* are **relative adjectives** when they modify nouns and introduce subordinate clauses (see page 483).

She couldn't decide <u>which</u> dessert she wanted to eat.

Proper adjectives are adjectives derived from proper nouns: *Spain* (noun), *Spanish* (adjective); *Freud* (noun), *Freudian* (adjective). (See page 451.) Most proper adjectives are capitalized.

Shakespeare lived in <u>Elizabethan</u> England.

The parrot knows many <u>French</u> expressions.

EXERCISE 3 ▶ Revise each of the following sentences by adding at least three adjectives.

EXAMPLE: The cat slept on the pillow.

REVISED: <u>The old yellow cat slept on the expensive pillow.</u>

1. Before leaving on a trip, the couple packed their suitcases.
   Before leaving on a long-awaited trip, the newlywed couple packed their tattered suitcases.

2. The tree dropped leaves all over the lawn. The old oak tree dropped yellow leaves all over the manicured lawn.

3. While riding the train, the passengers read newspapers.
   While riding the subway train, the bored passengers read daily newspapers.

4. The antiques dealer said that the desk was more valuable than the chair. The antiques dealer said that the cracked mahogany desk was more valuable than the worn upholstered chair.

5. As the play was ending, the audience clapped their hands and tossed roses onstage. As the mystery play was ending, the excited audience clapped their hands and tossed red roses onstage.

6. Stew is served nightly at the shelter. Tasty beef stew is served nightly at the homeless shelter.

7. The engine roared as the car stubbornly jerked into gear. _____
   The new engine roared as the dented car stubbornly jerked into first gear.

8. The tourists tossed pennies into the fountain. The Spanish tourists tossed shiny pennies into the flowing fountain.

9. Computer disks were stacked on the desk next to the monitor.
   Used computer disks were stacked on the metal desk next to the large monitor.

10. Marina's belt and shoes were made of the same material and complemented her dress. Marina's green belt and shoes were made of the same material and complemented her fashionable new dress.

A.5 Adverbs

Adverbs modify verbs, adjectives, other adverbs, or entire sentences or clauses (see page 60 on clauses). Like adjectives, adverbs describe, qualify, or limit the meaning of the words they modify.

An adverb answers the question *How? When? Where? How often?* or *To what extent?* about the word it modifies.

HOW?	Cheryl moved <u>awkwardly</u> because of her stiff neck.
WHEN?	I arrived <u>yesterday</u>.
WHERE?	They searched <u>everywhere</u>.
HOW OFTEN?	He telephoned <u>repeatedly</u>.
TO WHAT EXTENT?	Simon was <u>rather</u> slow to answer his doorbell.

Many adverbs end in *-ly (lazily, happily)*; some adverbs do not *(fast, here, much, well, rather, everywhere, never, so)*; and some words that end in *-ly* are not adverbs *(lively, friendly, lonely)*. Like all parts of speech, an adverb may be best identified by examining its function within a sentence.

I <u>quickly</u> skimmed the book. [Modifies the verb *skimmed*.]

<u>Very</u> cold water came from the shower. [Modifies the adjective *cold*.]

He was injured <u>quite</u> seriously. [Modifies the adverb *seriously*.]

<u>Apparently</u>, the job was bungled. [Modifies the whole sentence.]

Like adjectives, adverbs have three forms: **positive** (does not suggest any comparison), **comparative** (compares two actions or conditions), and **superlative** (compares three or more actions or conditions). (See also page 144.)

Andy rose <u>early</u> [positive] and crept downstairs <u>quietly</u> [positive].

Jim rose <u>earlier</u> [comparative] than Andy and crept downstairs <u>more quietly</u> [comparative].

Bill rose <u>earliest</u> [superlative] of anyone in the house and crept downstairs <u>most quietly</u> [superlative].

Some adverbs, called **conjunctive adverbs** (or **adverbial conjunctions**)—such as *however, therefore,* and *besides*—connect the ideas of one sentence or clause to those of a previous sentence or clause. They can appear anywhere in a sentence. (See page 107 for how to punctuate sentences containing conjunctive adverbs.)

James did not want to go to the library on Saturday; <u>however</u> [conjunctive adverb], he knew he needed to research his paper.

The sporting-goods store was crowded because of the sale. Leila, <u>therefore</u> [conjunctive adverb], decided to come back another day.

Some common conjunctive adverbs are listed here, including several phrases that function as conjunctive adverbs.

accordingly	for example	meanwhile	otherwise
also	further	moreover	similarly
anyway	furthermore	namely	still
as a result	hence	nevertheless	then
at the same time	however	next	thereafter
besides	incidentally	nonetheless	therefore
certainly	indeed	now	thus
consequently	instead	on the contrary	undoubtedly
finally	likewise	on the other hand	

EXERCISE 4

Write a sentence using each of the following comparative or superlative adverbs.

EXAMPLE: better: _My car runs better now than ever before._

1. farther: Arthur traveled farther than James.

2. most: Sociology was the most interesting class of all.

3. more: The exam was more difficult than I expected.

4. best: Professor Sung is the best-trained musician on campus.

5. least neatly: Pam was dressed least neatly of all the players.

6. more loudly: We applauded more loudly than anyone else.

7. worse: Sarah performed worse than she feared.

8. less angrily: Ramón reacted less angrily than I did.

9. later: The play began later than scheduled.

10. earliest: My family arrived earliest of all.

A.6 Conjunctions

Conjunctions connect words, phrases, and clauses. There are three kinds of conjunctions: **coordinating, correlative,** and **subordinating. Coordinating** and **correlative conjunctions** connect words, phrases, or clauses of equal grammatical rank. (A **phrase** is a group of related words lacking a subject, a predicate, or both. A **clause** is a group of words containing a subject and a predicate. See pages 472 and 473.)

The **coordinating conjunctions** are *and, but, for, nor, or, so,* and *yet.* These words must connect words or word groups of the same kind. That is, two nouns may be connected by *and,* but a noun and a clause cannot be. *For* and *so* can connect only independent clauses.

coordinating
noun   conjunction   noun
We studied the novels of Toni Morrison and Alice Walker.

coordinating
conjunction
verb | verb
The copilot successfully flew and landed the disabled plane.

           coordinating   independent
independent clause   conjunction   clause
The carpentry course sounded interesting, so Meg enrolled.

          coordinating
subordinate clause   conjunction   subordinate clause

We hoped that the mail would come soon and that it would contain our bonus check.

Correlative conjunctions are pairs of words that link and relate grammatically equivalent parts of a sentence. Some common correlative conjunctions are *either/or, neither/nor, both/and, not/but, not only/but also,* and *whether/or.* Correlative conjunctions are always used in pairs.

— correlative conjunctions —
Either the electricity was off, or the bulb had burned out.

Subordinating conjunctions connect dependent, or subordinate, clauses to independent clauses (see page 110). Some common subordinating conjunctions are *although, because, if, since, until, when, where,* and *while.*

subordinating conjunction
Although the movie got bad reviews, it drew big crowds.

subordinating conjunction
She received a lot of mail because she was a reliable correspondent.

A.7 Prepositions

A **preposition** links and relates its **object** (a noun or a pronoun) to the rest of the sentence. Prepositions often show relationships of time, place, direction, and manner.

preposition   object of preposition
I walked around the block.

preposition   object of preposition
She called during our vacation.

Common Prepositions

along	besides	from	past	up
among	between	in	since	upon
around	beyond	near	through	with
at	by	off	till	within
before	despite	on	to	without
behind	down	onto	toward	
below	during	out	under	
beneath	except	outside	underneath	
beside	for	over	until	

Some prepositions consist of more than one word; they are called **phrasal prepositions** or **compound prepositions**.

phrasal preposition   object of preposition

According to our records, you have enough credits to graduate.

phrasal preposition   object of preposition

We decided to make the trip in spite of the snowstorm.

Common Compound Prepositions

according to	in addition to	on account of
aside from	in front of	out of
as of	in place of	prior to
as well as	in regard to	with regard to
because of	in spite of	with respect to
by means of	instead of	

The object of the preposition often has modifiers.

prep.   modifier prep.   prep.   modifier obj. of prep.

Not a sound came from the child's room except a gentle snoring.

Sometimes a preposition has more than one object (a **compound object**).

preposition   compound object of preposition

The laundromat was between campus and home.

Usually the preposition comes before its object. In interrogative sentences, however, the preposition sometimes follows its object.

object of preposition   preposition

What did your supervisor ask you about?

The preposition, the object or objects of the preposition, and the object's modifiers all form a **prepositional phrase**.

prepositional phrase
The scientist conducted her experiment throughout the afternoon and early evening.

There may be many prepositional phrases in a sentence.

prepositional phrase   prepositional phrase
The water from the open hydrant flowed into the street.

The noisy kennel was underneath the beauty salon, despite the complaints of customers.

Alongside the weedy railroad tracks, an old hotel stood with faded grandeur near the abandoned brick station on the edge of town.

Prepositional phrases frequently function as adjectives or adverbs. If a prepositional phrase modifies a noun or pronoun, it functions as an adjective. If it modifies a verb, adjective, or adverb, it functions as an adverb.

The auditorium inside the new building has a special sound system. [Adjective modifying the noun *auditorium*.]

The doctor looked cheerfully at the patient and handed the lab results across the desk. [Adverbs modifying the verbs *looked* and *handed*.]

EXERCISE 5 Expand each of the following sentences by adding a prepositional phrase in the blank.

EXAMPLE: A cat hid __under the car__ when the garage door opened.

1. Fish nibbled __at the bait__ as the fisherman waited.

2. The librarian explained that the books about Africa are located __on the second floor__.

3. When the bullet hit the window, shards flew __in the air__.

4. __In Florida__, there is a restaurant that serves alligator meat.

5. Polar bears are able to swim __in icy waters__.

6. Heavy winds blowing __across the lake__ caused the waves to hit the house.

7. One student completed her exam __in record time__.

8. A frog jumped __across our pond__.

9. The bus was parked __beside another__.

10. Stacks of books were piled __on the table__.

A.8 Interjections

Interjections are words that express emotion or surprise. They are followed by an exclamation point, comma, or period, depending on whether they stand alone or serve as part or all of a sentence. Interjections are used in speech more than in writing.

<u>Wow!</u> What a hat!

<u>So,</u> was that lost letter ever found?

<u>Well,</u> I'd better be going.

Understanding the Parts of Sentences

A sentence is a group of words that expresses a complete thought about something or someone. A sentence must contain a **subject** and a **predicate**.

Subject	Predicate
Children	grow.
Cecilia	laughed.
Time	will tell.

Depending on their purpose and punctuation, sentences are **declarative, interrogative, exclamatory,** or **imperative.**

A **declarative sentence** makes a statement. It ends with a period.

subject predicate
The snow fell steadily.

An **interrogative sentence** asks a question. It ends with a question mark (?).

subject predicate
Who called?

An **exclamatory sentence** conveys strong emotion. It ends with an exclamation point (!).

subject predicate
Your picture is in the paper!

An **imperative sentence** gives an order or makes a request. It ends with either a period or an exclamation point, depending on how mild or strong the command or request is. In an imperative sentence, the subject is *you,* but this often is not included.

predicate
Get me a fire extinguisher now! [The subject *you* is understood: (*You*) get me a fire extinguisher now!]

B.1 Subjects

The subject of a sentence is who or what the sentence is about. It is who or what performs or receives the action expressed in the predicate. The subject is often a **noun,** a word that names a person, place, thing, or idea.

> Whitney Houston released a new video.

> The rose bushes must be watered.

> Honesty is the best policy.

The subject of a sentence can also be a **pronoun,** a word that refers to or substitutes for a noun.

> They saw the movie three times.

> I will attend the rally.

> Although the ink spilled, it did not go on my shirt.

The subject of a sentence can also be a group of words used as a noun.

> Lying on a beach is my idea of a good time.

Simple Versus Complete Subjects

The **simple subject** is the noun or pronoun that names what the sentence is about. It does not include any **modifiers**—that is, words that describe, identify, qualify, or limit the meaning of the noun or pronoun.

> simple subject
> The bright red concert poster caught everyone's eye.

> simple subject
> High-speed computers have revolutionized the banking industry.

When the subject of a sentence is a proper noun (a name of a particular person, place, or thing), the entire name is considered the simple subject.

> ⎡—— simple subject ——⎤
> Martin Luther King, Jr. was a famous leader.

The simple subject of an imperative sentence is you.

> simple subject
> [You] Remember to bring the cooler.

The **complete subject** is the simple subject plus its modifiers.

> ⎡——— complete subject———⎤
> simple subject
> The sleek, black limousine waited outside the church.

complete subject

Fondly remembered as a gifted songwriter, fiddle player, and storyteller, <u>Quintin Lotus Dickey</u> lived in a cabin in Paoli, Indiana.

simple subject

Compound Subjects

Some sentences contain two or more subjects joined with a coordinating conjunction (*and, but, for, nor, or, so, yet*). Those subjects together form a **compound subject.**

compound   subject

Neither <u>Maria</u> nor <u>I</u> completed the marathon.

compound subject

The microwave <u>oven</u>, the <u>dishwasher</u>, and the <u>refrigerator</u> were not usable during the blackout.

B.2 Predicates

The **predicate** indicates what the subject does, what happened to the subject, or what is being said about the subject. The predicate must include a **verb,** a word or group of words that expresses an action or a state of being (for example, *run, invent, build, know, become*).

Joy <u>swam</u> sixty laps.

The thunderstorm <u>replenished</u> the reservoir.

Sometimes the verb consists of only one word, as in the above examples. Often, however, the main verb is accompanied by a **helping verb** (see page 456).

helping   main
verb   verb

By the end of the week, I <u>will have</u> <u>worked</u> twenty-five hours.

helping main
verb   verb

The play <u>had</u> <u>begun</u>.

helping main
verb   verb

The professor <u>did</u> <u>return</u> the journal assignments.

Simple Versus Complete Predicates

The **simple predicate** is the main verb plus its helping verbs (together known as the **verb phrase**). The simple predicate does not include any modifiers.

simple predicate
The proctor hastily collected the blue books.

⌐ simple predicate ¬
The moderator had introduced the next speaker.

The **complete predicate** consists of the simple predicate, its modifiers, and any complements (words that complete the meaning of the verb; see page 475). In general, the complete predicate includes everything in the sentence except the complete subject.

────────── complete predicate ──────────
simple predicate
The music sounds better from the back of the room.

────────── complete predicate ──────────
simple predicate
Bill decided to change the name of his band to something less controversial and confusing.

Compound Predicates

Some sentences have two or more predicates joined by a coordinating conjunction (*and, or, but,* or *nor*). These predicates together form a **compound predicate.**

┌──── compound predicate ────┐
Marcia unlocked her bicycle and rode away.

┌──── compound predicate ────┐
The supermarket owner will survey his customers and order the specialized foods they desire.

EXERCISE 6 ▶ Underline the simple subject(s) and circle the simple predicate(s) in each of the following sentences.

EXAMPLE: Pamela Wong (photographed) a hummingbird.

1. A flock of geese (flew) over the park on its way south for the winter.
2. The campground for physically challenged children (is funded) and (supported) by the Rotary Club.
3. Forty doctors and lawyers (had attended) the seminar on malpractice insurance.
4. Sullivan Beach (will) not (reopen) because of pollution.
5. The boys (ran) to the store and (rushed) home with ice cream.

6. Greenpeace is an environmentalist organization.
7. Talented dancers and experienced musicians performed and received much applause at the open-air show.
8. Some undergraduate students have been using empty classrooms for group study.
9. A police officer, with the shoplifter in handcuffs, entered the police station.
10. The newly elected senator walked up to the podium and began her first speech to her constituents.

B.3 Complements

A **complement** is a word or group of words used to complete the meaning of a subject or object. There are four kinds of complements: **subject complements,** which follow linking verbs; **direct objects** and **indirect objects,** which follow transitive verbs (verbs that take an object); and **object complements,** which follow direct objects.

Linking Verbs and Subject Complements

A linking verb (such as *be, become, seem, feel, taste*) links the subject to a **subject complement,** a noun or adjective that renames or describes the subject. (See page 456 for more about linking verbs.) Nouns that function as complements are called **predicate nominatives** or **predicate nouns.** Adjectives that function as complements are called **predicate adjectives.**

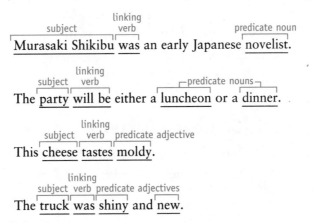

Direct Objects

A **direct object** is a noun or pronoun that receives the action of a transitive verb (see page 455). A direct object answers the question *What?* or *Whom?*

transitive verb   direct object

The pharmacist helped us. [The pharmacist helped *whom?*]

transitive verb   ⌐direct objects⌐

Jillian borrowed a bicycle and a visor. [Jillian borrowed *what?*]

Indirect Objects

An **indirect object** is a noun or pronoun that receives the action of the verb indirectly. Indirect objects name the person or thing *to whom* or *for whom* something is done.

transitive verb — indirect object   direct object

The oil-delivery man gave me the bill. [He gave the bill *to whom?*]

transitive verb   indirect objects   direct objects

Eric bought his wife and son some sandwiches and milk. [He bought food *for whom?*]

Object Complements

An **object complement** is a noun that renames the direct object or an adjective that modifies the direct object. Object complements appear with verbs like *name, find, think, elect, appoint, choose,* and *consider.*

direct object   noun as object complement

We appointed Dean our representative. [*Representative* renames the direct object, *Dean.*]

direct object adjective as object complement

The judge found the defendant innocent of the charges. [*Innocent* modifies the direct object, *defendant.*]

B.4 Basic Sentence Patterns

There are five basic sentence patterns in English. They are built with combinations of subjects, predicates, and complements. The order of these elements within a sentence may vary, or a sentence may become long and complicated when modifiers, phrases, or clauses are added. Nonetheless, one of five basic patterns stands at the heart of every sentence.

Pattern 1

Subject + Predicate
　　　　I　　shivered.
　　Cynthia　swam.

Pattern 2

Subject	+ Predicate	+ Direct Object
Anthony	bought	a sofa.
We	wanted	freedom.

Pattern 3

Subject	+ Predicate	+ Subject Complement
The woman	was	a welder.
Our course	is	interesting.

Pattern 4

Subject	+ Predicate	+ Indirect Object	+ Direct Object
My friend	loaned	me	a typewriter.
The company	sent	employees	a questionnaire.

Pattern 5

Subject	+ Predicate	+ Direct Object	+ Object Complement
I	consider	her singing	exceptional.
Lampwick	called	Jiminy Cricket	a beetle.

EXERCISE 7 ▶ Complete each sentence with a word or words that will function as the type of complement indicated.

EXAMPLE: The scientist acted ___proud___ as he announced his latest
invention.
<u>predicate adjective</u>

1. The delivery person handed ___George___ the large brown package.
<u>indirect object</u>

2. George Bush was an American ___president___.
<u>predicate noun</u>

3. The chairperson appointed Judith our ___representative___.
<u>object complement</u>

4. Protesters stood on the corner and handed out ___pamphlets___.
<u>direct object</u>

5. The secretary gave ___Anne___ the messages.
<u>indirect object</u>

6. Before the storm, many clouds were ___gray___.
<u>predicate adjective</u>

7. The beer advertisement targeted ___young adults___.
<u>direct object</u>

8. The Super Bowl players were ___professionals___.
<u>predicate noun</u>

9. The diplomat declared the Olympics ___successful___.
<u>object complement</u>

10. Shopping malls are ___crowded___ before Christmas.
<u>predicate adjective</u>

B.5 Expanding the Sentence with Adjectives and Adverbs

A sentence may consist of just a subject and a verb.

Linda studied.

Rumors circulated.

Most sentences, however, contain additional information about the subject and the verb. Information is commonly added in three ways:

- by using adjectives and adverbs.
- by using phrases (groups of words that lack either a subject or a predicate or both).
- by using clauses (groups of words that contain both a subject and a predicate).

Using Adjectives and Adverbs to Expand Your Sentences

Adjectives are words that modify or describe nouns and pronouns. (See page 461.) Adjectives answer questions about nouns and pronouns, such as *Which one? What kind? How many?* Using adjectives is one way to add detail and information to sentences.

> WITHOUT ADJECTIVES: Dogs barked at cats.
>
> WITH ADJECTIVES: Our three large brown dogs barked at the two terrified spotted cats.

Note: Sometimes nouns and participles are used as adjectives. (See page 480 on participles.)

noun used as adjective
People are rediscovering the milk bottle.

present participle   past participle
used as adjective   used as adjective
Mrs. Simon had a swimming pool with a broken drain.

Adverbs add information to sentences by modifying or describing verbs, adjectives, or other adverbs (see page 464). An adverb usually answers the question *How? When? Where? How often?* or *To what extent?*

> WITHOUT ADVERBS: I will clean.
> The audience applauded.
>
> WITH ADVERBS: I will clean very thoroughly tomorrow.
> The audience applauded loudly and enthusiastically.

B.6 Expanding the Sentence with Phrases

A **phrase** is a group of related words that lacks a subject, a predicate, or both. A phrase cannot stand alone as a sentence. Phrases can appear at the beginning, middle, or end of a sentence.

WITHOUT PHRASES: I noticed the stain.
Sal researched the topic.
Manuela arose.

WITH PHRASES: Upon entering the room, I noticed the stain on the expensive carpet.
At the local aquarium, Sal researched the topic of shark attacks.
An amateur astronomer, Manuela arose in the middle of the night to observe the lunar eclipse but, after waiting ten minutes in the cold, gave up.

There are eight kinds of phrases: **noun; verb; prepositional;** three kinds of **verbal,** which consist of **participial, gerund,** and **infinitive; appositive;** and **absolute.**

Noun and Verb Phrases

A noun plus its modifiers is a **noun phrase** (*red shoes, the quiet house*). A main verb plus its helping verb is a **verb phrase** (*had been exploring, is sleeping*). (See page 456 on helping verbs.)

Prepositional Phrases

A **prepositional phrase** consists of a preposition (such as *in, above, with, at, behind*), an object of the preposition (a noun or pronoun), and any modifiers of the object. (See page 468 for a list of common prepositions.) A prepositional phrase functions like an adjective (modifying a noun or pronoun) or an adverb (modifying a verb, adjective, or adverb). You can use prepositional phrases to tell more about people, places, objects, or actions. A prepositional phrase usually adds information about time, place, direction, manner, or degree.

As Adjectives

The woman with the briefcase is giving a presentation on meditation techniques.

Both of the telephones behind the partition were ringing.

As Adverbs

The fire drill occurred <u>in the morning</u>.

I was curious <u>about the new coffee shop</u>.

My niece came <u>from Australia</u>.

<u>With horror</u>, the crowd watched the rhinoceros's tether stretch <u>to the breaking point</u>.

A prepositional phrase can function as part of the complete subject or as part of the complete predicate but should not be confused with the simple subject or simple predicate.

```
         ┌──────────── complete subject ────────────┐   ┌───── complete predicate ─────┐
                    simple       prepositional          simple       prepositional
                    subject         phrase              predicate       phrase
         ┌──────────┐┌────────────────────┐  ┌────────┐┌──────────────────┐
The red leather-bound volumes on the dusty shelf were filled with obscure
facts.
```

```
                    ┌──────── complete predicate ────────┐
                    simple predicate   prepositional phrase
         ┌──────┐ ┌───────────────┐┌───────────────────┐
Pat ducked quickly behind the potted fern.
```

Verbal Phrases

A **verbal** is a verb form used as a noun, adjective, or adverb. It cannot function as the main verb of a sentence. The three kinds of verbals are **participles, gerunds,** and **infinitives.** A **verbal phrase** consists of a verbal and its modifiers.

Participles and Participial Phrases

All verbs have two participles: present and past. The **present participle** is formed by adding -ing to the infinitive form (*walking, riding, being*). The **past participle** of regular verbs is formed by adding -d or -ed to the infinitive form (*walked, baked*). The past participle of irregular verbs has no set pattern (*ridden, been*). (See page 457 for a list of common irregular verbs and their past participles.) Both the present participle and the past participle can function as adjectives modifying nouns and pronouns.

```
past participle                    present participle
as adjective                       as adjective
┌──────────┐                       ┌──────────┐
Irritated, Martha circled the confusing traffic rotary once again.
```

A **participial phrase** consists of a participle and any of its modifiers.

```
                    ┌──────── participial phrase ────────┐
                    participle
                    ┌────────┐
We listened for Isabella climbing the rickety stairs.
```

```
           ┌─────participial phrase──────┐
  ┌participle┐
```
Disillusioned with the whole system, Kay sat down to think.

```
              ┌──────participial phrase──────┐
     ┌participle┐
```
The singer, having caught a bad cold, canceled his performance.

Gerunds and Gerund Phrases

A **gerund** is the present participle (the *-ing* form) of the verb used as a noun.

Shoveling is good exercise.

Rex enjoyed gardening.

A **gerund phrase** consists of a gerund and its modifiers. A gerund phrase, like a gerund, is used as a noun and can therefore function in a sentence as a subject, a direct or indirect object, an object of a preposition, a subject complement, or an appositive.

```
┌──── gerund phrase ────┐
```
Knitting the sweater took longer than Alice anticipated. [Subject.]

```
                        ┌────────── gerund phrase ──────────┐
```
The director considered making another monster movie. [Direct object.]

```
          ┌──── gerund phrase ────┐
```
She gave running three miles daily credit for her health. [Indirect object.]

```
        ┌─gerund phrase─┐
```
Before learning Greek, Omar spoke only English. [Object of the preposition.]

```
          ┌────── gerund phrase ──────┐
```
Her business is designing collapsible furniture. [Subject complement.]

```
          ┌───── gerund phrase─────┐
```
Wayne's trick, memorizing license plates, has come in handy. [Appositive.]

Infinitives and Infinitive Phrases

The **infinitive** is the base form of the verb as it appears in the dictionary preceded by the word *to*. An **infinitive phrase** consists of the word *to*, the infinitive, and any modifiers. An infinitive phrase can function as a noun, an adjective, or an adverb. When it is used as a noun, an infinitive phrase can be a subject, object, complement, or appositive.

```
┌──infinitive phrase──┐
```
To love one's enemies is a noble goal. [Noun used as subject.]

```
       ┌infinitive phrase┐
```
The season to plant bulbs is the fall. [Adjective modifying *season*.]

┌──────────── infinitive phrase────────────┐

The chess club met <u>to practice</u> for the state championship. [Adverb modifying *met*.]

Sometimes the *to* in an infinitive phrase is understood but not written.

Frank helped us <u>learn</u> the dance. [The *to* before *learn* is understood.]

Note: Do not confuse infinitive phrases with prepositional phrases beginning with the preposition *to*. In an infinitive phrase, *to* is followed by a verb; in a prepositional phrase, *to* is followed by a noun or pronoun.

Appositive Phrases

An **appositive** is a noun that explains, restates, or adds new information about another noun. An **appositive phrase** consists of an appositive and its modifiers. (See page 493 for punctuation of appositive phrases.)

┌─ appositive ─┐

Claude Monet completed the painting <u>*Water Lilies*</u> around 1903. [Adds information about the noun *painting*.]

┌────────── appositive phrase──────────┐
┌ appositive ┐

Francis, <u>my neighbor</u> with a large workshop, lent me a wrench. [Adds information about the noun *Francis*.]

Absolute Phrases

An **absolute phrase** consists of a noun or pronoun and any modifiers followed by a participle or a participial phrase (see page 480). An absolute phrase modifies an entire sentence, not any particular word within the sentence. It can appear anywhere in a sentence and is set off from the rest of the sentence with a comma or commas. There may be more than one absolute phrase in a sentence.

┌──absolute phrase──┐

The winter being over, the geese returned.

┌────────absolute phrase────────┐

Senator Arden began his speech, his voice rising to be heard over the loud <u>applause</u>.

┌──absolute phrase──┐

A vacancy having occurred, the cottage owner called the first name on the rental waiting list.

EXERCISE 8 ▶ Expand each of the following sentences by adding adjectives, adverbs, and/or phrases (prepositional, verbal, appositive, or absolute).

EXAMPLE: The professor lectured.

EXPANDED: <u>Being an expert on animal behavior, the professor lectured</u> <u>about animal intelligence studies.</u>

1. Samantha will work. <u>Samantha, my cousin, plans to work at Niagara</u> <u>Mohawk in May after graduation.</u>

2. The play began. <u>The play, one of the most popular to ever run in Boston,</u> <u>began its fifth year this fall.</u>

3. The Watkins are leaving. <u>Unhappy with the cold, rainy weather, the</u> <u>Watkins are leaving London after their son graduates.</u>

4. Juan walked quickly. <u>Having decided to finish his research for his</u> <u>sociology paper, Juan walked quickly to the library.</u>

5. Arturio repairs jet engines. <u>Using the experience he gained in the</u> <u>military, Arturio repairs jet engines for Boeing.</u>

6. The party was loud. <u>The party, attended by approximately thirty</u> <u>teenagers, was understandably loud.</u>

7. My paper is due Friday. <u>My paper on drug-abuse counseling is still</u> <u>due on Friday.</u>

8. I unlocked my car door. <u>Prior to saying farewell to my friends, I</u> <u>unlocked my car door.</u>

9. Yolanda added a porch. <u>To improve her house's property value,</u> <u>Yolanda added a porch to the front.</u>

10. Fran goes snowboarding. <u>Fran, an avid cold-weather enthusiast, goes</u> <u>snowboarding each weekend.</u>

B.7 Expanding the Sentence with Clauses

A **clause** is a group of words that contains a subject and a predicate. A clause is either **independent** (also called **main**) or **dependent** (also called **subordinate**).

An **independent clause** can stand alone as a grammatically complete sentence.

```
    independent clause      independent clause
      subject  predicate      subject  predicate
The rooster crowed, and I awoke.
```

```
    independent clause           independent clause
      subject    predicate         subject      predicate
The scientist worried. The experiment might fail.
```

```
    independent clause          independent clause
  subject predicate           subject    predicate
He bandaged his ankle. It had been sprained.
```

A **dependent clause** has a subject and a predicate, but it cannot stand alone as a grammatically complete sentence because it does not express a complete thought. Most dependent clauses begin with either a **subordinating conjunction** or a **relative pronoun**. These words connect the dependent clause to an independent clause.

Common Subordinating Conjunctions

after	inasmuch as	that
although	in case that	though
as	in order that	unless
as if	insofar as	until
as far as	in that	when
as soon as	now that	whenever
as though	once	where
because	provided that	wherever
before	rather than	whether
even if	since	while
even though	so that	why
how	supposing that	
if	than	

Relative Pronouns

that	which
what	who (whose, whom)
whatever	whoever (whomever)

```
subordinating
conjunction   subject   predicate
because the rooster crowed
```

```
subordinating
conjunction   subject    predicate
that the experiment might fail
```

```
    relative pronoun
      (subject)        predicate
  which  had been sprained
```

These clauses do not express complete thoughts and therefore cannot stand alone as sentences. When joined to independent clauses, dependent clauses function as adjectives, known as **adjective** (or **relative**) **clauses**; as adverbs, known as **adverb clauses**; and as nouns, known as **noun clauses.** Noun clauses can function as subjects, objects, or complements.

Adjective Clause

```
                      ┌───── dependent clause ─────┐
```
He bandaged his ankle, which had been sprained. [Modifies *ankle.*]

Adverb Clause

```
  ┌───── dependent clause ─────┐
```
Because the rooster crowed, I awoke. [Modifies *awoke.*]

Noun Clause

```
                      ┌───── dependent clause ─────┐
```
The scientist worried that the experiment might fail. [Direct object of *worried.*]

Sometimes the relative pronoun or subordinating conjunction is implied or understood rather than stated. Also, a dependent clause may contain an implied predicate. When a dependent clause is missing an element that can clearly be supplied from the context of the sentence, it is called an **elliptical clause.**

```
                      ┌──── elliptical clause ────┐
```
The circus is more entertaining than television [is]. [*Is* is the understood predicate in the elliptical dependent clause.]

```
                      ┌──── elliptical clause ────┐
```
Canadian history is among the subjects [that] the book discusses. [*That* is the understood relative pronoun in the elliptical dependent clause.]

Relative pronouns are generally the subject or object in their clauses. *Who* and *whoever* change to *whom* and *whomever* when they function as objects.

B.8 Basic Sentence Classifications

Depending on its structure, a sentence can be classified as one of four basic types: **simple, compound, complex,** or **compound-complex.**

Simple Sentences

A **simple sentence** has one independent (main) clause and no dependent (subordinate) clauses. (See page 60.) A simple sentence contains at least one subject and one predicate. It may have a compound subject, a compound predicate, and various phrases, but it has only one clause.

subject predicate
Sap rises.

subject   compound predicate
In the spring the sap rises in the maple trees and is boiled to make a thick, delicious syrup.

Compound Sentences

A **compound sentence** has at least two independent clauses and no dependent clauses. (See page 102.) The two independent clauses are usually joined with a comma and a coordinating conjunction (*and, but, for, nor, or, so,* or *yet*). Sometimes the two clauses are joined with a semicolon and no coordinating conjunction or with a semicolon and a conjunctive adverb like *nonetheless* or *still* followed by a comma. (See page 465 on conjunctive adverbs and page 107 on punctuation.)

independent clause
Reading a novel by Henry James is not like reading a thriller, but with patience the rewards are greater.
independent clause

independent clause   independent clause
I set out to explore the North River near home; I ended up at Charlie's Clam Bar.

Complex Sentences

A **complex sentence** has one independent clause and one or more dependent clauses. (See page 102.) The clauses are joined to the independent clause by subordinating conjunctions or relative pronouns. (See page 65.)

independent clause   dependent clause
We tried to find topics to talk about while we waited for the bus.

independent clause   dependent clause   dependent clause
The butcher greeted me warmly as I entered the shop because I hadn't seen him in a long time.

Compound-Complex Sentences

A **compound-complex sentence** contains two or more independent clauses and one or more dependent clauses. (See page 102.)

┌────────dependent clause────────┐┌────────────independent clause────────────┐ ┌────
If students work part time, they must plan their studies carefully and they must limit their social lives.
└──┘
               independent clause

┌─independent clause─┐   ┌──────────independent clause──────────┐┌─independent clause─
It was mid-March and the pond had begun to melt; I walked toward it expectantly as I wondered if I could go skating one last time.
                   └──────dependent clause──────┘   dependent clause

EXERCISE ▶ 9

Combine each of the following pairs of sentences into a single sentence by forming independent and/or dependent clauses. You may need to add, change, or delete words.

EXAMPLE: a. The levee broke.
              b. The flood waters rose rapidly.

COMBINED: After the levee broke, the flood waters rose rapidly.

1. a. Margot is a picky eater.
   b. Ivan, Margot's cousin, will eat anything.

   Margot is a picky eater, but Ivan, Margot's cousin, will eat anything.

2. a. Joe broke his wrist rollerblading.
   b. Joe started to wear protective gear.

   After Joe broke his wrist rollerblading, he started to wear protective gear.

3. a. Rick waited in line at the Department of Motor Vehicles.
   b. At the same time, Jean waited in line at the bank.

   While Rick waited in line at the Department of Motor Vehicles, Jean waited in line at the bank.

4. a. Beer is high in calories.
   b. Some beer companies now make low-calorie beer.

   Beer is high in calories, but some beer companies now make low-calorie beer.

5. a. Keith says he is politically active.
   b. Keith is not registered to vote.

   Although Keith says he is politically active, he is not registered to vote.

   _____

6. a. Miguel sprained his ankle.
   b. His friends drove him to the hospital.

   When Miguel sprained his ankle, his friends drove him to the hospital.

   _____

7. a. The boat sped by.
   b. The Coast Guard was in hot pursuit.

   The boat sped by, and the Coast Guard was in hot pursuit.

   _____

8. a. The weather report predicted rain.
   b. I brought my umbrella.

   Because the weather report predicted rain, I brought my umbrella.

   _____

9. a. Graffiti had been spray-painted on the subway wall.
   b. Maintenance workers were scrubbing it off.

   Graffiti had been spray-painted on the subway wall, so maintenance

   workers were scrubbing it off.

10. a. Shoppers were crowding around a display table.
    b. Everything on the table was reduced by 50 percent.

    Shoppers were crowding around a display table because everything on the

    table was reduced by 50 percent.

Using Punctuation Correctly

C.1 End Punctuation

When to Use Periods

Use a period in the following situations:

1. To end a sentence unless it is a question or an exclamation.

We washed the car even though we knew a thunderstorm was imminent.

Note: Use a period to end a sentence that states an indirect question or indirectly quotes someone's words or thoughts.

INCORRECT: Margaret wondered if she would be on time?
CORRECT: Margaret wondered if she would be on time.

2. To punctuate many abbreviations.

M.D.   B.A.   P.M.   B.C.   Mr.   Ms.

Do not use periods in acronyms, such as *NATO* and *AIDS,* or in abbreviations for most organizations, such as *NBC* and *NAACP.* (See page 501.)

Note: If a sentence ends with an abbreviation, end the sentence with only one period, not two.

The train was due to arrive at 7:00 P.M.

When to Use Question Marks

Use question marks after direct questions. Place the question mark within the closing quotation marks.

She asked the grocer, "How old is this cheese?"

Note: Use a period, not a question mark, after an indirect question.

She asked the grocer how old the cheese was.

489

When to Use Exclamation Points

Use an exclamation point at the end of a sentence that expresses particular emphasis, excitement, or an urgency. Use exclamation points sparingly, however, especially in academic writing.

What a beautiful day it is!   Dial 911 right now!

C.2 Commas

The comma is used to separate parts of a sentence from one another. If you omit a comma when it is needed, you risk making a clear and direct sentence confusing.

When to Use Commas

Use a comma in the following situations:

1. Before a coordinating conjunction that joins two independent clauses. (See page 79.)

Terry had planned to leave work early, but he was delayed.

2. To separate a dependent (subordinate) clause from an independent clause when the dependent clause comes first in the sentence. (See page 111.)

After I left the library, I went to the computer lab.

3. To separate introductory words and phrases from the rest of the sentence.

Unfortunately, I forgot my umbrella.

To pass the baton, I will need to locate my teammate.

Exuberant over their victory, the football team members carried the quarterback on their shoulders.

4. To separate a nonrestrictive phrase or clause from the rest of a sentence. When a **nonrestrictive** phrase or clause is added to a sentence, it does not change the sentence's basic meaning.

To determine whether an element is nonrestrictive, read the sentence without the element. If the meaning of the sentence does not essentially change, then the commas are *necessary*.

My sister, who is a mail carrier, is afraid of dogs. [The essential meaning of this sentence does not change if we read the sentence without the subordinate clause: *My sister is afraid of dogs.* Therefore, commas are needed.]

Mail carriers who have been bitten by dogs are afraid of them. [If we read this sentence without the subordinate clause, its meaning changes considerably: *Mail carriers are afraid of (dogs).* It says that *all* mail carriers are afraid of dogs. In this case, adding commas is not correct.]

5. To separate three or more items in a series.

I plan to take math, psychology, and writing next semester.

Note: A comma is *not* used after the *last* item in the series.

6. To separate coordinate adjectives (two or more adjectives that are not joined by a coordinating conjunction and that equally modify the same noun or pronoun).

The thirsty, hungry children returned from a day at the beach.

To determine if a comma is needed between two adjectives, use the following test. Insert the word *and* between the two adjectives. Also try reversing the order of the two adjectives. If the phrase makes sense in either case, then a comma is needed. If the phrase does not make sense, do not use a comma.

The tired, angry child fell asleep. [*The tired and angry child* makes sense; so does *The angry, tired child.* Consequently, the comma is needed.]

Sarah is an excellent psychology student. [*Sarah is an excellent and psychology student* does not make sense, nor does *Sarah is a psychology, excellent student.* A comma is therefore not needed.]

7. To separate parenthetical expressions from the clauses they modify. Parenthetical expressions are additional pieces of information that are not essential to the meaning of the sentence.

Most students, I imagine, can get jobs on campus.

8. To separate a transition from the clause it modifies.

In addition, I will rake leaves.

9. To separate a quotation from the words that introduce or explain it.

"Shopping," Barbara explained, "is a form of relaxation for me."

Barbara explained, "Shopping is a form of relaxation for me."

Note: The comma goes *inside* the closed quotation marks.

10. To separate dates, place names, and long numbers.

October 10, 1961, is my birthday.

Dayton, Ohio, was the first stop on the tour.

Participants numbered 1,777,716.

11. To separate phrases expressing contrast.

Sam's good nature, not his wealth, explains his popularity.

EXERCISE 10 ▷ Revise each of the following sentences by adding commas where needed.

EXAMPLE: Until the judge entered, the courtroom was noisy.

1. "Hello," said her group of friends when Joan entered the room.
2. Robert DeNiro, the actor in the film, was very handsome.
3. My parents frequently vacation in Miami, Florida.
4. Drunk drivers, I suppose, may not realize they are not competent to drive.
5. Jeff purchased a television, couch, and dresser for his new apartment.
6. Luckily, the windstorm did not do any damage to our town.
7. Frieda has an early class, and she has to go to work afterward.
8. After taking a trip to the Galápagos Islands, Mark Twain wrote about them.
9. The old dilapidated stadium was opened to the public on September 15, 1931.
10. Afterward, we will go out for ice cream.

C.3 Unnecessary Commas

It is as important to know where *not* to place commas as it is to know where to place them. The following rules explain where it is incorrect to place commas.

1. Do not place a comma between subject and verb, between verb and complement, or between an adjective and the word it modifies.

INCORRECT: The stunning, imaginative, and intriguing, painting, became the hit of the show.

CORRECT: The stunning, imaginative, and intriguing painting became the hit of the show.

2. Do not place a comma between two verbs, subjects, or complements used as compounds.

┌─ compound verb ─┐
INCORRECT: Sue called, and asked me to come by her office.
CORRECT: Sue called and asked me to come by her office.

3. Do not place a comma before a coordinating conjunction joining two dependent clauses. (See page 483.)

┌──── dependent clause ────┐
INCORRECT: The city planner examined blueprints that the park designer had submitted, and that the budget officer had approved.
└──────── dependent clause ────────┘

CORRECT: The city planner examined blueprints that the park designer had submitted and that the budget officer had approved.

4. Do not place commas around restrictive clauses, phrases, or appositives. Restrictive clauses, phrases, and appositives are modifiers that are essential to the meaning of the sentence.

INCORRECT: The girl, who grew up down the block, became my lifelong friend.
CORRECT: The girl who grew up down the block became my life-long friend.

5. Do not place a comma before the word *than* in a comparison or after the words *like* and *such as* in an introduction to a list.

INCORRECT: Some snails, such as, the Oahu Tree Snail, have more colorful shells, than other snails.
CORRECT: Some snails, such as the Oahu Tree Snail, have more colorful shells than other snails.

6. Do not place a comma next to a period, a question mark, an exclamation point, a dash, or an opening parenthesis.

INCORRECT: "When will you come back?," Dillon's son asked him.
CORRECT: "When will you come back?" Dillon's son asked him.

INCORRECT: The bachelor button, (also known as the cornflower) grows well in ordinary garden soil.
CORRECT: The bachelor button (also known as the cornflower) grows well in ordinary garden soil.

7. Do not place a comma between cumulative adjectives. Cumulative adjectives, unlike coordinate adjectives (see page 491), cannot be joined by *and* or rearranged.

INCORRECT: The light, yellow, rose blossom was a pleasant birthday surprise. [*The light and yellow and rose blossom* does not make sense, so the commas are incorrect.]

CORRECT: The light yellow rose blossom was a pleasant birthday surprise.

C.4 Colons and Semicolons

When to Use a Colon

A colon follows an independent clause and usually signals that the clause is to be explained or elaborated on. Use a colon in the following situations:

1. To introduce items in a series after an independent clause. The series can consist of words, phrases, or clauses.

I am wearing three popular colors: magenta, black, and white.

2. To signal a list or a statement introduced by an independent clause ending with *the following* or *as follows*.

The directions are as follows: take Main Street to Oak Avenue and then turn left.

3. To introduce a quotation that follows an introductory independent clause.

My brother made his point quite clear: "Never borrow my car without asking me first!"

4. To introduce an explanation.

Mathematics is enjoyable: it requires a high degree of accuracy and peak concentration.

5. To separate titles and subtitles of books.

Biology: A Study of Life

Note: A colon must always follow an independent clause. It should not be used in the middle of a clause.

INCORRECT: My favorite colors are: red, pink, and green.
CORRECT: My favorite colors are red, pink, and green.

When to Use a Semicolon

Use a semicolon in the following situations:

1. To separate two closely related independent clauses not connected by a coordinating conjunction. (See page 83.)

Sam had a 99 average in math; he earned an A in the course.

2. To separate two independent clauses joined by a conjunctive adverb. (See page 107.)

Margaret earned an A on her term paper; consequently, she was exempt from the final exam.

3. To separate independent clauses joined by a coordinating conjunction if the clauses are very long or if they contain numerous commas.

By late afternoon, having tried on every pair of black checked pants in the mall, Marsha was tired and cranky; but she still had not found what she needed to complete her outfit for the play.

4. To separate items in a series if the items are lengthy or contain commas.

The soap opera characters include Marianne Loundsberry, the heroine; Ellen and Sarah, her children; Barry, her ex-husband; and Louise, her best friend.

5. To revise a comma splice or run-on sentence. (See pages 91 and 81.)

EXERCISE 11

Correct each of the following sentences by placing colons and semicolons where necessary. Delete any incorrect punctuation.

EXAMPLE: Samuel Clemens disliked his name; therefore, he used Mark Twain as his pen name.

1. The large, modern, and airy gallery houses works of art by important artists; however, it has not yet earned national recognition as an important gallery.

2. Rita suggested several herbs to add to my spaghetti sauce: oregano, basil, and thyme.

3. Vic quickly typed the paper; it was due in less than an hour.

4. Furniture refinishing is a great hobby; it is satisfying to be able to make a piece of furniture look new again.

5. The bridesmaids in my sister's wedding are as follows: Judy, her best friend; Kim, our sister; Franny, our cousin; and Sue, a family friend.

6. Mac got a speeding ticket; he has to go to court next Tuesday.

7. I will go for a swim when the sun comes out; it will not be so chilly then.

8. Will was hungry after his hockey game, consequently, he ordered four hamburgers.

9. Sid went to the bookstore to purchase *Physical Anthropology: Man and His Makings*, it is required for one of his courses.

10. Here is an old expression, "The way to a man's heart is through his stomach."

C.5 Dashes, Parentheses, Hyphens, Apostrophes, Quotation Marks

Dashes (—)

The dash is used to (1) separate inessential elements from the main part of the sentence, (2) create a stronger separation, or interruption, than commas or parentheses, (3) emphasize an idea, create a dramatic effect, or indicate a sudden change in thought.

> My sister—the friendliest person I know—will visit me this weekend.

> My brother's most striking quality is his ability to make money—or so I thought until I heard of his bankruptcy.

When typing, use two hyphens (--) to indicate a dash. No space appears between the dash and the words it separates.

Parentheses ( )

Parentheses are used in pairs to separate extra or inessential information that often amplifies, clarifies, or acts as an aside to the main point. Unlike dashes, parentheses de-emphasize information.

> Some large breeds of dogs (golden retrievers and Newfoundlands) are susceptible to hip deformities.

> The prize was dinner for two (maximum value $50.00) at a restaurant of one's choice.

Hyphens (-)

Hyphens have the following primary uses:

1. To split a word when dividing it between two lines of writing or typing (see page 503).

2. To join two or more words that function as a unit, either as a noun or as a noun modifier.

mother-in-law

twenty-year-old

state-of-the-art sound system

single-parent families

school-age children

Apostrophes (')

Use apostrophes in the following ways.

1. To show ownership or possession. When the person, place, or thing doing the possessing is a singular noun, add -'s to the end of it, regardless of what its final letter is.

The man's CD player   John Keats's poetry

Aretha's best friend

With plural nouns that end in -s, add only an apostrophe to the end of the word.

the twins' bedroom   postal workers' hours

teachers' salaries   Smiths' new car

With plural nouns that do not end in -s, add 's.

children's books   men's slacks

Do not use an apostrophe with the possessive adjective *its*.

INCORRECT: It's frame is damaged.
CORRECT: Its frame is damaged.

2. To indicate omission of one or more letters in a word or number. Contractions are used in informal writing, but not in academic writing.

it's [it is]   hasn't [has not]

doesn't [does not]   '57 Ford [1957 Ford]

you're [you are]   class of '89 [class of 1989]

Quotation Marks (" ")

Quotation marks separate a direct quotation from the sentence that contains it. Here are some rules to follow in using quotation marks.

1. Quotation marks are always used in pairs.

Marge declared, "I never expected Peter to give me a watch for Christmas."

"I never expected Peter to give me a watch for Christmas," Marge declared.

Note: A punctuation mark goes at the end of the quotation, inside the quotation marks.

2. Use single quotation marks for a quotation within a quotation.

My literature professor said, "Byron's line 'She walks in beauty like the night' is one of his most sensual."

Note: When quoting long prose passages of more than four typed lines, do not use quotation marks. Instead, set off the quotation from the rest of the text by indenting each line ten spaces from the left margin. This format is called a **block quotation.**

The opening lines of the Declaration of Independence establish the purpose of the document:

> When in the Course of human events it becomes necessary for one people to dissolve the political bonds which have connected them with another, and to assume among the powers of the earth, the separate and equal station to which the Laws of Nature and of Nature's God entitle them, a decent respect to the opinions of mankind requires that they should declare the causes which impel them to the separation.

3. Use quotation marks to indicate titles of songs, short stories, poems, reports, articles, and essays. Books, movies, plays, operas, paintings, statues, and the names of television series are italicized (or underlined to indicate italics).

"Rappaccini's Daughter" (short story)
60 Minutes [or 60 Minutes] (television stories)
"The Road Not Taken" (poem)

EXERCISE 12

To the following sentences, add dashes, apostrophes, parentheses, hyphens, and quotation marks where necessary.

EXAMPLE: "You are not going out dressed that way!" said Frank's roommate.

1. My daughter-in-law recently entered medical school.

2. At the bar I worked in last summer, the waitresses' tips were always pooled and equally divided.

3. You're going to Paris next summer, aren't you?

4. The career counselor said, "The computer field is not as open as it used to be."

5. We heard Peter, Paul, and Mary sing "Puff, the Magic Dragon" in concert.

6. Frank asked me if I wanted to rent a big-screen television for our Super Bowl party.

7. Rachel, she was the teaching assistant for my linguistics class, spent last year in China.

8. Macy's is having a sale on women's boots next week.

9. Trina said, "My one-year-old's newest word is 'Bzz,' which she says whenever she sees a fly."

10. Some animals (horses and donkeys) can interbreed, but they produce infertile offspring.

Managing Mechanics and Spelling

D.1 Capitalization

In general, capital letters are used to mark the beginning of a sentence, to mark the beginning of a quotation, and to identify proper nouns. Here are some guidelines on capitalization.

What to Capitalize	*Example*
1. First word in every sentence	Prewriting is useful.
2. First word in a direct quotation	Sarah commented, "That exam was difficult!"
3. Names of people and animals, including the pronoun *I*	Aladdin Janet Reno Spot
4. Names of specific places, cities, states, nations, geographic areas, or regions	New Orleans the Southwest Lake Erie
5. Government and public offices, departments, buildings	Williamsville Library House of Representatives
6. Names of social, political, business, sporting, cultural organizations	Boy Scouts Buffalo Bills
7. Names of months, days of the week, holidays	August Tuesday Halloween
8. In titles of works: the first word following a colon, the first and last words, and all other words except articles, prepositions, and conjunctions	"Once More to the Lake" *Biology: A Study of Life*

9. Races, nationalities, languages — African American, Italian, English
10. Religions, religious figures, sacred books — Hindu, Hinduism, God, Allah, the Bible
11. Names of products — Tide, Buick
12. Personal titles when they come right before a name — Professor Rodriguez, Senator Hatch
13. Major historic events — World War I
14. Specific course titles — History 201, Introduction to Psychology

EXERCISE 13

Capitalize words as necessary in the following sentences.

EXAMPLE: Farmers in the **M**idwest were devastated by floods last summer.

1. My mother is preparing some special foods for our **H**anukkah meal; **R**abbi **E**pstein will join us.

2. My **A**merican **P**olitics professor used to be a judge in the town of **E**vans.

3. A restaurant in the **G**alleria **M**all serves **K**orean food.

4. A graduate student I know is writing a book about **B**uddha entitled *_**T**he **G**reat **O**ne: **W**ays to **E**nlightenment_.

5. **A**t the concert last night, **C**her changed into many different outfits.

6. An employee announced over the loudspeaker, "**A**ttention, customers! **W**e have **P**epsi on sale in aisle ten for a very low price!"

7. Karen's father was stationed at **F**ort **B**radley during the **V**ietnam **W**ar.

8. Last **T**uesday the state assembly passed **G**overnor **A**llen's budget.

9. Boston is an exciting city; be sure to visit the **M**useum of **F**ine **A**rts.

10. Dan asked if **I** wanted to go see the **B**olshoi **B**allet at **S**hea's **T**heatre in **N**ovember.

D.2 Abbreviations

An abbreviation is a shortened form of a word or phrase that is used to represent the whole word or phrase. The following is a list of common acceptable abbreviations.

What to Abbreviate	*Example*
1. Some titles before or after people's names	Mr. Ling Samuel Rosen, M.D. *but* Professor Ashe
2. Names of familiar organizations, corporations, countries	CIA, IBM, VISTA, USA
3. Time references preceded or followed by a number	7:00 A.M. 3:00 P.M. A.D. 1973
4. Latin terms when used in footnotes, reference lists, or parentheses	i.e. [*id est,* "that is"] et al. [*et alii,* "and others"]

Here is a list of things that are usually *not* abbreviated.

	Example	
What Not to Abbreviate	*Incorrect*	*Correct*
1. Units of measurement	thirty in.	thirty inches
2. Geographic or other place names when used in sentences	N.Y. Elm St.	New York Elm Street
3. Parts of written works when used in sentences	ch. 3	chapter 3
4. Names of days, months, holidays	Tues.	Tuesday
5. Names of subject areas	psych.	psychology

EXERCISE 14

Correct the inappropriate use of abbreviations in the following sentences. If a sentence contains no errors, write *Correct* beside it.

EXAMPLE: We live thirty ~~mi.~~ miles outside ~~NYC~~ New York City.

1. Frank enjoys going swimming at the YMCA on Oak ~~St.~~ Street

2. ~~Prof.~~ Professor Jorge asked the class to turn to ~~pg.~~ page 8.

3. Because he is seven ~~ft.~~ feet tall, my brother was recruited for the high-school ~~b-ball~~ basketball team.

4. When I asked Ron why he hadn't called me, he said it was Northeast Bell's fault—~~i.e.,~~ that is, his phone hadn't been working.

5. Tara is flying TWA to ~~KC~~ Kansas City to visit her parents next ~~Wed.~~ Wednesday.

Correct

6. At 11:30 P.M., we turned on NBC to watch *The Tonight Show.*
7. Last ~~wk.~~ I missed my ~~chem.~~ lab.

   week *chemistry*
8. The exam wasn't too difficult; only ~~ques. no.~~ 15 and ~~ques. no.~~ 31 were extremely difficult.

   question number *question number*
9. Dr. Luc removed the mole from my ~~rt.~~ hand with lasers.

   right
10. Mark drove out to ~~L.A.~~ to audition for a role in MGM's new movie.

    Los Angeles

D.3 Hyphenation and Word Division

On occasion you must divide and hyphenate a word on one line and continue it on the next. Here are some guidelines for dividing words.

1. Divide words only when absolutely necessary. Frequent word divisions make a paper difficult to read.

2. Divide words between syllables. Consult a dictionary if you are unsure how to break a word into syllables.

   di-vi-sion   pro-tect

3. Do not divide one-syllable words.

4. Do not divide a word so that a single letter is left at the end of a line.

   INCORRECT: a-typical
   CORRECT: atyp-ical

5. Do not divide a word so that fewer than three letters begin the new line.

   INCORRECT: visu-al
   CORRECT: vi-sual
   INCORRECT: caus-al [This word cannot be divided at all.]

6. Divide compound words only between the words.

   some-thing   any-one

7. Divide words that are already hyphenated only at the hyphen.

   ex-policeman

EXERCISE 15 ▶ Insert a diagonal (/) mark where each word should be divided. Mark "N" in the margin if the word should not be divided.

> EXAMPLE: every/where

1. en/close
2. houseN
3. sax/ophone
4. hardlyN
5. well-/known

6. dis/gusted
7. chan/delier
8. head/phones
9. swings N
10. abyss N

D.4 Numbers

Numbers can be written as numerals (600) or words (six hundred). Here are some guidelines on when to use numerals and when to use words.

When to Use Numerals	*Example*
1. Numbers that are spelled with more than two words	375 students
2. Days and years	August 10, 1993
3. Decimals, percentages, fractions	56.7 59 percent 1¾ cups
4. Exact times	9:27 A.M.
5. Pages, chapters, volumes; acts and lines from plays	chapter 12 volume 4
6. Addresses	122 Peach Street
7. Exact amounts of money	$5.60
8. Scores and statistics	23–6 5 of every 12

When to Use Words	*Example*
1. Numbers that begin sentences	Two hundred ten students attended the lecture.
2. Numbers of one or two words	sixty students, two hundred women

EXERCISE 16 ▶ Correct the misuse of numbers in the following sentences. If a sentence contains no errors, write *Correct* next to it.

> five hundred
>
> EXAMPLE: The reception hall was filled with ~~500~~ guests.

1. At 6:52 A.M. my roommate's alarm clock went off. Correct

2. I purchased ~~9~~ *nine* turtlenecks for ~~one dollar and fifty-five cents~~ *$1.55* each.

3. ~~35~~ *Thirty-five* floats were entered in the parade, but only 4 received prizes.

4. Act ~~three~~ *3* of *Othello* is very exciting.

5. Almost ~~fifty~~ *50* percent of all marriages end in divorce.

6. The Broncos won the game 21–7. Correct

7. We were assigned volume ~~two~~ *2* of *Don Quixote*, beginning on page 351.

8. The hardware store is located at ~~three forty-four~~ *344* Elm Street, ~~2~~ *two* doors down from my grandmother's house.

9. Maryanne's new car is a ~~2~~ *two*-door V-8.

10. Our anniversary is June ~~ninth, nineteen eighty-nine~~ *9* *1989*.

D.5 Suggestions for Improving Spelling

Correct spelling is important to a well-written paragraph or essay. The following suggestions will help you submit papers without misspellings.

1. Do not worry about spelling as you write your first draft. Checking a word in a dictionary at this point will interrupt your flow of ideas. If you do not know how a word is spelled, spell it the way it sounds and circle or underline it so you remember to check it later.

2. Keep a list of words you commonly misspell. This list can be part of your error log.

3. Every time you catch an error or find a misspelled word in a paper returned by your instructor, add it to your list.

4. Study your list. Ask a friend to quiz you on the words. Eliminate words from the list after you have passed several quizzes on them.

5. Develop a spelling awareness. You'll find that your spelling will improve just by being aware that spelling is important. When you encounter a new word, notice how it is spelled and practice writing it.

6. Pronounce words you are having difficulty spelling. Pronounce each syllable distinctly.

7. Review basic spelling rules. Your college library or learning lab may have manuals, workbooks, or computer programs that cover basic rules and provide guided practice.

8. Be sure to have a dictionary close by when you write.

9. Read your final draft through once, checking only for spelling errors. Look at each word carefully, and check the spelling of those words you don't know well.

D.6 Six Useful Spelling Rules

The following six rules focus on common spelling trouble spots.

1. Is it *ei* or *ie*?

    Rule: Use *i* before *e*, except after *c* or when the syllable is pronounced *ay,* as in the word *weigh.*

    EXAMPLE: *i* before *e*: believe, niece

    except after *c:* receive, conceive

    or when pronounced *ay:* neighbor, sleigh

    Exceptions:

    | either | neither | foreign | forfeit |
    | height | leisure | weird | seize |

2. When adding an ending, do you keep or drop the final *e*?

    Rules: a. Keep the final *e* when adding an ending that begins with a consonant. (Vowels are *a, e, i, o, u,* and sometimes *y;* all other letters are consonants.)

    hope → hopeful   aware → awareness
    live → lively   force → forceful

    b. Drop the final *e* when adding an ending that begins with a vowel.

    hope → hoping   file → filing
    note → notable   write → writing

    Exceptions: argument   truly   changeable
    awful   manageable   courageous
    judgment   noticeable   outrageous
    acknowledgment

3. When adding an ending, do you keep the final *y*, change it to *i*, or drop it?

    Rules: a. Keep the *y* if the letter before the *y* is a vowel.

$$\text{del\underline{ay}} \rightarrow \text{del\underline{ay}ing} \qquad \text{b\underline{uy}} \rightarrow \text{b\underline{uy}ing} \qquad \text{pr\underline{ey}} \rightarrow \text{pr\underline{ey}ed}$$

b. Change the *y* to *i* if the letter before the *y* is a consonant, but keep the *y* for the *-ing* ending.

$$\text{de\underline{fy}} \rightarrow \text{defiance} \qquad \text{mar\underline{ry}} \rightarrow \text{married}$$
$$\rightarrow \text{de\underline{fy}ing} \qquad \rightarrow \text{mar\underline{ry}ing}$$

4. **When adding an ending to a one-syllable word, when do you double the final letter if it is a consonant?**

   Rules: a. In one-syllable words, double the final consonant when a single vowel comes before it.

   $$\text{dr\underline{op}} \rightarrow \text{dr\underline{opp}ed} \qquad \text{sh\underline{op}} \rightarrow \text{sh\underline{opp}ed} \qquad \text{p\underline{it}} \rightarrow \text{p\underline{itt}ed}$$

   b. In one-syllable words, *don't* double the final consonant when two vowels or another consonant comes before it.

   $$\text{soun\underline{d}} \rightarrow \text{soun\underline{d}ed} \qquad \text{re\underline{al}} \rightarrow \text{re\underline{al}ize}$$

5. **When adding an ending to a word with more than one syllable, when do you double the final letter if it is a consonant?**

   Rules: a. In multisyllable words, double the final consonant when a single vowel comes before it *and* the stress falls on the last syllable.

   $$\text{begin}' \rightarrow \text{beg\underline{inn}ing} \qquad \text{transmit}' \rightarrow \text{transm\underline{itt}ed}$$
   $$\text{repel}' \rightarrow \text{rep\underline{ell}ing}$$

   b. In multisyllable words, do *not* double the final consonant when two vowels or a vowel and another consonant come before it *or* when the stress is not on the last syllable.

   $$\text{desp\underline{air}} \rightarrow \text{desp\underline{air}ing} \qquad \text{ben}'\text{e\underline{fit}} \rightarrow \text{bene\underline{fit}ed}$$
   $$\text{conc\underline{eal}} \rightarrow \text{conc\underline{eal}ing}$$

6. **To form a plural, do you add *-s* or *-es*?**

   Rules: a. For most nouns, add *-s*.

   $$\text{cat} \rightarrow \text{cat\underline{s}} \qquad \text{house} \rightarrow \text{house\underline{s}}$$

   b. Add *-es* to words that end in *-o* if the *-o* is preceded by a consonant.

   $$\text{her\underline{o}} \rightarrow \text{her\underline{o}es} \qquad \text{potat\underline{o}} \rightarrow \text{potat\underline{o}es}$$

   c. Add *-es* to words ending in *-ch*, *-sh*, *-ss*, *-x*, or *-z*.

   $$\text{chur\underline{ch}} \rightarrow \text{chur\underline{ch}es} \qquad \text{di\underline{sh}} \rightarrow \text{di\underline{sh}es} \qquad \text{fo\underline{x}} \rightarrow \text{fo\underline{x}es}$$

TEXT AND CARTOON CREDITS

Chapter 1   Page 8, drawing by Barsotti, © 1977. The New Yorker Magazine, Inc.; page 13, reading from *Fatherhood* by Bill Cosby. Copyright © 1986 by William H. Cosby, Jr. Used by permission of Doubleday, a division of Bantam Doubleday Dell Publishing Group, Inc.

Chapter 2   Page 40, reading reprinted by permission of John Rosemond.

Chapter 3   Page 71, reading, "John Corcoran–The Man Who Couldn't Read" from *Chicken Soup for the Soul: 101 Stories to Open the Heart and Rekindle the Spirit*, Jack Canfield and Mark Victor Hansen, Editors (Deerfield Beach, FL: Health Communications, 1993). Reprinted by permission of John Corcoran, author of *The Teacher Who Couldn't Read*.

Chapter 4   Page 95, reading by Pride, W.M, Hughes, R.J., Kapoor, J.R., *Business*, third edition. Copyright © 1991 by Houghton Mifflin Company.

Chapter 5   Page 119, reading from *Newsweek*, February 24, © 1997, Newsweek, Inc. All rights reserved. Used by permission.

Chapter 6   Page 133, drawing by Ziegler, © 1983. The New Yorker Magazine, Inc.; page 151, reading, copyright © 1980 by Elizabeth Wong.

Chapter 7   Page 177, reading, copyright © 1996 by The New York Times Company. Reprinted by permission.

Chapter 8   Page 211, reading by Ober, Scott, *Contemporary Business Communication*, second edition. Copyright © 1995 by Houghton Mifflin Company.

Chapter 9   Page 218, drawing by Barsotti, © 1981. The New Yorker Magazine, Inc.; page 234, reading, copyright © 1997 by The New York Times Company. Reprinted by permission.

Chapter 10   Page 248, drawing by Booth, © 1976. The New Yorker Magazine, Inc.; page 261, reading reprinted by permission of Rosemary Bray. "Toys Aren't Us," *Redbook* Magazine. December 1994. Copyright 1994. All rights reserved.

Chapter 11   Page 288, reading from *Superstitious Minds*. Copyright 1988 by Letty Cottin Pogrebin. Originally appeared in *Ms.* Magazine. No part of this material may be reproduced in whole or part without the express written permission of the author or her agent.

Chapter 12   Page 312, reading adapted from "Halloween: Fun Without Cultural Guilt" by Maya Prestwich. From *The Daily Northwestern*, October 30, 1997; page 314, reading, copyright © 1996 by The New York Times Company. Reprinted by permission.

Chapter 13   Page 336, reading, copyright (June 1996), by *Hispanic,* Austin, TX 78701. Reprinted from *Hispanic.*

Chapter 14   Page 362, reading courtesy of *Mademoiselle.* Copyright © 1996 by The Condé Nast Publications, Inc.

Chapter 15   Page 391, reading adapted from *Utne Reader,* September/October 1992 from "The Lure of Gambling's Easy Money" by Robert McClory. Copyright © 1992.

Chapter 16   Page 421, reading by Mary Ellen Shearer, co-director of Medill News Service and associate professor at the Medill School of Journalism at Northwestern University. Jack Doppelt is an associate professor at the Medill School of Journalism at Northwestern University.

Additional Readings   Page 432, reading by Rubin, Z., Peplan, L.A., and Salovey, P., *Psychology,* first edition. Copyright © 1993 by Houghton Mifflin Company; page 433, reading from E.J. Kahn, Jr., *The Big Drink: The Story of Coca-Cola.* Copyright 1950, 1959, 1960 by E.J. Kahn, Jr. Reprinted by permission of Random House, Inc.; page 435, reading from Vickie Sears, Music Lady, as found in *Dancing on the Rim: An Anthology of Contemporary Northwest Native American Writing,* edited by Andrea Lerner. Copyright 1990 by Vickie Sears. Reprinted by permission of Firebrand Books, Ithaca, New York; page 438, reading reprinted by permission of The Putnam Publishing Group from *Word for Word* by Andy Rooney. Copyright © 1986 by Essay Productions, Inc.; page 440, reading from *Wouldn't Take Nothing for my Journey Now* by Maya Angelou. Copyright © 1993 by Maya Angelou. Reprinted by permission of Random House, Inc.; page 442, reading by Pride, W.M., Hughes, R.J., and Kapoor, J.R., *Business,* fourth edition. Copyright © 1993 by Houghton Mifflin Company; page 444, reading adapted from *Utne Reader,* January/February 1992 from "Can Self Esteem Fight Poverty and Drugs?" by Teo Furtado. Copyright © 1992.

INDEX

Selected Answer Key
Part II Skills Check   Paragraph 3

Our country has a problem because so many people are homeless. Now is the time for the government to take action on the problem of homelessness. For the past several years, the media have focused a great deal of attention on the homeless. Many college campuses have been holding "sleepouts," in order to call attention to the problems of the homeless. Religious groups have been trying to help and have been opening shelters for them. Still this is not enough because the problem is only getting worse. The government needs to be pushed to do something about this problem now. Religious groups and students should write their government officials, put pressure on members of Congress, and urge them to act on the problems of the homeless. Concerned citizens should become involved now because this problem is a disgrace to our country.

Part V Skills Check   Paragraph 1

Fog is caused by the natural movements of air from one place to another. Warm winds pass over the ocean or another large body of water. As these warm winds pass over the water, they pick up moisture. When this moist air that was picked up over warm water moves to cool land, or from warmer to cooler water, it cools down. As the moist air cools down, the molecules in the water vapor move more slowly and begin to stick together rather than to bounce off each other when they collide. When these water molecules condense into a liquid near the ground, fog forms.

Part V Skills Check   Paragraph 2

What instructors expect of college students is very different from what was expected in high school. In high school, there were almost no papers assigned. When we were given writing assignments, we were not expected to type them out on a word processor. It was acceptable to write papers using pencil and paper. My instructors at college not only expected me to type my papers neatly, but to write papers that provide objective support for an opinion. My first semester I spent nearly all of my time at the library trying to figure out how to write an objective paper instead of a paper with just my opinion. It didn't take me long to figure out that the requirements for college papers are very different from those assigned in high school. Furthermore, my high school teachers would take class time to help students review for exams and even small tests. As a result, I did very little studying on my own. In addition, most high school tests were objective tests, and essay questions were found only on final exams. College instructors expect students to prepare themselves for exams and only rarely are these exams objective ones. It was a real struggle for me to learn how to prepare for college exams and to write good essays, but now that I have two semesters experience, I think I am on the right track.

Part V Skills Check   Paragraph 3

My favorite room in the house is my bedroom, which is a deep shade of blue that contrasts with the long, white drapes on the two windows. A dark pine double bed, covered with a white down-filled comforter, extends from the middle of one wall to the center of the room. Across from the bed, on the opposite wall, is a dark pine dresser with a tall mirror and crystal lamps. Another tall pine chest of drawers stands against the wall opposite the door. Large, leafy green ferns hang in rustic clay pots in front of the multi-paned windows. It is always peaceful and quiet here, because the room is at the back of the house, away from street traffic, overlooking the wide, sunny back yard.

Part VI Skills Check   Paragraph 2

My family's trip through the Canadian Rockies and westward into British Columbia was an unforgettable experience. After flying to Chicago and on to Calgary, Alberta, we boarded a scenic cruiser of the Canadian Pacific Railway for a two day trip to Vancouver, B.C. We quickly passed through rolling foothills and began our steep ascent into the mountains. On our way to our first stop, Banff, we were enchanted by the beauty of the mountains and the many sightings of wildlife. After a brief stopover, we reboarded the train for perhaps the most scenic and longest portion of our trip. Along this stretch the railroad crossed a number of trestle bridges towering over wild river valleys, hugged the cliffs along the Columbia and Thompson Rivers, and tunneled through mountains. By the time we reached Kamloops, B.C., at the end of the first day, it seemed as if our eyes could not take in even one more breathtaking scene. The next morning, we continued our journey down the western slope of the Rockies. We followed the Thompson and Frasier Rivers, but the railroad bed was perched less perilously than in the earlier part of the trip. We were struck by the lush greenness of the slopes facing the Pacific. As we slowly descended to the Pacific coast our excitement about exploring the beautiful city of Vancouver increased. By early afternoon we arrived at Vancouver's historic railroad terminal, tired and inspired by what we had seen.

Part VI Skills Check   Paragraph 3

A. Point-by-Point Revision:

Cross-country skis and downhill skis are different in many aspects. Cross-country skis are intended for gliding over fairly level terrain, whereas downhill skis are used to ski down steep slopes with frequent turns. Cross-country skis are lightweight and very narrow, and the bottom is curved so the ski does not lie flat on the snow. Downhill skis are broader and heavier, and they have a flatter bottom. Unlike cross-country skis, downhill skis have steel edges, and the bindings keep the entire boot clamped to the ski. On the other hand, the bindings on cross-country skis do not keep the heel clamped down, since the long running strides used in cross-country skiing depend on free movement of the heel.

B. Subject-by-Subject Revision:

Cross-country and downhill skis are different in many aspects. Cross-country skis are intended for gliding over fairly level terrain. They are lightweight and very narrow with a curved bottom so the ski does not lie flat on the snow. The bindings on cross-country skis do not keep the heel clamped down, since the long running strides used in cross-country skiing depend on free movement of the heel. On the other hand, downhill skis are used to ski down steep slopes with frequent turns. They are broader and heavier, and have a flatter bottom. Unlike cross-country skis, downhill skis have steel edges, and the bindings keep the entire foot clamped to the ski.

Part VII Skills Check   Paragraph 1

Studying history can benefit you by enriching your life in a number of ways. First, studying history gives you a new way of looking at your own life. When you learn about the past, you begin to see that your lifetime is only part of a larger picture. Second, history can help you understand problems better. You begin to see why the world is as it is and what events caused it to be this way. Finally, history allows you to think of yourself in a different way. In looking at everything that has happened before us, we as individuals seem small and unimportant.

Part VII Skills Check   Paragraph 2   Revision Map

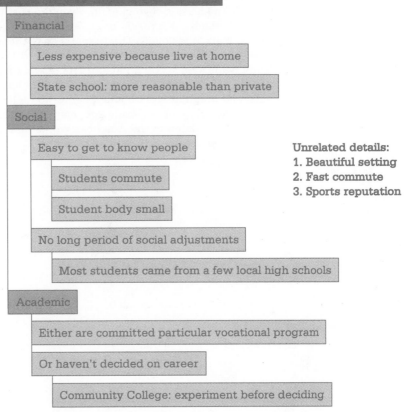

REASONS STUDENTS ATTEND MY COLLEGE

Financial
- Less expensive because live at home
- State school: more reasonable than private

Social
- Easy to get to know people
- Students commute
- Student body small
- No long period of social adjustments
- Most students came from a few local high schools

Academic
- Either are committed particular vocational program
- Or haven't decided on career
- Community College: experiment before deciding

Unrelated details:
1. Beautiful setting
2. Fast commute
3. Sports reputation

Part VII Skills Check   Paragraph 2   Revision

Students attend my college for financial, social, and academic reasons. The college I attend is a community college, which makes it somewhat less expensive because the students still live at home. Also, it is a state school, so the cost of tuition is more reasonable than it might be in a private college. Since the students commute to school and the student body is small, it is easy to get to know a lot of people. Most of the students are people who came from a few local high schools, so there is not a long period of social adjustments. Finally, many of the students who attend my college are either committed to a particular vocational program, or they have not yet made up their minds about a career. A community college gives them the opportunity to experiment for a couple of years before they decide.

Part VII Skills Check   Paragraph 3

The average American worker is worse off today than at any time in the past decade. In the past decade, we have seen a decline in good manufacturing jobs which previously were a mainstay of American employment. Businesses have been downsizing, reorganizing, and just plain shipping American jobs overseas where labor is far cheaper. The result is that the American worker has suffered. For industries to remain competitive in world markets, workers have experienced a net reduction in salaries during this decade. While this has been happening, living expenses have continued to increase. Taxes seem to go up every year. The cost of family medical insurance, of which employers have been paying less and less, is skyrocketing. Even the cost of food and clothing has continued to climb. As a result, more families now need both spouses to work in order to make ends meet. The "experts" say that we have added more jobs to the economy than we have lost. Take a look at those jobs, though. Many are minimum wage jobs slinging hamburgers or working at other low-paying positions in the service sector. These jobs offer little hope of advancement, very few benefits, and irregular work hours. In order to replace the salary earned in a good manufacturing job a decade ago, many workers now need to work two or more jobs. If you listen to the American worker and not the "experts," it will be clear that we are certainly worse off today.